TRANS-METRO-POLITAN:
BACK ON THE STREET

Warren_Ellis 😶
Writer

Darick_Robertson
Penciller

Rodney_Ramos, Keith_Aiken Jerome_K._Moore, Kim_DeMulder Ray_Kryssing, Dick_Giordano Inkers

Nathan_Eyring Colorist

Clem_Robins Letterer

Geof_Darrow (#1-3) Frank_Quitely (#4-6) Original Series Covers

TRANSMETROPOLITAN created by Warren_Ellis and Darick_Robertson

Special thanks to Michael_O'Brien
and André_Ricciardi

Dedicated to Meredith, for your unlimited support and love, and to the memory of my father, Ira D. Robertson, for his.

— Darick_Robertson

For my daughter Lilith, who makes the world new for me, and for Niki, whom I love more each day.

— Warren_Ellis

Stuart Moore Editor – Original Series Julie Rottenberg Associate Editor – Original Series
Scott Nybakken Editor Robbin Brosterman Design Director – Books Louis Prandi Publication Design
Shelly Bond Executive Editor – Vertigo Hank Kanalz Senior VP – Vertigo and Integrated Publishing Diane Nelson President
Dan DiDio and Jim Lee Co-Publishers Geoff Johns Chief Creative Officer John Rood Executive VP – Sales, Marketing and Business Development Amy Genkins Senior VP – Business and Legal Affairs Nairi Gardiner Senior VP – Finance Jeff Boison VP – Publishing Planning Mark Chiarello VP – Art Direction and Design John Cunningham VP – Marketing Terri Cunningham VP – Editorial Administration Alison Gill Senior VP – Manufacturing and Operations Jay Kogan VP – Business and Legal Affairs, Publishing Jack Mahan VP – Business Affairs, Talent Nick Napolitano VP – Manufacturing Administration Sue Pohja VP – Book Sales Courtney Simmons Senior VP – Publicity Bob Wayne Senior VP – Sales

Cover illustration by Geof_Darrow.

TRANSMETROPOLITAN: BACK ON THE STREET

DC Comics, 1700 Broadway, New York, NY 10019 A Warner Bros. Entertainment Company. Printed in Canada. Seventh Printing. ISBN: 978-1-4012-2084-6

Library of Congress Cataloging-in-Publication Data

Ellis, Warren.
Transmetropolitan : back on the street / Warren Ellis, writer ; Darick Robertson, penciller.
p. cm.
"Originally published in single magazine form as TRANSMETROPOLITAN 1-6."
Includes bibliographical references and index.
ISBN 978-1-4012-2084-6 (alk. paper)
1. Journalists–Comic books, strips, etc. 2. Graphic novels.
I. Robertson, Darick. II. Title.
PN6728.T68E4325 2012
741.5'973-dc23

2012017896

SUSTAINABLE FORESTRY INITIATIVE
Certified Chain of Custody
Promoting Sustainable Forestry
www.sfiprogram.org
SFI-00507
This label only applies to the text section.

I think that the main reason I like Warren Ellis — not just as one of my best friends, but as one of my favorite writers — is that in him I recognize a kindred spirit.

This may not be a good thing for the advancement as a race of cosmic star-beings walking hand-in-hand to take their place in a bold new dawn of universal and spiritual unity, but bollocks to that: Warren doesn't like "nice" things. He distrusts "nice" people. They make him suspicious. And I know how he feels.

I've been lucky, though, because I've been able to channel this venomous attitude into a number of projects and stories. Not so Mr. Ellis, forced to filter his own poison through the dubious medium of the super-hero story. The work's been great, but at the end of the day it's still about grown men in tights (with the glorious exception of Warren's old *Lazarus Churchyard* series, and if someone could publish this I would be very, very grateful, because I want to know what happens next).

TRANSMETROPOLITAN changed all that. Drawn by the highly talented Darick Robertson, who really has no idea what he's getting into, this story represents Warren's work at its finest and purest. These are the tales he wants to tell, the way he wants to tell them, and there's not a writer worth his salt who won't do his best work under those conditions. I was actually privy to much of the development of the book, and I knew it was precisely this kind of creative freedom that would make it great: and that would ensure its success. Warren, meanwhile, was convinced it would roll over and die in about six months...

"First issue's sold fuck all. We're doomed."

"Warren, Warren, the whole industry's in a slump. Give it time, word'll spread. Sales'll pick up."

"Sales always fall on issue two. It's traditional. We're doomed."

"Honestly, mate, it'll be rightly. The book'll get a reputation, people'll check it out. It's too good for them not to."

"These are the end times. It rained cheese last night. The Black Squirrel has been seen as far afield as Luton."

"Warren..."

"And I behold a pale horse, and his name that sat on him was Death. And —"

But Warren was wrong. What he seemed to have forgotten was that he had written an excellent story. That Darick, delighted to be let loose on something as foul and fabulous as this after years of super-hero comics, was matching that story with the richest, darkest artwork of his career. That sometimes — *sometimes* — that combination is all you need.

Here then, collected in one neat volume, is the very first story in the saga of TRANSMETROPOLITAN. Here is a city filled with every sin you can imagine, and a few that have been imagined for you. Here is Spider Jerusalem, the cranky, miserable bastard who will guide you through this future Babylon. Here is the finest, blackest humor, and the purest hate, and a sense of justice hissed through gritted teeth. And here, as unexpected and natural as a stripper's tears, is a little vein of ordinary humanity.

Fuck you.
If anyone in this shithole city gave two tugs of a dead dog's cock about Truth, this wouldn't be happening.

That's Warren talking.

— Garth Ennis
**Bloody London,
October 1997**

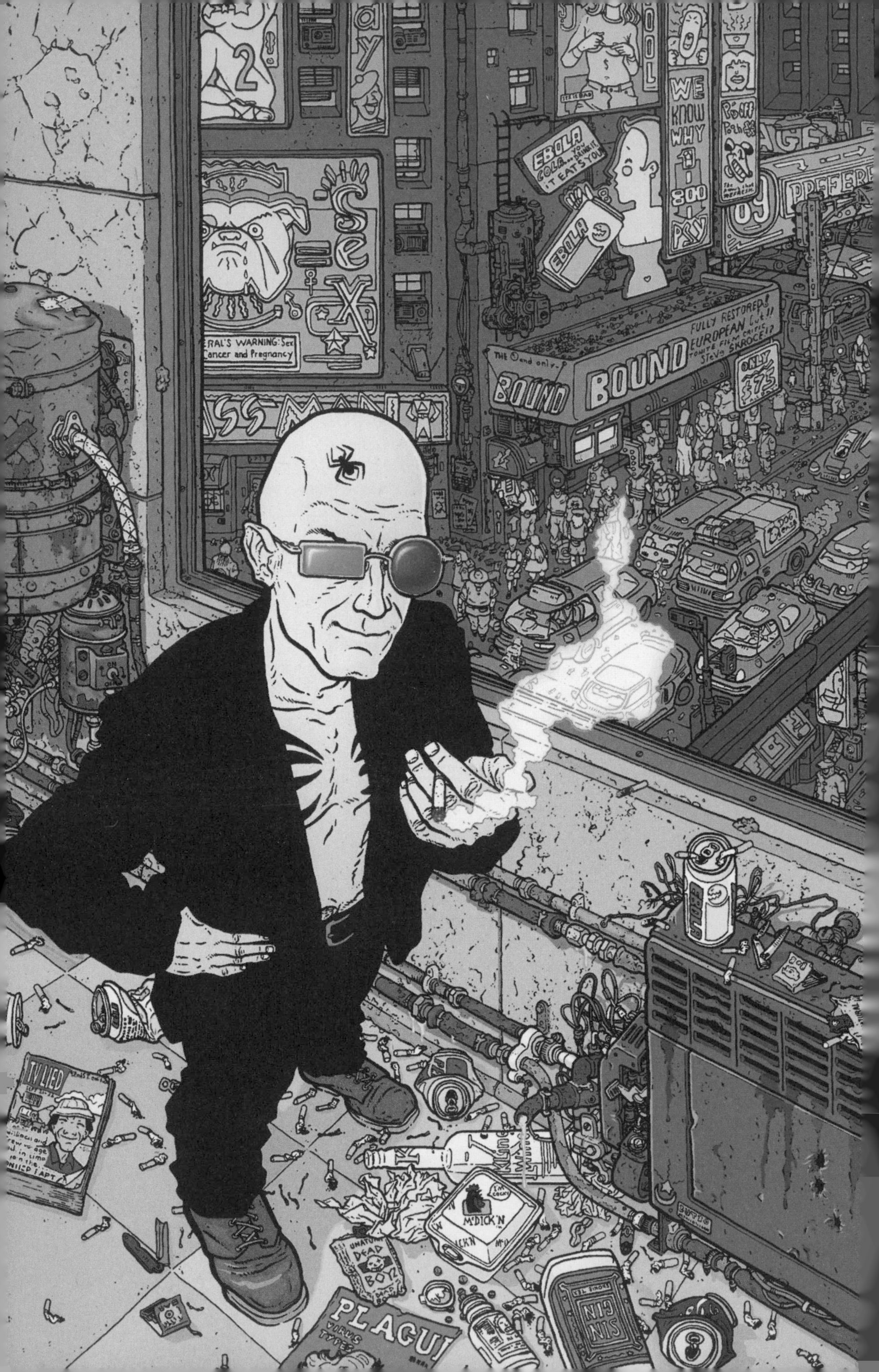

EBOLA COLA... YOU DRINK IT, IT EATS YOU
WE KNOW WHY 1 800 PSY
EBOLA
FULLY RESTORED! EUROPEAN Cut!! TONITE FILM CRITIC STeVe SKROCE!?
BOUND
BOUND
ONLY $75
ERAL'S WARNING: Sex
Cancer and Pregnancy
TV LIED
I'M COCKY
M'DICK'N
DEAD BOYZ
PLAGU
VIRUS TYPES
SIN GIN

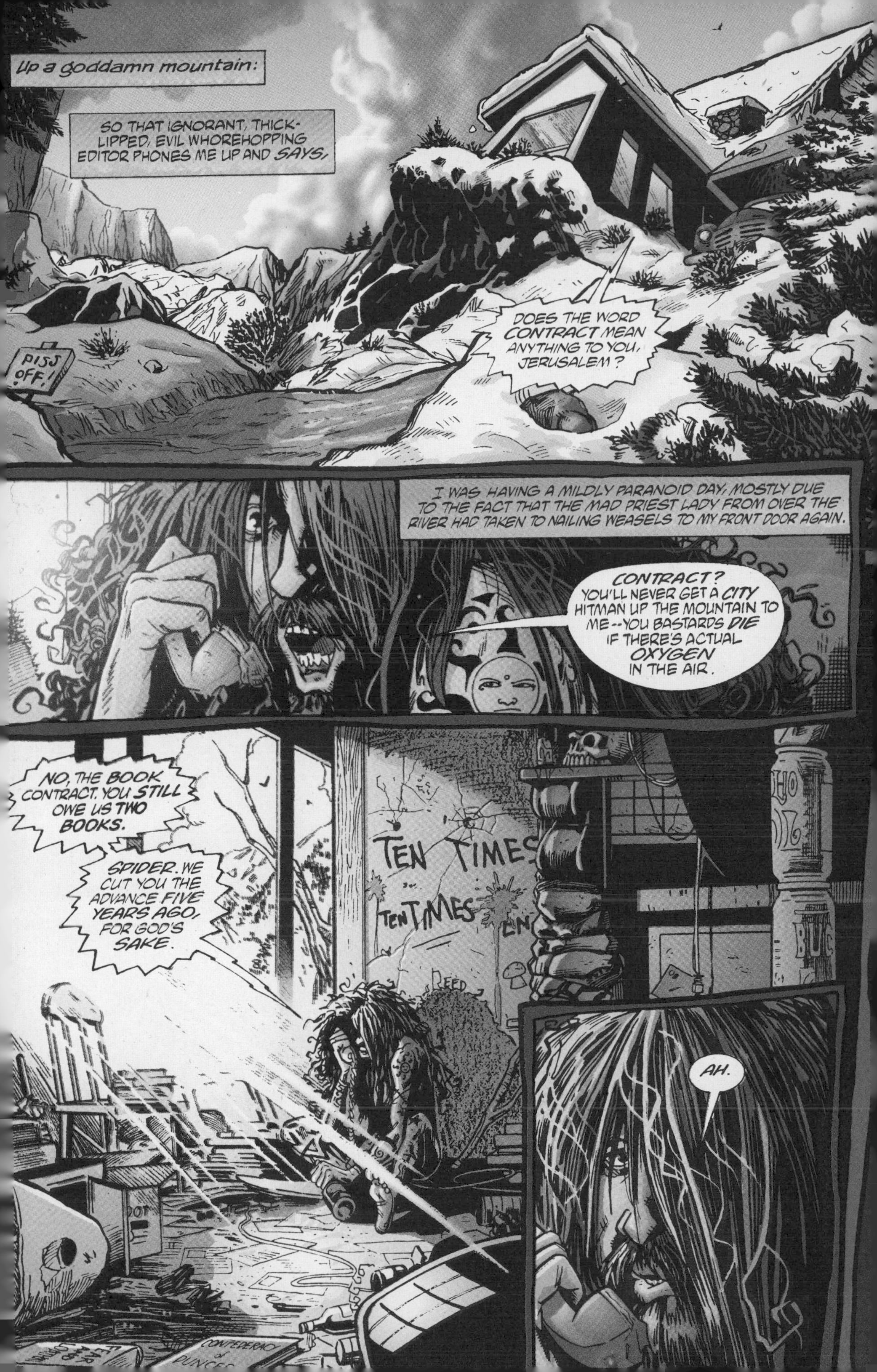

Up a goddamn mountain:
SO THAT IGNORANT, THICK-LIPPED, EVIL WHOREHOPPING EDITOR PHONES ME UP AND SAYS,
DOES THE WORD CONTRACT MEAN ANYTHING TO YOU, JERUSALEM?
PISS OFF!
I WAS HAVING A MILDLY PARANOID DAY, MOSTLY DUE TO THE FACT THAT THE MAD PRIEST LADY FROM OVER THE RIVER HAD TAKEN TO NAILING WEASELS TO MY FRONT DOOR AGAIN.
CONTRACT? YOU'LL NEVER GET A CITY HITMAN UP THE MOUNTAIN TO ME--YOU BASTARDS DIE IF THERE'S ACTUAL OXYGEN IN THE AIR.
NO, THE BOOK CONTRACT. YOU STILL OWE US TWO BOOKS.
SPIDER. WE CUT YOU THE ADVANCE FIVE YEARS AGO, FOR GOD'S SAKE.
TEN TIMES
TEN TIMES
AH.
CONFEDERACY of DUNCES

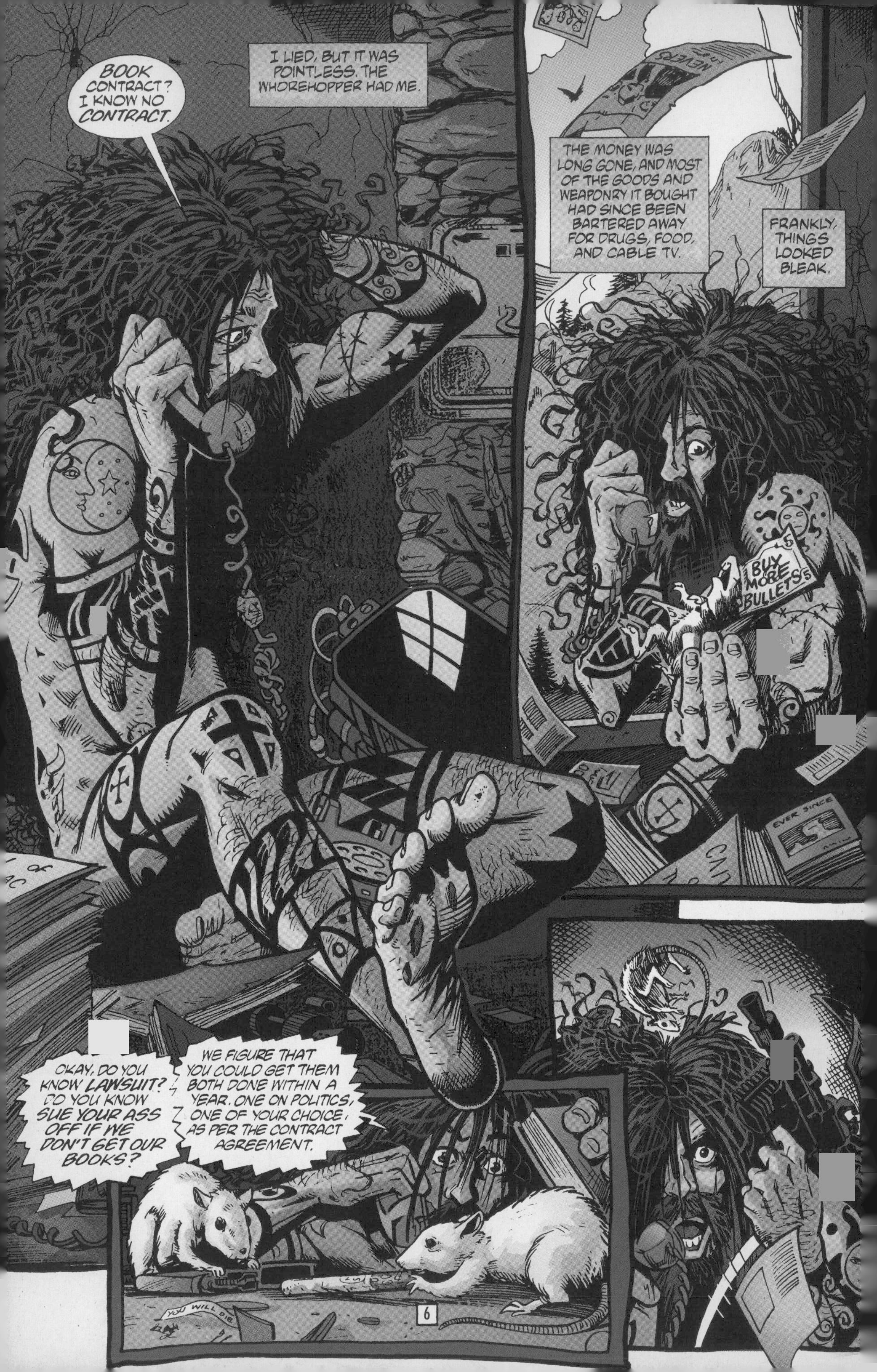

BOOK CONTRACT? I KNOW NO CONTRACT.
I LIED, BUT IT WAS POINTLESS. THE WHOREHOPPER HAD ME.
THE MONEY WAS LONG GONE, AND MOST OF THE GOODS AND WEAPONRY IT BOUGHT HAD SINCE BEEN BARTERED AWAY FOR DRUGS, FOOD, AND CABLE TV.
FRANKLY, THINGS LOOKED BLEAK.
BUY MORE BULLETS
OKAY, DO YOU KNOW LAWSUIT? DO YOU KNOW SUE YOUR ASS OFF IF WE DON'T GET OUR BOOKS?
WE FIGURE THAT YOU COULD GET THEM BOTH DONE WITHIN A YEAR. ONE ON POLITICS, ONE OF YOUR CHOICE, AS PER THE CONTRACT AGREEMENT.
YOU WILL DIE

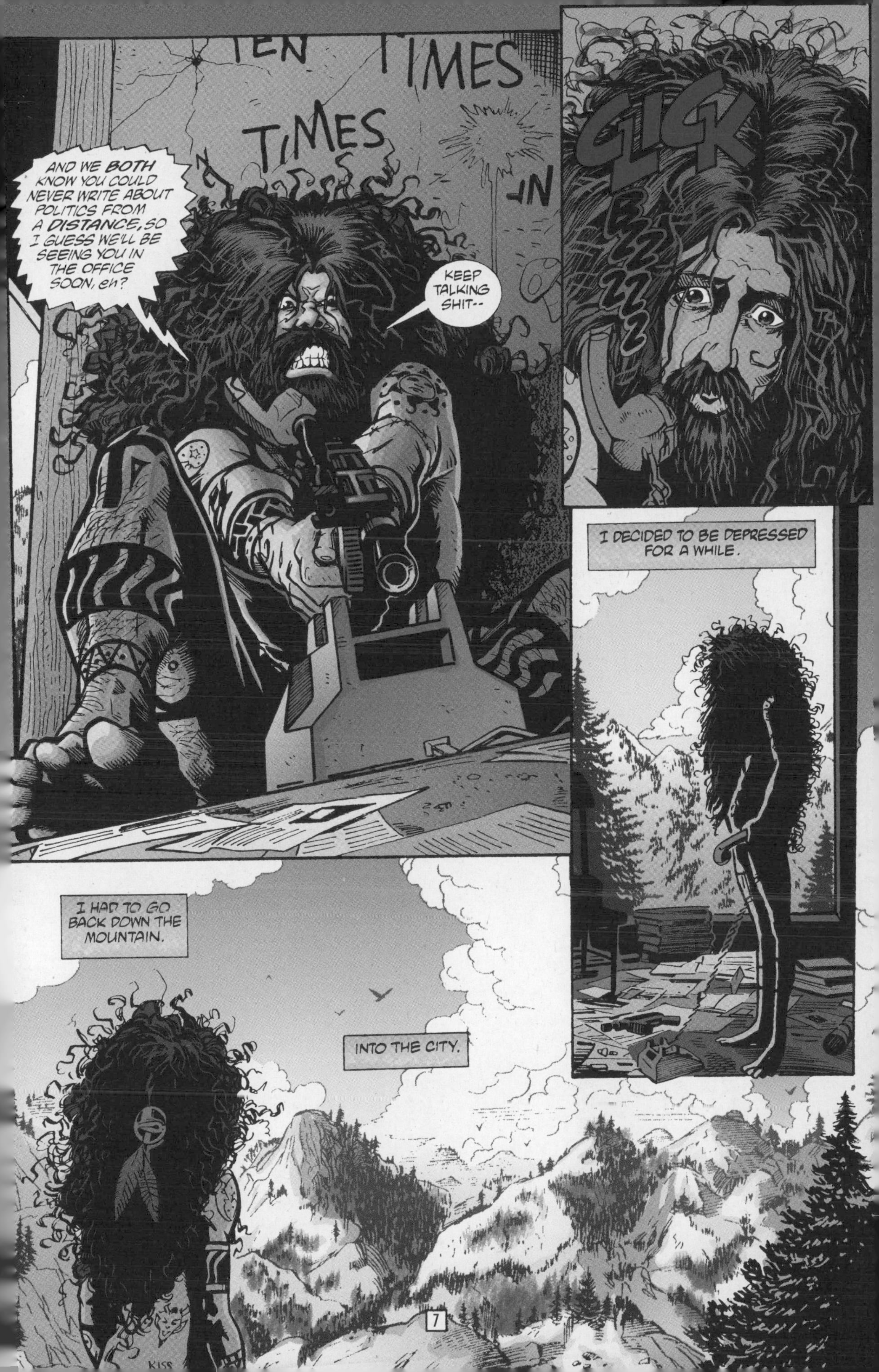
TEN TIMES
TIMES
AND WE BOTH KNOW YOU COULD NEVER WRITE ABOUT POLITICS FROM A DISTANCE, SO I GUESS WE'LL BE SEEING YOU IN THE OFFICE SOON, eh?
KEEP TALKING SHIT--
CLICK
I DECIDED TO BE DEPRESSED FOR A WHILE.
I HAD TO GO BACK DOWN THE MOUNTAIN.
INTO THE CITY.

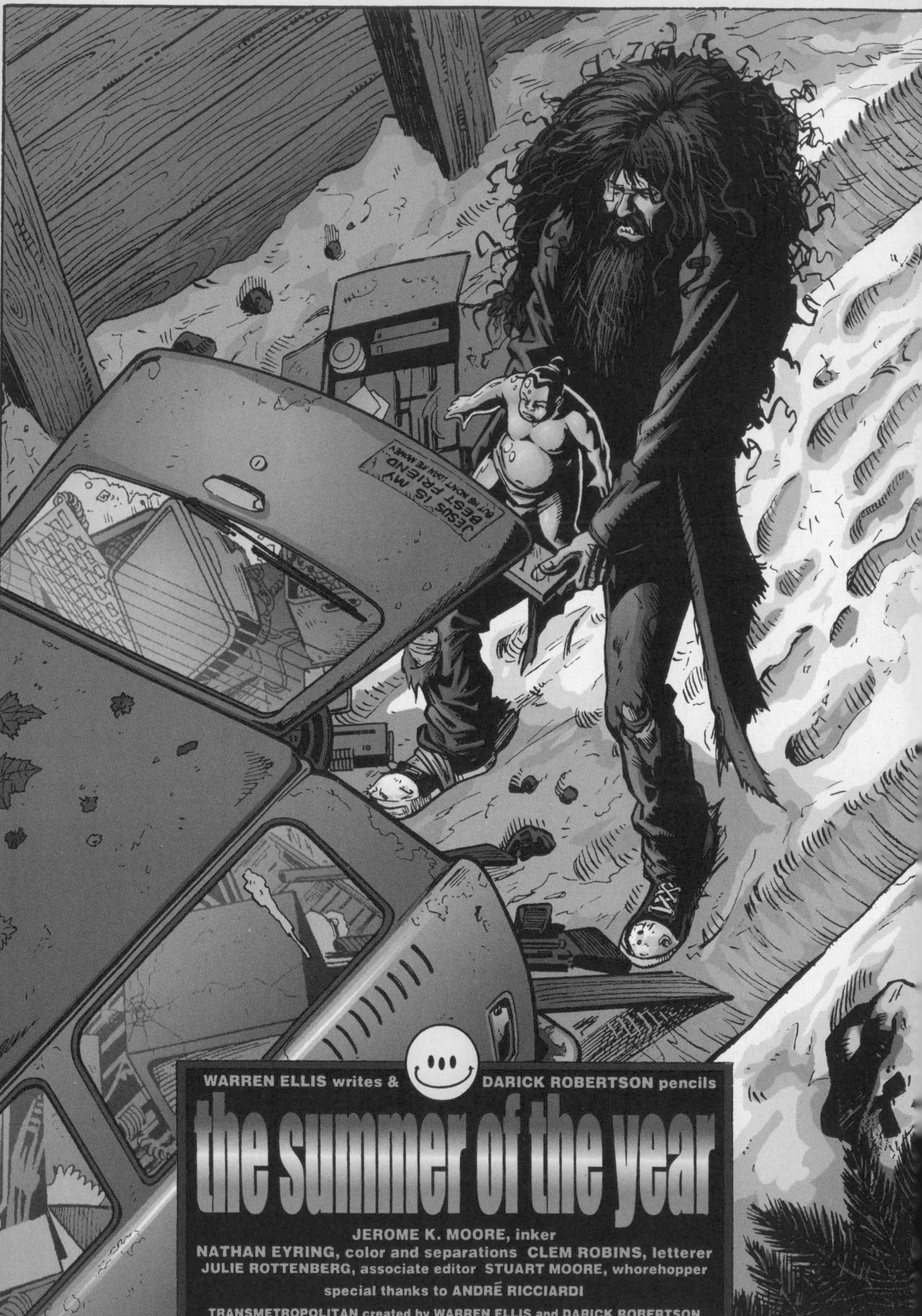

JESUS IS MY BEST FRIEND
BUT HE WON'T LOAN ME MONEY...
WARREN ELLIS writes & DARICK ROBERTSON pencils
the summer of the year
JEROME K. MOORE, inker
NATHAN EYRING, color and separations CLEM ROBINS, letterer
JULIE ROTTENBERG, associate editor STUART MOORE, whorehopper
special thanks to ANDRÉ RICCIARDI
TRANSMETROPOLITAN created by WARREN ELLIS and DARICK ROBERTSON

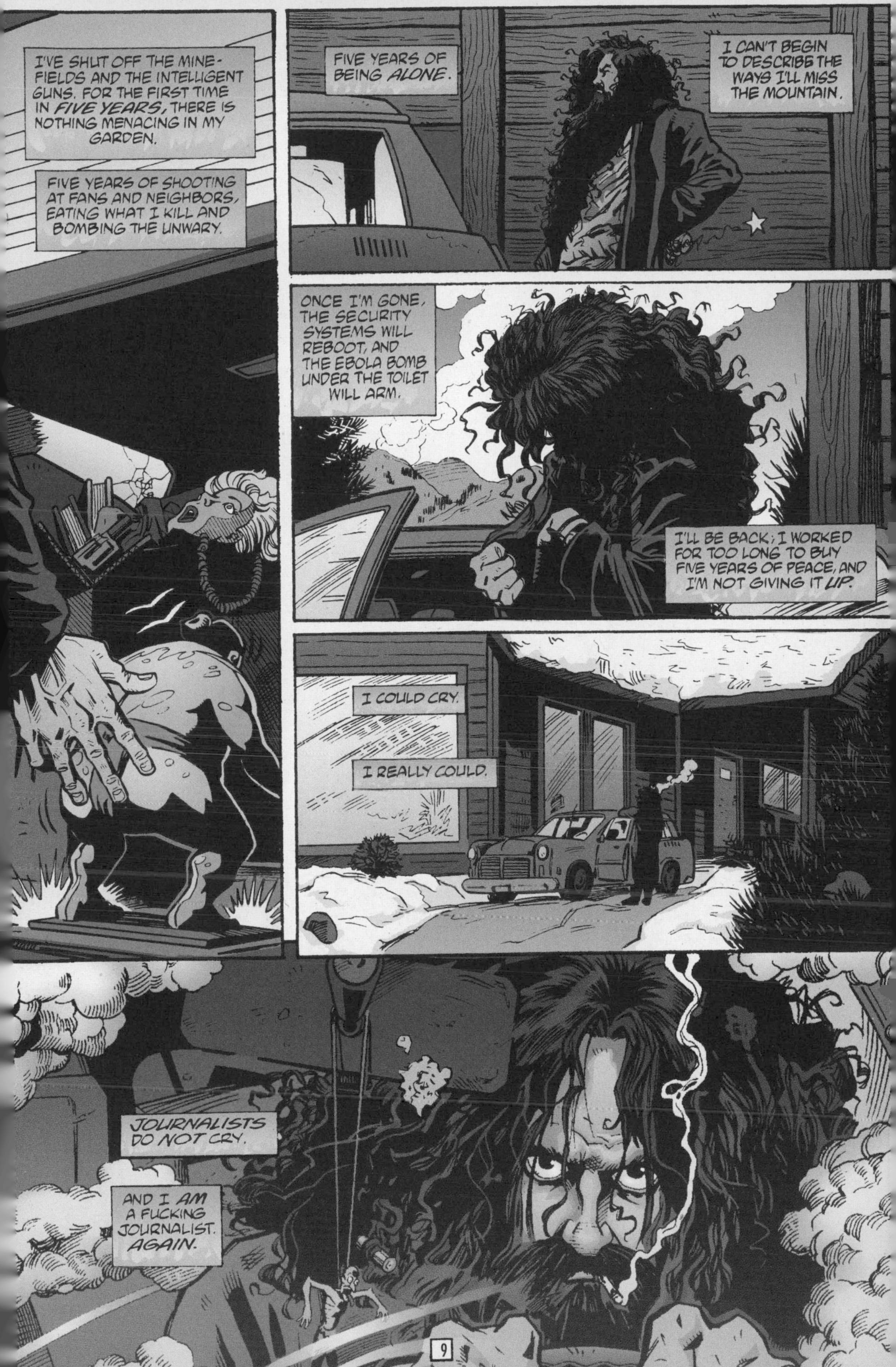
I'VE SHUT OFF THE MINE-FIELDS AND THE INTELLIGENT GUNS. FOR THE FIRST TIME IN FIVE YEARS, THERE IS NOTHING MENACING IN MY GARDEN.
FIVE YEARS OF SHOOTING AT FANS AND NEIGHBORS, EATING WHAT I KILL AND BOMBING THE UNWARY.
FIVE YEARS OF BEING ALONE.
I CAN'T BEGIN TO DESCRIBE THE WAYS I'LL MISS THE MOUNTAIN.
ONCE I'M GONE, THE SECURITY SYSTEMS WILL REBOOT, AND THE EBOLA BOMB UNDER THE TOILET WILL ARM.
I'LL BE BACK; I WORKED FOR TOO LONG TO BUY FIVE YEARS OF PEACE, AND I'M NOT GIVING IT UP.
I COULD CRY.
I REALLY COULD.
JOURNALISTS DO NOT CRY.
AND I AM A FUCKING JOURNALIST. AGAIN.

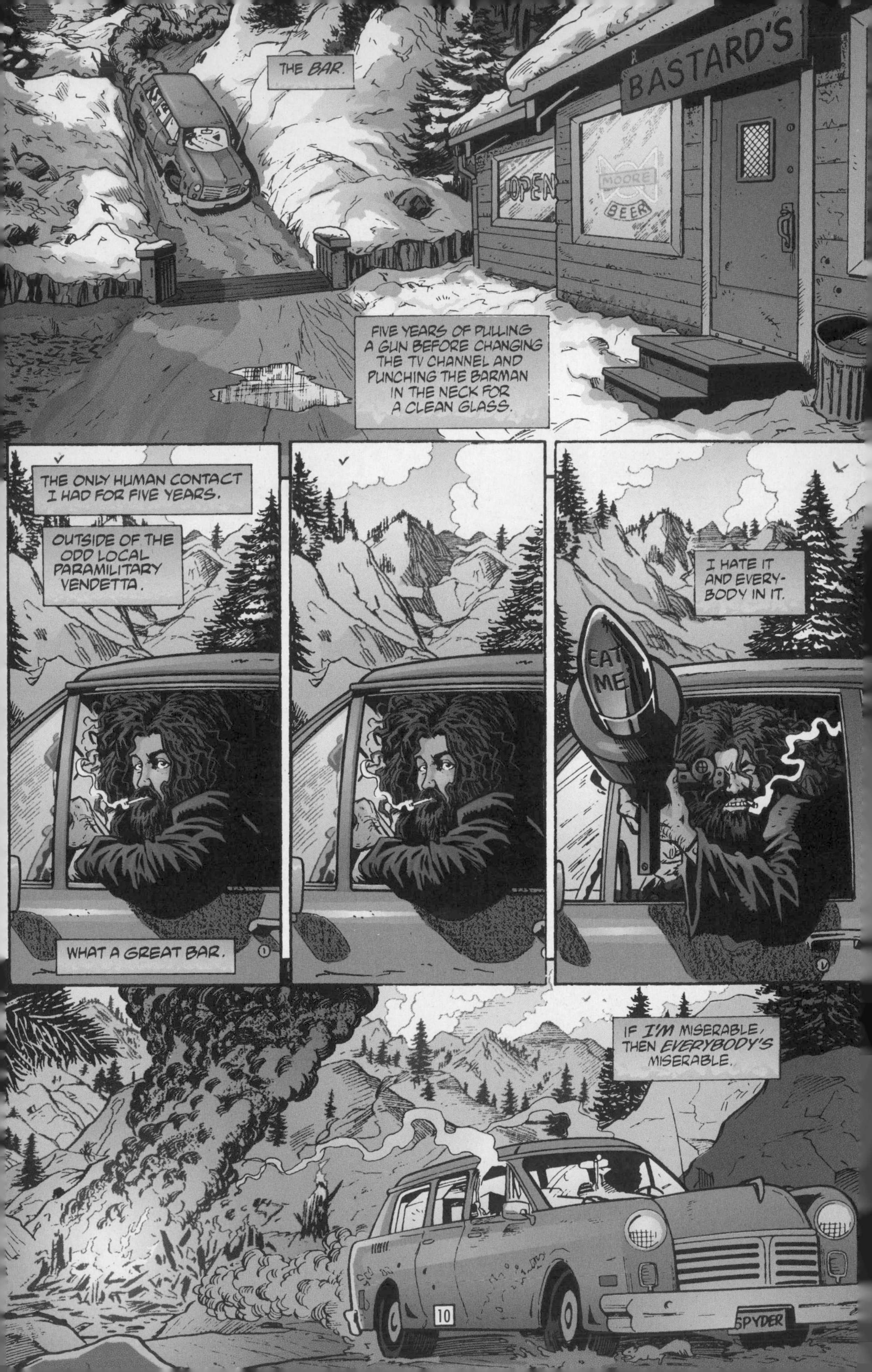
BASTARD'S
THE *BAR*.
OPEN
MOORE
BEER
FIVE YEARS OF PULLING A GUN BEFORE CHANGING THE TV CHANNEL AND PUNCHING THE BARMAN IN THE NECK FOR A CLEAN GLASS.
THE ONLY HUMAN CONTACT I HAD FOR FIVE YEARS.
OUTSIDE OF THE ODD LOCAL PARAMILITARY VENDETTA.
WHAT A GREAT BAR.
I HATE IT AND EVERYBODY IN IT.
EAT ME
IF *I'M* MISERABLE, THEN *EVERYBODY'S* MISERABLE.
SPYDER

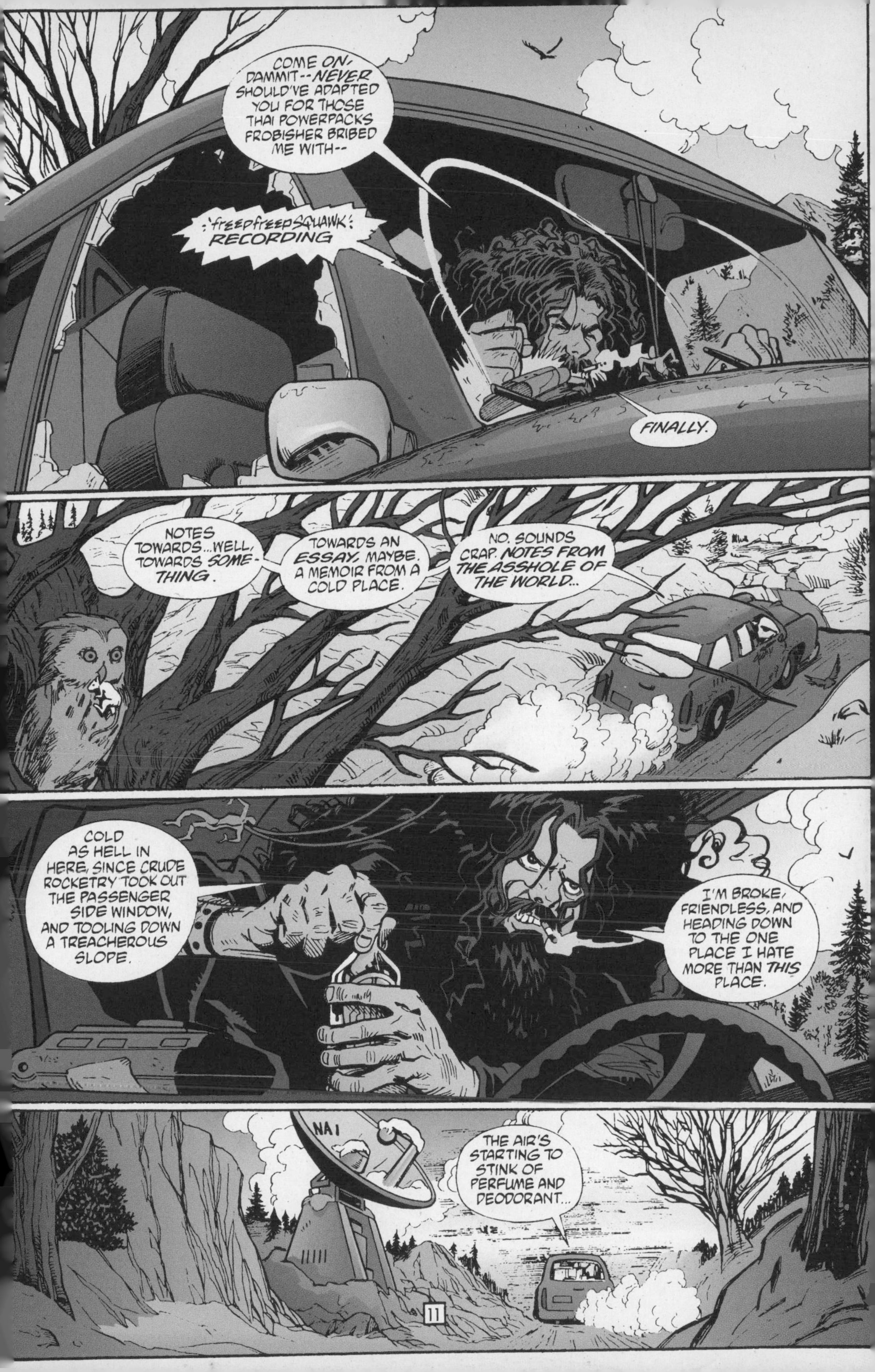

COME ON, DAMMIT--NEVER SHOULD'VE ADAPTED YOU FOR THOSE THAI POWERPACKS FROBISHER BRIBED ME WITH--
:freepfreepSQUAWK: RECORDING
FINALLY.
NOTES TOWARDS...WELL, TOWARDS SOMETHING.
TOWARDS AN ESSAY, MAYBE. A MEMOIR FROM A COLD PLACE.
NO. SOUNDS CRAP. NOTES FROM THE ASSHOLE OF THE WORLD...
COLD AS HELL IN HERE, SINCE CRUDE ROCKETRY TOOK OUT THE PASSENGER SIDE WINDOW, AND TOOLING DOWN A TREACHEROUS SLOPE.
I'M BROKE, FRIENDLESS, AND HEADING DOWN TO THE ONE PLACE I HATE MORE THAN THIS PLACE.
NAI
THE AIR'S STARTING TO STINK OF PERFUME AND DEODORANT...

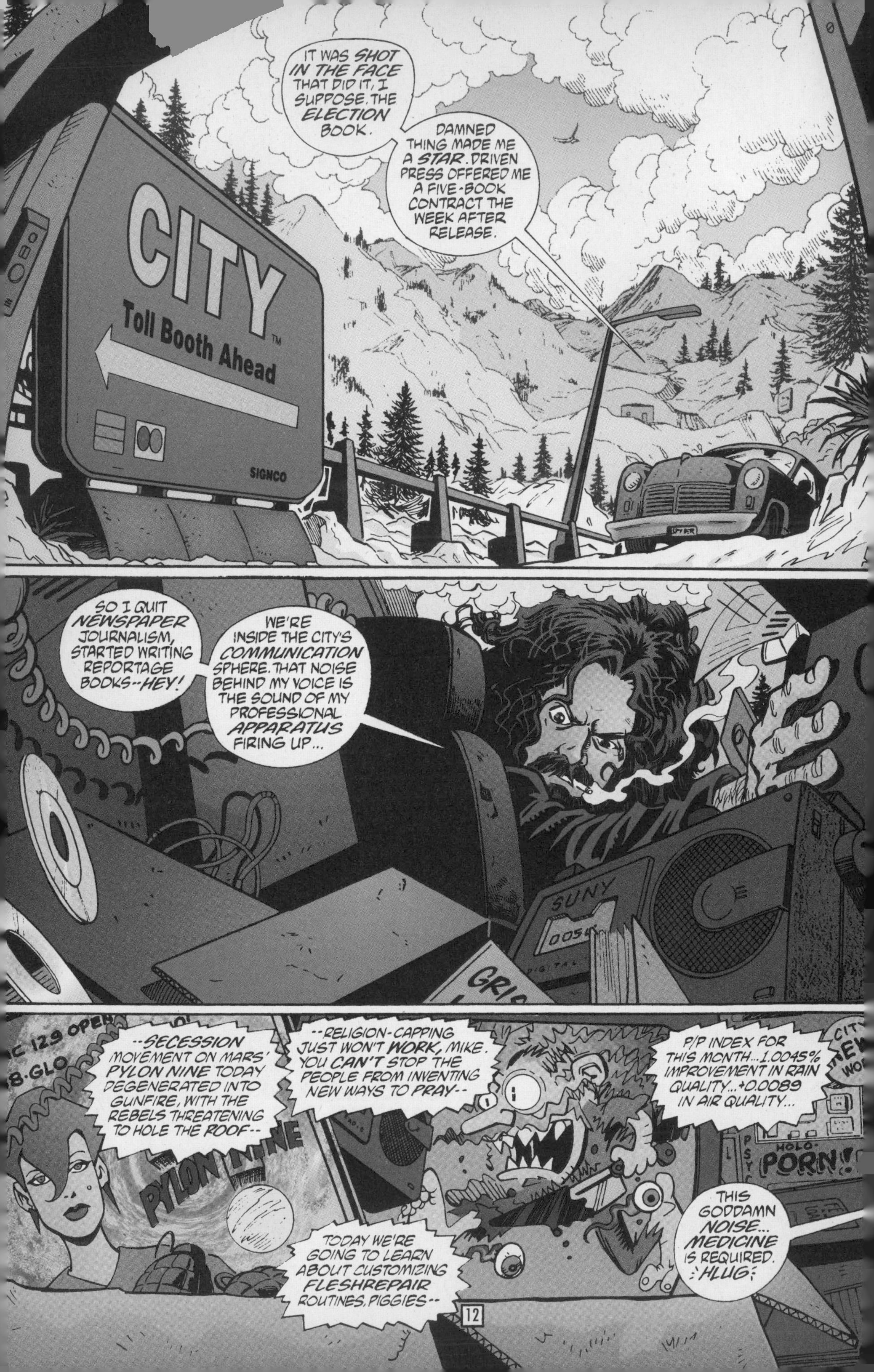
IT WAS SHOT IN THE FACE THAT DID IT, I SUPPOSE. THE ELECTION BOOK.
DAMNED THING MADE ME A STAR. DRIVEN PRESS OFFERED ME A FIVE-BOOK CONTRACT THE WEEK AFTER RELEASE.
CITY
Toll Booth Ahead
SIGNCO
SO I QUIT NEWSPAPER JOURNALISM, STARTED WRITING REPORTAGE BOOKS--HEY!
WE'RE INSIDE THE CITY'S COMMUNICATION SPHERE. THAT NOISE BEHIND MY VOICE IS THE SOUND OF MY PROFESSIONAL APPARATUS FIRING UP...
SUNY
--SECESSION MOVEMENT ON MARS' PYLON NINE TODAY DEGENERATED INTO GUNFIRE, WITH THE REBELS THREATENING TO HOLE THE ROOF--
PYLON NINE
--RELIGION-CAPPING JUST WON'T WORK, MIKE. YOU CAN'T STOP THE PEOPLE FROM INVENTING NEW WAYS TO PRAY--
P/P INDEX FOR THIS MONTH...1.0045% IMPROVEMENT IN RAIN QUALITY...+0.0089 IN AIR QUALITY...
HOLO-PORN!
TODAY WE'RE GOING TO LEARN ABOUT CUSTOMIZING FLESHREPAIR ROUTINES, PIGGIES--
THIS GODDAMN NOISE... MEDICINE IS REQUIRED. :HLUG:

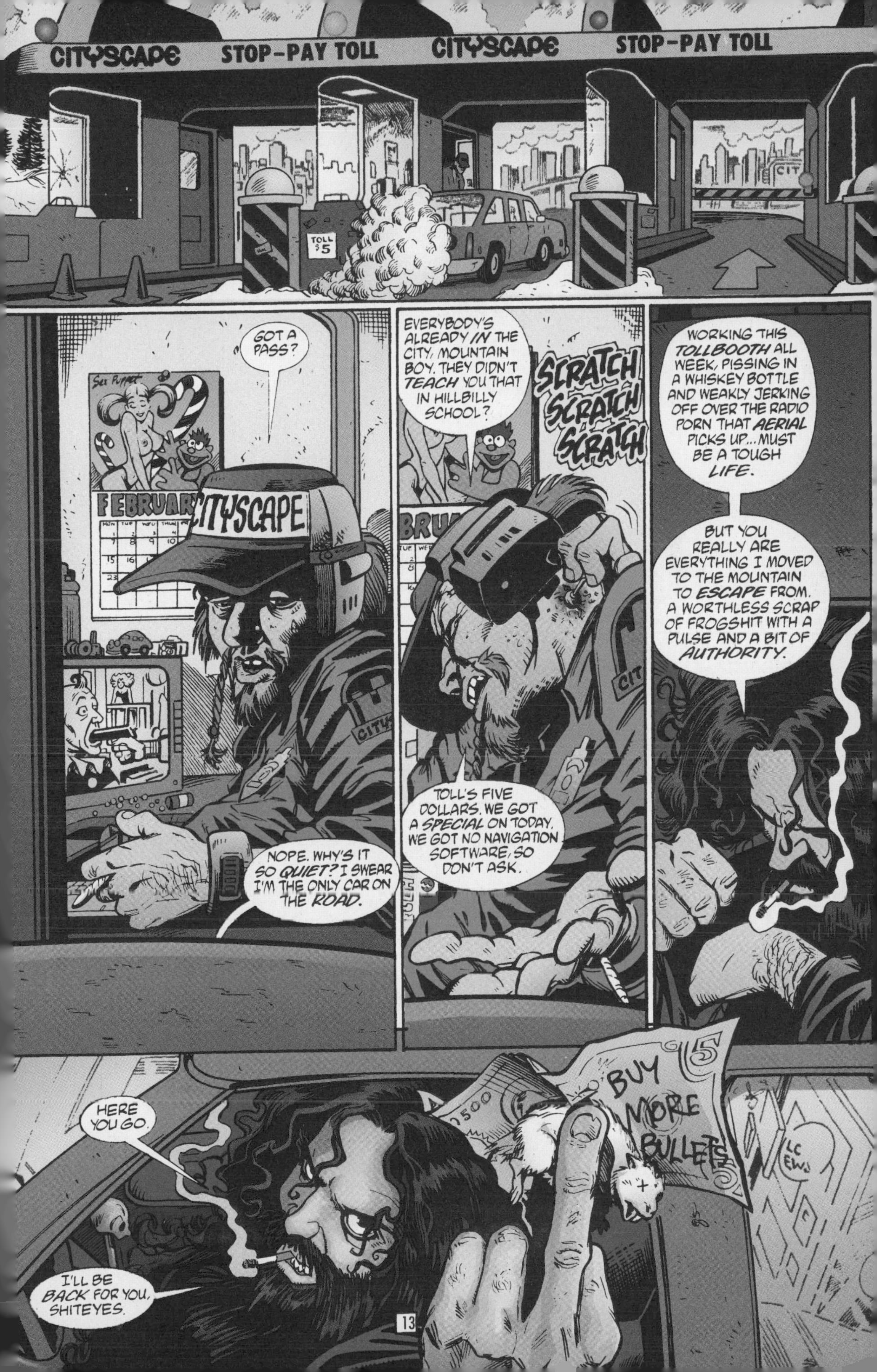
CITYSCAPE
STOP-PAY TOLL
CITYSCAPE
STOP-PAY TOLL
TOLL $5
GOT A PASS?
CITYSCAPE
FEBRUARY
NOPE. WHY'S IT SO QUIET? I SWEAR I'M THE ONLY CAR ON THE ROAD.
EVERYBODY'S ALREADY IN THE CITY, MOUNTAIN BOY. THEY DIDN'T TEACH YOU THAT IN HILLBILLY SCHOOL?
SCRATCH SCRATCH SCRATCH
TOLL'S FIVE DOLLARS. WE GOT A SPECIAL ON TODAY. WE GOT NO NAVIGATION SOFTWARE, SO DON'T ASK.
WORKING THIS TOLLBOOTH ALL WEEK, PISSING IN A WHISKEY BOTTLE AND WEAKLY JERKING OFF OVER THE RADIO PORN THAT AERIAL PICKS UP... MUST BE A TOUGH LIFE.
BUT YOU REALLY ARE EVERYTHING I MOVED TO THE MOUNTAIN TO ESCAPE FROM. A WORTHLESS SCRAP OF FROGSHIT WITH A PULSE AND A BIT OF AUTHORITY.
HERE YOU GO.
BUY MORE BULLETS
I'LL BE BACK FOR YOU, SHITEYES.

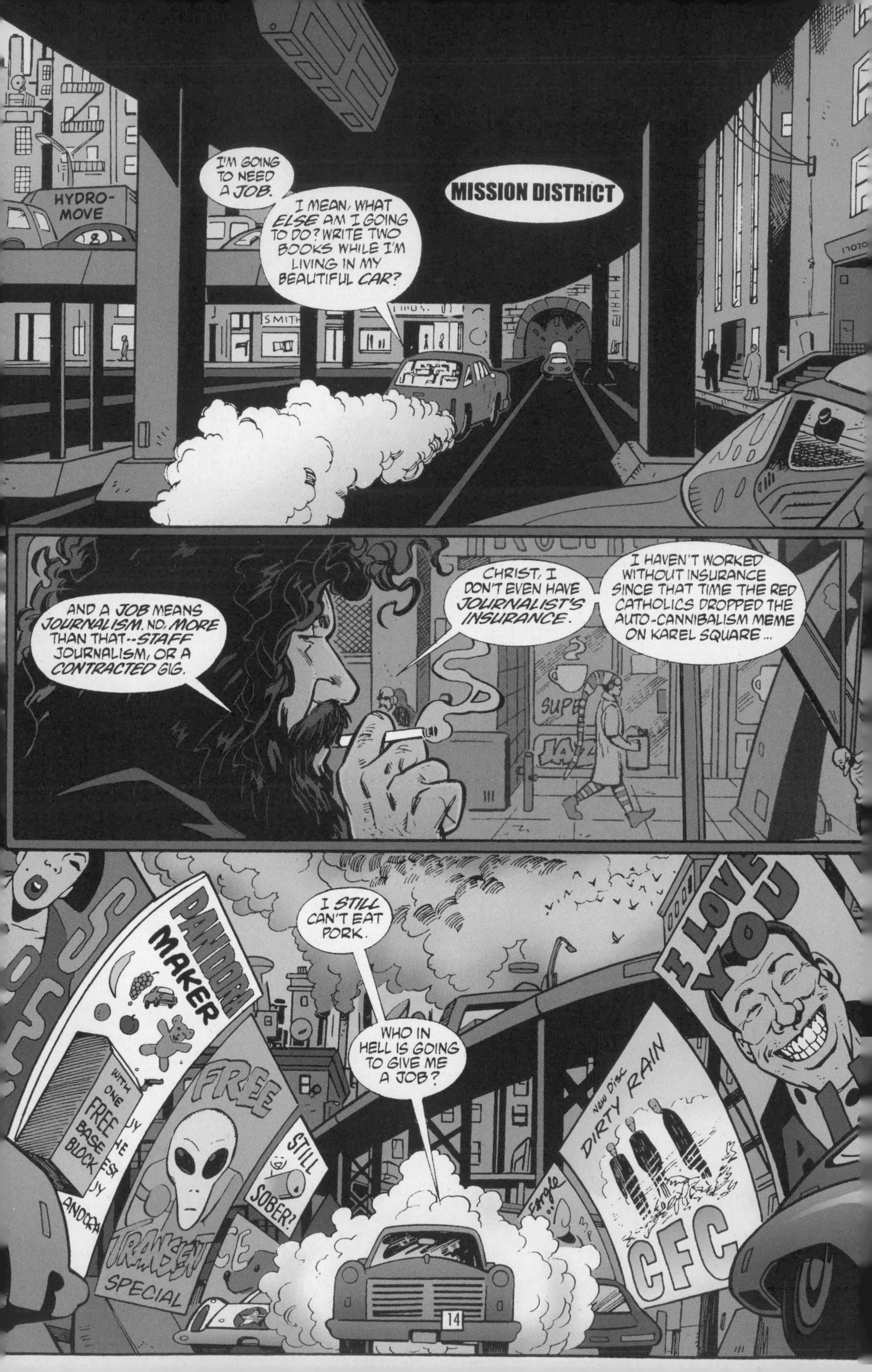
HYDRO-MOVE
I'M GOING TO NEED A JOB.
MISSION DISTRICT
I MEAN, WHAT ELSE AM I GOING TO DO? WRITE TWO BOOKS WHILE I'M LIVING IN MY BEAUTIFUL CAR?
SMITH
AND A JOB MEANS JOURNALISM. NO, MORE THAN THAT--STAFF JOURNALISM, OR A CONTRACTED GIG.
CHRIST, I DON'T EVEN HAVE JOURNALIST'S INSURANCE.
I HAVEN'T WORKED WITHOUT INSURANCE SINCE THAT TIME THE RED CATHOLICS DROPPED THE AUTO-CANNIBALISM MEME ON KAREL SQUARE ...
SUPE
PANDORA MAKER
WITH ONE FREE BASE BLOCK
FREE
TRANSIENT SPECIAL
STILL SOBER?
I STILL CAN'T EAT PORK.
WHO IN HELL IS GOING TO GIVE ME A JOB?
I LOVE YOU
New Disc DIRTY RAIN
CFC
14

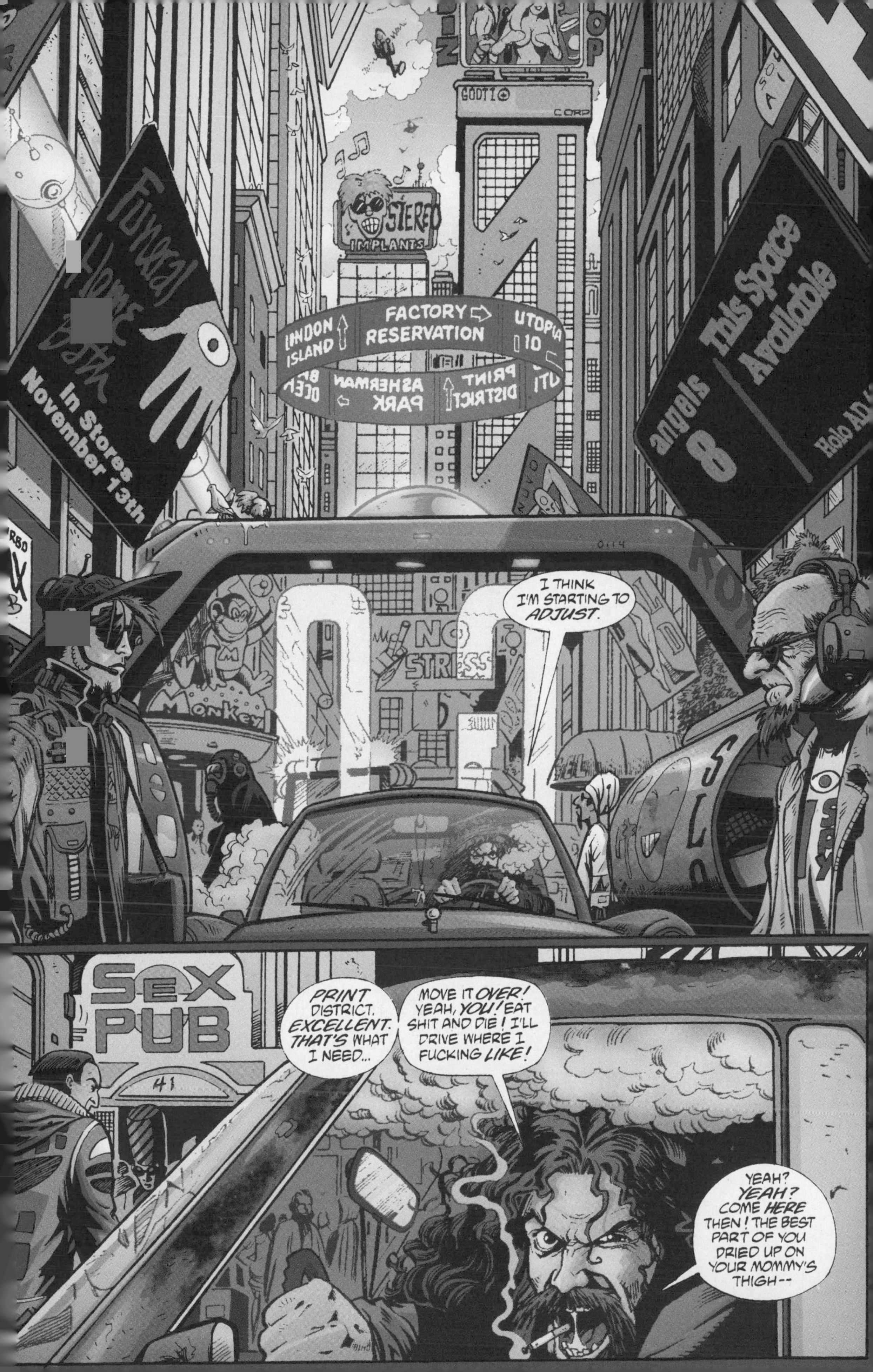
STEREO
IMPLANTS
FACTORY
RESERVATION
LONDON
ISLAND
UTOPIA
10
ASHERMAN
PARK
PRINT
DISTRICT
In Stores
November 13th
This Space
Available
angels
8
NO
STRESS
Monkey
I THINK I'M STARTING TO ADJUST.
SEX
PUB
41
PRINT DISTRICT. EXCELLENT. THAT'S WHAT I NEED...
MOVE IT OVER! YEAH, YOU! EAT SHIT AND DIE! I'LL DRIVE WHERE I FUCKING LIKE!
YEAH? YEAH? COME HERE THEN! THE BEST PART OF YOU DRIED UP ON YOUR MOMMY'S THIGH--

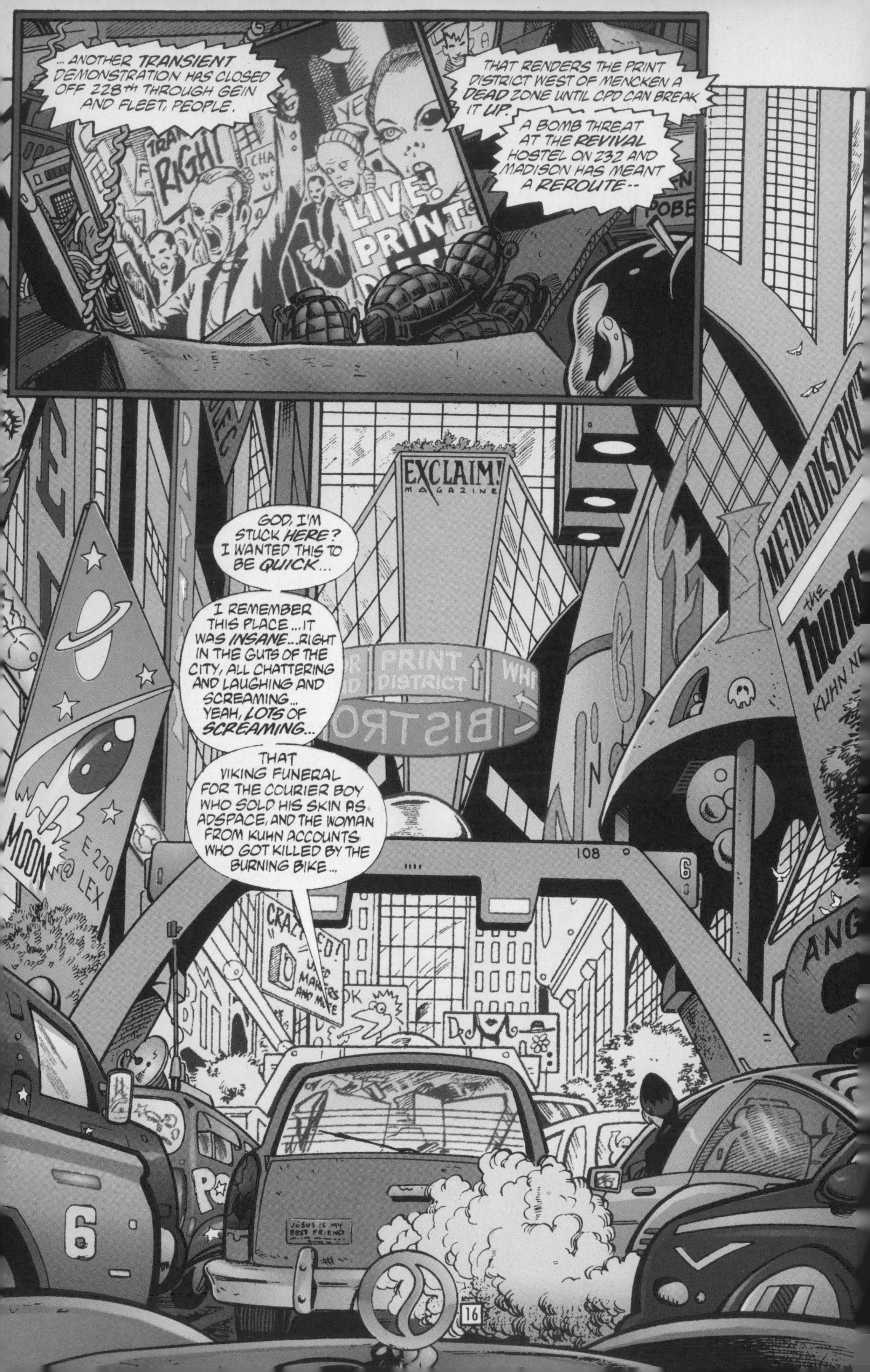
...ANOTHER TRANSIENT DEMONSTRATION HAS CLOSED OFF 228th THROUGH GEIN AND FLEET, PEOPLE.
THAT RENDERS THE PRINT DISTRICT WEST OF MENCKEN A DEAD ZONE UNTIL CPD CAN BREAK IT UP.
A BOMB THREAT AT THE REVIVAL HOSTEL ON 232 AND MADISON HAS MEANT A REROUTE--
LIVE! PRINT
EXCLAIM! MAGAZINE
MEDIA DISTRICT
GOD, I'M STUCK HERE? I WANTED THIS TO BE QUICK...
I REMEMBER THIS PLACE...IT WAS INSANE...RIGHT IN THE GUTS OF THE CITY, ALL CHATTERING AND LAUGHING AND SCREAMING... YEAH, LOTS OF SCREAMING...
PRINT DISTRICT
BISTRO
THAT VIKING FUNERAL FOR THE COURIER BOY WHO SOLD HIS SKIN AS ADSPACE, AND THE WOMAN FROM KUHN ACCOUNTS WHO GOT KILLED BY THE BURNING BIKE...
MOON @ E 270 LEX
108
JESUS IS MY BEST FRIEND

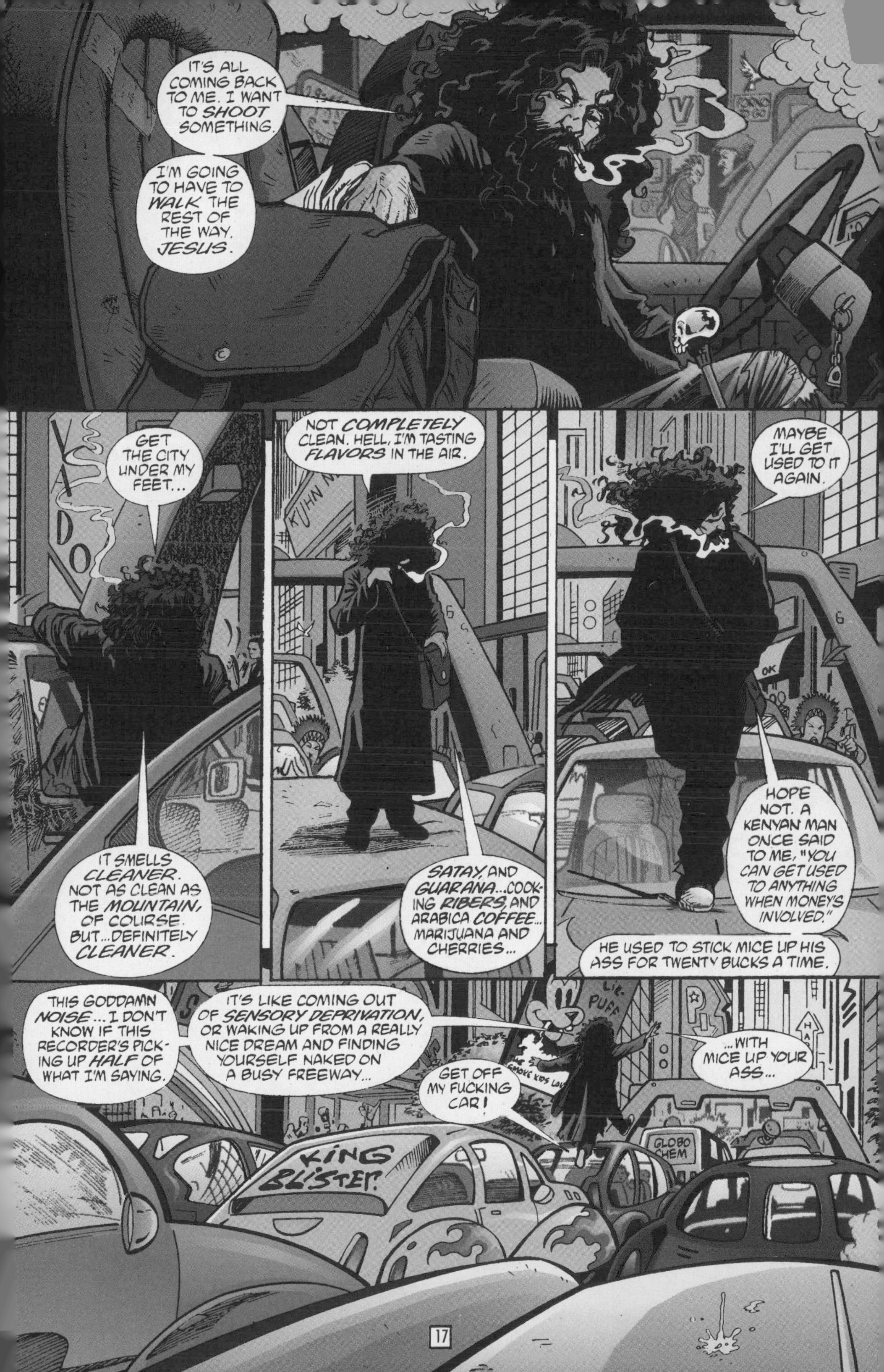
IT'S ALL COMING BACK TO ME. I WANT TO *SHOOT* SOMETHING.
I'M GOING TO HAVE TO *WALK* THE REST OF THE WAY. *JESUS*.
PORNO GO GO
GET THE CITY UNDER MY FEET...
IT SMELLS *CLEANER*. NOT AS CLEAN AS THE *MOUNTAIN*, OF COURSE. BUT...DEFINITELY *CLEANER*.
NOT *COMPLETELY* CLEAN. HELL, I'M TASTING *FLAVORS* IN THE AIR.
SATAY, AND *GUARANA*...COOKING *RIBERS*, AND ARABICA *COFFEE*... MARIJUANA AND CHERRIES...
MAYBE I'LL GET USED TO IT AGAIN.
OK
HOPE NOT. A KENYAN MAN ONCE SAID TO ME, "YOU CAN GET USED TO ANYTHING WHEN MONEY'S INVOLVED."
HE USED TO STICK MICE UP HIS ASS FOR TWENTY BUCKS A TIME.
THIS GODDAMN *NOISE*... I DON'T KNOW IF THIS RECORDER'S PICKING UP *HALF* OF WHAT I'M SAYING.
IT'S LIKE COMING OUT OF *SENSORY DEPRIVATION*, OR WAKING UP FROM A REALLY NICE DREAM AND FINDING YOURSELF NAKED ON A BUSY FREEWAY...
...WITH MICE UP YOUR ASS...
GET OFF MY FUCKING CAR!
KING BLISTER
GLOBO CHEM

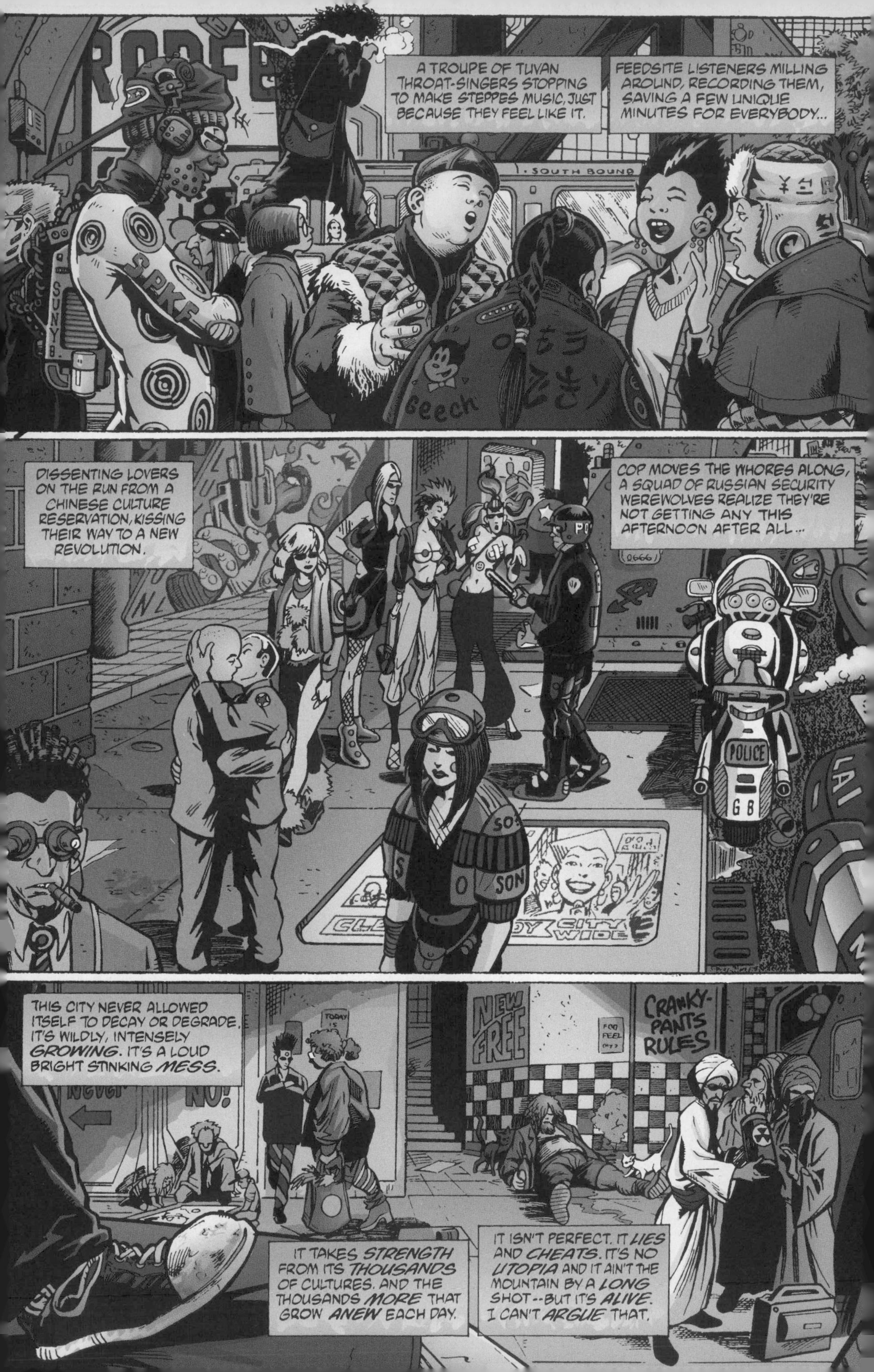
A TROUPE OF TUVAN THROAT-SINGERS STOPPING TO MAKE STEPPES MUSIC, JUST BECAUSE THEY FEEL LIKE IT.
FEEDSITE LISTENERS MILLING AROUND, RECORDING THEM, SAVING A FEW UNIQUE MINUTES FOR EVERYBODY...
SOUTH BOUND
DISSENTING LOVERS ON THE RUN FROM A CHINESE CULTURE RESERVATION, KISSING THEIR WAY TO A NEW REVOLUTION.
COP MOVES THE WHORES ALONG, A SQUAD OF RUSSIAN SECURITY WEREWOLVES REALIZE THEY'RE NOT GETTING ANY THIS AFTERNOON AFTER ALL...
POLICE
GB
CITY WIDE
THIS CITY NEVER ALLOWED ITSELF TO DECAY OR DEGRADE. IT'S WILDLY, INTENSELY *GROWING*. IT'S A LOUD BRIGHT STINKING *MESS*.
NEW FREE
CRANKY-PANTS RULES
NO!
IT TAKES *STRENGTH* FROM ITS *THOUSANDS* OF CULTURES. AND THE THOUSANDS *MORE* THAT GROW *ANEW* EACH DAY.
IT ISN'T PERFECT. IT *LIES* AND *CHEATS*. IT'S NO *UTOPIA* AND IT AIN'T THE MOUNTAIN BY A *LONG* SHOT--BUT IT'S *ALIVE*. I CAN'T *ARGUE* THAT.

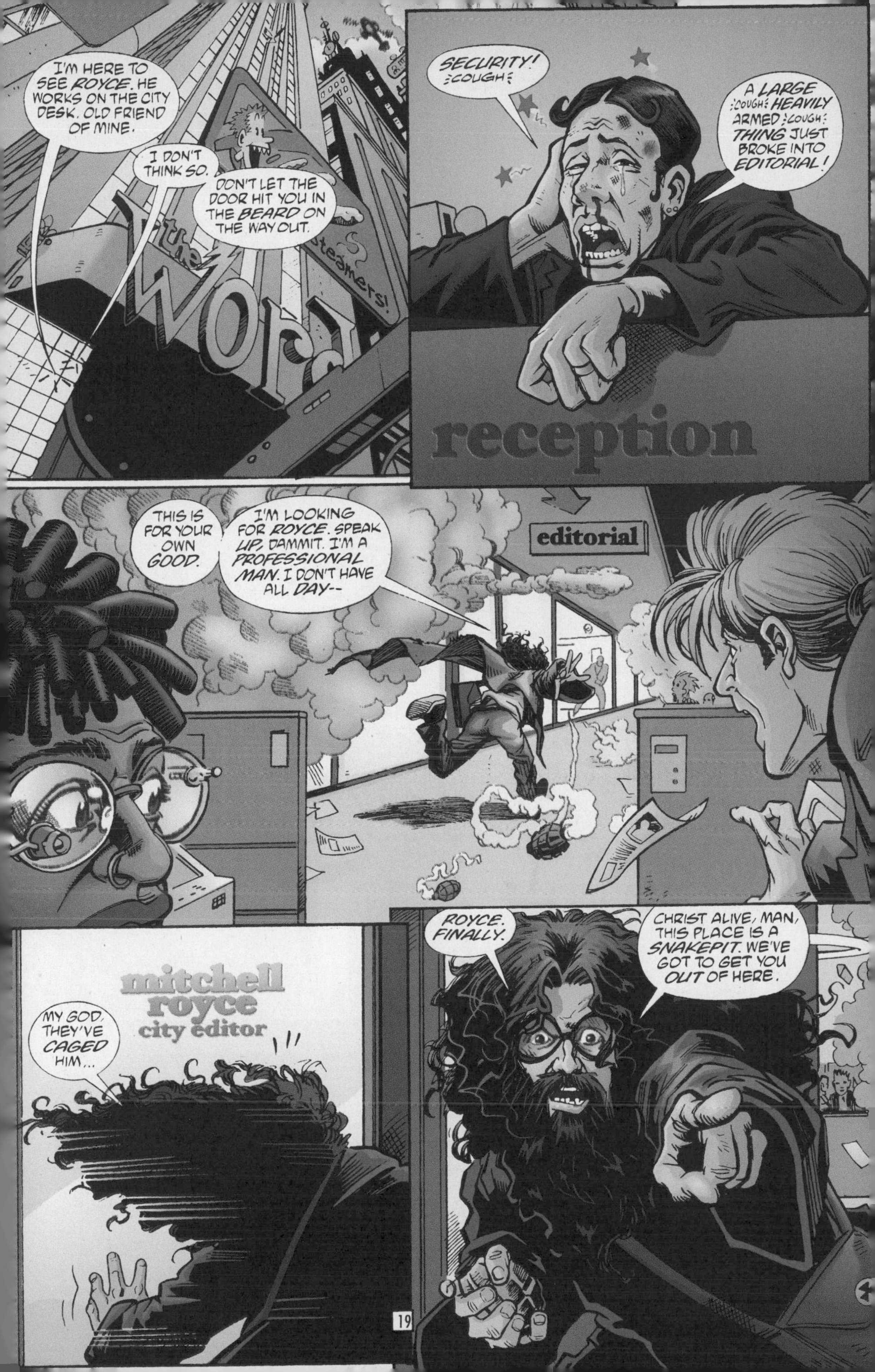
I'M HERE TO SEE ROYCE. HE WORKS ON THE CITY DESK. OLD FRIEND OF MINE.
I DON'T THINK SO.
DON'T LET THE DOOR HIT YOU IN THE BEARD ON THE WAY OUT.
the WORD
steamers!
SECURITY! :COUGH:
A LARGE :COUGH: HEAVILY ARMED :COUGH: THING JUST BROKE INTO EDITORIAL!
reception
editorial
THIS IS FOR YOUR OWN GOOD.
I'M LOOKING FOR ROYCE. SPEAK UP, DAMMIT. I'M A PROFESSIONAL MAN. I DON'T HAVE ALL DAY--
mitchell royce city editor
MY GOD. THEY'VE CAGED HIM...
ROYCE. FINALLY.
CHRIST ALIVE, MAN, THIS PLACE IS A SNAKEPIT. WE'VE GOT TO GET YOU OUT OF HERE.

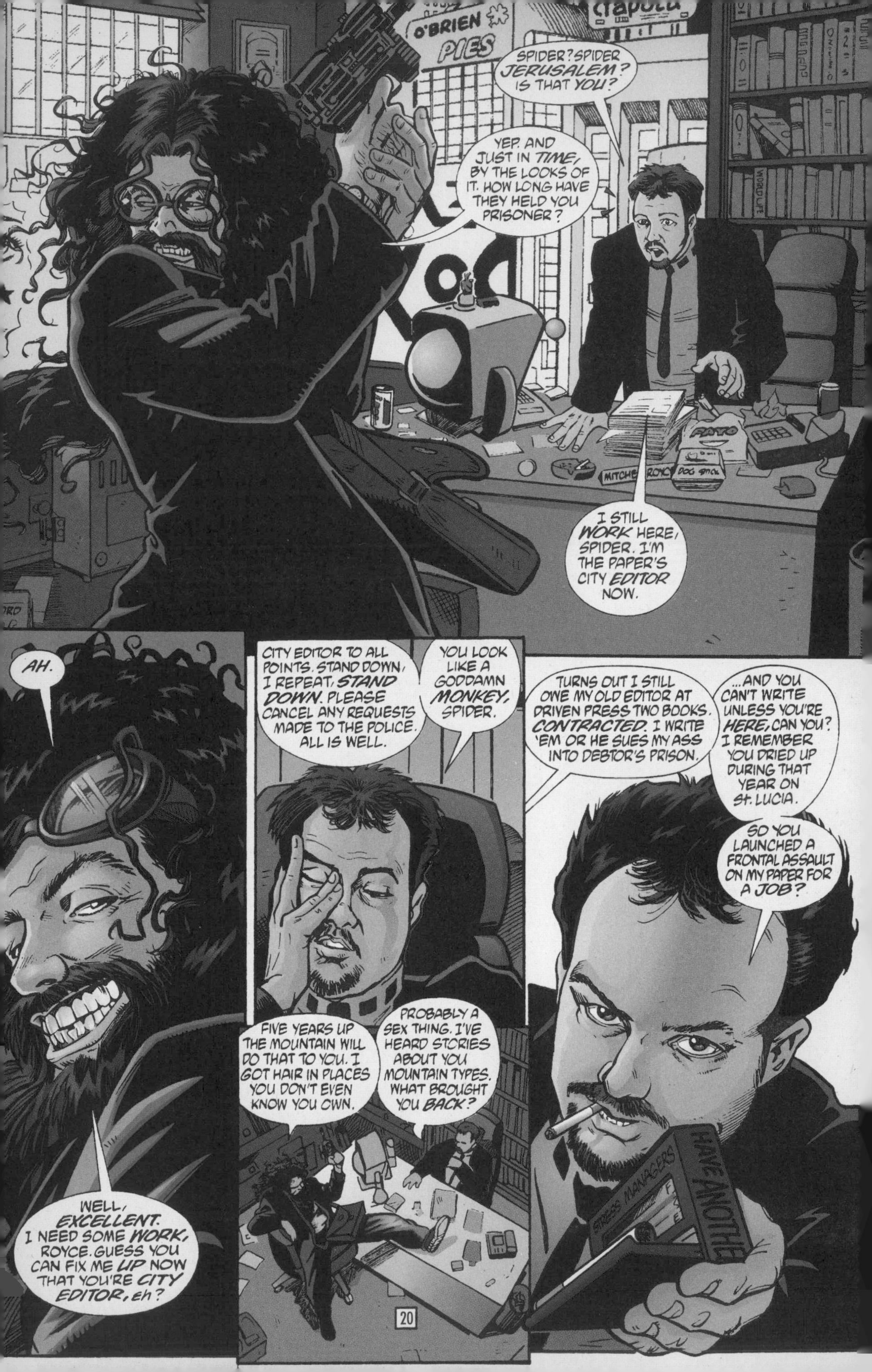
O'BRIEN PIES
SPIDER? SPIDER JERUSALEM? IS THAT YOU?
YEP. AND JUST IN TIME, BY THE LOOKS OF IT. HOW LONG HAVE THEY HELD YOU PRISONER?
I STILL WORK HERE, SPIDER. I'M THE PAPER'S CITY EDITOR NOW.
AH.
WELL, EXCELLENT. I NEED SOME WORK, ROYCE. GUESS YOU CAN FIX ME UP NOW THAT YOU'RE CITY EDITOR, eh?
CITY EDITOR TO ALL POINTS. STAND DOWN, I REPEAT, STAND DOWN. PLEASE CANCEL ANY REQUESTS MADE TO THE POLICE. ALL IS WELL.
YOU LOOK LIKE A GODDAMN MONKEY, SPIDER.
FIVE YEARS UP THE MOUNTAIN WILL DO THAT TO YOU. I GOT HAIR IN PLACES YOU DON'T EVEN KNOW YOU OWN.
PROBABLY A SEX THING. I'VE HEARD STORIES ABOUT YOU MOUNTAIN TYPES. WHAT BROUGHT YOU BACK?
TURNS OUT I STILL OWE MY OLD EDITOR AT DRIVEN PRESS TWO BOOKS. CONTRACTED. I WRITE 'EM OR HE SUES MY ASS INTO DEBTOR'S PRISON.
...AND YOU CAN'T WRITE UNLESS YOU'RE HERE, CAN YOU? I REMEMBER YOU DRIED UP DURING THAT YEAR ON St. LUCIA.
SO YOU LAUNCHED A FRONTAL ASSAULT ON MY PAPER FOR A JOB?
STRESS MANAGERS
HAVE ANOTHE
20

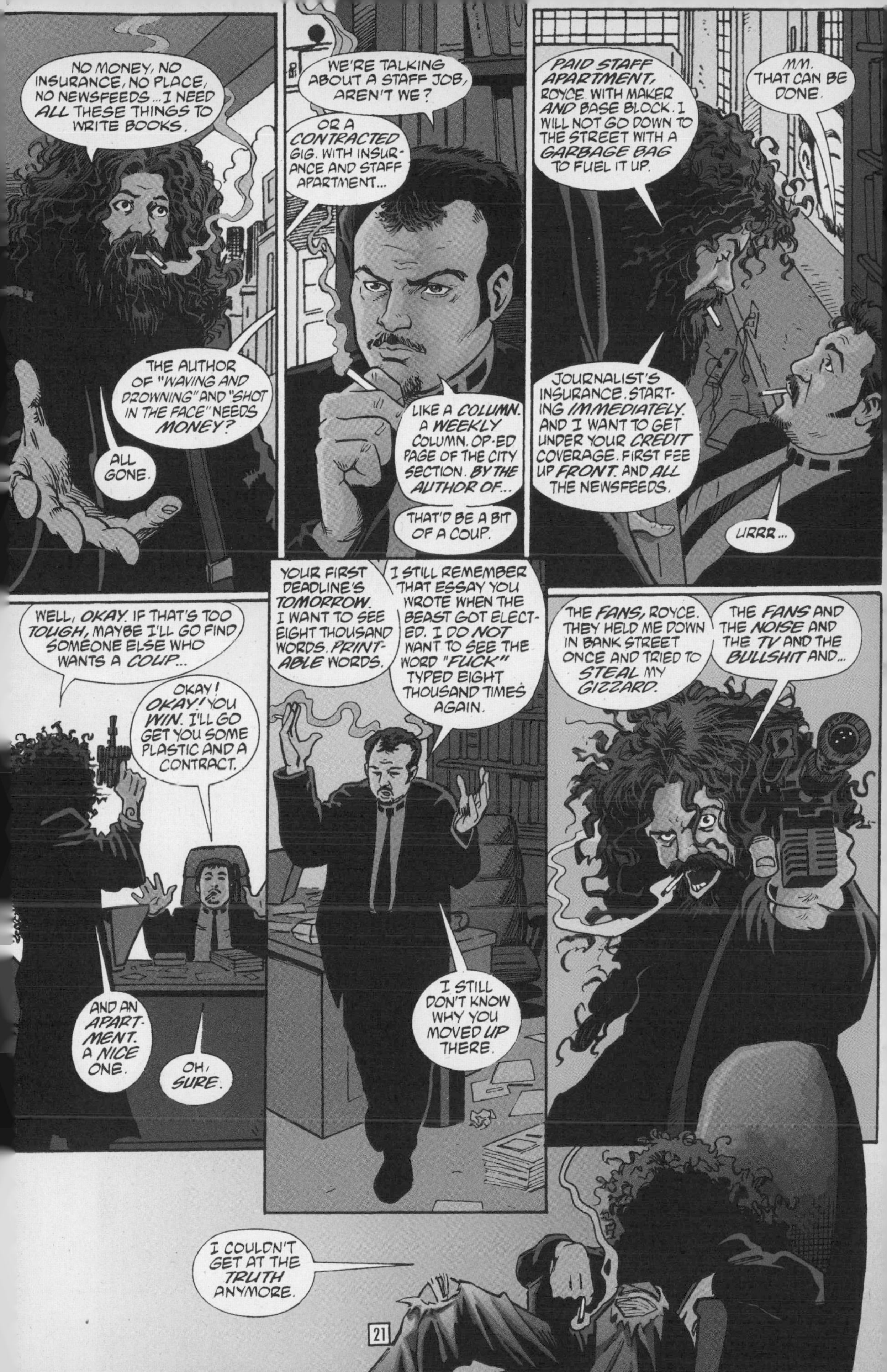
NO MONEY, NO INSURANCE, NO PLACE, NO NEWSFEEDS... I NEED ALL THESE THINGS TO WRITE BOOKS.
THE AUTHOR OF "WAVING AND DROWNING" AND "SHOT IN THE FACE" NEEDS MONEY?
ALL GONE.
WE'RE TALKING ABOUT A STAFF JOB, AREN'T WE?
OR A CONTRACTED GIG. WITH INSURANCE AND STAFF APARTMENT...
LIKE A COLUMN. A WEEKLY COLUMN. OP-ED PAGE OF THE CITY SECTION. BY THE AUTHOR OF...
THAT'D BE A BIT OF A COUP.
PAID STAFF APARTMENT, ROYCE. WITH MAKER AND BASE BLOCK. I WILL NOT GO DOWN TO THE STREET WITH A GARBAGE BAG TO FUEL IT UP.
MM. THAT CAN BE DONE.
JOURNALIST'S INSURANCE. STARTING IMMEDIATELY. AND I WANT TO GET UNDER YOUR CREDIT COVERAGE. FIRST FEE UP FRONT. AND ALL THE NEWSFEEDS.
URRR...
WELL, OKAY. IF THAT'S TOO TOUGH, MAYBE I'LL GO FIND SOMEONE ELSE WHO WANTS A COUP...
OKAY! OKAY! YOU WIN. I'LL GO GET YOU SOME PLASTIC AND A CONTRACT.
AND AN APARTMENT. A NICE ONE.
OH, SURE.
YOUR FIRST DEADLINE'S TOMORROW. I WANT TO SEE EIGHT THOUSAND WORDS. PRINTABLE WORDS.
I STILL REMEMBER THAT ESSAY YOU WROTE WHEN THE BEAST GOT ELECTED. I DO NOT WANT TO SEE THE WORD "FUCK" TYPED EIGHT THOUSAND TIMES AGAIN.
I STILL DON'T KNOW WHY YOU MOVED UP THERE.
THE FANS, ROYCE. THEY HELD ME DOWN IN BANK STREET ONCE AND TRIED TO STEAL MY GIZZARD.
THE FANS AND THE NOISE AND THE TV AND THE BULLSHIT AND...
I COULDN'T GET AT THE TRUTH ANYMORE.

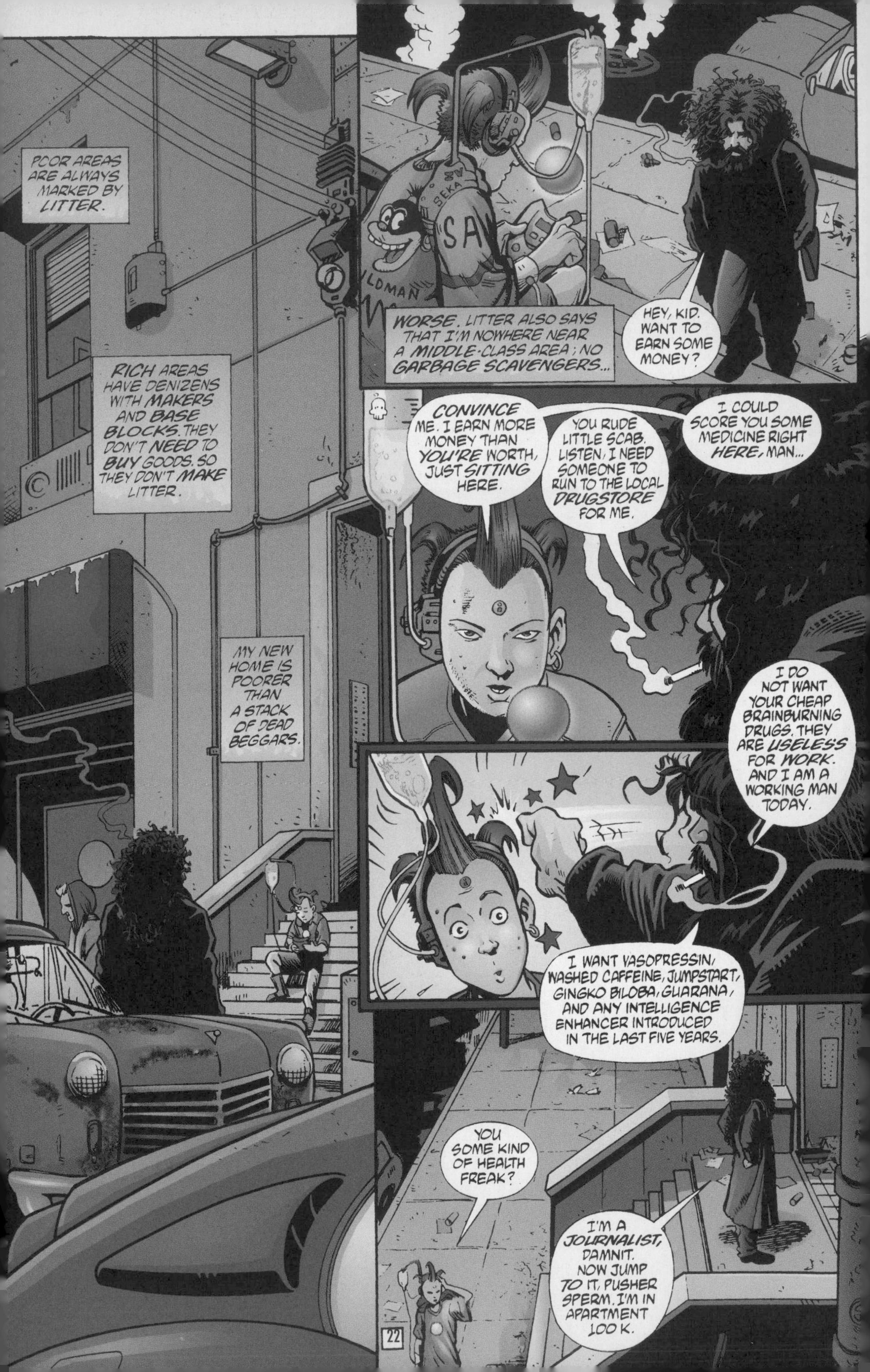

POOR AREAS ARE ALWAYS MARKED BY LITTER.
RICH AREAS HAVE DENIZENS WITH MAKERS AND BASE BLOCKS. THEY DON'T NEED TO BUY GOODS. SO THEY DON'T MAKE LITTER.
MY NEW HOME IS POORER THAN A STACK OF DEAD BEGGARS.
WORSE. LITTER ALSO SAYS THAT I'M NOWHERE NEAR A MIDDLE-CLASS AREA; NO GARBAGE SCAVENGERS...
HEY, KID. WANT TO EARN SOME MONEY?
CONVINCE ME. I EARN MORE MONEY THAN YOU'RE WORTH, JUST SITTING HERE.
YOU RUDE LITTLE SCAB. LISTEN, I NEED SOMEONE TO RUN TO THE LOCAL DRUGSTORE FOR ME.
I COULD SCORE YOU SOME MEDICINE RIGHT HERE, MAN...
I DO NOT WANT YOUR CHEAP BRAINBURNING DRUGS. THEY ARE USELESS FOR WORK. AND I AM A WORKING MAN TODAY.
I WANT VASOPRESSIN, WASHED CAFFEINE, JUMPSTART, GINGKO BILOBA, GUARANA, AND ANY INTELLIGENCE ENHANCER INTRODUCED IN THE LAST FIVE YEARS.
YOU SOME KIND OF HEALTH FREAK?
I'M A JOURNALIST, DAMNIT. NOW JUMP TO IT, PUSHER SPERM. I'M IN APARTMENT 100 K.

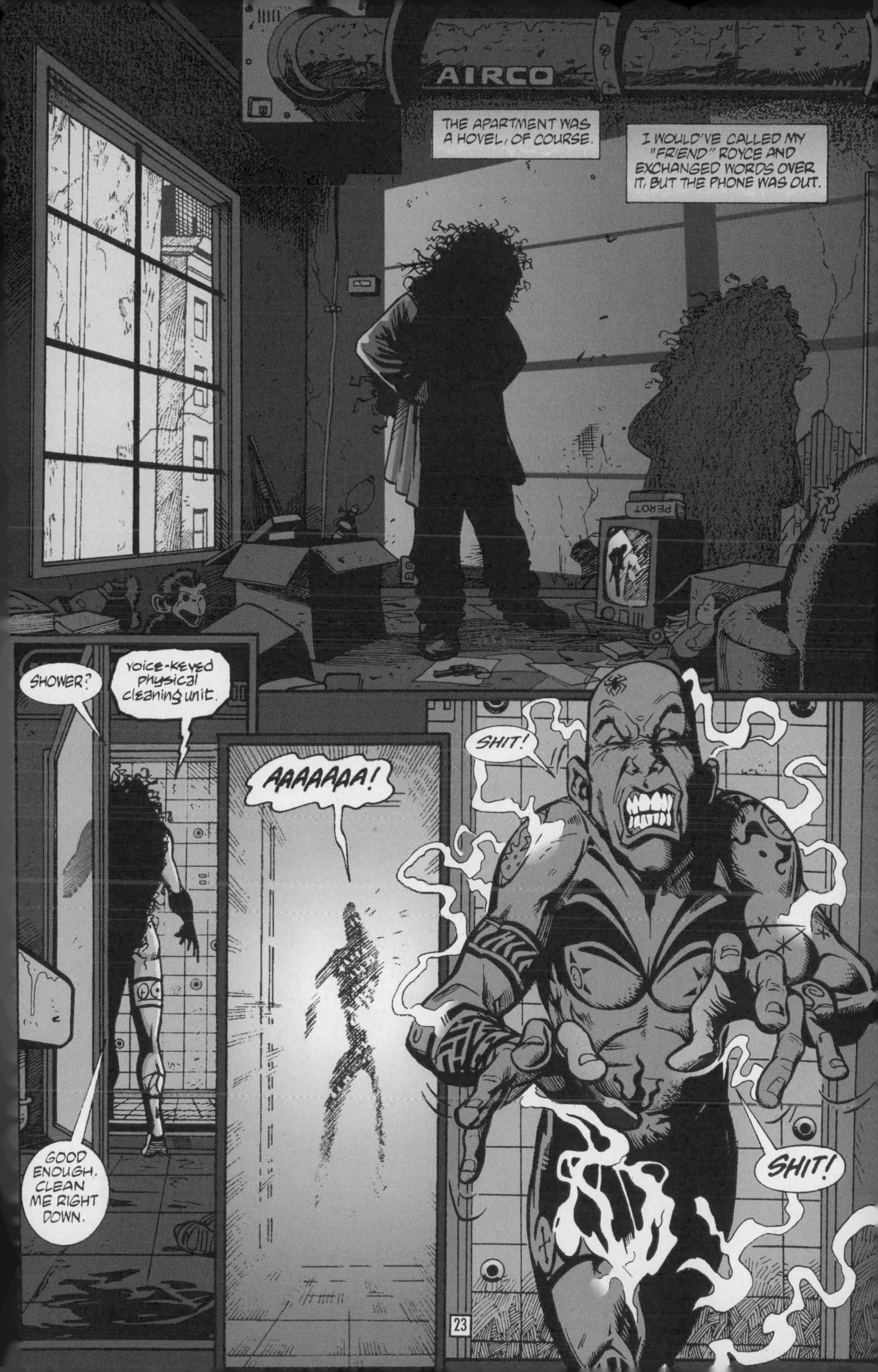
AIRCO
THE APARTMENT WAS A HOVEL, OF COURSE.
I WOULD'VE CALLED MY "FRIEND" ROYCE AND EXCHANGED WORDS OVER IT, BUT THE PHONE WAS OUT.
PEROT
SHOWER?
voice-keyed physical cleaning unit.
GOOD ENOUGH. CLEAN ME RIGHT DOWN.
AAAAAAA!
SHIT!
SHIT!

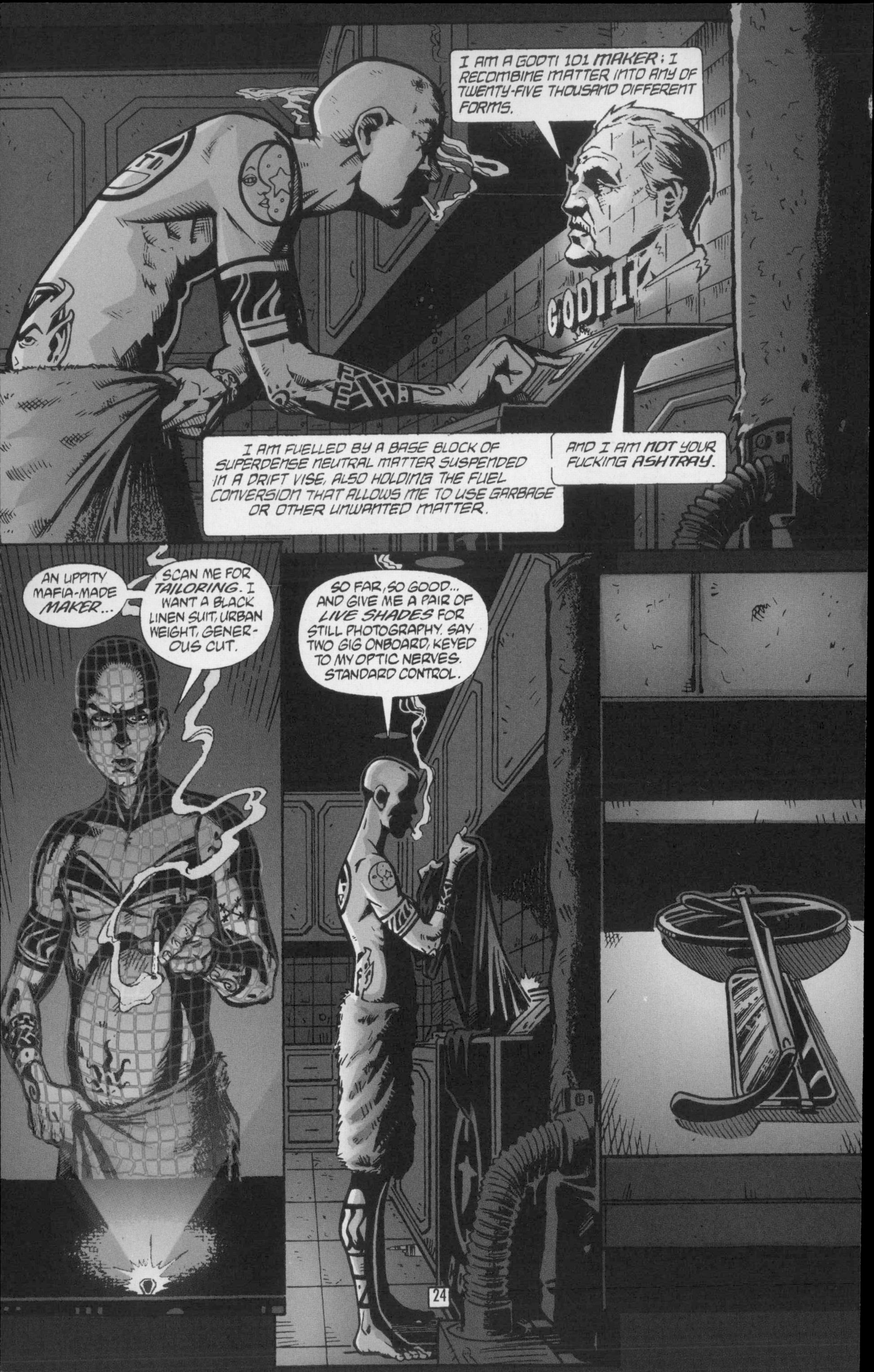

I AM A GODTI 101 MAKER; I RECOMBINE MATTER INTO ANY OF TWENTY-FIVE THOUSAND DIFFERENT FORMS.
GODTIT
I AM FUELLED BY A BASE BLOCK OF SUPERDENSE NEUTRAL MATTER SUSPENDED IN A DRIFT VISE, ALSO HOLDING THE FUEL CONVERSION THAT ALLOWS ME TO USE GARBAGE OR OTHER UNWANTED MATTER.
AND I AM NOT YOUR FUCKING ASHTRAY.
AN UPPITY MAFIA-MADE MAKER...
SCAN ME FOR TAILORING. I WANT A BLACK LINEN SUIT, URBAN WEIGHT, GENEROUS CUT.
SO FAR, SO GOOD... AND GIVE ME A PAIR OF LIVE SHADES FOR STILL PHOTOGRAPHY. SAY TWO GIG ONBOARD, KEYED TO MY OPTIC NERVES. STANDARD CONTROL.

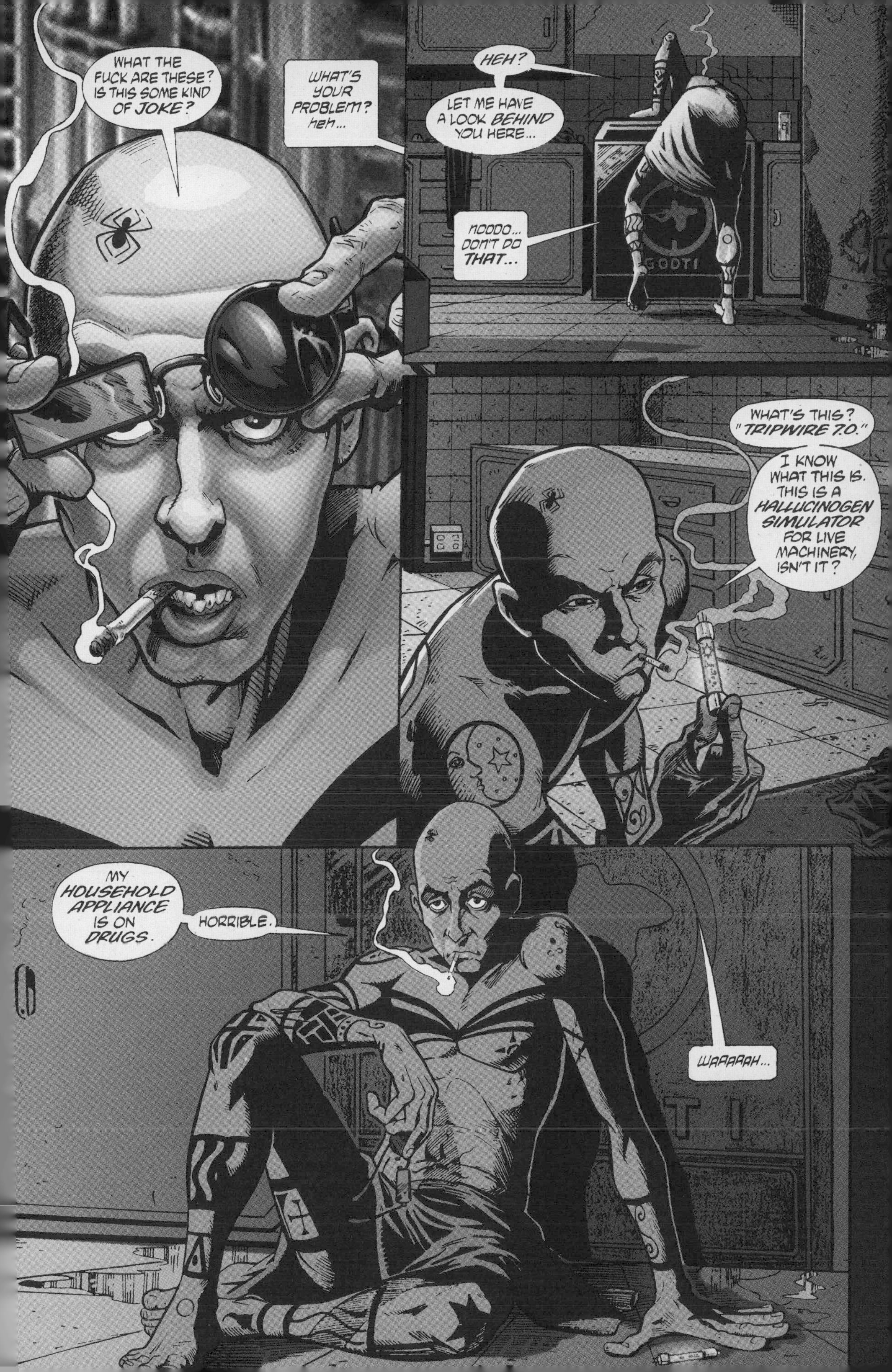
WHAT THE FUCK ARE THESE? IS THIS SOME KIND OF JOKE?
WHAT'S YOUR PROBLEM? heh...
HEH?
LET ME HAVE A LOOK BEHIND YOU HERE...
NOOOO... DON'T DO THAT...
WHAT'S THIS? "TRIPWIRE 7.0."
I KNOW WHAT THIS IS. THIS IS A HALLUCINOGEN SIMULATOR FOR LIVE MACHINERY, ISN'T IT?
MY HOUSEHOLD APPLIANCE IS ON DRUGS.
HORRIBLE.
WAAAAAH...
GODTI

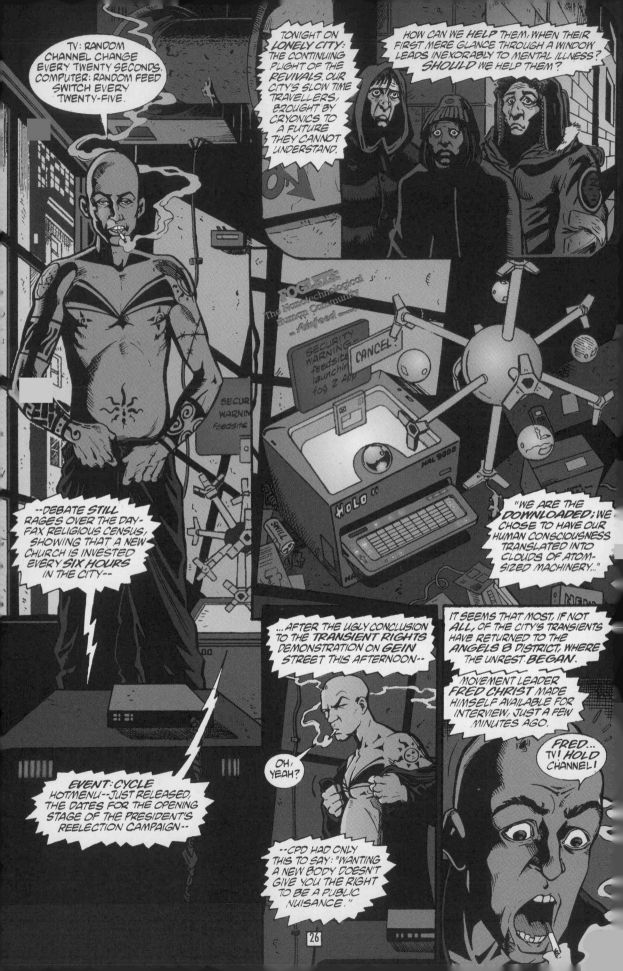

TV: RANDOM CHANNEL CHANGE EVERY TWENTY SECONDS. COMPUTER: RANDOM FEED SWITCH EVERY TWENTY-FIVE.

TONIGHT ON *LONELY CITY:* THE CONTINUING PLIGHT OF THE *REVIVALS.* OUR CITY'S SLOW TIME TRAVELLERS, BROUGHT BY CRYONICS TO A FUTURE THEY CANNOT UNDERSTAND.

HOW CAN WE *HELP* THEM, WHEN THEIR FIRST, MERE GLANCE THROUGH A WINDOW LEADS INEXORABLY TO MENTAL ILLNESS? *SHOULD* WE HELP THEM?

SECURITY WARNING: feedsite launching fog 2 App

CANCEL

HAL 9000

--DEBATE *STILL* RAGES OVER THE DAY-FAX RELIGIOUS CENSUS, SHOWING THAT A NEW CHURCH IS INVESTED *EVERY SIX HOURS* IN THE CITY--

"WE ARE THE *DOWNLOADED;* WE CHOSE TO HAVE OUR HUMAN CONSCIOUSNESS TRANSLATED INTO CLOUDS OF ATOM-SIZED MACHINERY..."

IT SEEMS THAT MOST, IF NOT ALL, OF THE CITY'S TRANSIENTS HAVE RETURNED TO THE *ANGELS 8 DISTRICT,* WHERE THE UNREST *BEGAN.*

...AFTER THE UGLY CONCLUSION TO THE *TRANSIENT RIGHTS* DEMONSTRATION ON *GEIN* STREET THIS AFTERNOON--

MOVEMENT LEADER *FRED CHRIST* MADE HIMSELF AVAILABLE FOR INTERVIEW, JUST A FEW MINUTES AGO.

OH, YEAH?

FRED... TV! *HOLD* CHANNEL!

EVENT-CYCLE HOTMENU--JUST RELEASED, THE DATES FOR THE OPENING STAGE OF THE PRESIDENT'S REELECTION CAMPAIGN--

--CPD HAD ONLY THIS TO SAY: "WANTING A NEW BODY DOESN'T GIVE YOU THE RIGHT TO BE A PUBLIC NUISANCE."

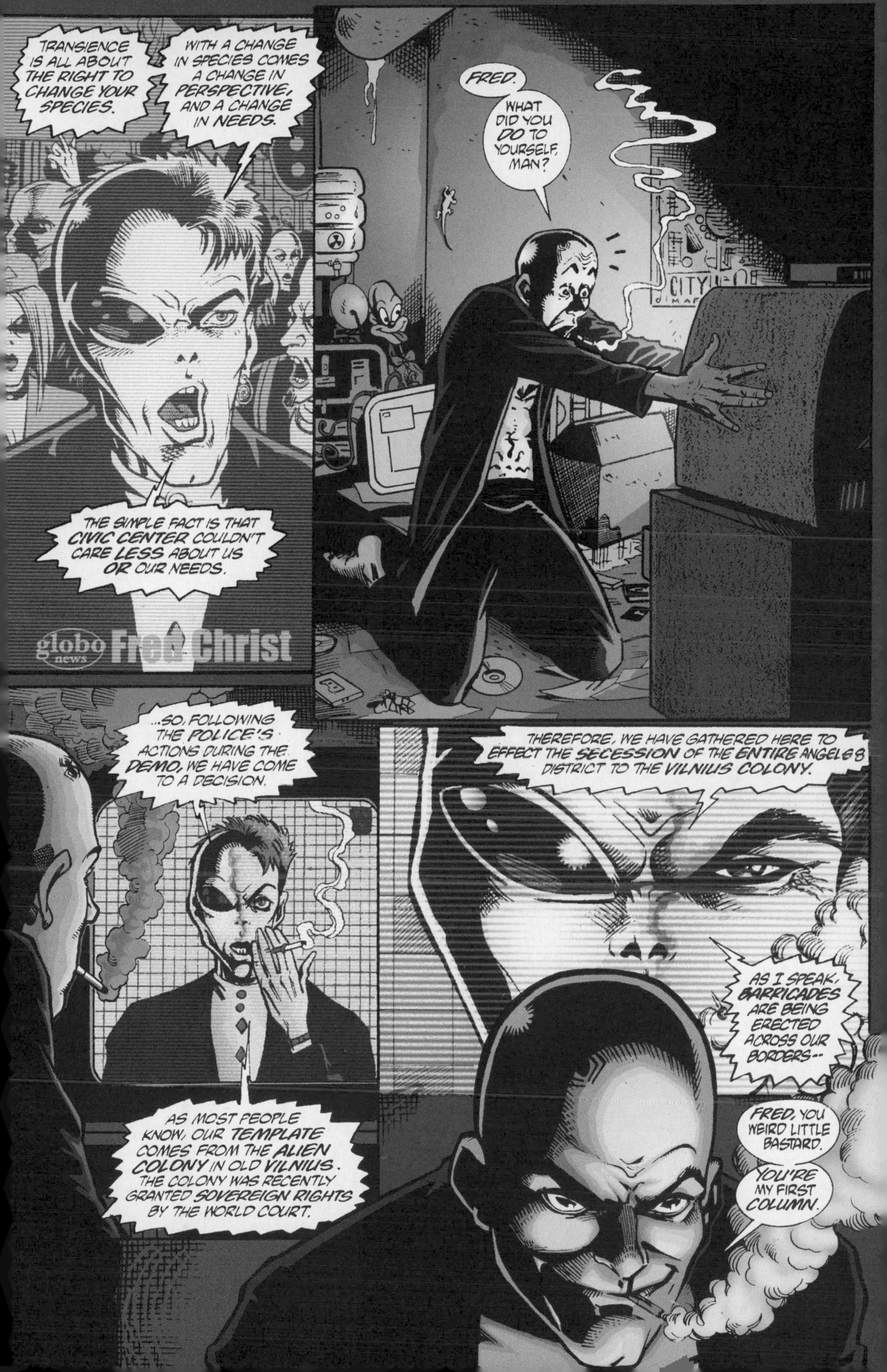
TRANSIENCE IS ALL ABOUT THE RIGHT TO CHANGE YOUR SPECIES.
WITH A CHANGE IN SPECIES COMES A CHANGE IN PERSPECTIVE, AND A CHANGE IN NEEDS.
THE SIMPLE FACT IS THAT CIVIC CENTER COULDN'T CARE LESS ABOUT US OR OUR NEEDS.
globo news Fred Christ
FRED.
WHAT DID YOU DO TO YOURSELF, MAN?
CITY
...SO, FOLLOWING THE POLICE'S ACTIONS DURING THE DEMO, WE HAVE COME TO A DECISION.
AS MOST PEOPLE KNOW, OUR TEMPLATE COMES FROM THE ALIEN COLONY IN OLD VILNIUS. THE COLONY WAS RECENTLY GRANTED SOVEREIGN RIGHTS BY THE WORLD COURT.
THEREFORE, WE HAVE GATHERED HERE TO EFFECT THE SECESSION OF THE ENTIRE ANGELS 8 DISTRICT TO THE VILNIUS COLONY.
AS I SPEAK, BARRICADES ARE BEING ERECTED ACROSS OUR BORDERS--
FRED, YOU WEIRD LITTLE BASTARD.
YOU'RE MY FIRST COLUMN.

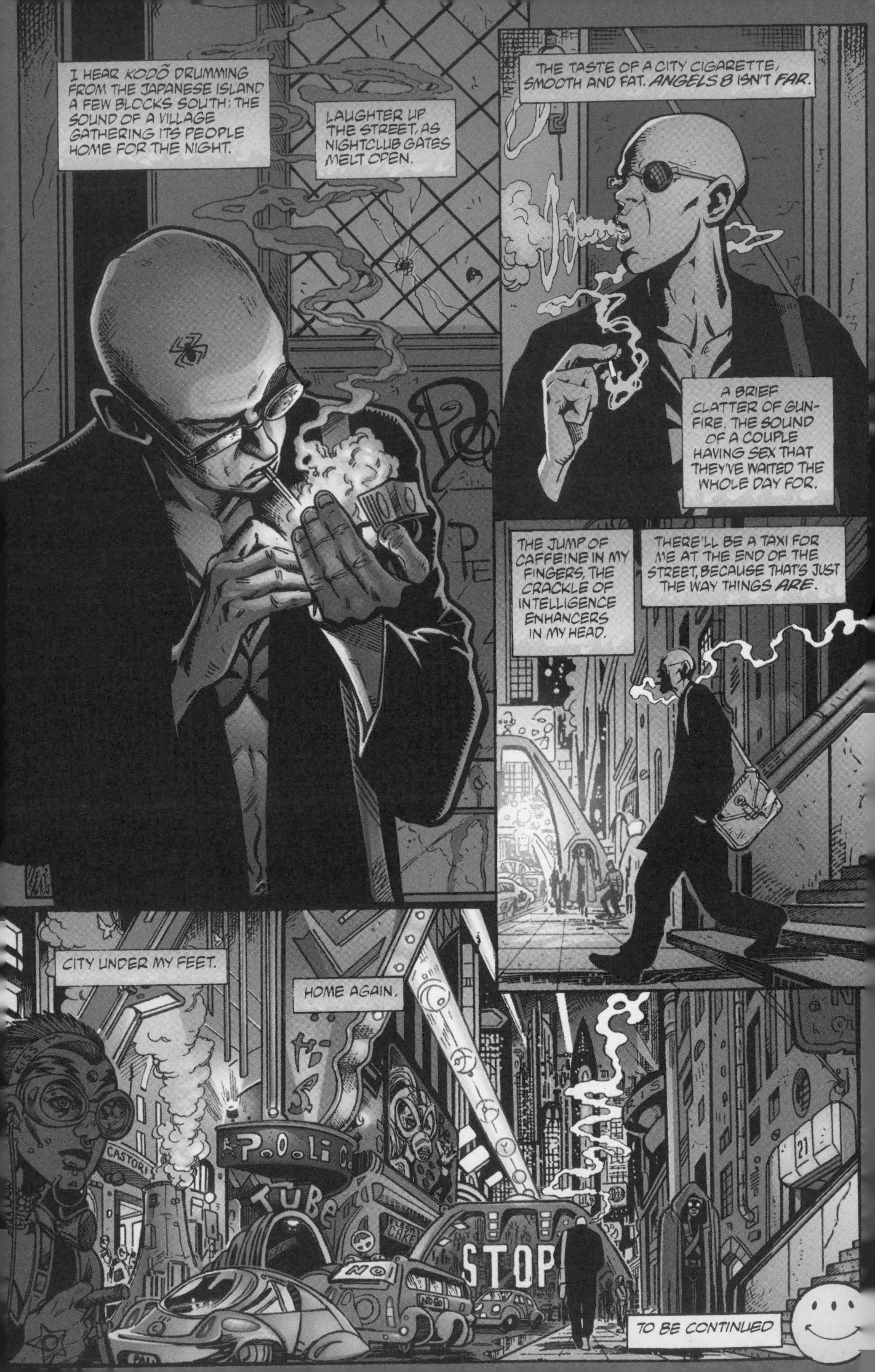

I HEAR KODŌ DRUMMING FROM THE JAPANESE ISLAND A FEW BLOCKS SOUTH; THE SOUND OF A VILLAGE GATHERING ITS PEOPLE HOME FOR THE NIGHT.
LAUGHTER UP THE STREET, AS NIGHTCLUB GATES MELT OPEN.
THE TASTE OF A CITY CIGARETTE, SMOOTH AND FAT. ANGELS 8 ISN'T FAR.
A BRIEF CLATTER OF GUN-FIRE. THE SOUND OF A COUPLE HAVING SEX THAT THEY'VE WAITED THE WHOLE DAY FOR.
THE JUMP OF CAFFEINE IN MY FINGERS, THE CRACKLE OF INTELLIGENCE ENHANCERS IN MY HEAD.
THERE'LL BE A TAXI FOR ME AT THE END OF THE STREET, BECAUSE THAT'S JUST THE WAY THINGS ARE.
CITY UNDER MY FEET.
HOME AGAIN.
CASTORI
P.O.LiC
TUBE
STOP
21
TO BE CONTINUED

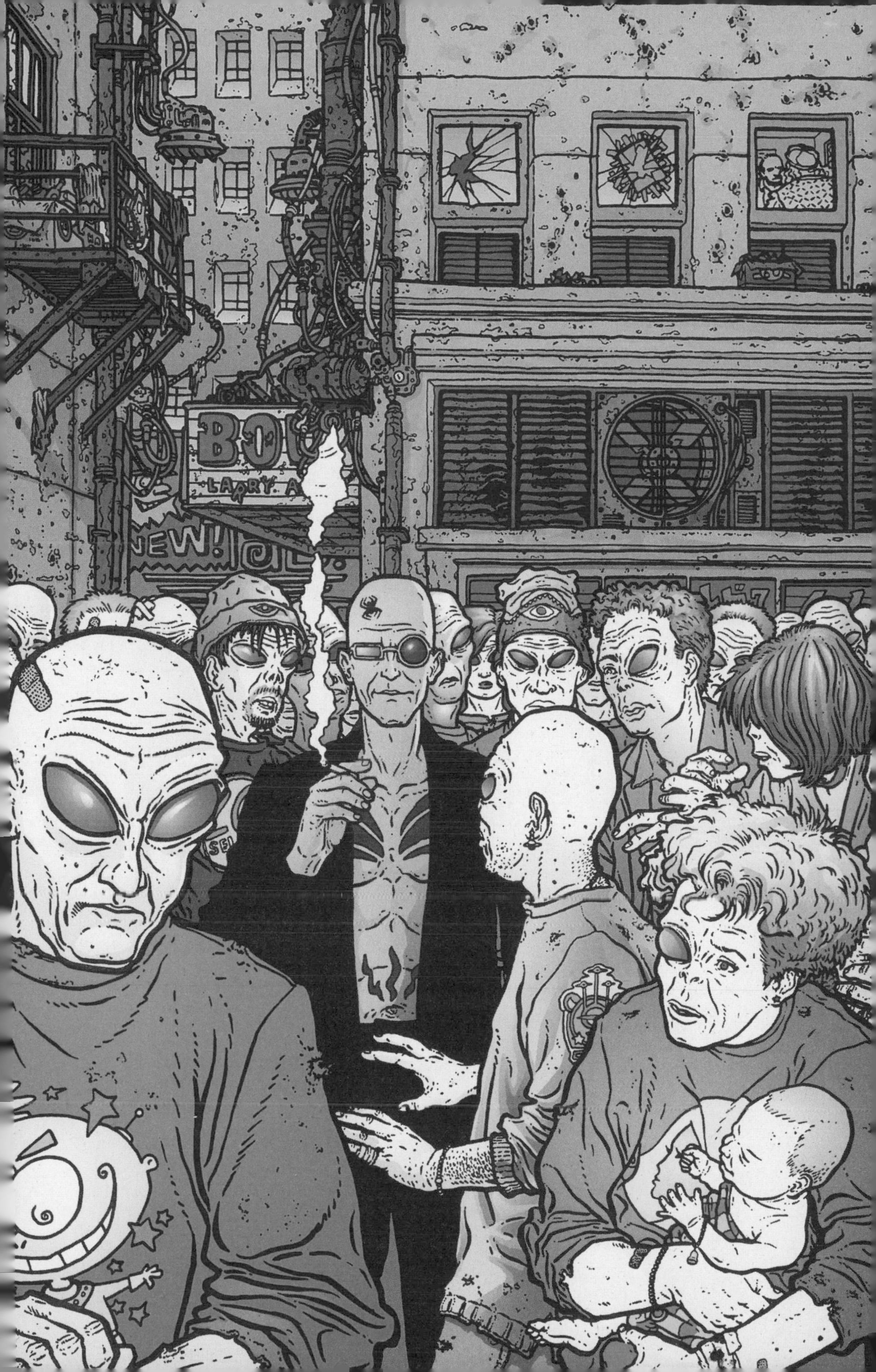
NEW!

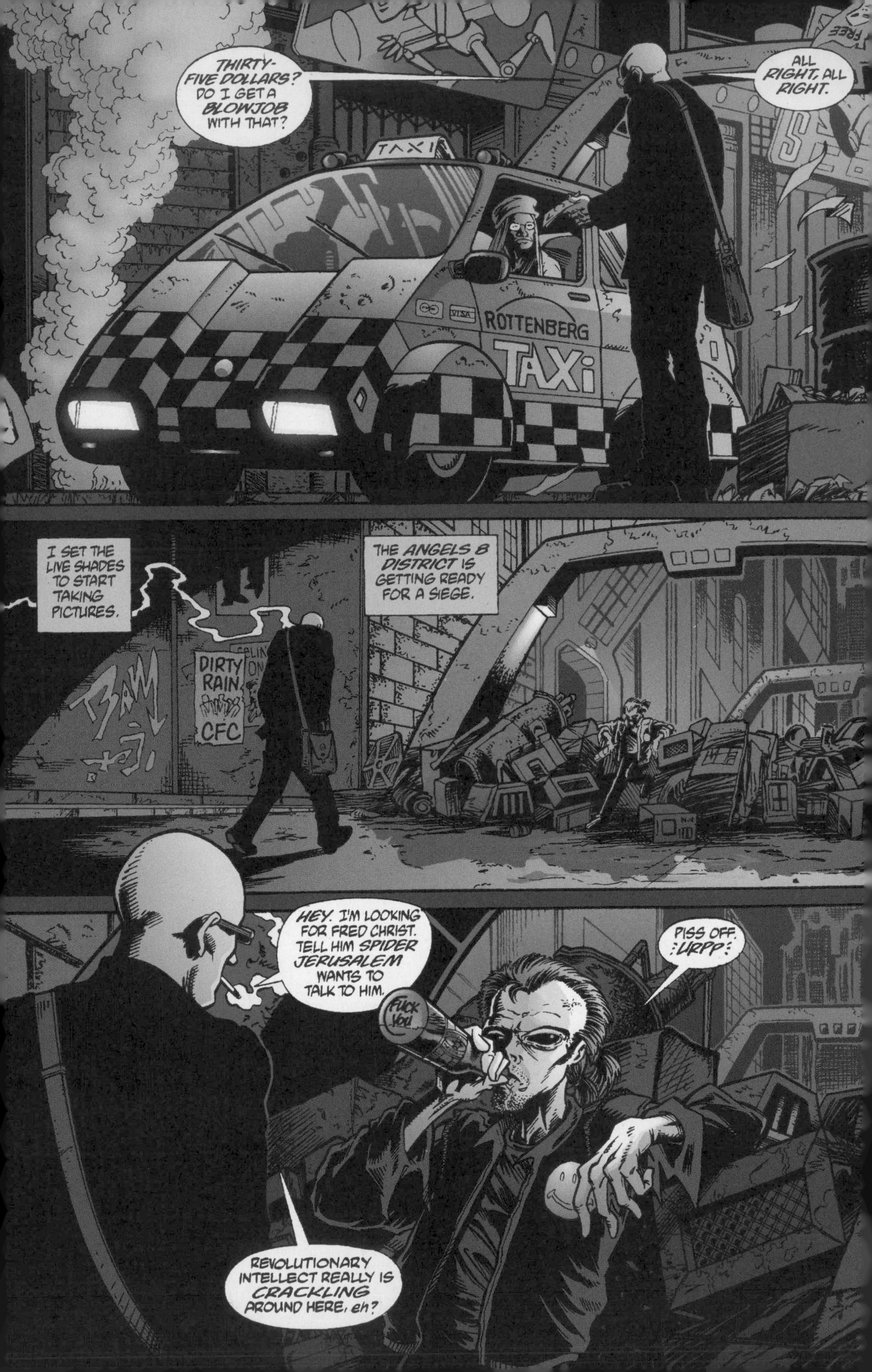
THIRTY-FIVE DOLLARS? DO I GET A BLOWJOB WITH THAT?
ALL RIGHT, ALL RIGHT.
TAXI
ROTTENBERG TAXi
I SET THE LIVE SHADES TO START TAKING PICTURES.
THE ANGELS 8 DISTRICT IS GETTING READY FOR A SIEGE.
DIRTY RAIN CFC
HEY. I'M LOOKING FOR FRED CHRIST. TELL HIM SPIDER JERUSALEM WANTS TO TALK TO HIM.
PISS OFF. URPP
FUCK YOU
REVOLUTIONARY INTELLECT REALLY IS CRACKLING AROUND HERE, eh?

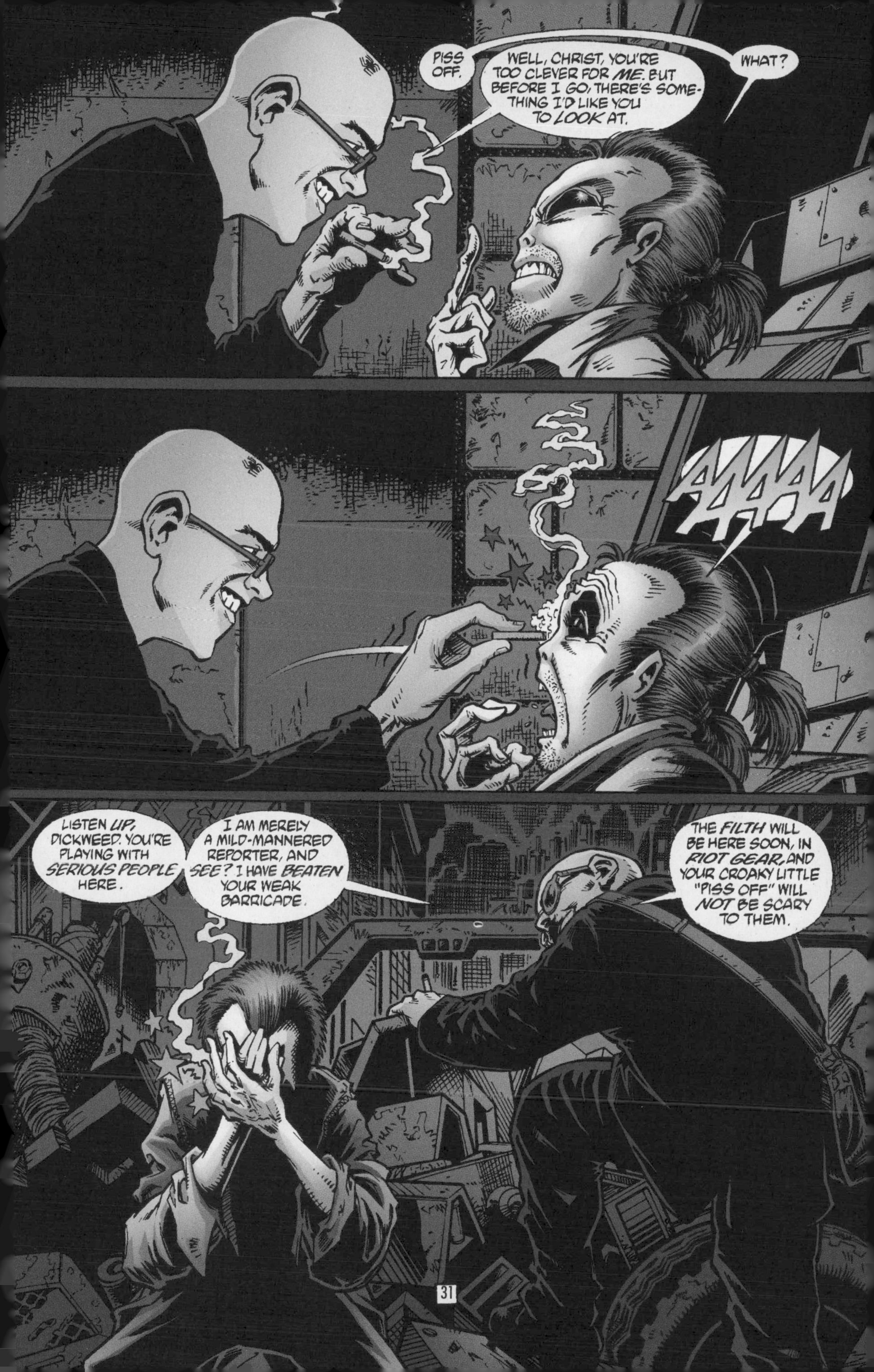

PISS OFF.
WELL, CHRIST, YOU'RE TOO CLEVER FOR ME. BUT BEFORE I GO, THERE'S SOMETHING I'D LIKE YOU TO LOOK AT.
WHAT?
AAAAA
LISTEN UP, DICKWEED. YOU'RE PLAYING WITH SERIOUS PEOPLE HERE.
I AM MERELY A MILD-MANNERED REPORTER, AND SEE? I HAVE BEATEN YOUR WEAK BARRICADE.
THE FILTH WILL BE HERE SOON, IN RIOT GEAR, AND YOUR CROAKY LITTLE "PISS OFF" WILL NOT BE SCARY TO THEM.

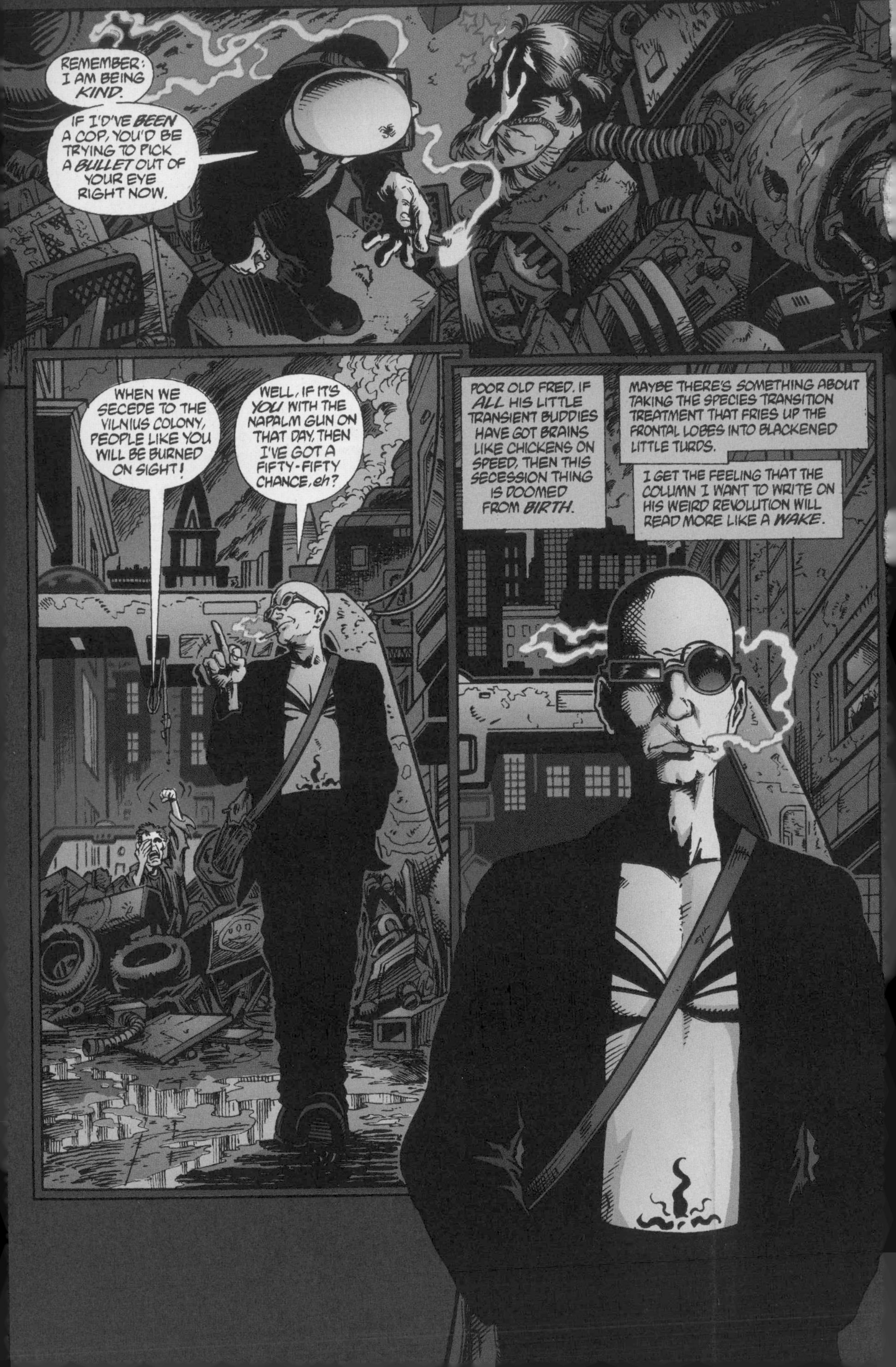
REMEMBER: I AM BEING KIND.
IF I'D'VE BEEN A COP, YOU'D BE TRYING TO PICK A BULLET OUT OF YOUR EYE RIGHT NOW.
WHEN WE SECEDE TO THE VILNIUS COLONY, PEOPLE LIKE YOU WILL BE BURNED ON SIGHT!
WELL, IF IT'S YOU WITH THE NAPALM GUN ON THAT DAY, THEN I'VE GOT A FIFTY-FIFTY CHANCE, eh?
POOR OLD FRED. IF ALL HIS LITTLE TRANSIENT BUDDIES HAVE GOT BRAINS LIKE CHICKENS ON SPEED, THEN THIS SECESSION THING IS DOOMED FROM BIRTH.
MAYBE THERE'S SOMETHING ABOUT TAKING THE SPECIES TRANSITION TREATMENT THAT FRIES UP THE FRONTAL LOBES INTO BLACKENED LITTLE TURDS.
I GET THE FEELING THAT THE COLUMN I WANT TO WRITE ON HIS WEIRD REVOLUTION WILL READ MORE LIKE A WAKE.

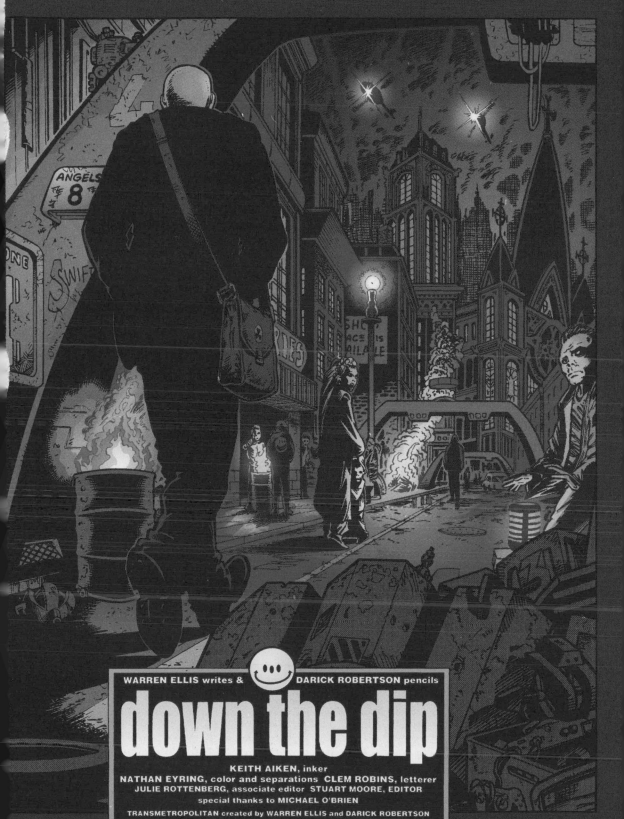

WARREN ELLIS writes & DARICK ROBERTSON pencils

down the dip

KEITH AIKEN, inker
NATHAN EYRING, color and separations   CLEM ROBINS, letterer
JULIE ROTTENBERG, associate editor   STUART MOORE, EDITOR
special thanks to MICHAEL O'BRIEN

TRANSMETROPOLITAN created by WARREN ELLIS and DARICK ROBERTSON

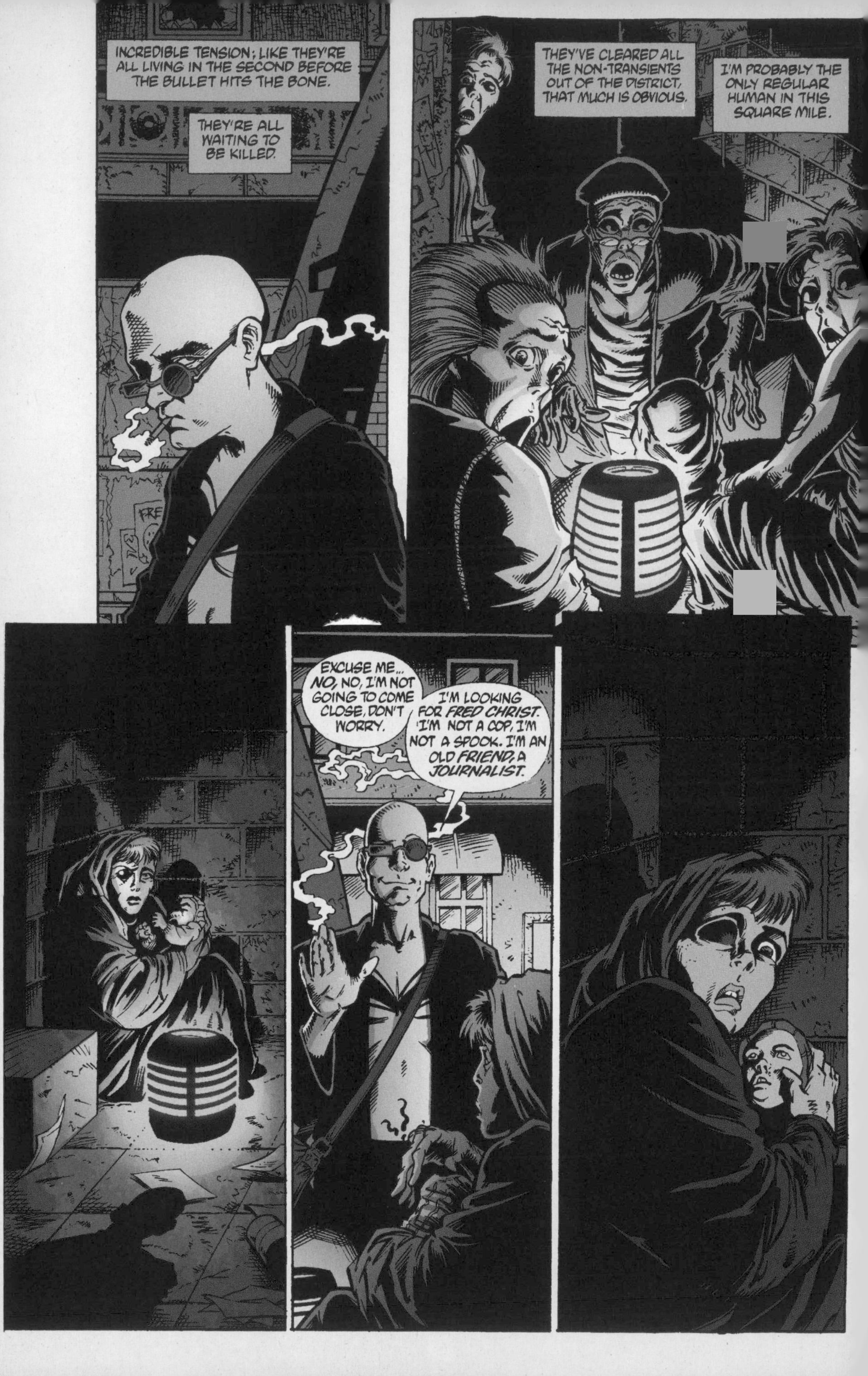
INCREDIBLE TENSION; LIKE THEY'RE ALL LIVING IN THE SECOND BEFORE THE BULLET HITS THE BONE.
THEY'RE ALL WAITING TO BE KILLED.
THEY'VE CLEARED ALL THE NON-TRANSIENTS OUT OF THE DISTRICT, THAT MUCH IS OBVIOUS.
I'M PROBABLY THE ONLY REGULAR HUMAN IN THIS SQUARE MILE.
EXCUSE ME... NO, NO, I'M NOT GOING TO COME CLOSE, DON'T WORRY.
I'M LOOKING FOR FRED CHRIST. I'M NOT A COP, I'M NOT A SPOOK. I'M AN OLD FRIEND, A JOURNALIST.

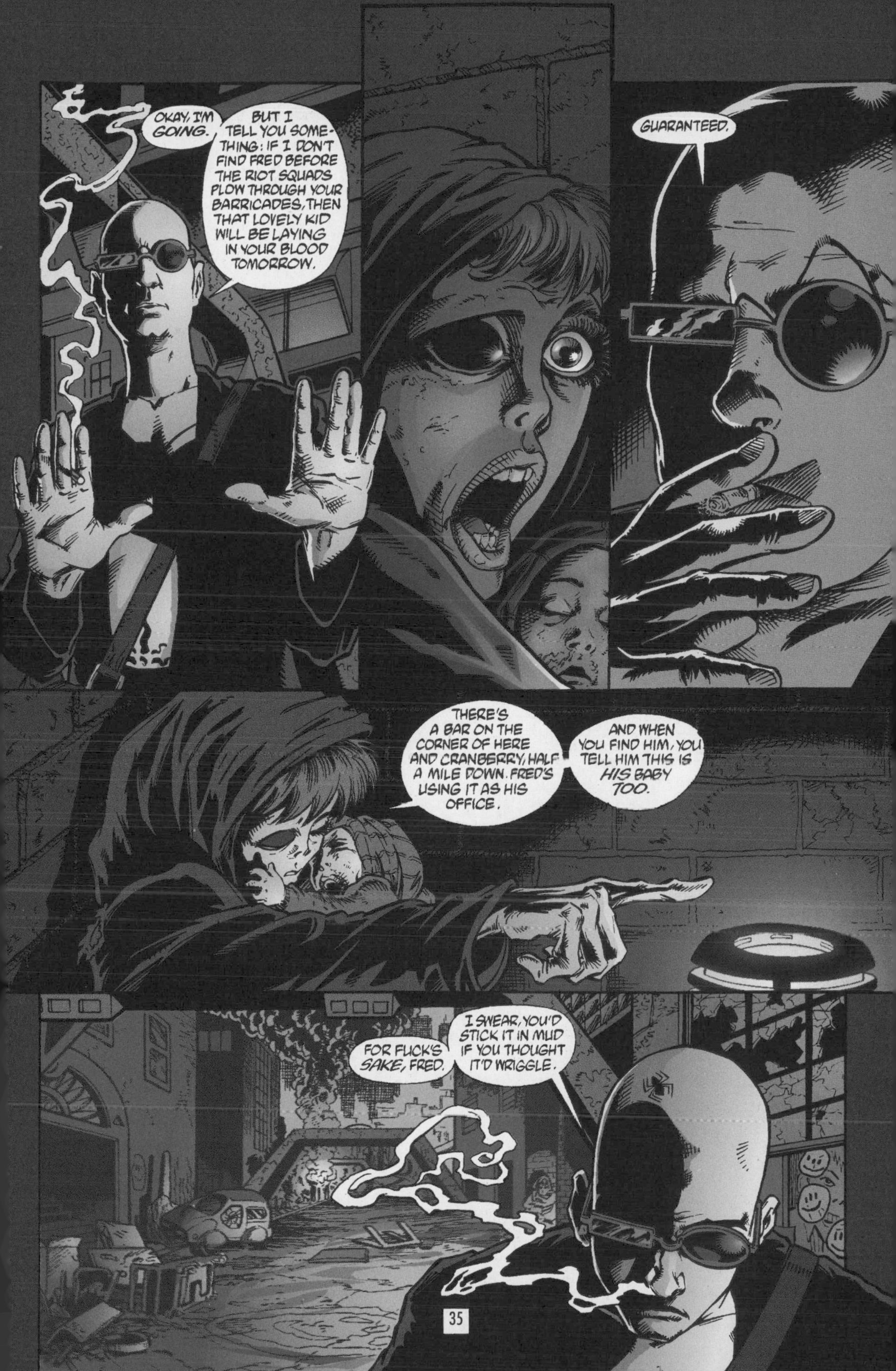

OKAY, I'M GOING.
BUT I TELL YOU SOMETHING: IF I DON'T FIND FRED BEFORE THE RIOT SQUADS PLOW THROUGH YOUR BARRICADES, THEN THAT LOVELY KID WILL BE LAYING IN YOUR BLOOD TOMORROW.
GUARANTEED.
THERE'S A BAR ON THE CORNER OF HERE AND CRANBERRY, HALF A MILE DOWN. FRED'S USING IT AS HIS OFFICE.
AND WHEN YOU FIND HIM, YOU TELL HIM THIS IS HIS BABY TOO.
FOR FUCK'S SAKE, FRED.
I SWEAR, YOU'D STICK IT IN MUD IF YOU THOUGHT IT'D WRIGGLE.

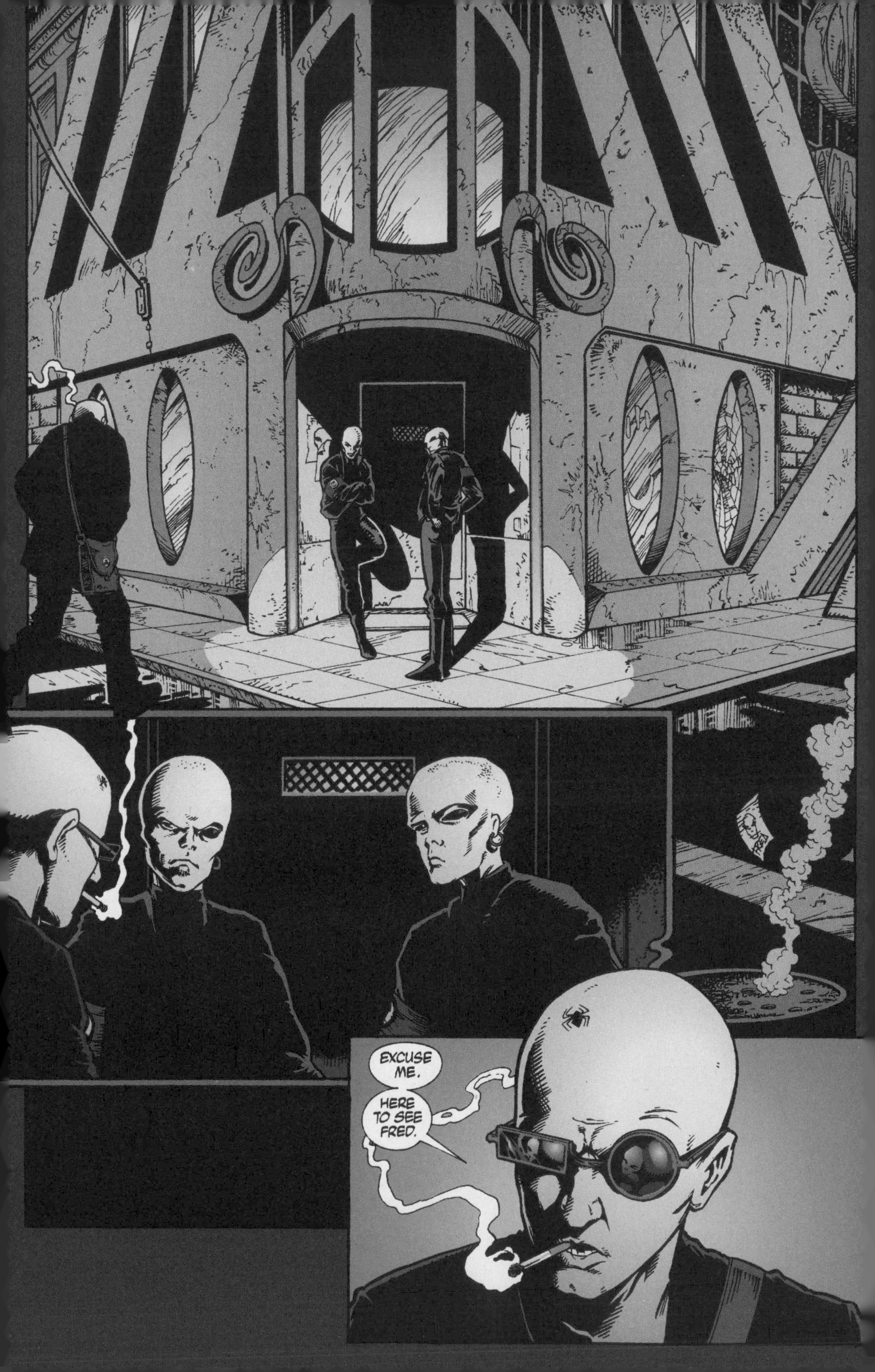
EXCUSE ME.
HERE TO SEE FRED.

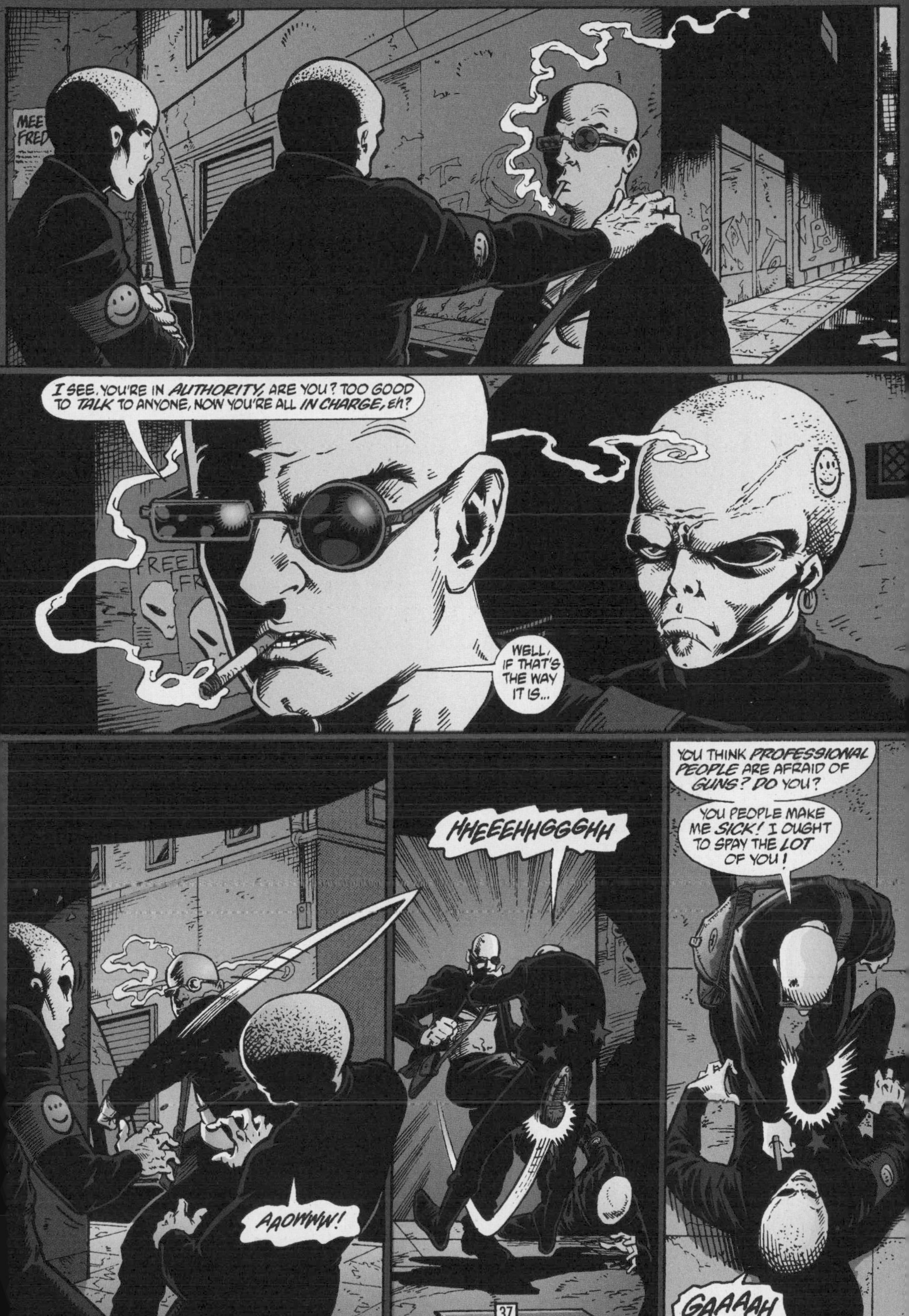
MEET FRED
I SEE. YOU'RE IN AUTHORITY, ARE YOU? TOO GOOD TO TALK TO ANYONE, NOW YOU'RE ALL IN CHARGE, EH?
FREE
WELL, IF THAT'S THE WAY IT IS...
AAOWWW!
HHEEEHHGGGHH
YOU THINK PROFESSIONAL PEOPLE ARE AFRAID OF GUNS? DO YOU?
YOU PEOPLE MAKE ME SICK! I OUGHT TO SPAY THE LOT OF YOU!
GAAAAH

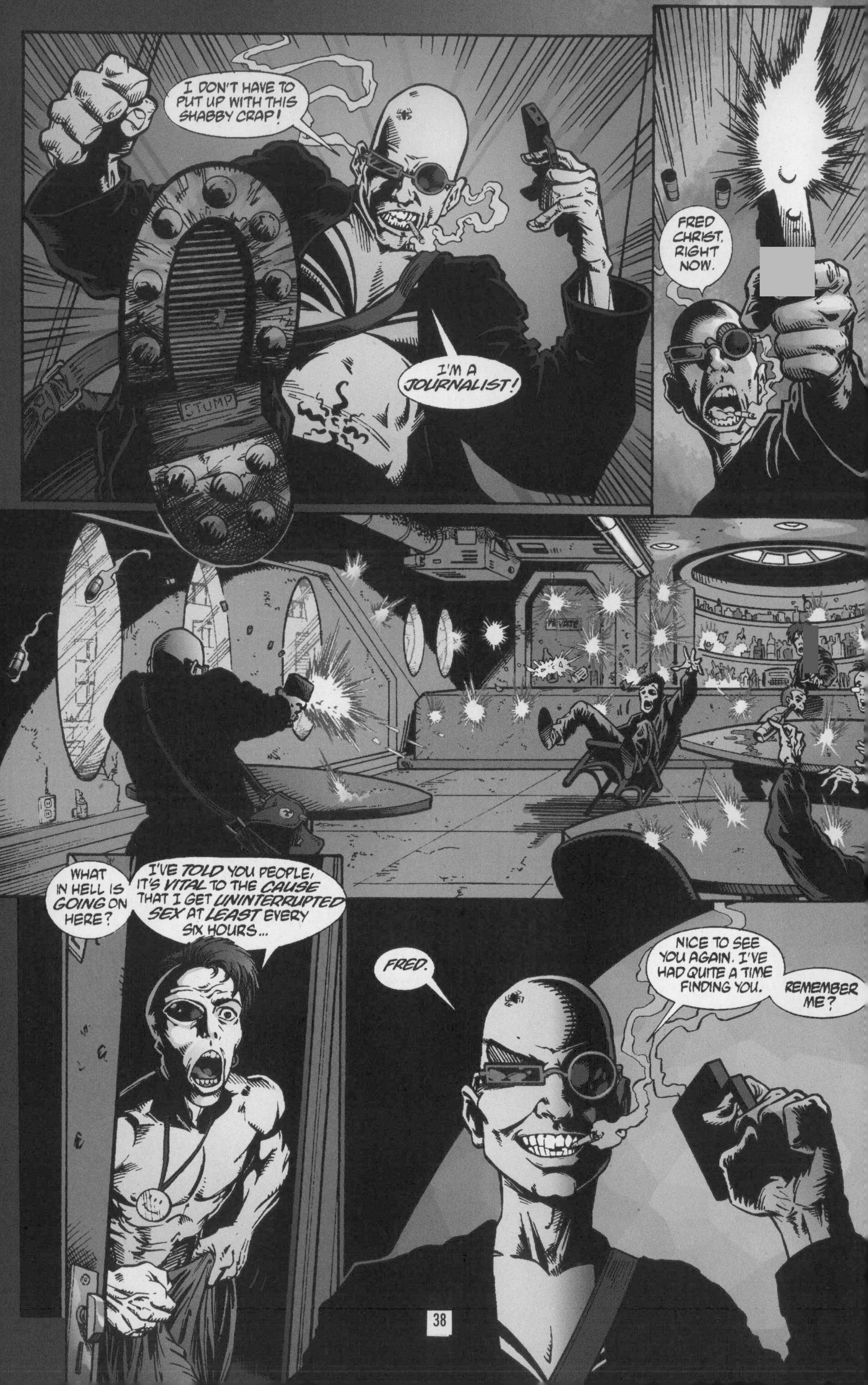

I DON'T HAVE TO PUT UP WITH THIS SHABBY CRAP!
STUMP
I'M A JOURNALIST!
FRED CHRIST. RIGHT NOW.
WHAT IN HELL IS GOING ON HERE?
I'VE TOLD YOU PEOPLE, IT'S VITAL TO THE CAUSE THAT I GET UNINTERRUPTED SEX AT LEAST EVERY SIX HOURS...
FRED.
NICE TO SEE YOU AGAIN. I'VE HAD QUITE A TIME FINDING YOU.
REMEMBER ME?

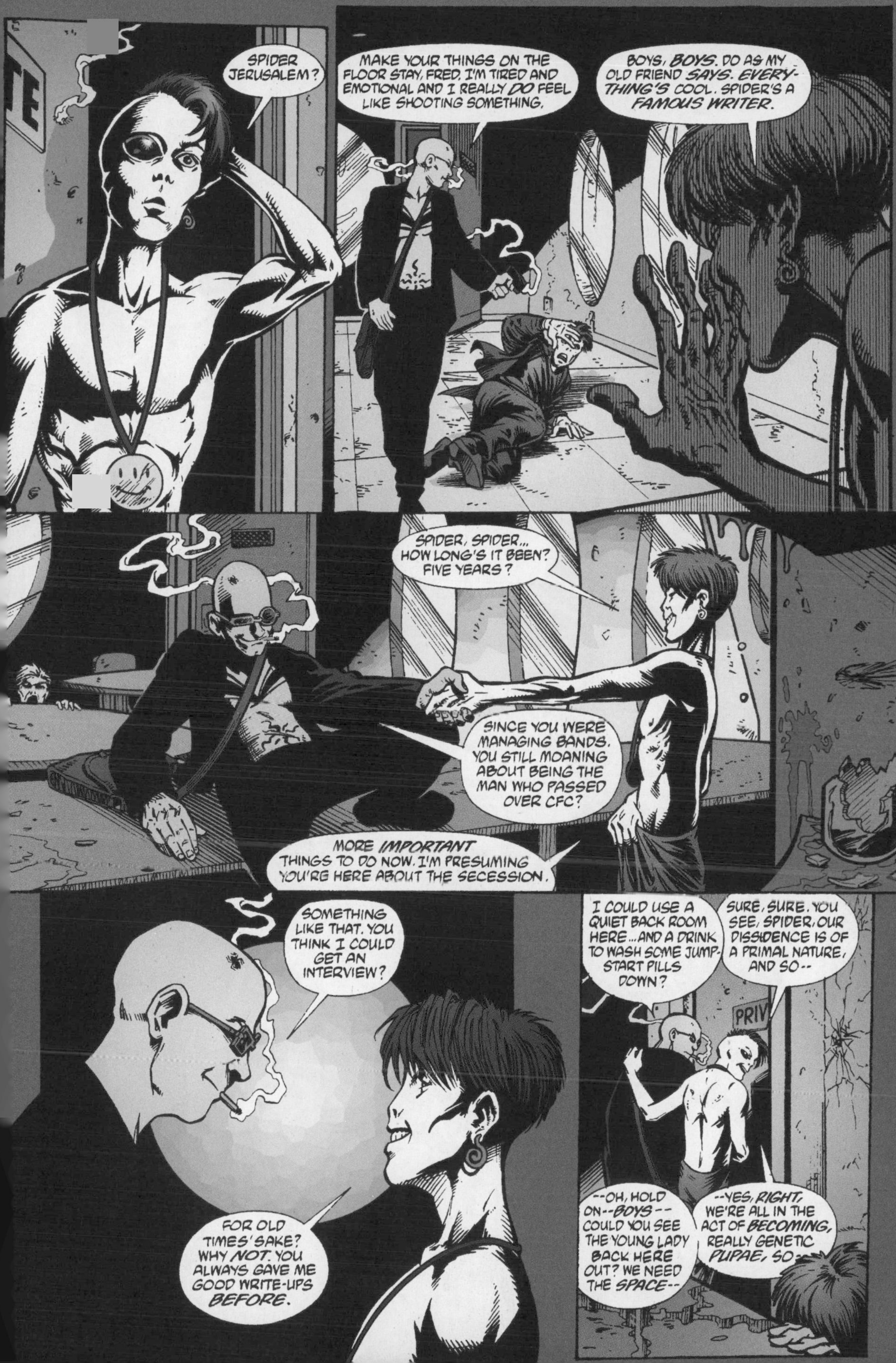

SPIDER JERUSALEM?
MAKE YOUR THINGS ON THE FLOOR STAY, FRED, I'M TIRED AND EMOTIONAL AND I REALLY *DO* FEEL LIKE SHOOTING SOMETHING.
BOYS, *BOYS*. DO AS MY OLD FRIEND *SAYS*. *EVERYTHING'S* COOL. SPIDER'S A *FAMOUS WRITER*.
SPIDER, SPIDER... HOW LONG'S IT BEEN? FIVE YEARS?
SINCE YOU WERE MANAGING BANDS. YOU STILL MOANING ABOUT BEING THE MAN WHO PASSED OVER CFC?
MORE *IMPORTANT* THINGS TO DO NOW. I'M PRESUMING YOU'RE HERE ABOUT THE SECESSION.
SOMETHING LIKE THAT. YOU THINK I COULD GET AN INTERVIEW?
FOR OLD TIMES' SAKE? WHY *NOT*. YOU ALWAYS GAVE ME GOOD WRITE-UPS *BEFORE*.
I COULD USE A QUIET BACK ROOM HERE...AND A DRINK TO WASH SOME JUMP-START PILLS DOWN?
SURE, SURE. YOU SEE, SPIDER, OUR DISSIDENCE IS OF A PRIMAL NATURE, AND SO--
--OH, HOLD ON--*BOYS*--COULD YOU SEE THE YOUNG LADY BACK HERE OUT? WE NEED THE *SPACE*--
--YES, *RIGHT*, WE'RE ALL IN THE ACT OF *BECOMING*, REALLY GENETIC *PUPAE*, SO--

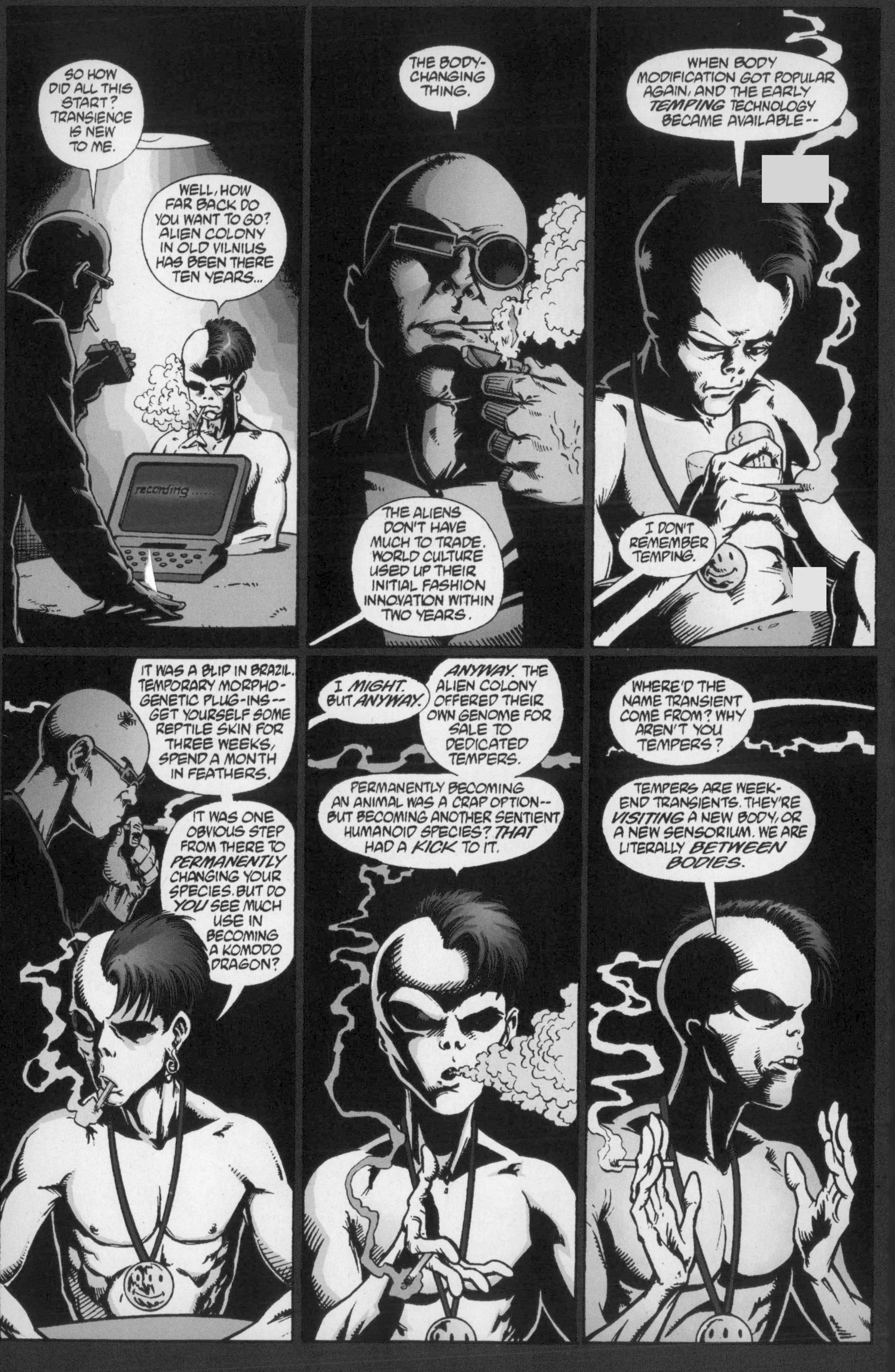
SO HOW DID ALL THIS START? TRANSIENCE IS NEW TO ME.
WELL, HOW FAR BACK DO YOU WANT TO GO? ALIEN COLONY IN OLD VILNIUS HAS BEEN THERE TEN YEARS...
recording......
THE BODY-CHANGING THING.
THE ALIENS DON'T HAVE MUCH TO TRADE. WORLD CULTURE USED UP THEIR INITIAL FASHION INNOVATION WITHIN TWO YEARS.
WHEN BODY MODIFICATION GOT POPULAR AGAIN, AND THE EARLY *TEMPING* TECHNOLOGY BECAME AVAILABLE--
I DON'T REMEMBER TEMPING.
IT WAS A BLIP IN BRAZIL. TEMPORARY MORPHOGENETIC PLUG-INS-- GET YOURSELF SOME REPTILE SKIN FOR THREE WEEKS, SPEND A MONTH IN FEATHERS.
IT WAS ONE OBVIOUS STEP FROM THERE TO *PERMANENTLY* CHANGING YOUR SPECIES. BUT DO *YOU* SEE MUCH USE IN BECOMING A KOMODO DRAGON?
I *MIGHT.* BUT *ANYWAY.*
ANYWAY. THE ALIEN COLONY OFFERED THEIR OWN GENOME FOR SALE TO DEDICATED TEMPERS.
PERMANENTLY BECOMING AN ANIMAL WAS A CRAP OPTION-- BUT BECOMING ANOTHER SENTIENT HUMANOID SPECIES? *THAT* HAD A *KICK* TO IT.
WHERE'D THE NAME TRANSIENT COME FROM? WHY AREN'T YOU TEMPERS?
TEMPERS ARE WEEKEND TRANSIENTS. THEY'RE *VISITING* A NEW BODY, OR A NEW SENSORIUM. WE ARE LITERALLY *BETWEEN BODIES.*

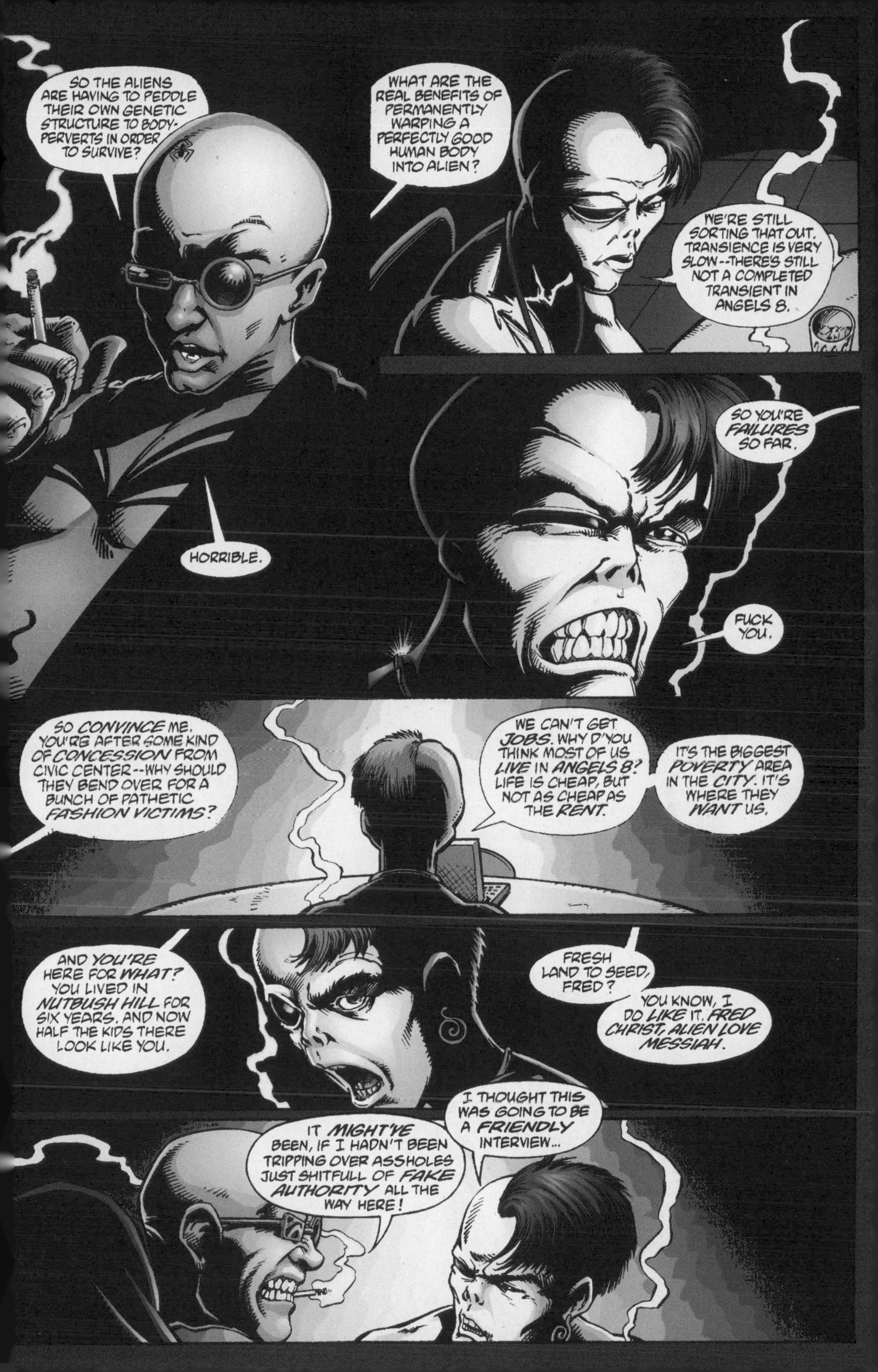
SO THE ALIENS ARE HAVING TO PEDDLE THEIR OWN GENETIC STRUCTURE TO BODY-PERVERTS IN ORDER TO SURVIVE?
WHAT ARE THE REAL BENEFITS OF PERMANENTLY WARPING A PERFECTLY GOOD HUMAN BODY INTO ALIEN?
WE'RE STILL SORTING THAT OUT. TRANSIENCE IS VERY SLOW--THERE'S STILL NOT A COMPLETED TRANSIENT IN ANGELS 8.
SO YOU'RE FAILURES SO FAR.
HORRIBLE.
FUCK YOU.
SO CONVINCE ME. YOU'RE AFTER SOME KIND OF CONCESSION FROM CIVIC CENTER--WHY SHOULD THEY BEND OVER FOR A BUNCH OF PATHETIC FASHION VICTIMS?
WE CAN'T GET JOBS. WHY D'YOU THINK MOST OF US LIVE IN ANGELS 8? LIFE IS CHEAP, BUT NOT AS CHEAP AS THE RENT.
IT'S THE BIGGEST POVERTY AREA IN THE CITY. IT'S WHERE THEY WANT US.
AND YOU'RE HERE FOR WHAT? YOU LIVED IN NUTBUSH HILL FOR SIX YEARS, AND NOW HALF THE KIDS THERE LOOK LIKE YOU.
FRESH LAND TO SEED, FRED?
YOU KNOW, I DO LIKE IT. FRED CHRIST, ALIEN LOVE MESSIAH.
I THOUGHT THIS WAS GOING TO BE A FRIENDLY INTERVIEW...
IT MIGHT'VE BEEN, IF I HADN'T BEEN TRIPPING OVER ASSHOLES JUST SHITFULL OF FAKE AUTHORITY ALL THE WAY HERE!

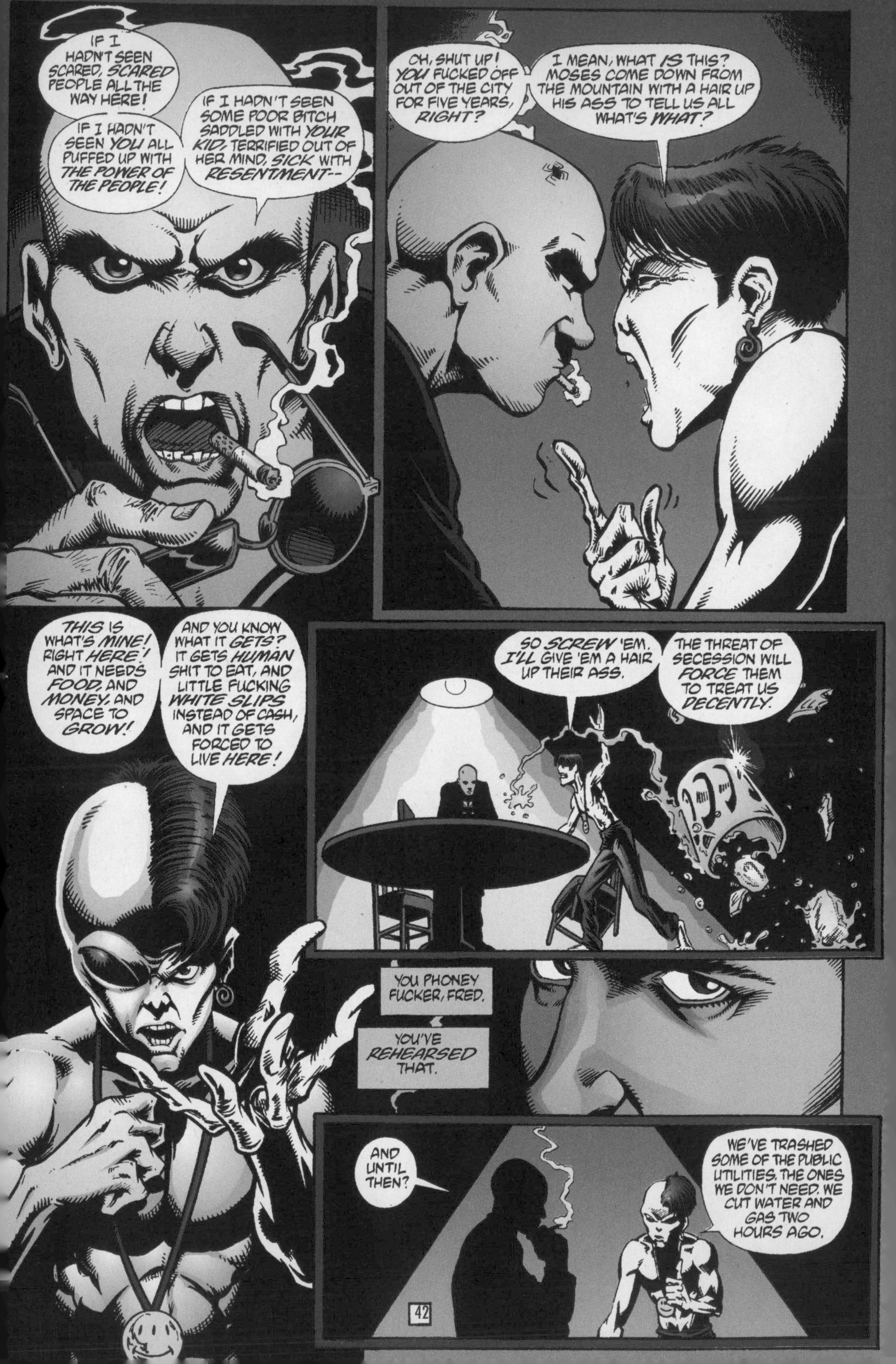
IF I HADN'T SEEN SCARED, SCARED PEOPLE ALL THE WAY HERE!
IF I HADN'T SEEN YOU ALL PUFFED UP WITH THE POWER OF THE PEOPLE!
IF I HADN'T SEEN SOME POOR BITCH SADDLED WITH YOUR KID, TERRIFIED OUT OF HER MIND, SICK WITH RESENTMENT--
OH, SHUT UP! YOU FUCKED OFF OUT OF THE CITY FOR FIVE YEARS, RIGHT?
I MEAN, WHAT IS THIS? MOSES COME DOWN FROM THE MOUNTAIN WITH A HAIR UP HIS ASS TO TELL US ALL WHAT'S WHAT?
THIS IS WHAT'S MINE! RIGHT HERE! AND IT NEEDS FOOD, AND MONEY, AND SPACE TO GROW!
AND YOU KNOW WHAT IT GETS? IT GETS HUMAN SHIT TO EAT, AND LITTLE FUCKING WHITE SLIPS INSTEAD OF CASH, AND IT GETS FORCED TO LIVE HERE!
SO SCREW 'EM. I'LL GIVE 'EM A HAIR UP THEIR ASS.
THE THREAT OF SECESSION WILL FORCE THEM TO TREAT US DECENTLY.
YOU PHONEY FUCKER, FRED.
YOU'VE REHEARSED THAT.
AND UNTIL THEN?
WE'VE TRASHED SOME OF THE PUBLIC UTILITIES. THE ONES WE DON'T NEED. WE CUT WATER AND GAS TWO HOURS AGO.

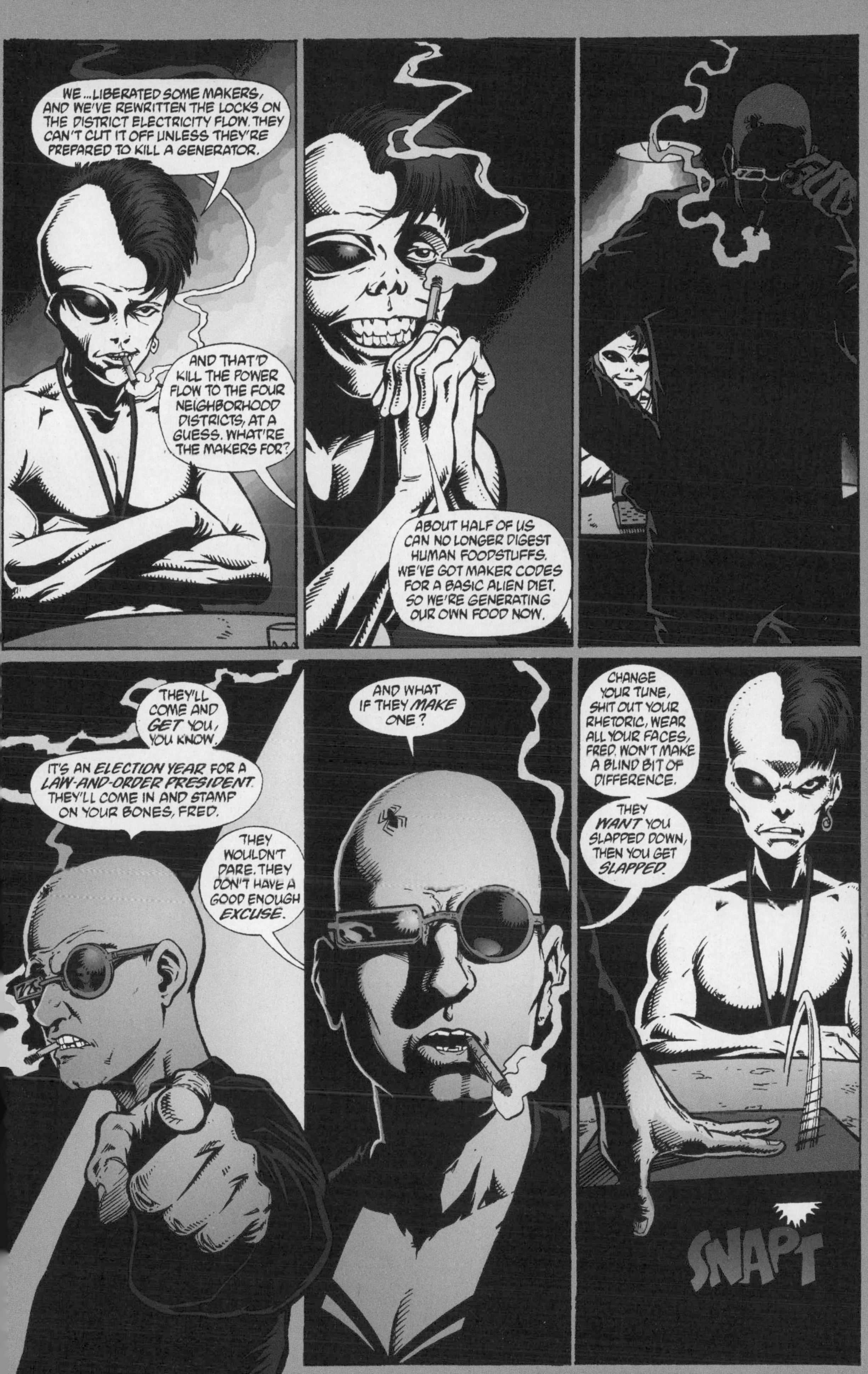
WE...LIBERATED SOME MAKERS, AND WE'VE REWRITTEN THE LOCKS ON THE DISTRICT ELECTRICITY FLOW. THEY CAN'T CUT IT OFF UNLESS THEY'RE PREPARED TO KILL A GENERATOR.
AND THAT'D KILL THE POWER FLOW TO THE FOUR NEIGHBORHOOD DISTRICTS, AT A GUESS. WHAT'RE THE MAKERS FOR?
ABOUT HALF OF US CAN NO LONGER DIGEST HUMAN FOODSTUFFS. WE'VE GOT MAKER CODES FOR A BASIC ALIEN DIET. SO WE'RE GENERATING OUR OWN FOOD NOW.
THEY'LL COME AND GET YOU, YOU KNOW.
IT'S AN ELECTION YEAR FOR A LAW-AND-ORDER PRESIDENT. THEY'LL COME IN AND STAMP ON YOUR BONES, FRED.
THEY WOULDN'T DARE. THEY DON'T HAVE A GOOD ENOUGH EXCUSE.
AND WHAT IF THEY MAKE ONE?
CHANGE YOUR TUNE, SHIT OUT YOUR RHETORIC, WEAR ALL YOUR FACES, FRED. WON'T MAKE A BLIND BIT OF DIFFERENCE.
THEY WANT YOU SLAPPED DOWN, THEN YOU GET SLAPPED.
SNAPT

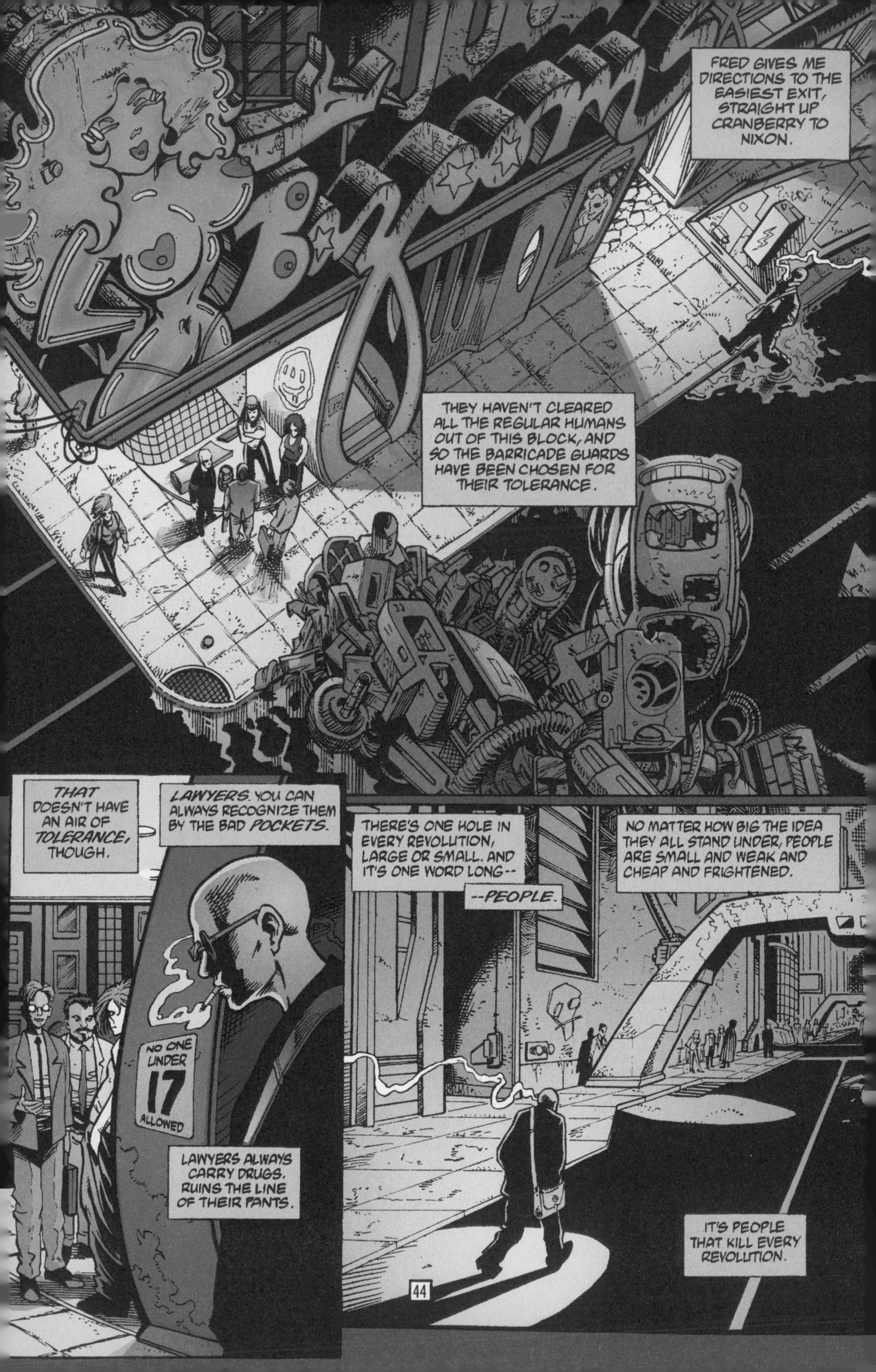
FRED GIVES ME DIRECTIONS TO THE EASIEST EXIT, STRAIGHT UP CRANBERRY TO NIXON.
THEY HAVEN'T CLEARED ALL THE REGULAR HUMANS OUT OF THIS BLOCK, AND SO THE BARRICADE GUARDS HAVE BEEN CHOSEN FOR THEIR TOLERANCE.
THAT DOESN'T HAVE AN AIR OF TOLERANCE, THOUGH.
LAWYERS. YOU CAN ALWAYS RECOGNIZE THEM BY THE BAD POCKETS.
NO ONE UNDER 17 ALLOWED
LAWYERS ALWAYS CARRY DRUGS. RUINS THE LINE OF THEIR PANTS.
THERE'S ONE HOLE IN EVERY REVOLUTION, LARGE OR SMALL. AND IT'S ONE WORD LONG--
--PEOPLE.
NO MATTER HOW BIG THE IDEA THEY ALL STAND UNDER, PEOPLE ARE SMALL AND WEAK AND CHEAP AND FRIGHTENED.
IT'S PEOPLE THAT KILL EVERY REVOLUTION.

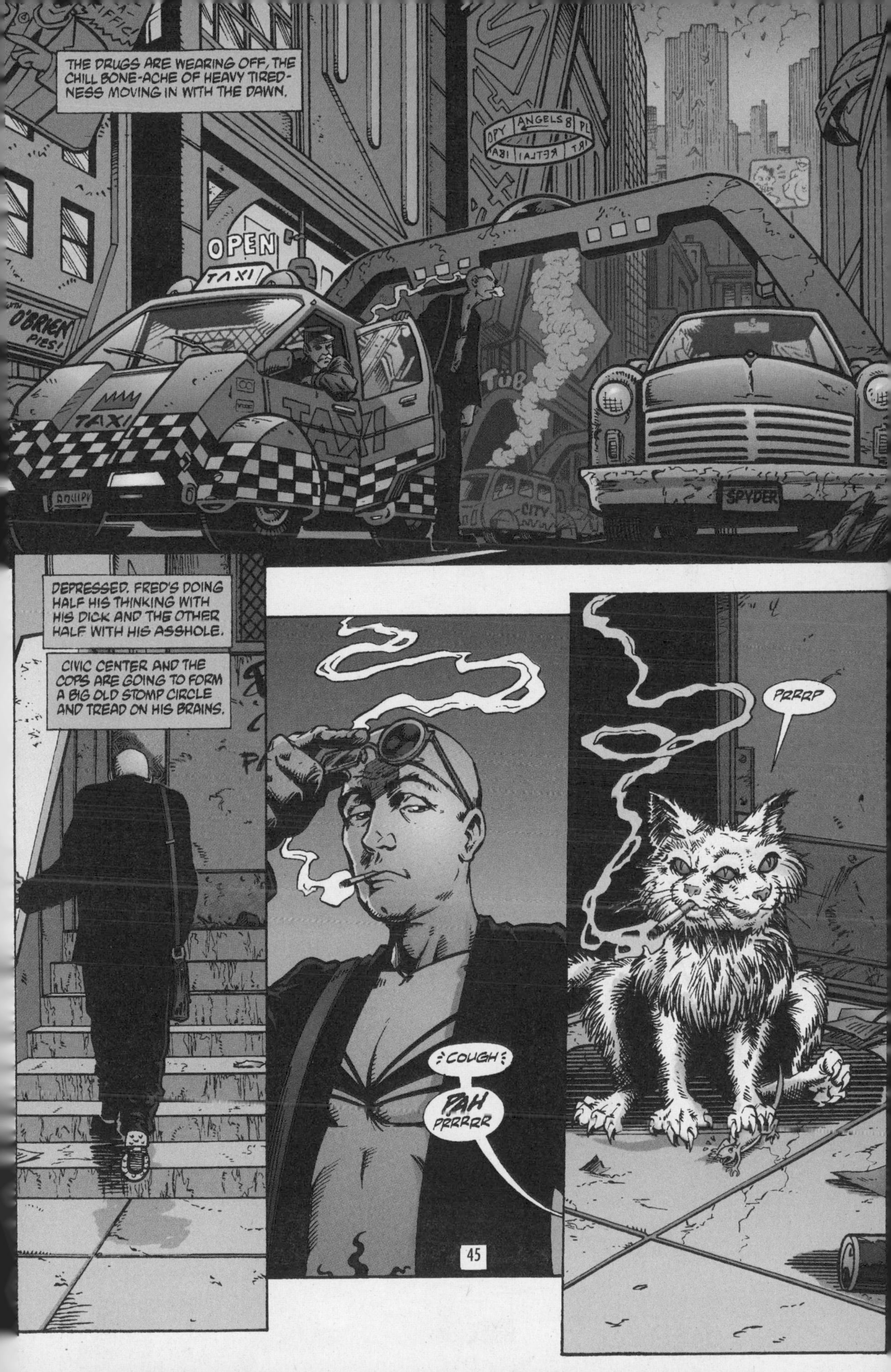
THE DRUGS ARE WEARING OFF, THE CHILL BONE-ACHE OF HEAVY TIREDNESS MOVING IN WITH THE DAWN.
OPEN
TAXI
O'BRIEN PIES!
ANGELS 8
SPYDER
CITY
DEPRESSED. FRED'S DOING HALF HIS THINKING WITH HIS DICK AND THE OTHER HALF WITH HIS ASSHOLE.
CIVIC CENTER AND THE COPS ARE GOING TO FORM A BIG OLD STOMP CIRCLE AND TREAD ON HIS BRAINS.
COUGH
PAH PRRRRR
PRRRP

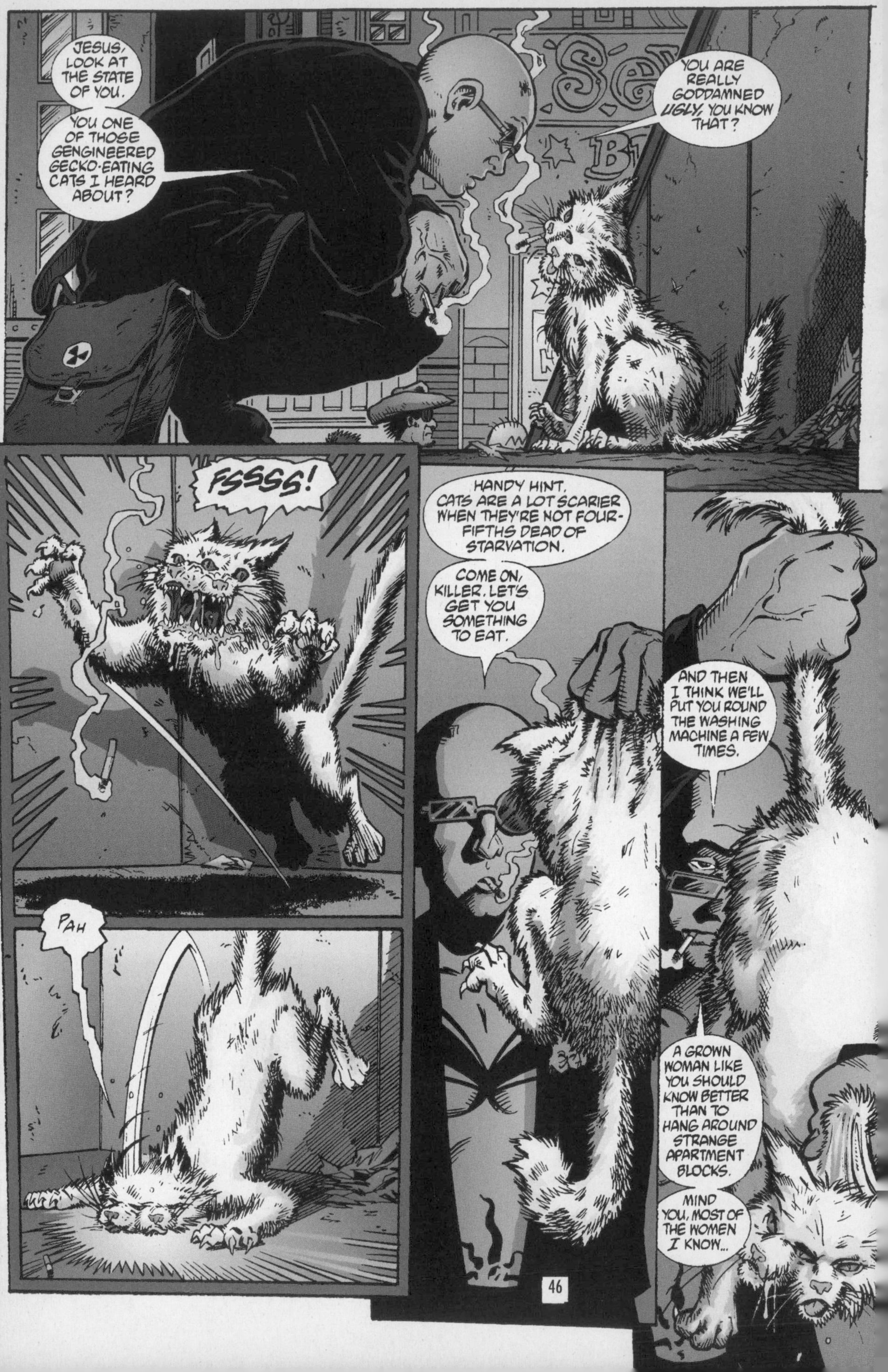
JESUS, LOOK AT THE STATE OF YOU.
YOU ONE OF THOSE GENGINEERED GECKO-EATING CATS I HEARD ABOUT?
YOU ARE REALLY GODDAMNED UGLY, YOU KNOW THAT?
FSSSS!
PAH
HANDY HINT. CATS ARE A LOT SCARIER WHEN THEY'RE NOT FOUR-FIFTHS DEAD OF STARVATION.
COME ON, KILLER. LET'S GET YOU SOMETHING TO EAT.
AND THEN I THINK WE'LL PUT YOU ROUND THE WASHING MACHINE A FEW TIMES.
A GROWN WOMAN LIKE YOU SHOULD KNOW BETTER THAN TO HANG AROUND STRANGE APARTMENT BLOCKS.
MIND YOU, MOST OF THE WOMEN I KNOW...

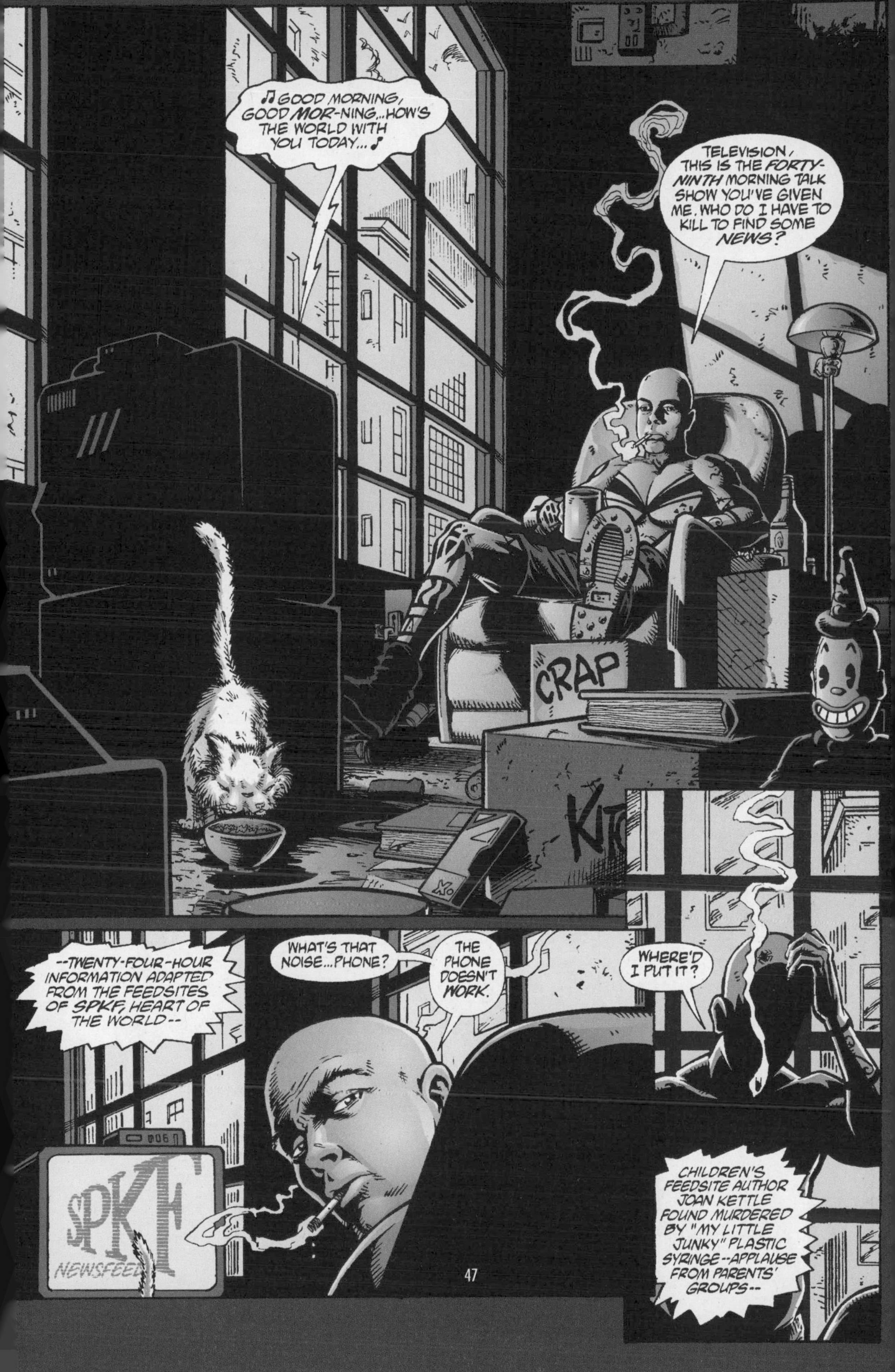
♫GOOD MORNING, GOOD MOR-NING...HOW'S THE WORLD WITH YOU TODAY...♪
TELEVISION, THIS IS THE FORTY-NINTH MORNING TALK SHOW YOU'VE GIVEN ME. WHO DO I HAVE TO KILL TO FIND SOME NEWS?
CRAP
--TWENTY-FOUR-HOUR INFORMATION ADAPTED FROM THE FEEDSITES OF SPKF, HEART OF THE WORLD--
WHAT'S THAT NOISE...PHONE?
THE PHONE DOESN'T WORK.
WHERE'D I PUT IT?
SPKF
NEWSFEED
CHILDREN'S FEEDSITE AUTHOR JOAN KETTLE FOUND MURDERED BY "MY LITTLE JUNKY" PLASTIC SYRINGE--APPLAUSE FROM PARENTS' GROUPS--

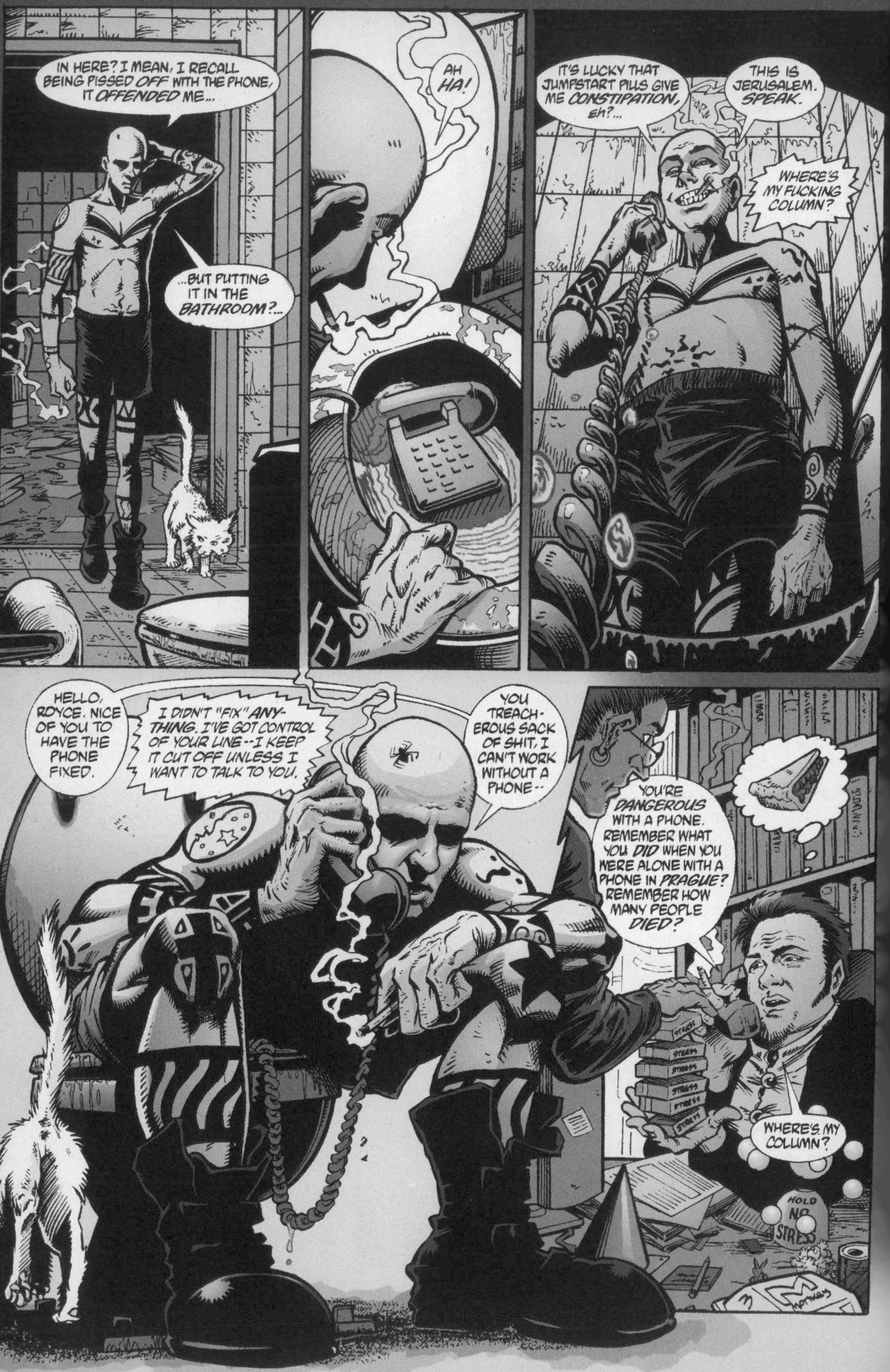
IN HERE? I MEAN, I RECALL BEING PISSED OFF WITH THE PHONE, IT OFFENDED ME...
...BUT PUTTING IT IN THE BATHROOM?...
AH HA!
IT'S LUCKY THAT JUMPSTART PILLS GIVE ME CONSTIPATION, eh?...
THIS IS JERUSALEM. SPEAK.
WHERE'S MY FUCKING COLUMN?
HELLO, ROYCE. NICE OF YOU TO HAVE THE PHONE FIXED.
I DIDN'T "FIX" ANYTHING. I'VE GOT CONTROL OF YOUR LINE -- I KEEP IT CUT OFF UNLESS I WANT TO TALK TO YOU.
YOU TREACHEROUS SACK OF SHIT, I CAN'T WORK WITHOUT A PHONE --
YOU'RE DANGEROUS WITH A PHONE. REMEMBER WHAT YOU DID WHEN YOU WERE ALONE WITH A PHONE IN PRAGUE? REMEMBER HOW MANY PEOPLE DIED?
WHERE'S MY COLUMN?
HOLD
NO
STRESS

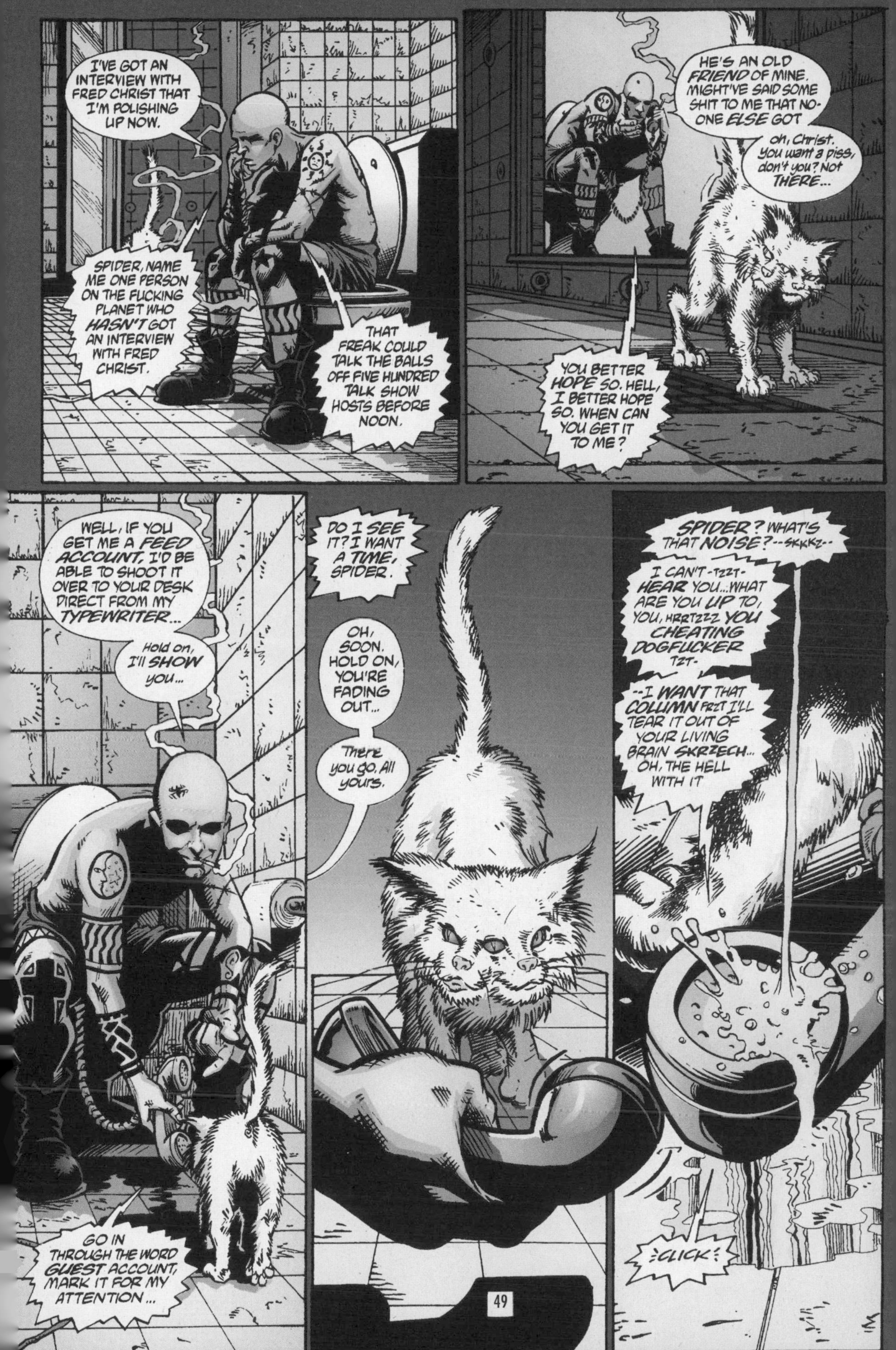
I'VE GOT AN INTERVIEW WITH FRED CHRIST THAT I'M POLISHING UP NOW.
SPIDER, NAME ME ONE PERSON ON THE FUCKING PLANET WHO HASN'T GOT AN INTERVIEW WITH FRED CHRIST.
THAT FREAK COULD TALK THE BALLS OFF FIVE HUNDRED TALK SHOW HOSTS BEFORE NOON.
HE'S AN OLD FRIEND OF MINE. MIGHT'VE SAID SOME SHIT TO ME THAT NO-ONE ELSE GOT
Oh, Christ. You want a piss, don't you? Not THERE...
YOU BETTER HOPE SO. HELL, I BETTER HOPE SO. WHEN CAN YOU GET IT TO ME?
WELL, IF YOU GET ME A FEED ACCOUNT, I'D BE ABLE TO SHOOT IT OVER TO YOUR DESK DIRECT FROM MY TYPEWRITER...
Hold on, I'll SHOW you...
GO IN THROUGH THE WORD GUEST ACCOUNT, MARK IT FOR MY ATTENTION...
DO I SEE IT? I WANT A TIME, SPIDER.
OH, SOON. HOLD ON, YOU'RE FADING OUT...
There you go. All yours.
SPIDER? WHAT'S THAT NOISE? --SKKKZ--
I CAN'T -TZZT- HEAR YOU... WHAT ARE YOU UP TO, YOU, HRRTZZZ YOU CHEATING DOGFUCKER TZT-
--I WANT THAT COLUMN FRZT I'LL TEAR IT OUT OF YOUR LIVING BRAIN SKRZECH... OH, THE HELL WITH IT
CLICK

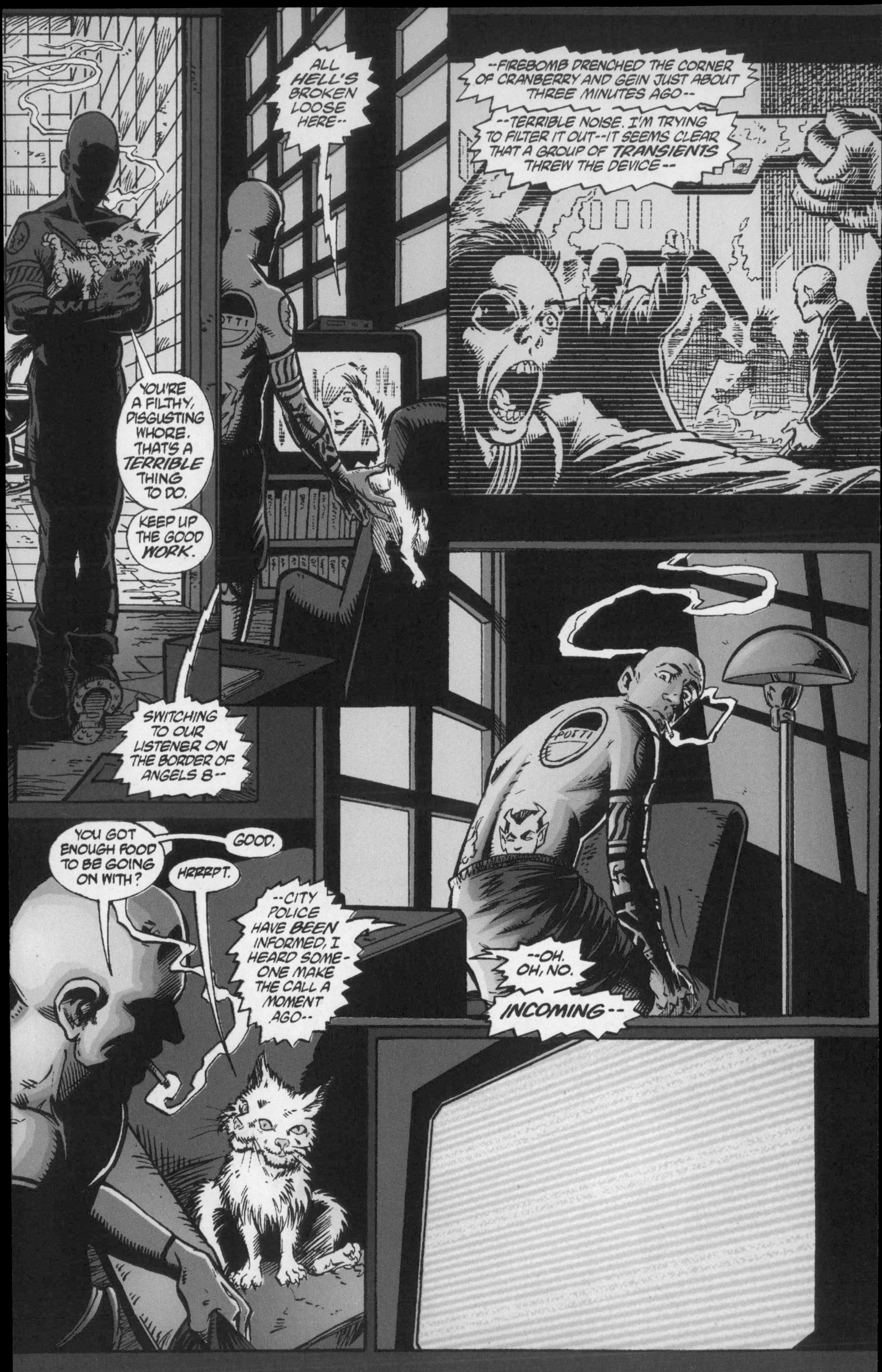
ALL HELL'S BROKEN LOOSE HERE--
--FIREBOMB DRENCHED THE CORNER OF CRANBERRY AND GEIN JUST ABOUT THREE MINUTES AGO--
--TERRIBLE NOISE. I'M TRYING TO FILTER IT OUT--IT SEEMS CLEAR THAT A GROUP OF TRANSIENTS THREW THE DEVICE--
YOU'RE A FILTHY, DISGUSTING WHORE. THAT'S A TERRIBLE THING TO DO.
KEEP UP THE GOOD WORK.
SWITCHING TO OUR LISTENER ON THE BORDER OF ANGELS 8--
YOU GOT ENOUGH FOOD TO BE GOING ON WITH?
GOOD.
HRRRPT.
--CITY POLICE HAVE BEEN INFORMED, I HEARD SOME-ONE MAKE THE CALL A MOMENT AGO--
--OH. OH, NO.
INCOMING--

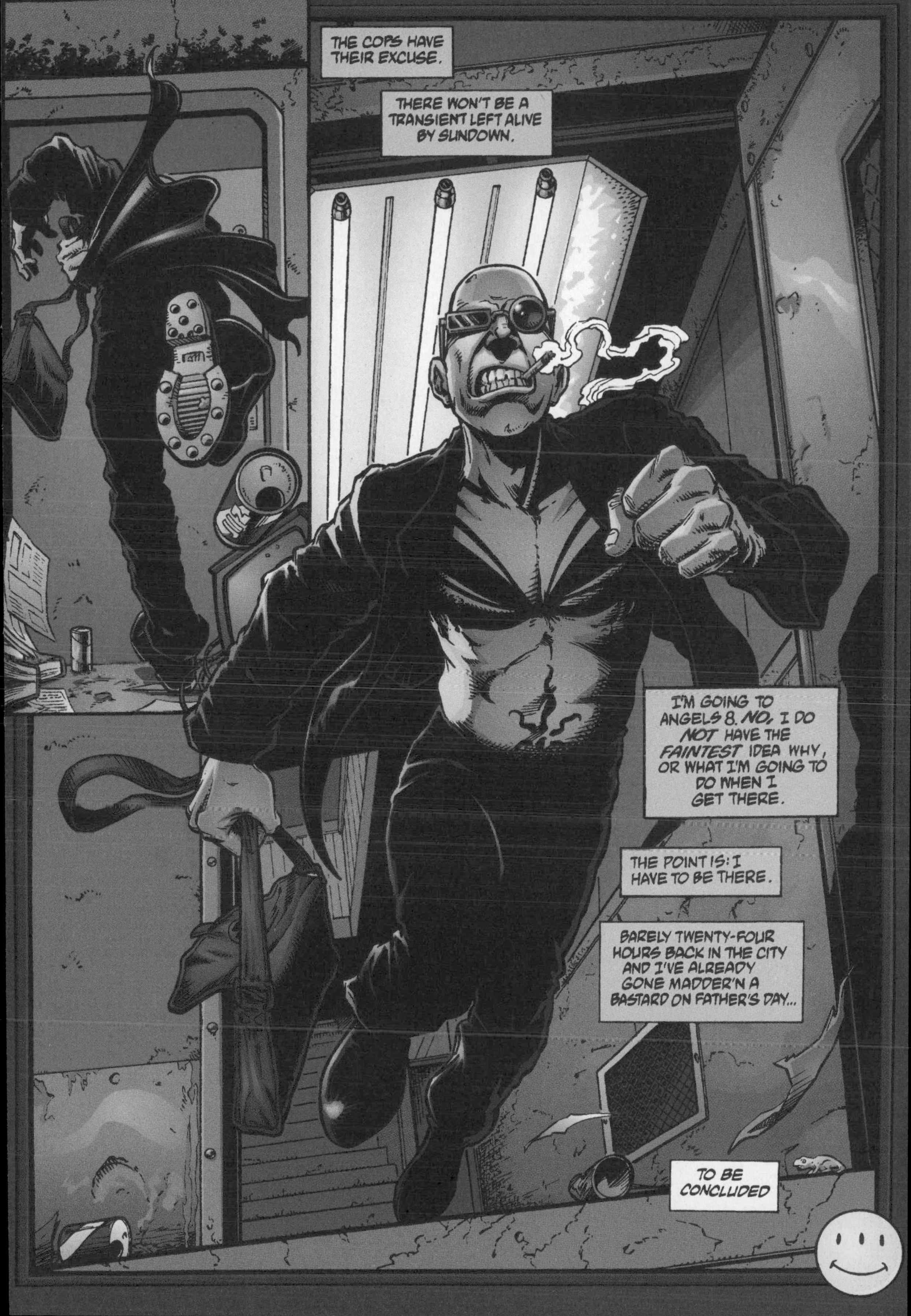
THE COPS HAVE THEIR EXCUSE.
THERE WON'T BE A TRANSIENT LEFT ALIVE BY SUNDOWN.
I'M GOING TO ANGELS 8. NO, I DO NOT HAVE THE FAINTEST IDEA WHY, OR WHAT I'M GOING TO DO WHEN I GET THERE.
THE POINT IS: I HAVE TO BE THERE.
BARELY TWENTY-FOUR HOURS BACK IN THE CITY AND I'VE ALREADY GONE MADDER'N A BASTARD ON FATHER'S DAY...
TO BE CONCLUDED

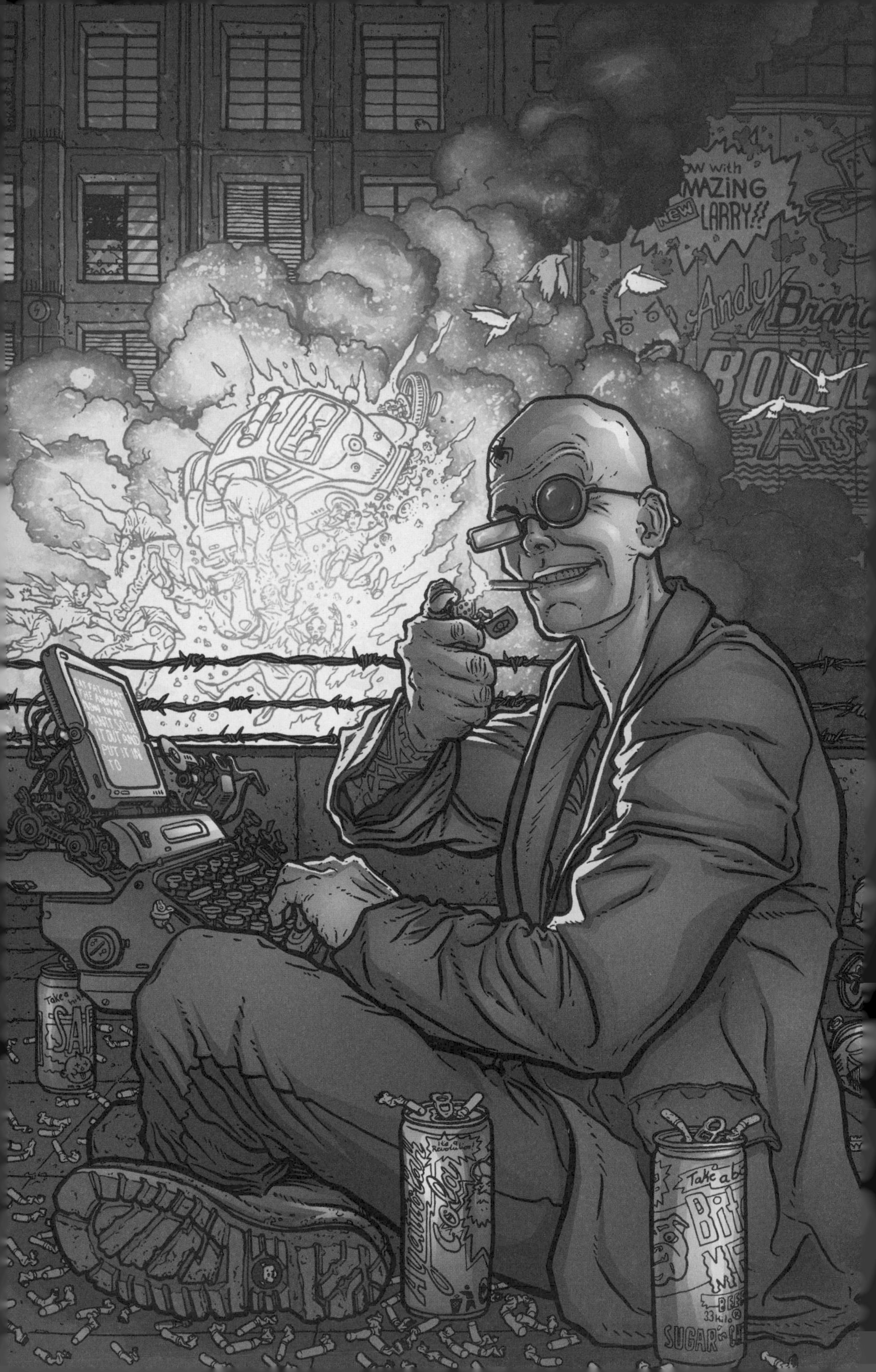
NEW
LARRY!!
It's a Revolution!
BEER
SUGAR

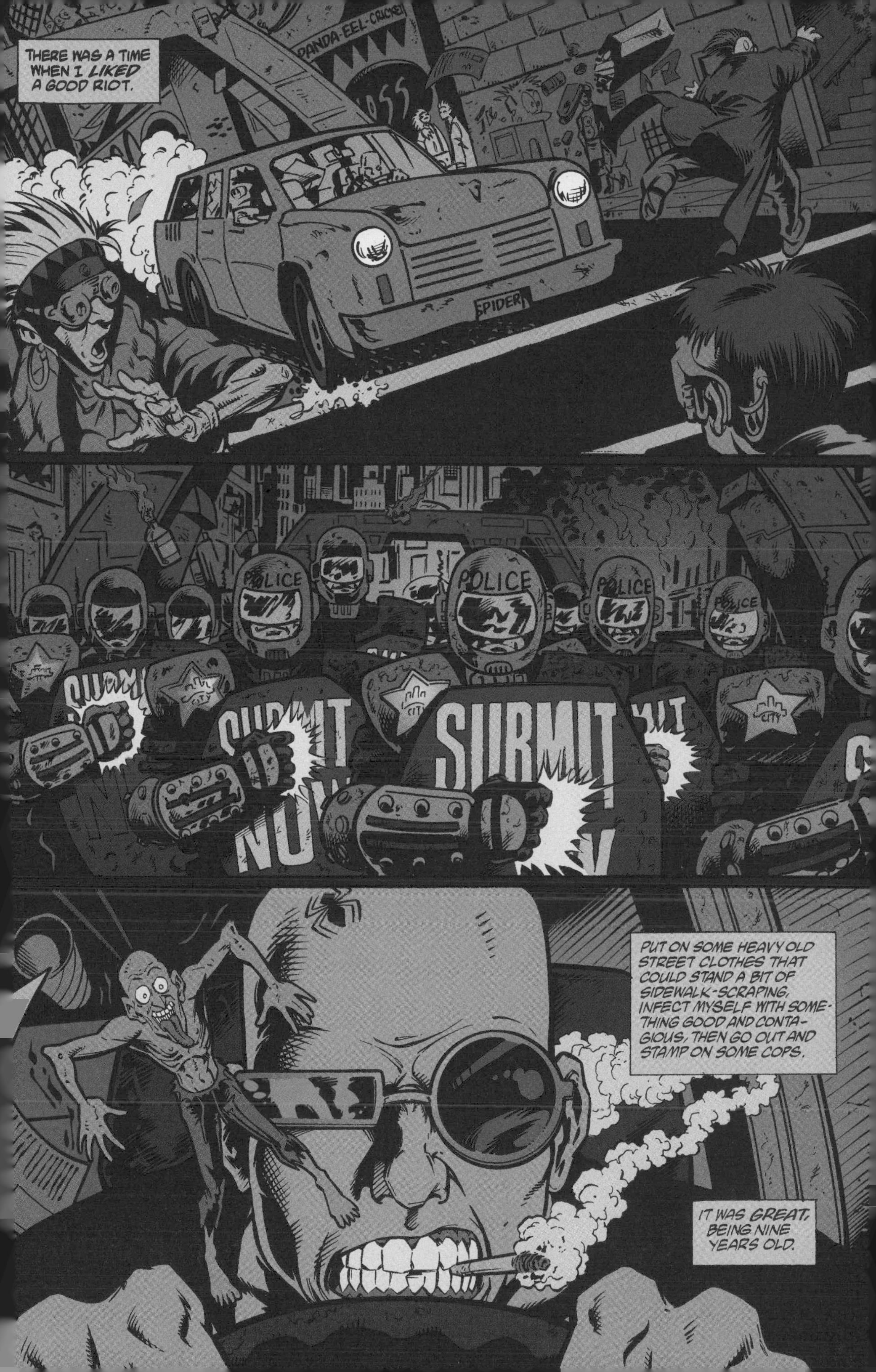
THERE WAS A TIME WHEN I *LIKED* A GOOD RIOT.
PANDA-EEL-CRICKET
SPIDER
POLICE
SURMIT
NOW
CITY
PUT ON SOME HEAVY OLD STREET CLOTHES THAT COULD STAND A BIT OF SIDEWALK-SCRAPING, INFECT MYSELF WITH SOMETHING GOOD AND CONTAGIOUS, THEN GO OUT AND STAMP ON SOME COPS.
IT WAS *GREAT*, BEING NINE YEARS OLD.

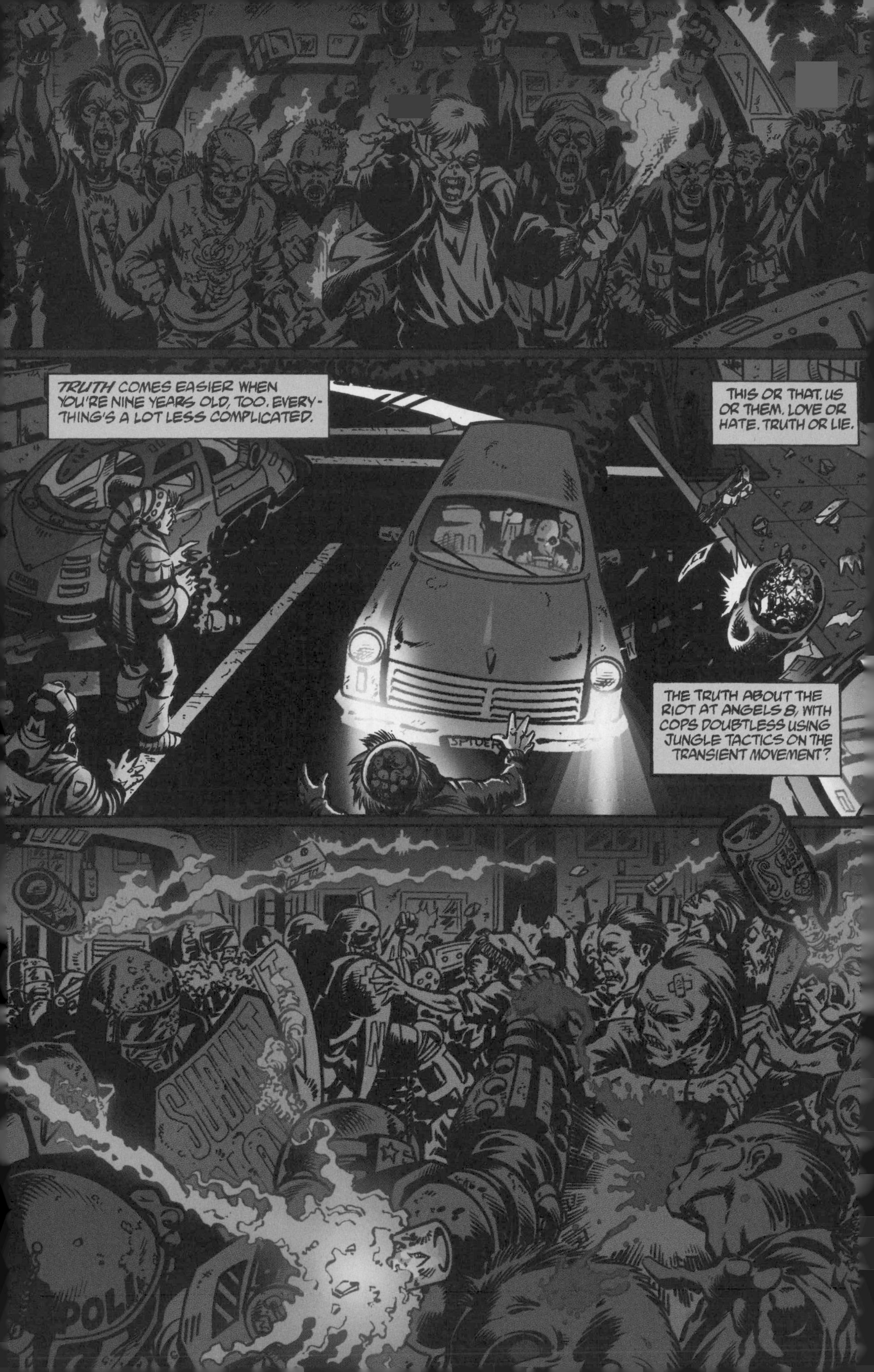
TRUTH COMES EASIER WHEN YOU'RE NINE YEARS OLD, TOO. EVERYTHING'S A LOT LESS COMPLICATED.
THIS OR THAT. US OR THEM. LOVE OR HATE. TRUTH OR LIE.
SPIDER
THE TRUTH ABOUT THE RIOT AT ANGELS 8, WITH COPS DOUBTLESS USING JUNGLE TACTICS ON THE TRANSIENT MOVEMENT?

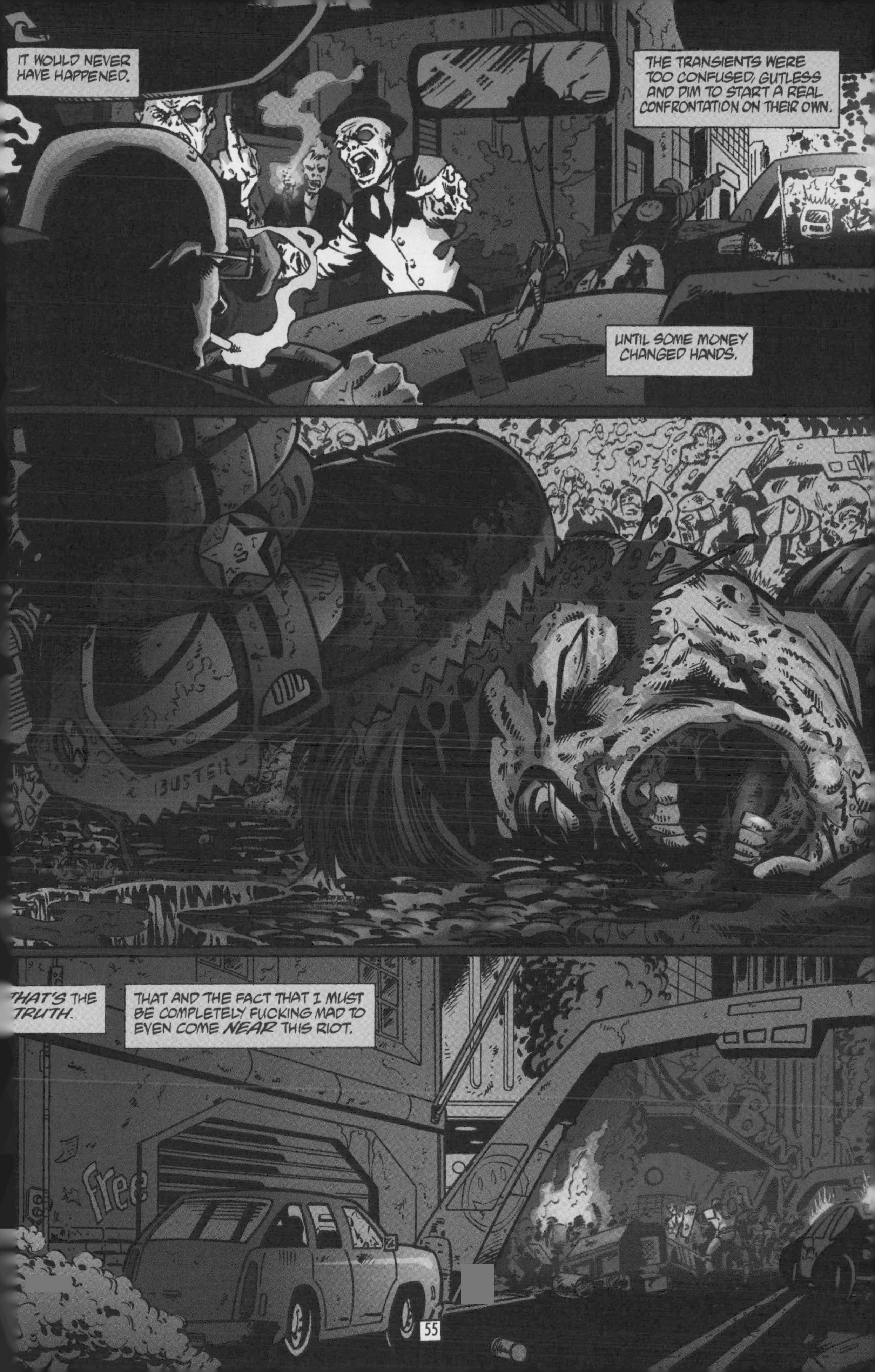
IT WOULD NEVER HAVE HAPPENED.
THE TRANSIENTS WERE TOO CONFUSED, GUTLESS AND DIM TO START A REAL CONFRONTATION ON THEIR OWN.
UNTIL SOME MONEY CHANGED HANDS.
BUSTER
THAT'S THE TRUTH.
THAT AND THE FACT THAT I MUST BE COMPLETELY FUCKING MAD TO EVEN COME NEAR THIS RIOT.
Free

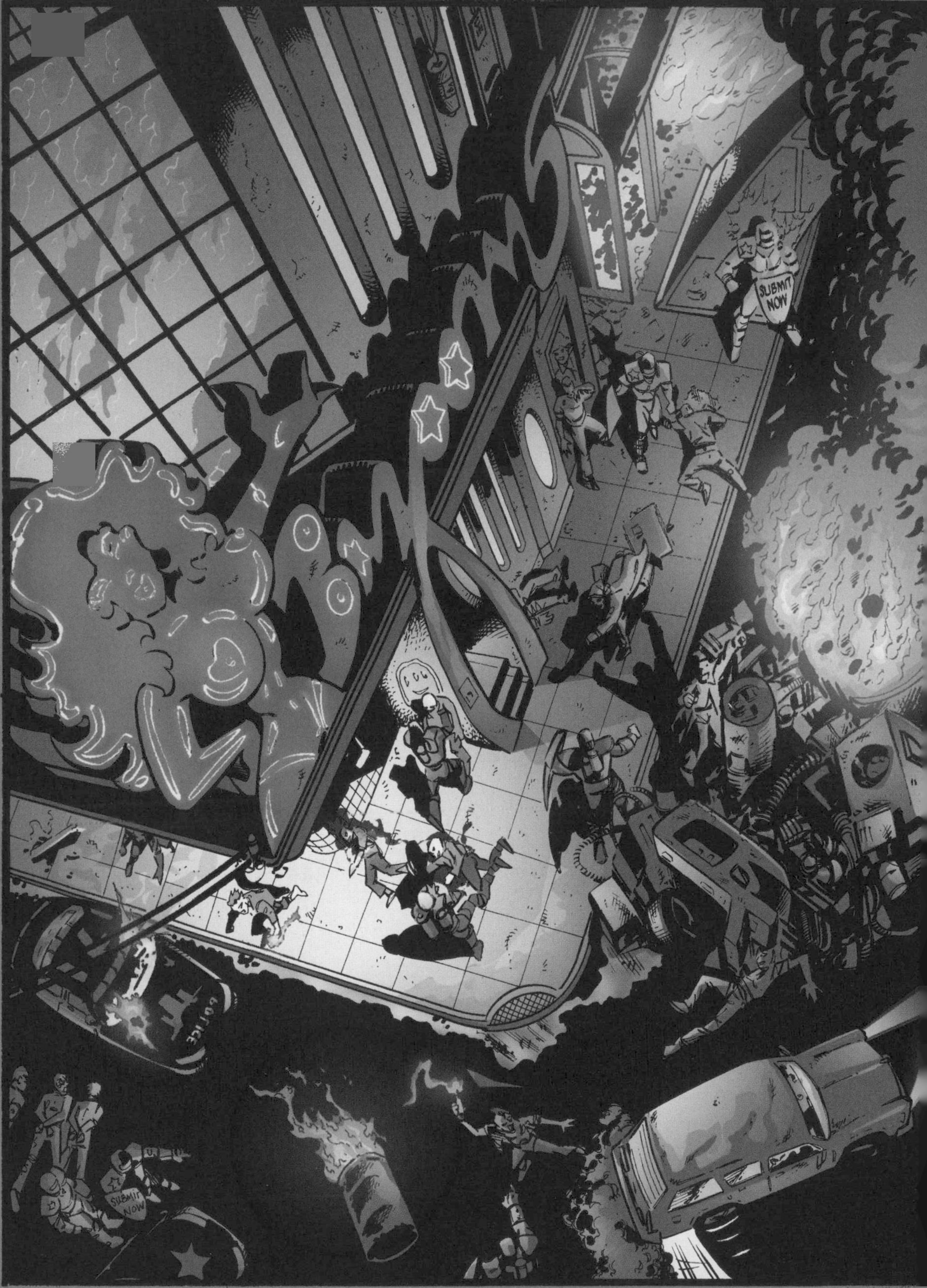
SUBMIT NOW
SUBMIT NOW

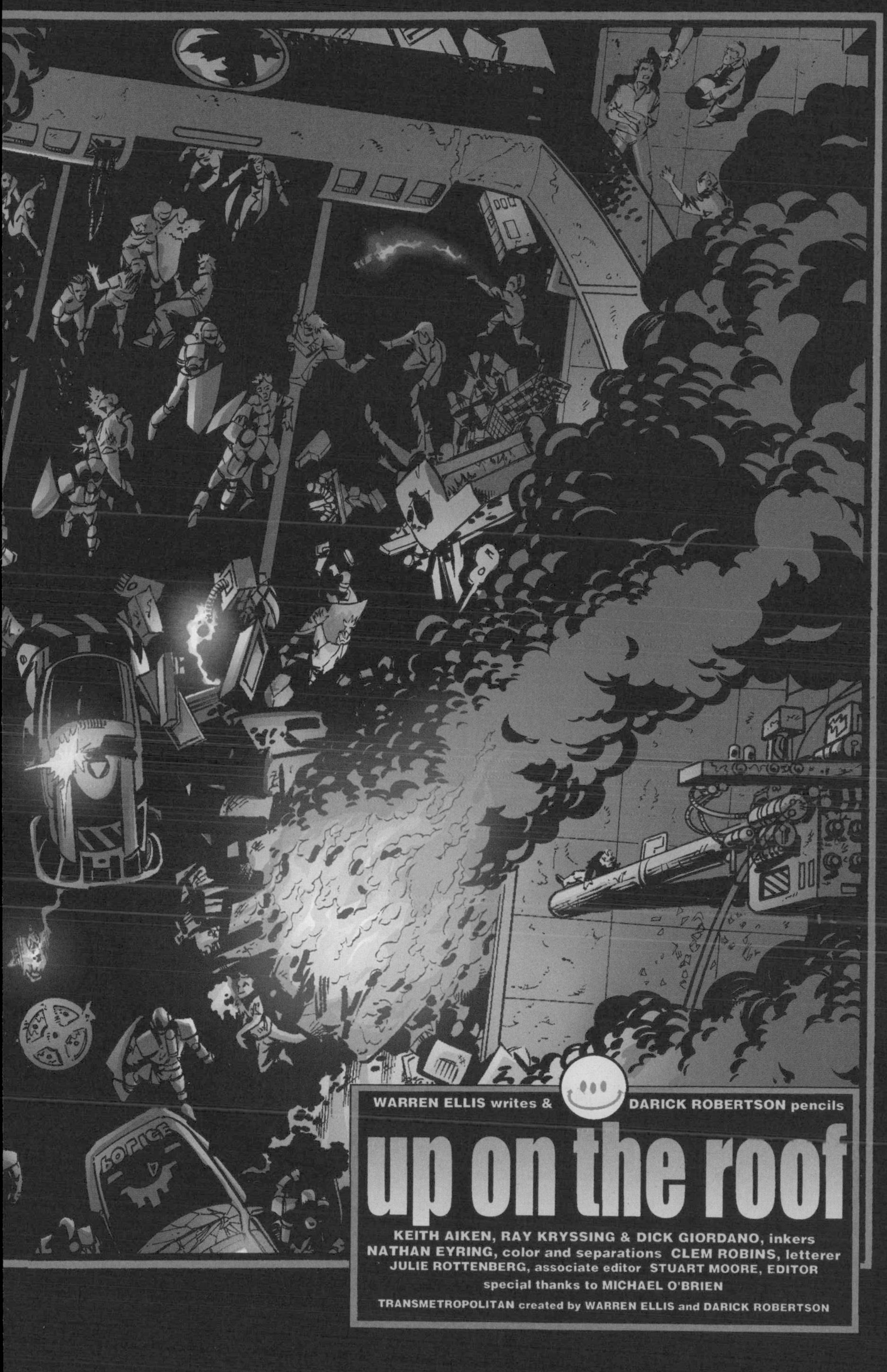
WARREN ELLIS writes & DARICK ROBERTSON pencils
up on the roof
KEITH AIKEN, RAY KRYSSING & DICK GIORDANO, inkers
NATHAN EYRING, color and separations CLEM ROBINS, letterer
JULIE ROTTENBERG, associate editor STUART MOORE, EDITOR
special thanks to MICHAEL O'BRIEN
TRANSMETROPOLITAN created by WARREN ELLIS and DARICK ROBERTSON

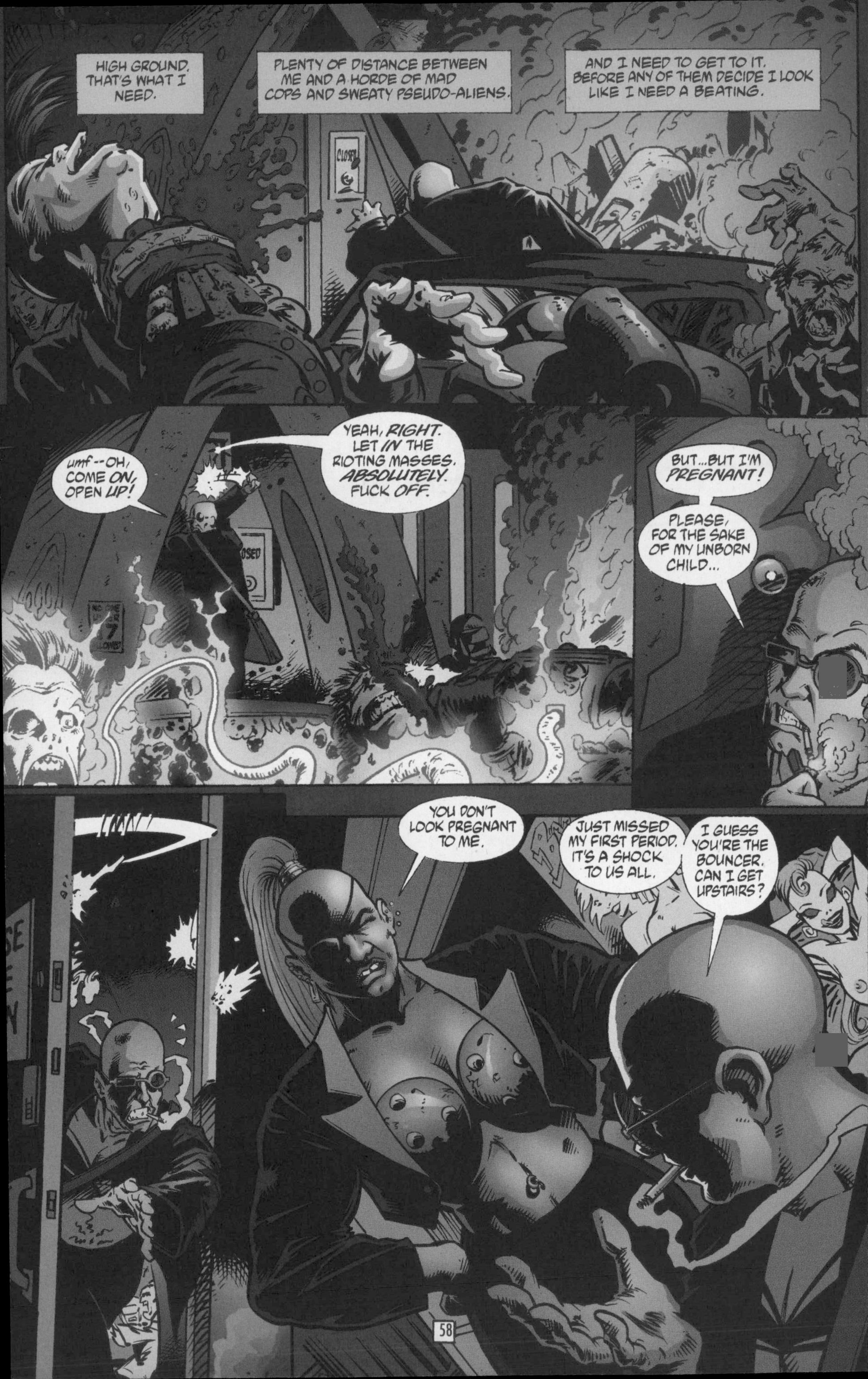

HIGH GROUND. THAT'S WHAT I NEED.
PLENTY OF DISTANCE BETWEEN ME AND A HORDE OF MAD COPS AND SWEATY PSEUDO-ALIENS.
AND I NEED TO GET TO IT. BEFORE ANY OF THEM DECIDE I LOOK LIKE I NEED A BEATING.
CLOSED
umf--OH, COME ON, OPEN UP!
YEAH, RIGHT. LET IN THE RIOTING MASSES. ABSOLUTELY. FUCK OFF.
BUT...BUT I'M PREGNANT!
PLEASE, FOR THE SAKE OF MY UNBORN CHILD...
YOU DON'T LOOK PREGNANT TO ME.
JUST MISSED MY FIRST PERIOD. IT'S A SHOCK TO US ALL.
I GUESS YOU'RE THE BOUNCER. CAN I GET UPSTAIRS?

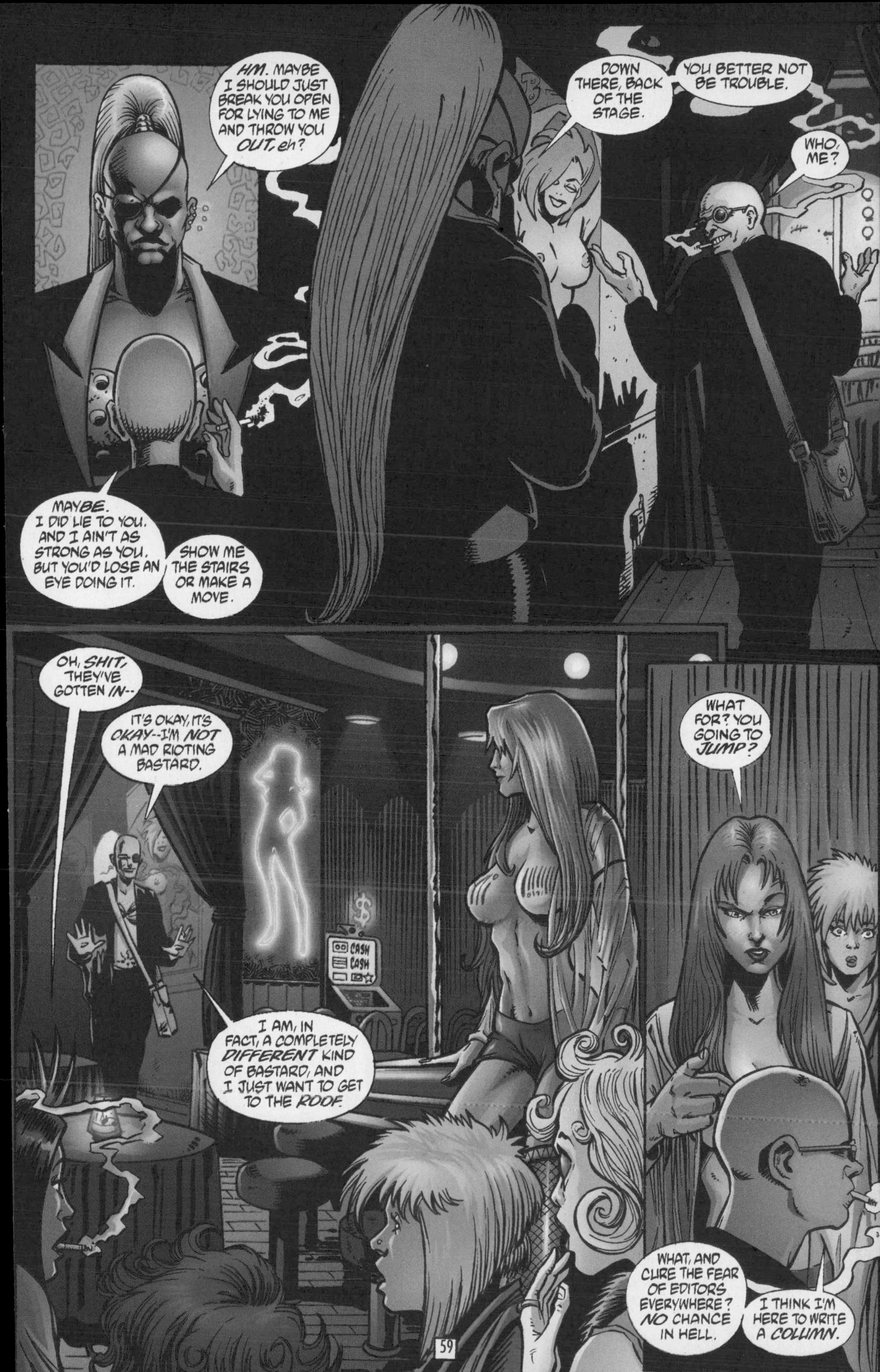
HM. MAYBE I SHOULD JUST BREAK YOU OPEN FOR LYING TO ME AND THROW YOU OUT, eh?
MAYBE. I DID LIE TO YOU. AND I AIN'T AS STRONG AS YOU. BUT YOU'D LOSE AN EYE DOING IT.
SHOW ME THE STAIRS OR MAKE A MOVE.
DOWN THERE, BACK OF THE STAGE.
YOU BETTER NOT BE TROUBLE.
WHO, ME?
OH, SHIT, THEY'VE GOTTEN IN--
IT'S OKAY, IT'S OKAY--I'M NOT A MAD RIOTING BASTARD.
I AM, IN FACT, A COMPLETELY DIFFERENT KIND OF BASTARD, AND I JUST WANT TO GET TO THE ROOF.
CASH
CASH
WHAT FOR? YOU GOING TO JUMP?
WHAT, AND CURE THE FEAR OF EDITORS EVERYWHERE? NO CHANCE IN HELL.
I THINK I'M HERE TO WRITE A COLUMN.

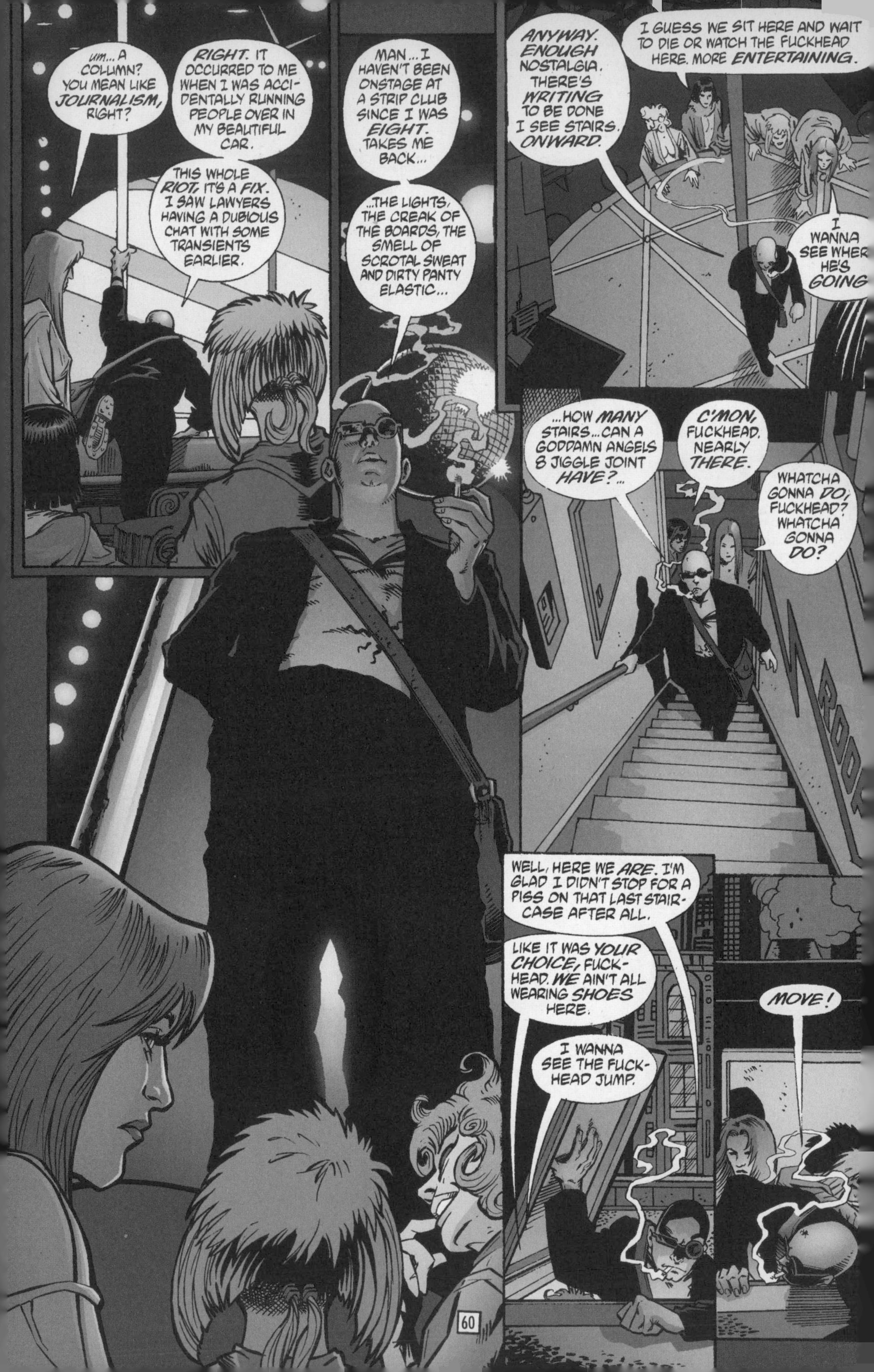

UM... A COLUMN? YOU MEAN LIKE JOURNALISM, RIGHT?
RIGHT. IT OCCURRED TO ME WHEN I WAS ACCIDENTALLY RUNNING PEOPLE OVER IN MY BEAUTIFUL CAR.
THIS WHOLE RIOT, IT'S A FIX. I SAW LAWYERS HAVING A DUBIOUS CHAT WITH SOME TRANSIENTS EARLIER.
MAN... I HAVEN'T BEEN ONSTAGE AT A STRIP CLUB SINCE I WAS EIGHT. TAKES ME BACK...
...THE LIGHTS, THE CREAK OF THE BOARDS, THE SMELL OF SCROTAL SWEAT AND DIRTY PANTY ELASTIC...
ANYWAY. ENOUGH NOSTALGIA. THERE'S WRITING TO BE DONE. I SEE STAIRS. ONWARD.
I GUESS WE SIT HERE AND WAIT TO DIE OR WATCH THE FUCKHEAD HERE. MORE ENTERTAINING.
I WANNA SEE WHER HE'S GOING
...HOW MANY STAIRS... CAN A GODDAMN ANGELS 8 JIGGLE JOINT HAVE?...
C'MON, FUCKHEAD. NEARLY THERE.
WHATCHA GONNA DO, FUCKHEAD? WHATCHA GONNA DO?
WELL, HERE WE ARE. I'M GLAD I DIDN'T STOP FOR A PISS ON THAT LAST STAIRCASE AFTER ALL.
LIKE IT WAS YOUR CHOICE, FUCKHEAD. WE AIN'T ALL WEARING SHOES HERE.
I WANNA SEE THE FUCKHEAD JUMP.
MOVE!

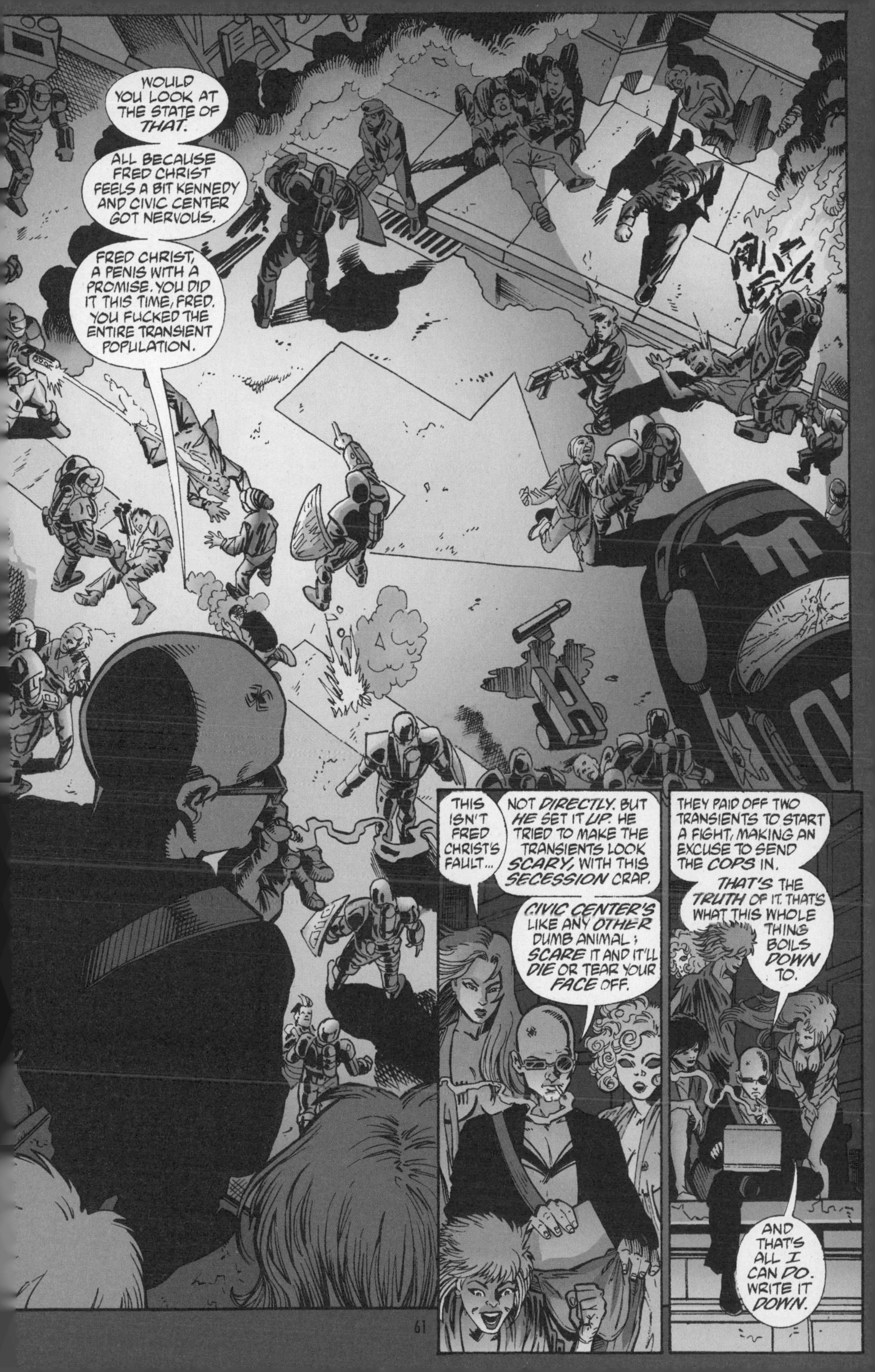
WOULD YOU LOOK AT THE STATE OF *THAT*.
ALL BECAUSE FRED CHRIST FEELS A BIT KENNEDY AND CIVIC CENTER GOT NERVOUS.
FRED CHRIST, A PENIS WITH A PROMISE. YOU DID IT THIS TIME, FRED. YOU FUCKED THE ENTIRE TRANSIENT POPULATION.
THIS ISN'T FRED CHRIST'S FAULT...
NOT *DIRECTLY*. BUT *HE* SET IT *UP*. HE TRIED TO MAKE THE TRANSIENTS LOOK *SCARY*, WITH THIS *SECESSION* CRAP.
CIVIC CENTER'S LIKE ANY *OTHER* DUMB ANIMAL; *SCARE* IT AND IT'LL *DIE* OR TEAR YOUR *FACE* OFF.
THEY PAID OFF TWO TRANSIENTS TO START A FIGHT, MAKING AN EXCUSE TO SEND THE *COPS* IN.
THAT'S THE *TRUTH* OF IT. THAT'S WHAT THIS WHOLE THING BOILS *DOWN* TO.
AND THAT'S ALL *I* CAN *DO*. WRITE IT *DOWN*.

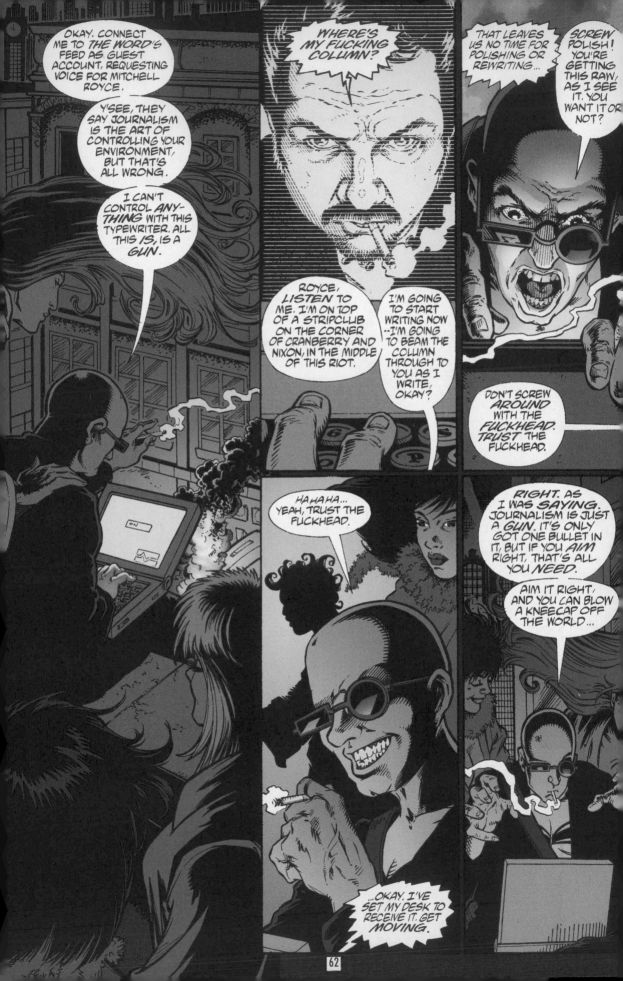

OKAY. CONNECT ME TO *THE WORD'S* FEED AS GUEST ACCOUNT, REQUESTING VOICE FOR MITCHELL ROYCE.

Y'SEE, THEY SAY JOURNALISM IS THE ART OF CONTROLLING YOUR ENVIRONMENT, BUT THAT'S ALL WRONG.

I CAN'T CONTROL *ANY-THING* WITH THIS TYPEWRITER. ALL THIS *IS*, IS A *GUN.*

WHERE'S MY FUCKING COLUMN?

ROYCE, *LISTEN* TO ME. I'M ON TOP OF A STRIPCLUB ON THE CORNER OF CRANBERRY AND NIXON, IN THE MIDDLE OF THIS RIOT.

I'M GOING TO START WRITING NOW --I'M GOING TO BEAM THE COLUMN THROUGH TO YOU AS I WRITE, OKAY?

THAT LEAVES US NO TIME FOR POLISHING OR REWRITING...

SCREW POLISH! YOU'RE GETTING THIS RAW, AS I SEE IT. YOU WANT IT OR NOT?

DON'T SCREW *AROUND* WITH THE *FUCKHEAD.* *TRUST* THE FUCKHEAD.

HA HA HA... YEAH, TRUST THE FUCKHEAD.

RIGHT. AS I WAS *SAYING.* JOURNALISM IS JUST A *GUN.* IT'S ONLY GOT ONE BULLET IN IT, BUT IF YOU *AIM* RIGHT, THAT'S ALL YOU *NEED.*

AIM IT RIGHT, AND YOU CAN BLOW A KNEECAP OFF THE WORLD...

...OKAY. I'VE SET MY DESK TO RECEIVE IT. GET *MOVING.*

I COULD NEVER WRITE UNLESS I WAS IN THE CITY.

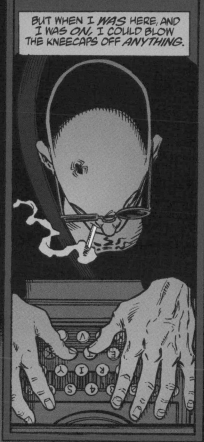

BUT WHEN I *WAS* HERE, AND I WAS *ON*, I COULD BLOW THE KNEECAPS OFF *ANYTHING*.

I'M NOT SCARED. I'M *NOT* SCARED. INDIRA, D'YOU KNOW HOW THE LIVE NEWSFEEDS ARE COVERING ANGELS 8?

THEY'RE HAVING SOME TROUBLE GETTING CLOSE. SOME PICTURES, NOT MUCH REPORTAGE.

mm. OKAY. GET ME A CONFERENCE CALL WITH THE CITY EDITOR AT *SPKF.* I THINK I HAVE SOMETHING TO *SELL* HER.

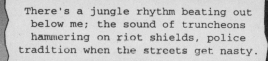

There's a jungle rhythm beating out below me; the sound of truncheons hammering on riot shields, police tradition when the streets get nasty.

I'm in Angels 8, above what will doubtless be called the Transient Riot. History's only written by the winners, after all, and if the cops want it called the Transient Riot, then that's how it'll be.

Because there's going to be Transient blood all over this place. And you know something?

It's not their fault.

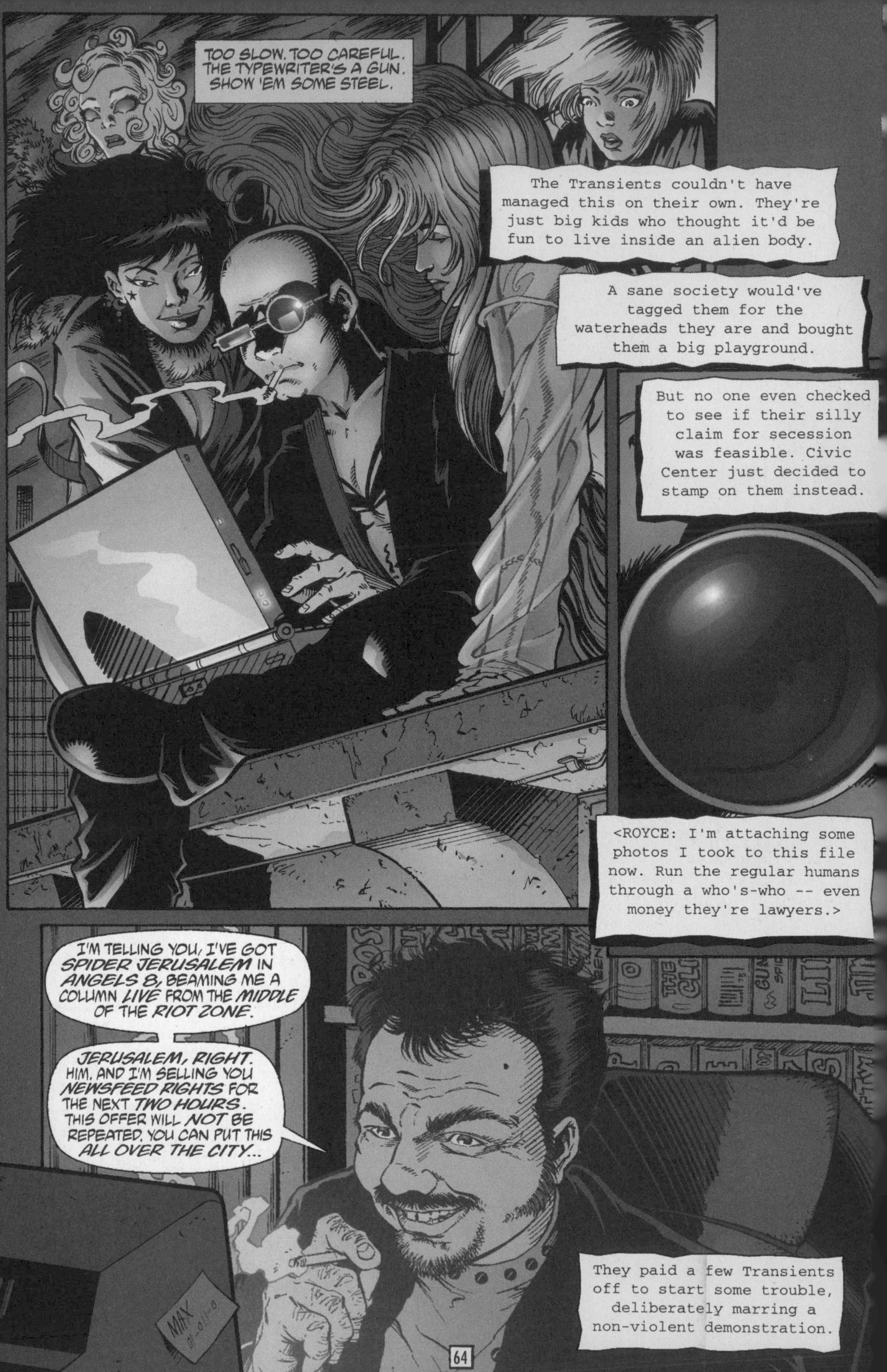
TOO SLOW. TOO CAREFUL. THE TYPEWRITER'S A GUN. SHOW 'EM SOME STEEL.
The Transients couldn't have managed this on their own. They're just big kids who thought it'd be fun to live inside an alien body.
A sane society would've tagged them for the waterheads they are and bought them a big playground.
But no one even checked to see if their silly claim for secession was feasible. Civic Center just decided to stamp on them instead.
<ROYCE: I'm attaching some photos I took to this file now. Run the regular humans through a who's-who -- even money they're lawyers.>
I'M TELLING YOU, I'VE GOT SPIDER JERUSALEM IN ANGELS 8, BEAMING ME A COLUMN LIVE FROM THE MIDDLE OF THE RIOT ZONE.
JERUSALEM, RIGHT. HIM. AND I'M SELLING YOU NEWSFEED RIGHTS FOR THE NEXT TWO HOURS. THIS OFFER WILL NOT BE REPEATED. YOU CAN PUT THIS ALL OVER THE CITY...
They paid a few Transients off to start some trouble, deliberately marring a non-violent demonstration.

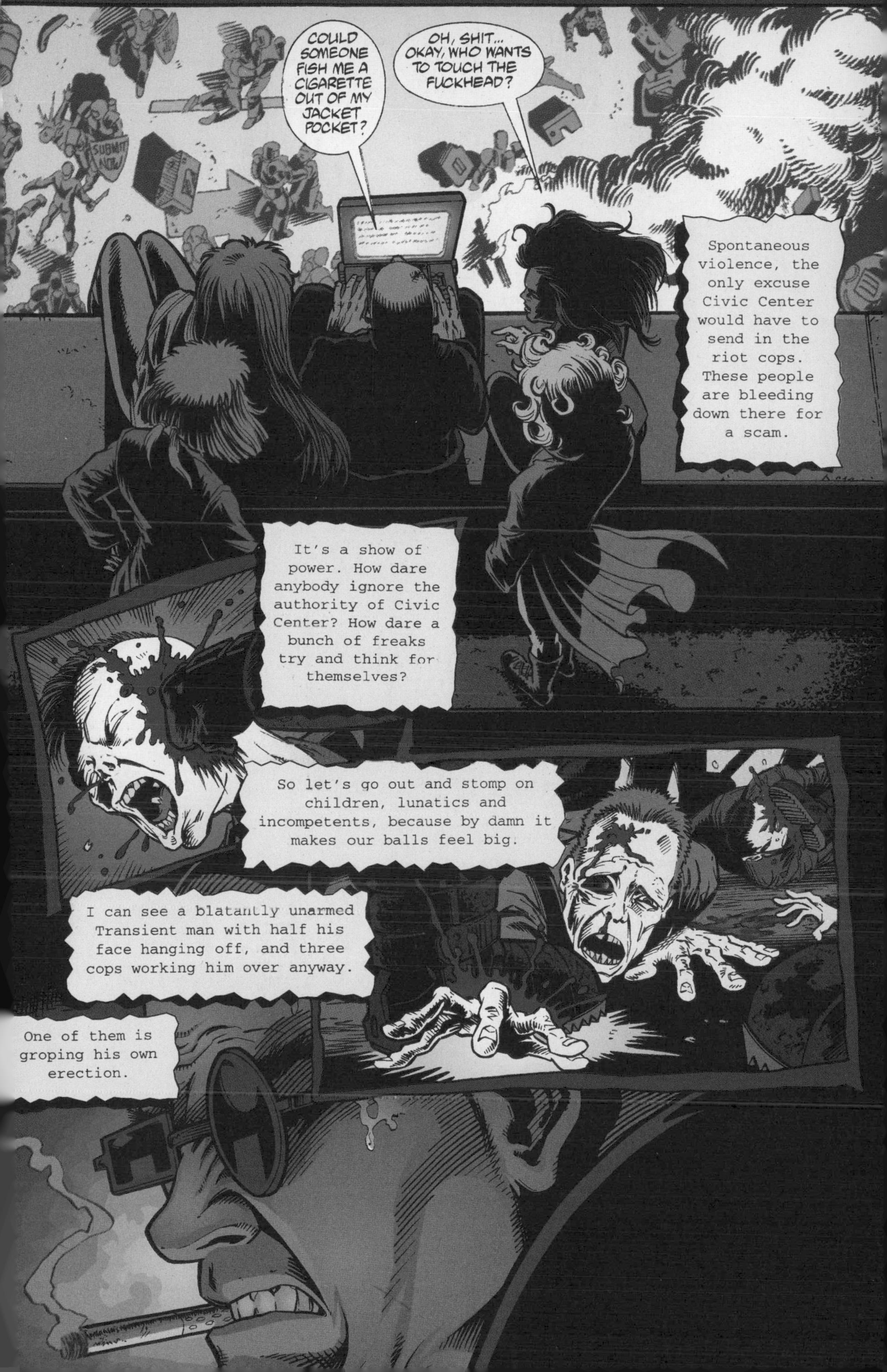

COULD SOMEONE FISH ME A CIGARETTE OUT OF MY JACKET POCKET?
OH, SHIT... OKAY, WHO WANTS TO TOUCH THE FUCKHEAD?
Spontaneous violence, the only excuse Civic Center would have to send in the riot cops. These people are bleeding down there for a scam.
It's a show of power. How dare anybody ignore the authority of Civic Center? How dare a bunch of freaks try and think for themselves?
So let's go out and stomp on children, lunatics and incompetents, because by damn it makes our balls feel big.
I can see a blatantly unarmed Transient man with half his face hanging off, and three cops working him over anyway.
One of them is groping his own erection.

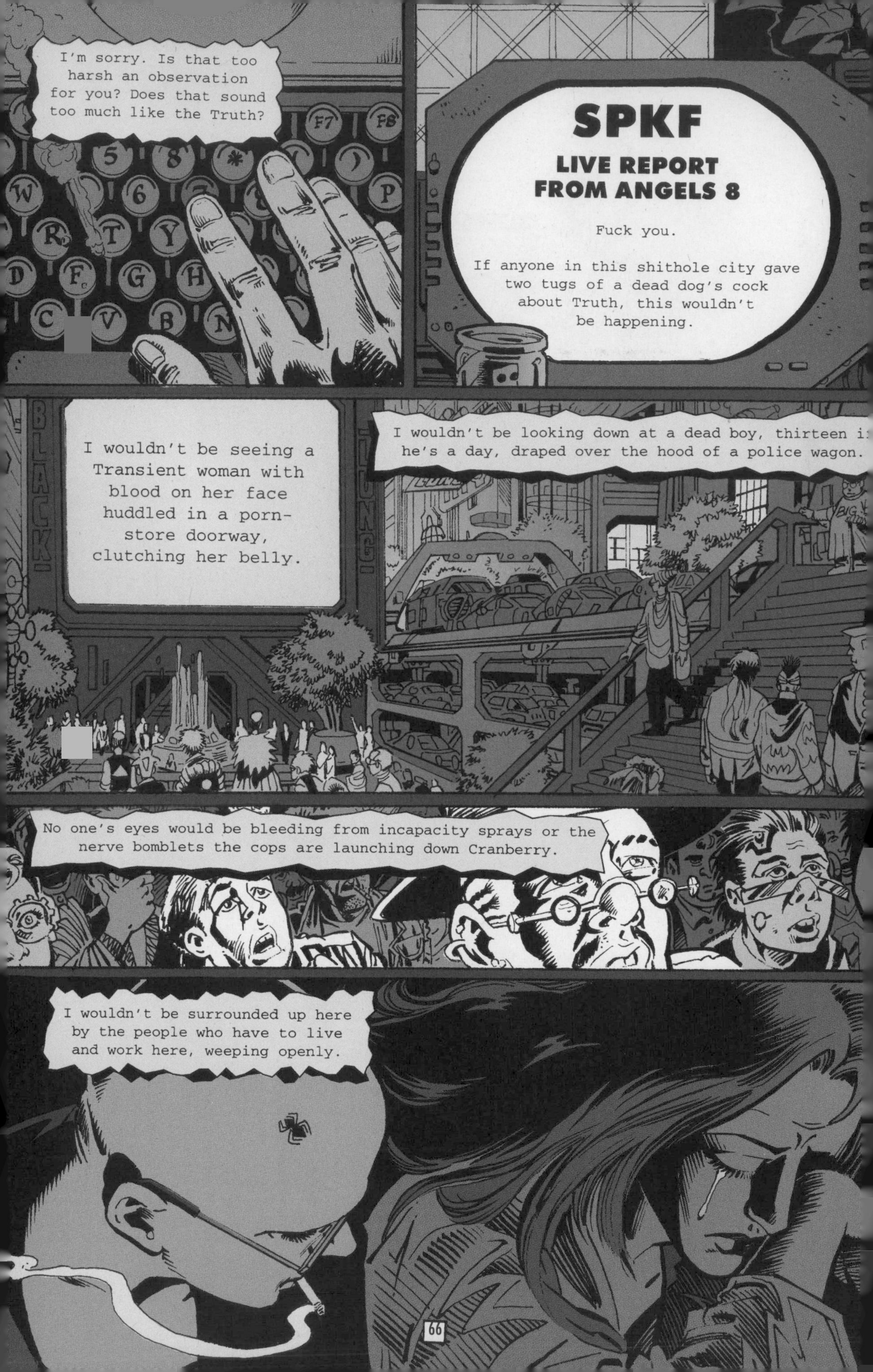

I'm sorry. Is that too harsh an observation for you? Does that sound too much like the Truth?
SPKF
LIVE REPORT FROM ANGELS 8
Fuck you.
If anyone in this shithole city gave two tugs of a dead dog's cock about Truth, this wouldn't be happening.
I wouldn't be seeing a Transient woman with blood on her face huddled in a porn-store doorway, clutching her belly.
I wouldn't be looking down at a dead boy, thirteen if he's a day, draped over the hood of a police wagon.
No one's eyes would be bleeding from incapacity sprays or the nerve bomblets the cops are launching down Cranberry.
I wouldn't be surrounded up here by the people who have to live and work here, weeping openly.

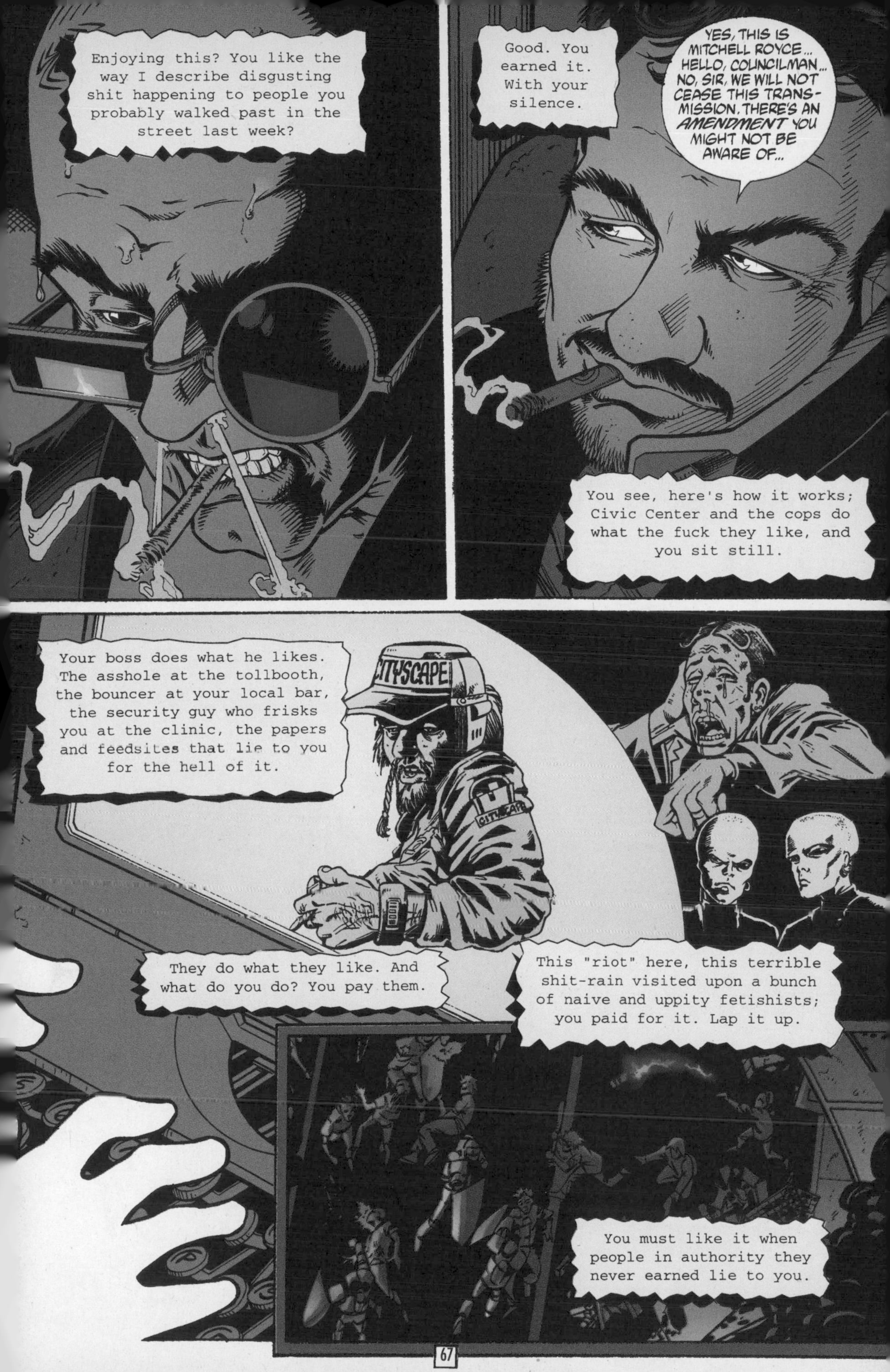
Enjoying this? You like the way I describe disgusting shit happening to people you probably walked past in the street last week?
Good. You earned it. With your silence.
YES, THIS IS MITCHELL ROYCE... HELLO, COUNCILMAN... NO, SIR, WE WILL NOT CEASE THIS TRANS-MISSION. THERE'S AN AMENDMENT YOU MIGHT NOT BE AWARE OF...
You see, here's how it works; Civic Center and the cops do what the fuck they like, and you sit still.
Your boss does what he likes. The asshole at the tollbooth, the bouncer at your local bar, the security guy who frisks you at the clinic, the papers and feedsites that lie to you for the hell of it.
CITYSCAPE
They do what they like. And what do you do? You pay them.
This "riot" here, this terrible shit-rain visited upon a bunch of naive and uppity fetishists; you paid for it. Lap it up.
You must like it when people in authority they never earned lie to you.

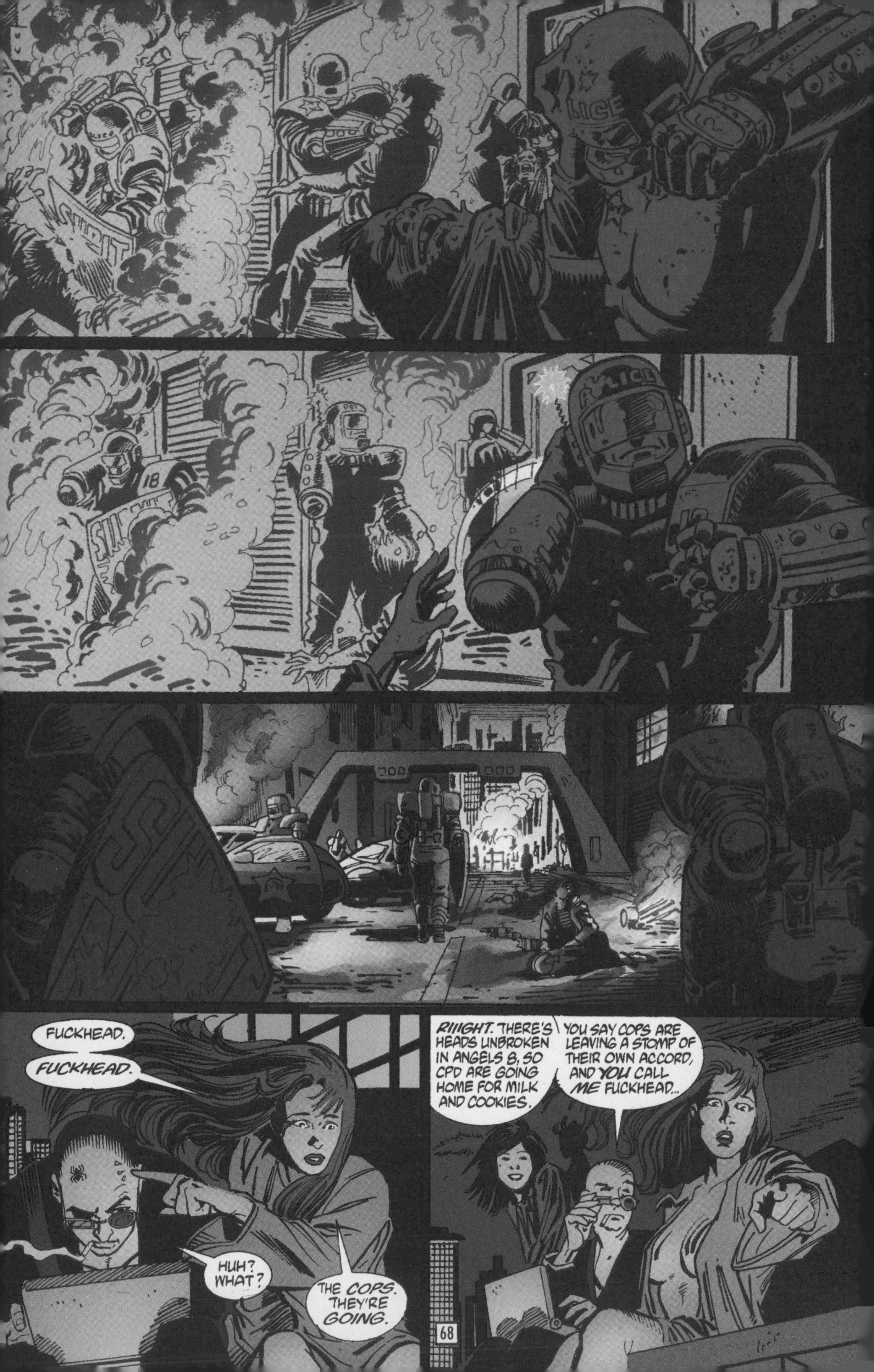

FUCKHEAD.
FUCKHEAD.
HUH? WHAT?
THE COPS. THEY'RE GOING.
RIIIGHT. THERE'S HEADS UNBROKEN IN ANGELS 8, SO CPD ARE GOING HOME FOR MILK AND COOKIES.
YOU SAY COPS ARE LEAVING A STOMP OF THEIR OWN ACCORD, AND YOU CALL ME FUCKHEAD...

CHRIST.
YOU'RE RIGHT.
THEY'RE PULLING RIGHT OUT. THERE'S COPS DOUBLE-TIMING IT UP CRANBERRY, NOT LAYING COVERING FIRE...
FUCK ME. THEY'RE REALLY GOING.
I AM SO TIRED.

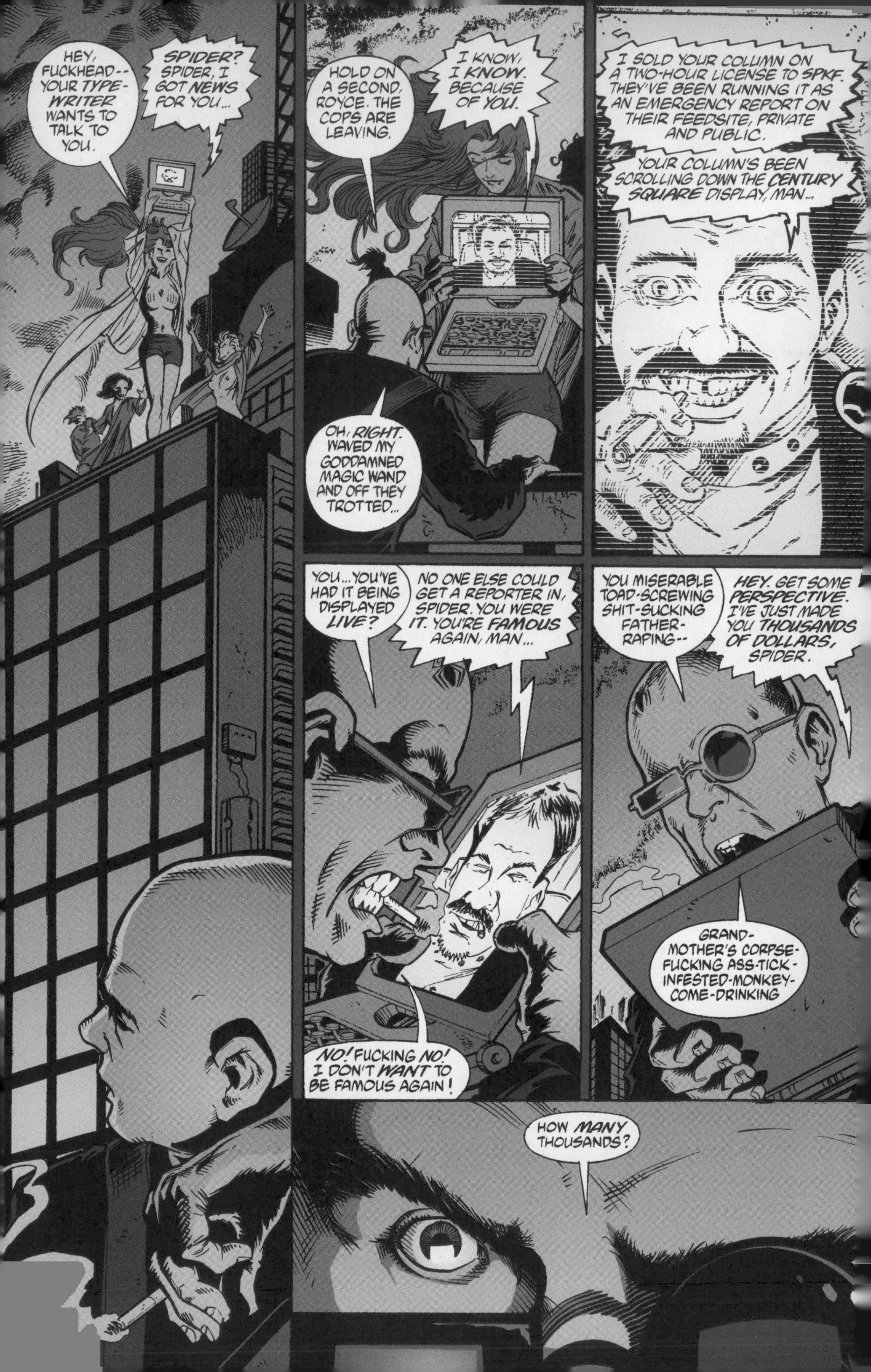
HEY, FUCKHEAD-- YOUR TYPEWRITER WANTS TO TALK TO YOU.
SPIDER? SPIDER, I GOT NEWS FOR YOU...
HOLD ON A SECOND, ROYCE. THE COPS ARE LEAVING.
I KNOW, I KNOW. BECAUSE OF YOU.
OH, RIGHT. WAVED MY GODDAMNED MAGIC WAND AND OFF THEY TROTTED...
I SOLD YOUR COLUMN ON A TWO-HOUR LICENSE TO SPKF. THEY'VE BEEN RUNNING IT AS AN EMERGENCY REPORT ON THEIR FEEDSITE, PRIVATE AND PUBLIC.
YOUR COLUMN'S BEEN SCROLLING DOWN THE CENTURY SQUARE DISPLAY, MAN...
YOU... YOU'VE HAD IT BEING DISPLAYED LIVE?
NO ONE ELSE COULD GET A REPORTER IN, SPIDER. YOU WERE IT. YOU'RE FAMOUS AGAIN, MAN...
NO! FUCKING NO! I DON'T WANT TO BE FAMOUS AGAIN!
YOU MISERABLE TOAD-SCREWING SHIT-SUCKING FATHER-RAPING--
HEY. GET SOME PERSPECTIVE. I'VE JUST MADE YOU THOUSANDS OF DOLLARS, SPIDER.
GRAND-MOTHER'S CORPSE-FUCKING ASS-TICK-INFESTED-MONKEY-COME-DRINKING
HOW MANY THOUSANDS?

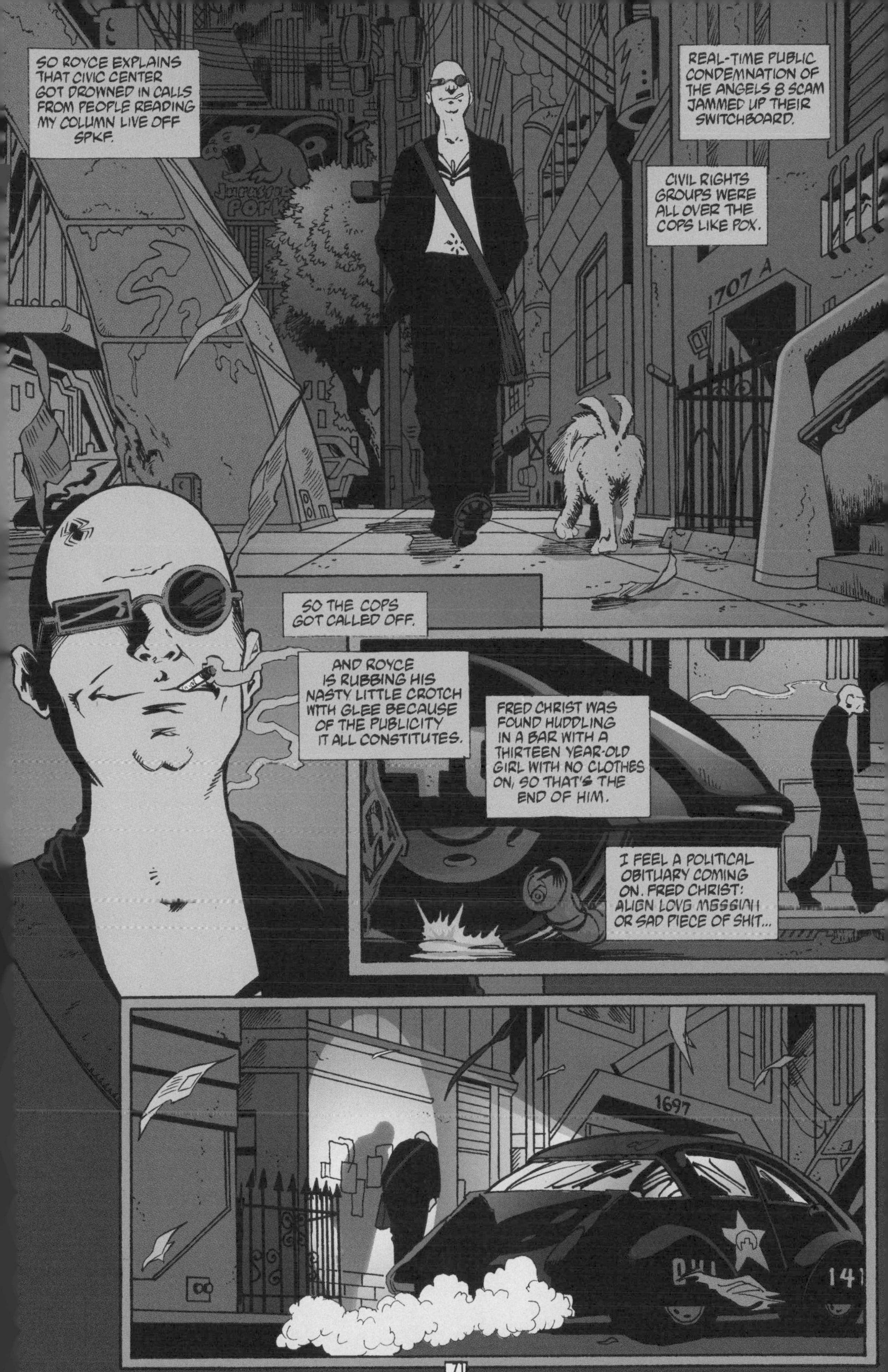
SO ROYCE EXPLAINS THAT CIVIC CENTER GOT DROWNED IN CALLS FROM PEOPLE READING MY COLUMN LIVE OFF SPKF.
REAL-TIME PUBLIC CONDEMNATION OF THE ANGELS 8 SCAM JAMMED UP THEIR SWITCHBOARD.
CIVIL RIGHTS GROUPS WERE ALL OVER THE COPS LIKE POX.
1707 A
SO THE COPS GOT CALLED OFF.
AND ROYCE IS RUBBING HIS NASTY LITTLE CROTCH WITH GLEE BECAUSE OF THE PUBLICITY IT ALL CONSTITUTES.
FRED CHRIST WAS FOUND HUDDLING IN A BAR WITH A THIRTEEN YEAR-OLD GIRL WITH NO CLOTHES ON, SO THAT'S THE END OF HIM.
I FEEL A POLITICAL OBITUARY COMING ON. FRED CHRIST: ALIEN LOVE MESSIAH OR SAD PIECE OF SHIT...
1697

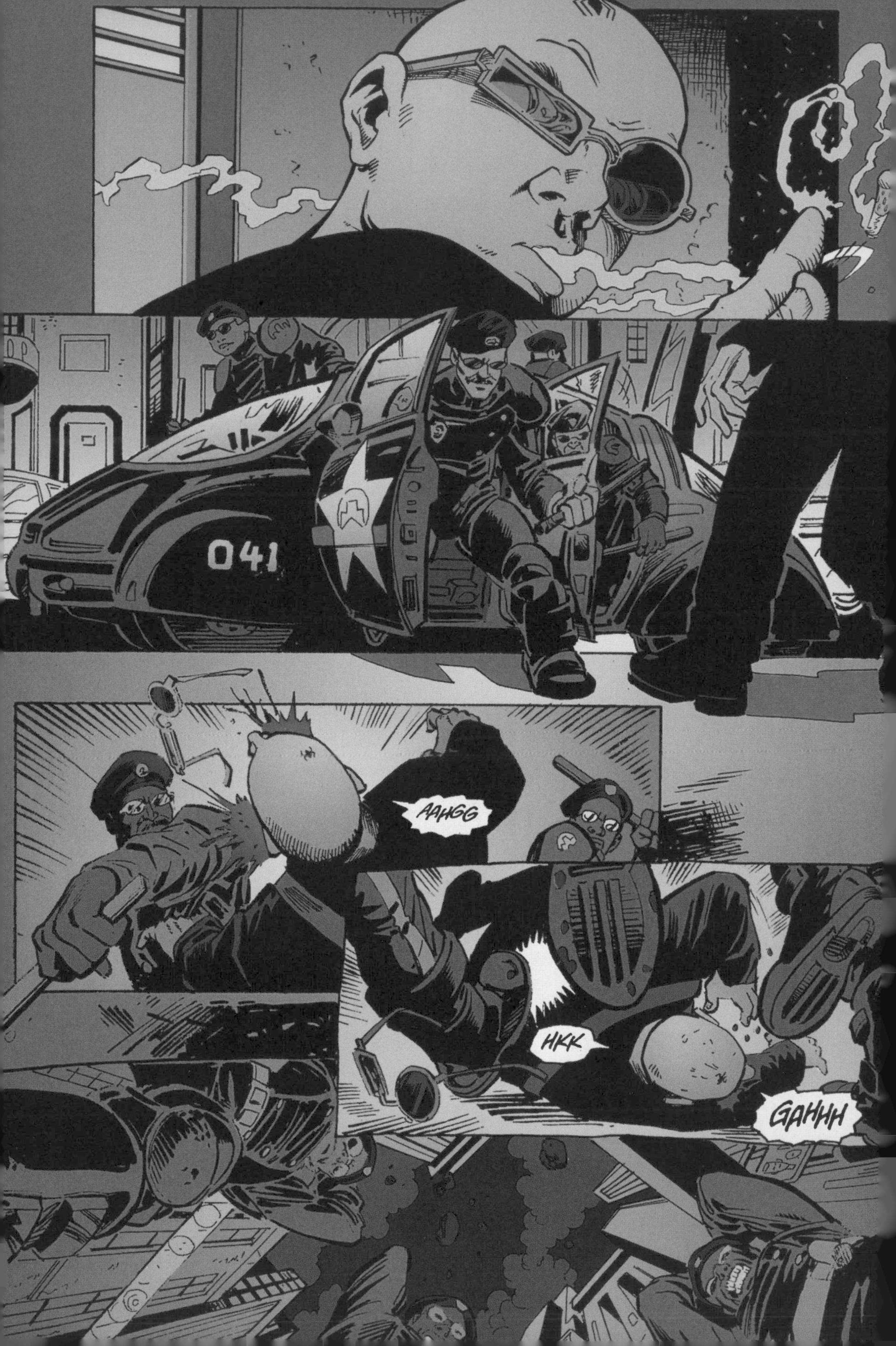
041
AAHGG
HKK
GAHHH

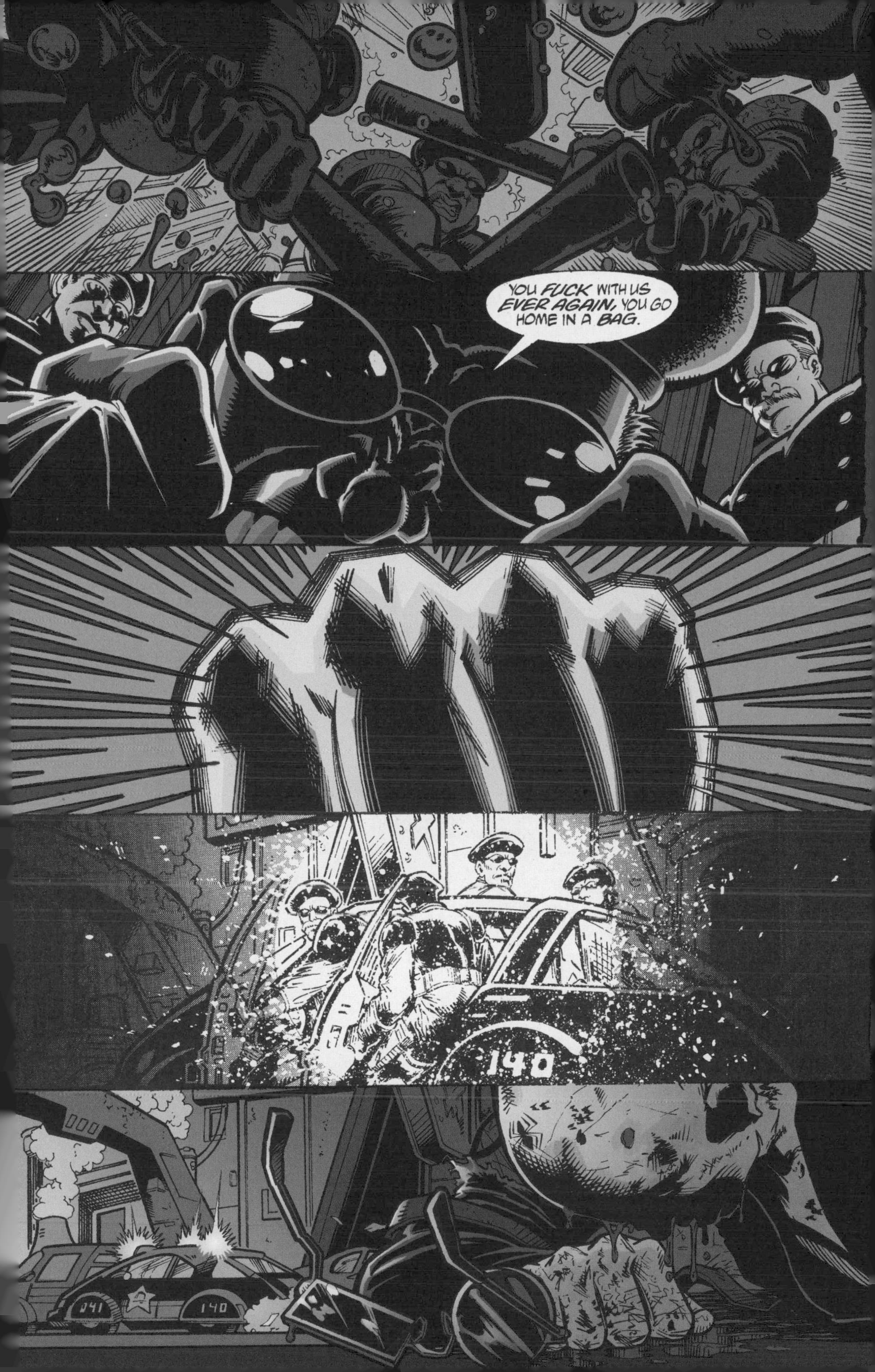
YOU FUCK WITH US EVER AGAIN, YOU GO HOME IN A BAG.
140
041
140

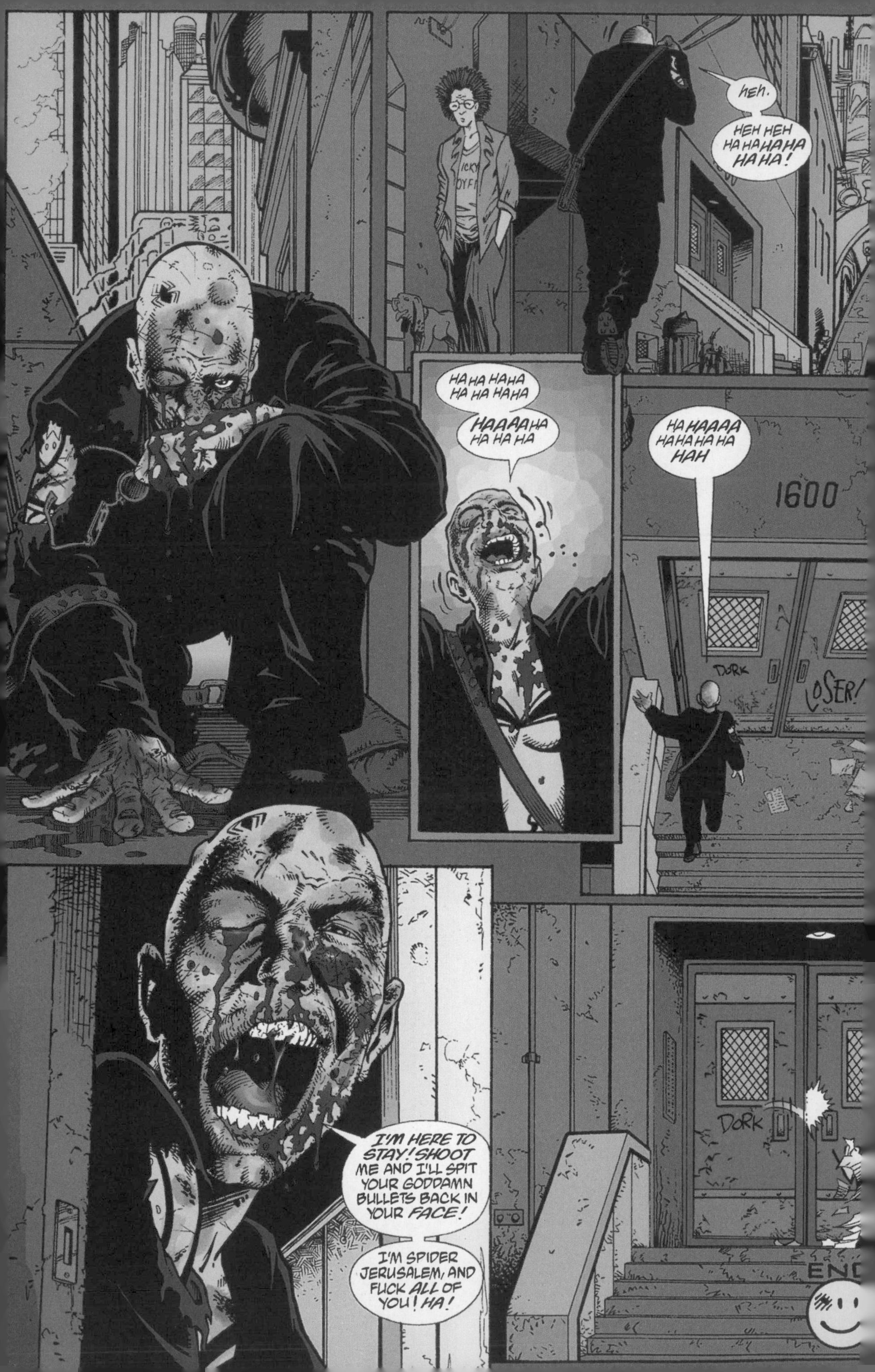
heh.
HEH HEH HA HA HAHA HA HA!
HA HA HAHA HA HA HAHA
HAAAAHA HA HA HA
HA HAAAA HA HA HA HA HAH
1600
DORK
LOSER!
DORK
I'M HERE TO STAY! SHOOT ME AND I'LL SPIT YOUR GODDAMN BULLETS BACK IN YOUR FACE!
I'M SPIDER JERUSALEM, AND FUCK ALL OF YOU! HA!
END

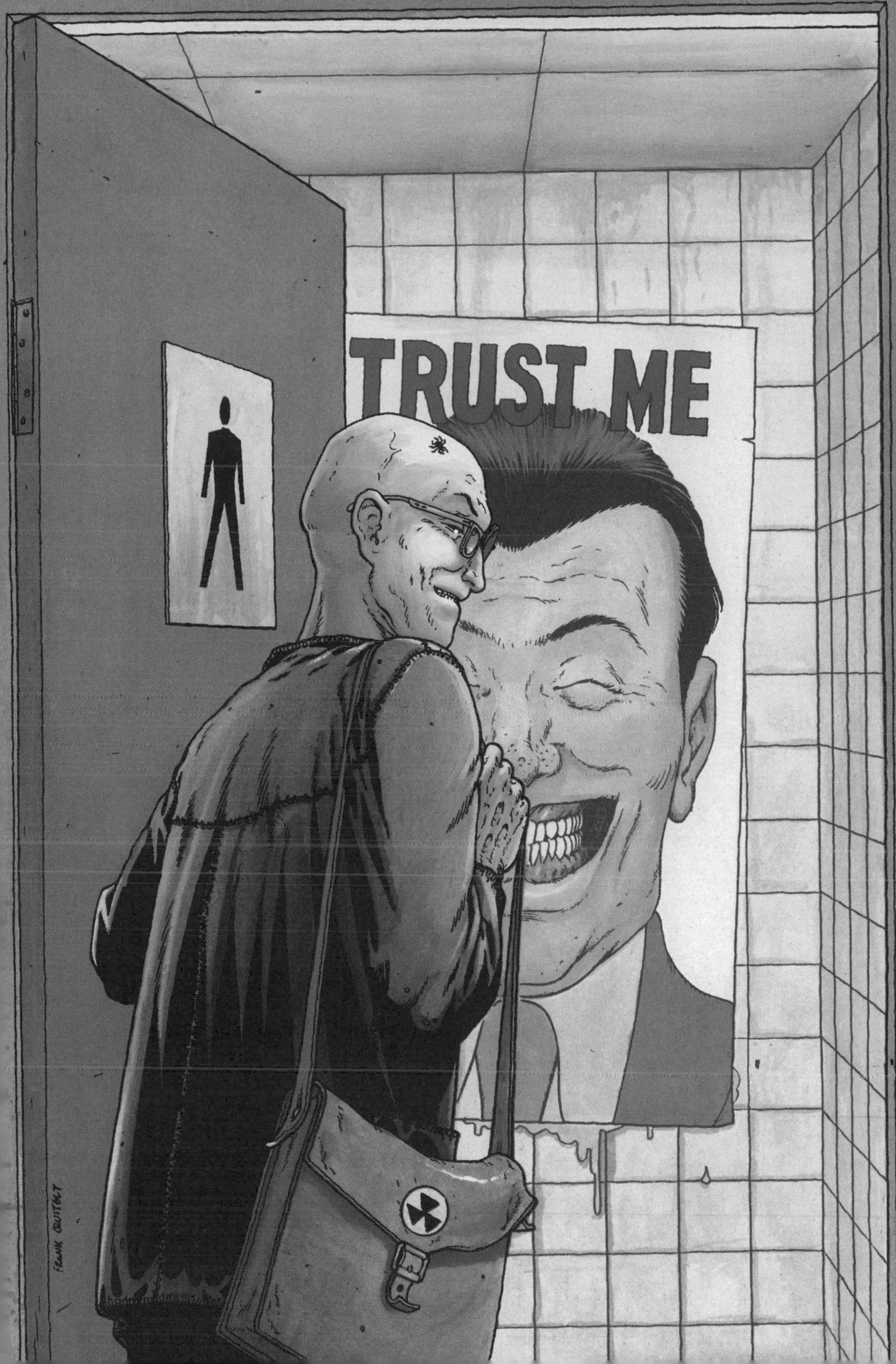
TRUST ME

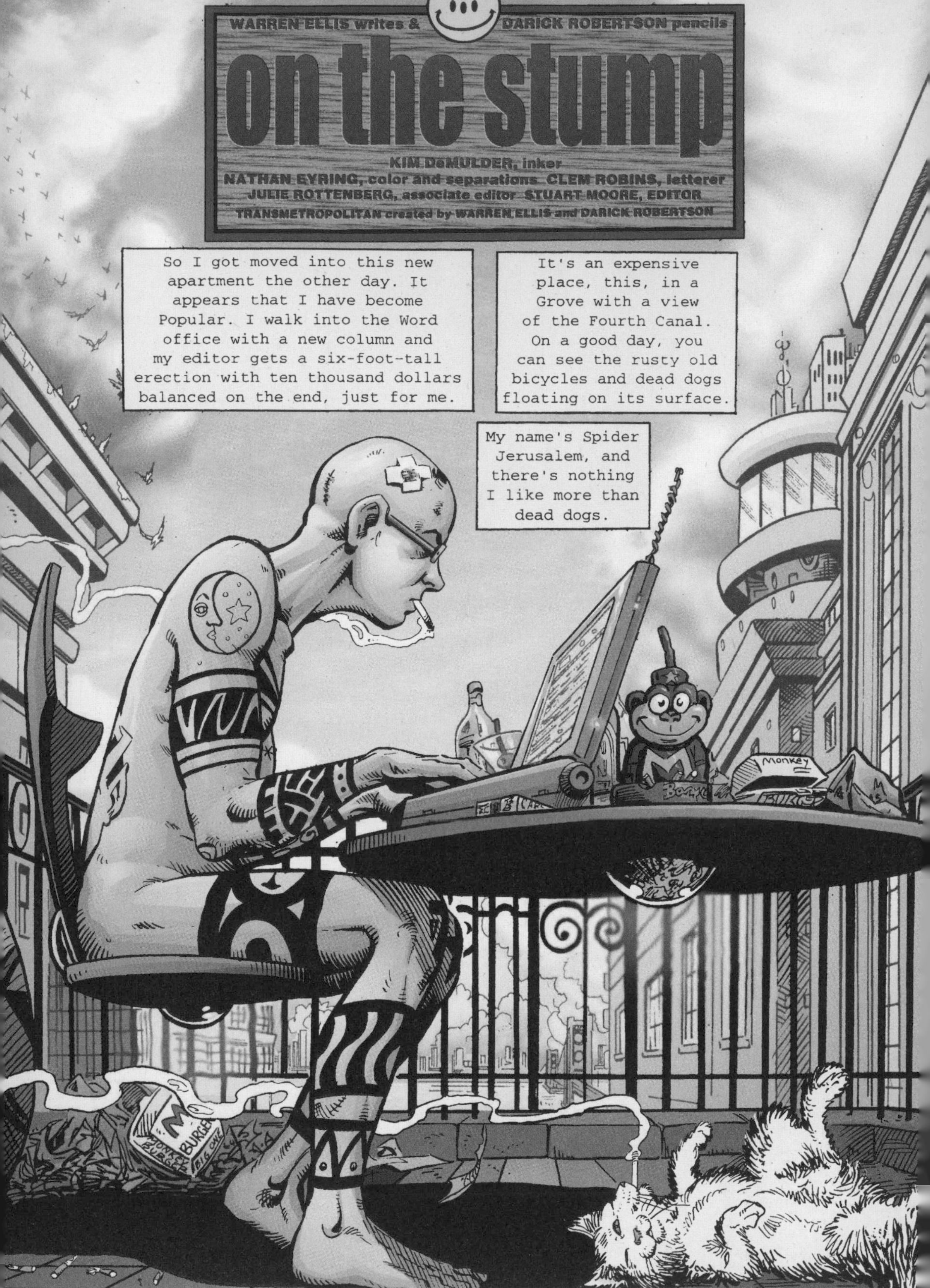
WARREN ELLIS writes & DARICK ROBERTSON pencils
on the stump
KIM DeMULDER, inker
NATHAN EYRING, color and separations CLEM ROBINS, letterer
JULIE ROTTENBERG, associate editor STUART MOORE, EDITOR
TRANSMETROPOLITAN created by WARREN ELLIS and DARICK ROBERTSON
So I got moved into this new apartment the other day. It appears that I have become Popular. I walk into the Word office with a new column and my editor gets a six-foot-tall erection with ten thousand dollars balanced on the end, just for me.
It's an expensive place, this, in a Grove with a view of the Fourth Canal. On a good day, you can see the rusty old bicycles and dead dogs floating on its surface.
My name's Spider Jerusalem, and there's nothing I like more than dead dogs.
Monkey
BURGER

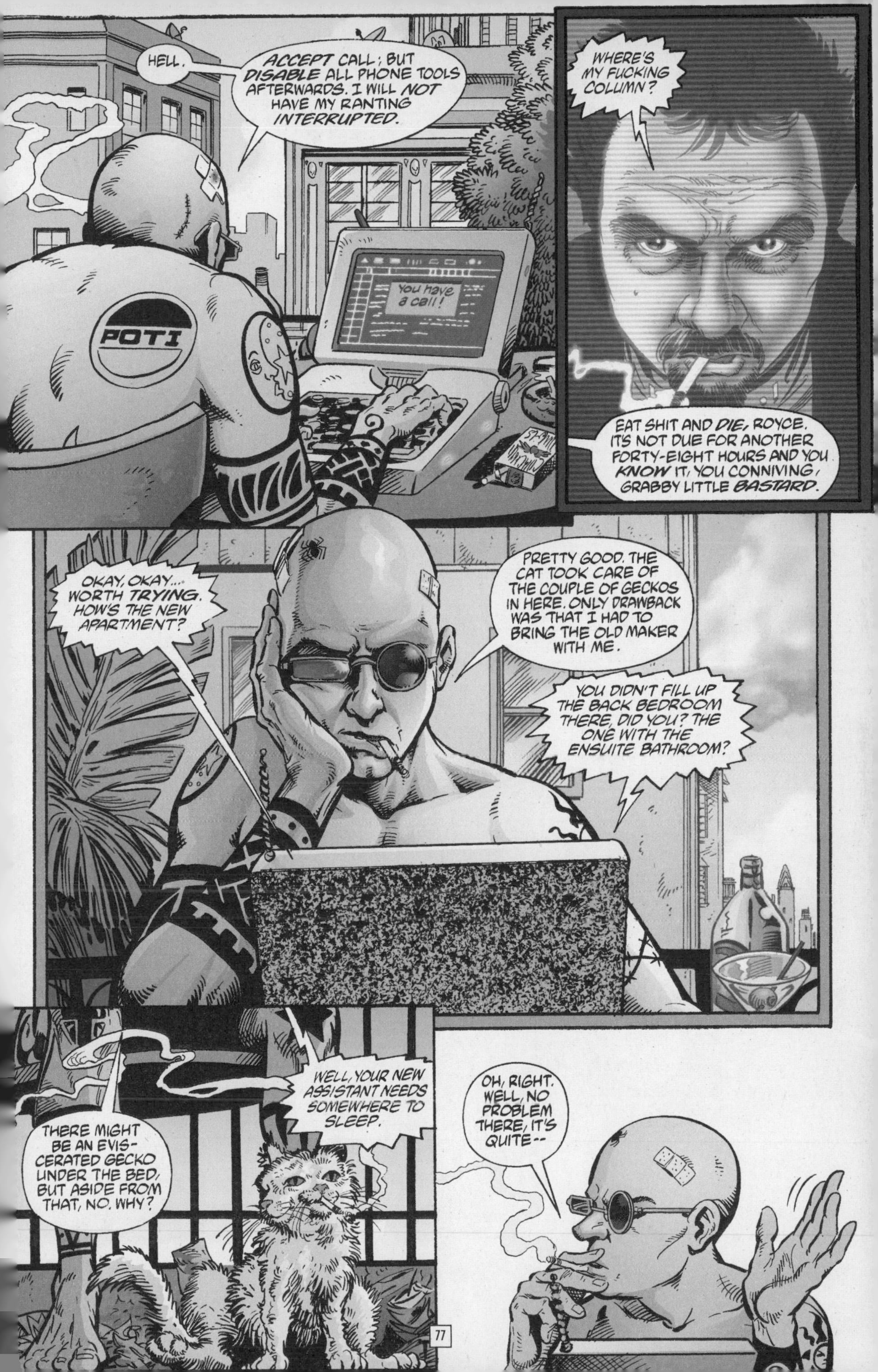
HELL.
ACCEPT CALL; BUT DISABLE ALL PHONE TOOLS AFTERWARDS. I WILL NOT HAVE MY RANTING INTERRUPTED.
POTI
You have a call!
WHERE'S MY FUCKING COLUMN?
EAT SHIT AND DIE, ROYCE. IT'S NOT DUE FOR ANOTHER FORTY-EIGHT HOURS AND YOU KNOW IT, YOU CONNIVING, GRABBY LITTLE BASTARD.
OKAY, OKAY... WORTH TRYING. HOW'S THE NEW APARTMENT?
PRETTY GOOD. THE CAT TOOK CARE OF THE COUPLE OF GECKOS IN HERE. ONLY DRAWBACK WAS THAT I HAD TO BRING THE OLD MAKER WITH ME.
YOU DIDN'T FILL UP THE BACK BEDROOM THERE, DID YOU? THE ONE WITH THE ENSUITE BATHROOM?
THERE MIGHT BE AN EVIS-CERATED GECKO UNDER THE BED, BUT ASIDE FROM THAT, NO. WHY?
WELL, YOUR NEW ASSISTANT NEEDS SOMEWHERE TO SLEEP.
OH, RIGHT. WELL, NO PROBLEM THERE, IT'S QUITE--

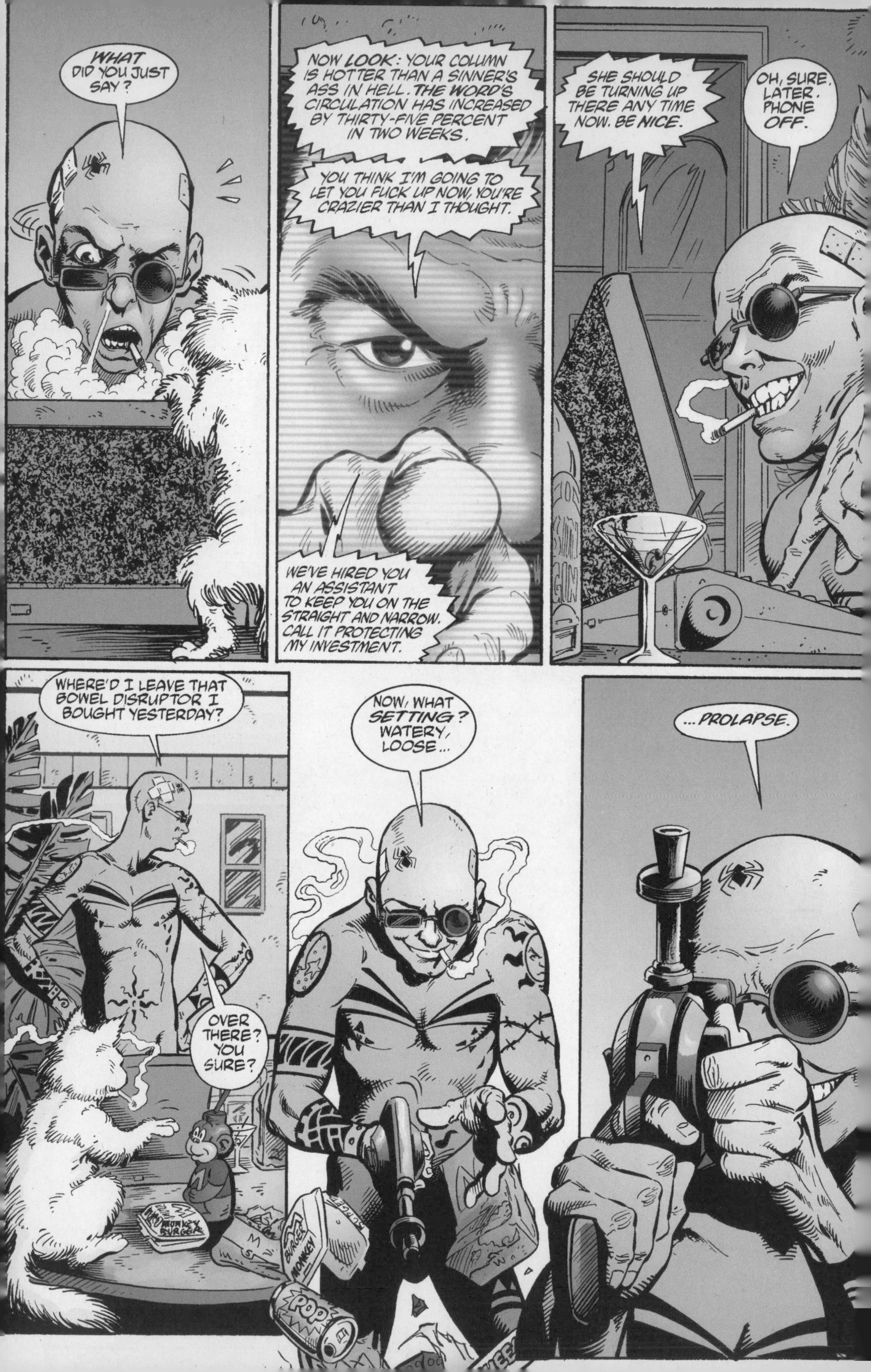
WHAT DID YOU JUST SAY?
NOW LOOK: YOUR COLUMN IS HOTTER THAN A SINNER'S ASS IN HELL. THE WORD'S CIRCULATION HAS INCREASED BY THIRTY-FIVE PERCENT IN TWO WEEKS.
YOU THINK I'M GOING TO LET YOU FUCK UP NOW, YOU'RE CRAZIER THAN I THOUGHT.
WE'VE HIRED YOU AN ASSISTANT TO KEEP YOU ON THE STRAIGHT AND NARROW. CALL IT PROTECTING MY INVESTMENT.
SHE SHOULD BE TURNING UP THERE ANY TIME NOW. BE NICE.
OH, SURE. LATER. PHONE OFF.
WHERE'D I LEAVE THAT BOWEL DISRUPTOR I BOUGHT YESTERDAY?
OVER THERE? YOU SURE?
NOW, WHAT SETTING? WATERY, LOOSE...
...PROLAPSE.

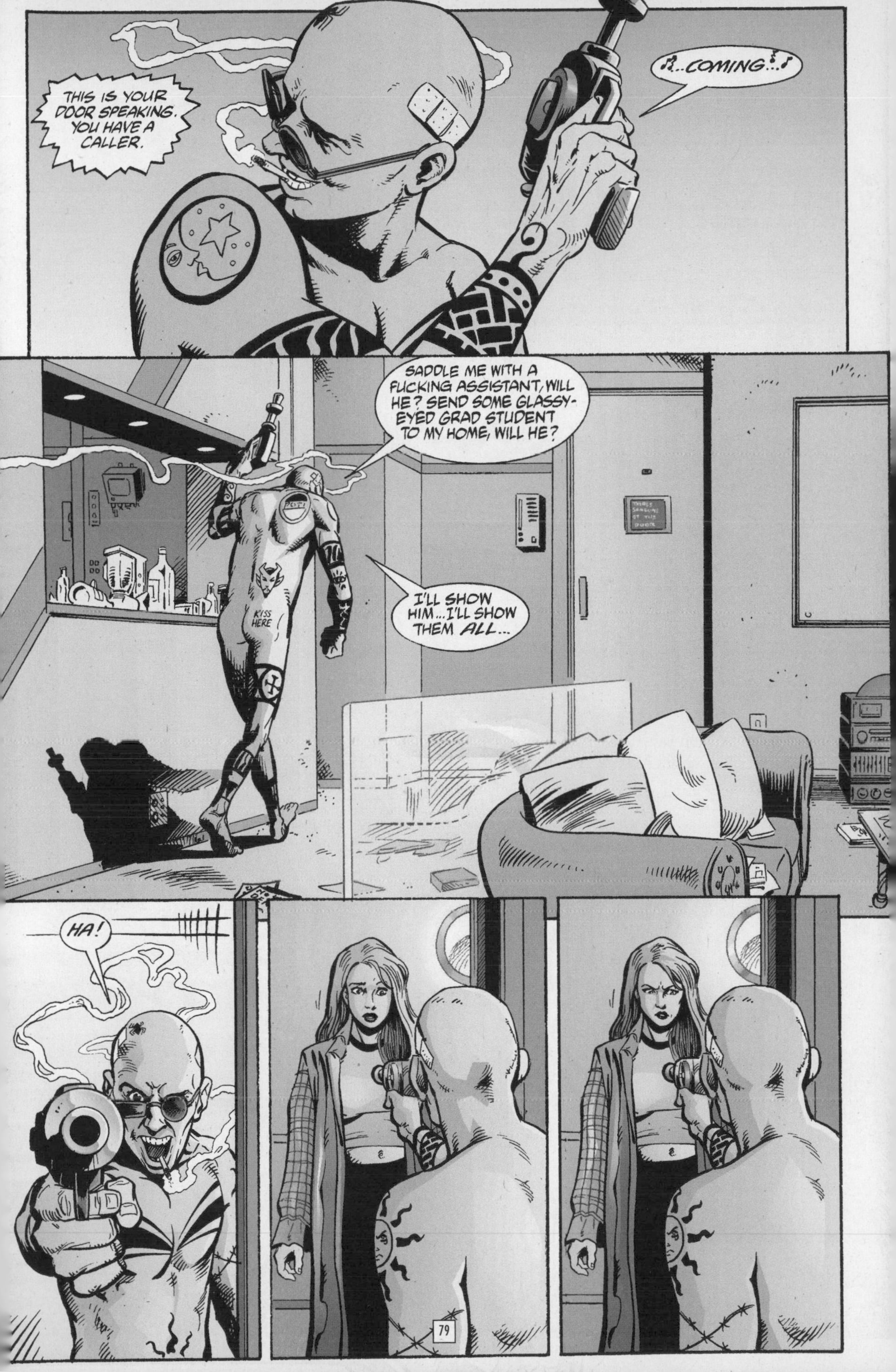
THIS IS YOUR DOOR SPEAKING. YOU HAVE A CALLER.
..COMING..
SADDLE ME WITH A FUCKING ASSISTANT, WILL HE? SEND SOME GLASSY-EYED GRAD STUDENT TO MY HOME, WILL HE?
I'LL SHOW HIM...I'LL SHOW THEM ALL...
HA!

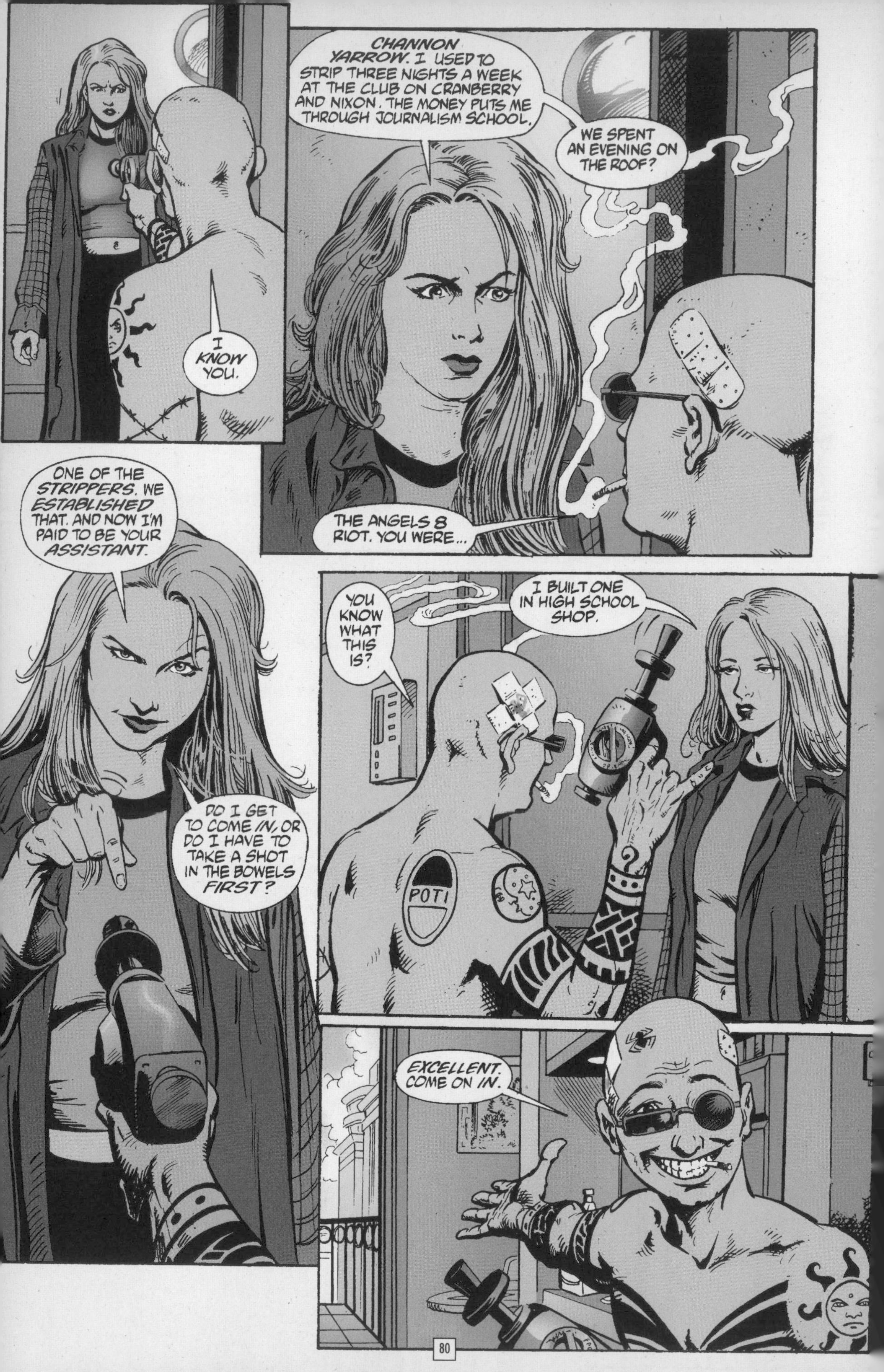
I KNOW YOU.
CHANNON YARROW. I USED TO STRIP THREE NIGHTS A WEEK AT THE CLUB ON CRANBERRY AND NIXON. THE MONEY PUTS ME THROUGH JOURNALISM SCHOOL.
WE SPENT AN EVENING ON THE ROOF?
THE ANGELS 8 RIOT. YOU WERE...
ONE OF THE STRIPPERS. WE ESTABLISHED THAT. AND NOW I'M PAID TO BE YOUR ASSISTANT.
DO I GET TO COME IN, OR DO I HAVE TO TAKE A SHOT IN THE BOWELS FIRST?
YOU KNOW WHAT THIS IS?
I BUILT ONE IN HIGH SCHOOL SHOP.
POTI
EXCELLENT. COME ON IN.

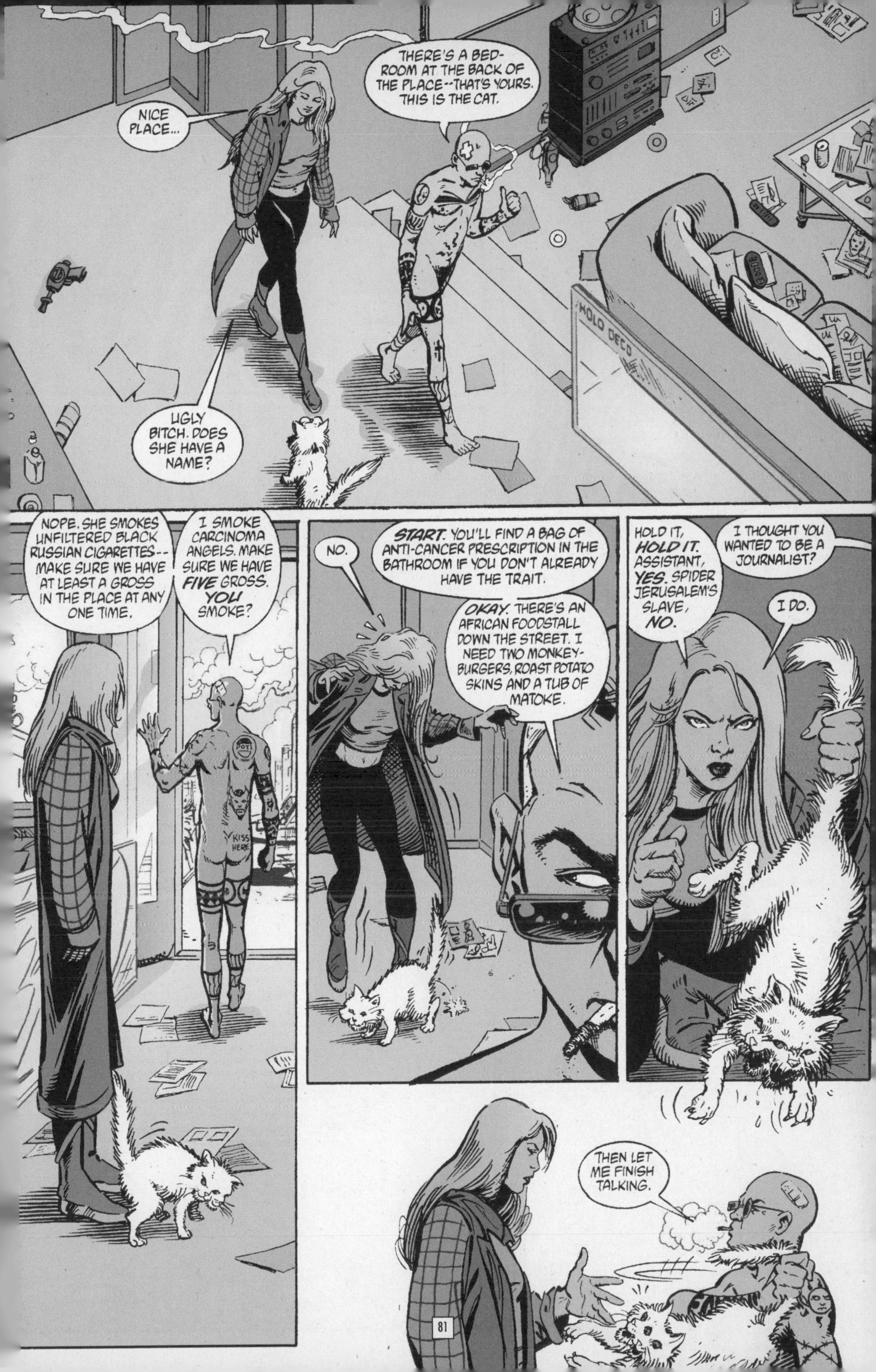
NICE PLACE...
THERE'S A BED-ROOM AT THE BACK OF THE PLACE--THAT'S YOURS. THIS IS THE CAT.
HOLO DECO
UGLY BITCH. DOES SHE HAVE A NAME?
NOPE. SHE SMOKES UNFILTERED BLACK RUSSIAN CIGARETTES--MAKE SURE WE HAVE AT LEAST A GROSS IN THE PLACE AT ANY ONE TIME.
I SMOKE CARCINOMA ANGELS. MAKE SURE WE HAVE FIVE GROSS. YOU SMOKE?
KISS HERE
NO.
START. YOU'LL FIND A BAG OF ANTI-CANCER PRESCRIPTION IN THE BATHROOM IF YOU DON'T ALREADY HAVE THE TRAIT.
OKAY. THERE'S AN AFRICAN FOODSTALL DOWN THE STREET. I NEED TWO MONKEY-BURGERS, ROAST POTATO SKINS AND A TUB OF MATOKE.
HOLD IT, HOLD IT. ASSISTANT, YES. SPIDER JERUSALEM'S SLAVE, NO.
I THOUGHT YOU WANTED TO BE A JOURNALIST?
I DO.
THEN LET ME FINISH TALKING.

WHEN YOU GET BACK, YOU'RE GOING TO SIT DOWN WITH ME OVER MONKEY-BURGERS AND TELL ME EVERY-THING YOU SAW ON THE WAY.

WHY?

BECAUSE IF YOU'RE GOING TO BE A *REAL* JOURNALIST, YOU'RE GOING TO NEED TO LEARN HOW TO *LOOK.*

NOW GET OUT OF HERE. I NEED MONKEY.

ONE REQUEST.

SHOOT.

BE *DRESSED* WHEN I GET BACK, OKAY? I'M NEVER GOING TO BE ABLE TO KEEP FOOD DOWN IF I HAVE TO WATCH *THAT* WHILE I'M EATING.

POTI

KISS HERE

DOOR CLOSING

EVERYONE'S A FUCKING EDITOR.

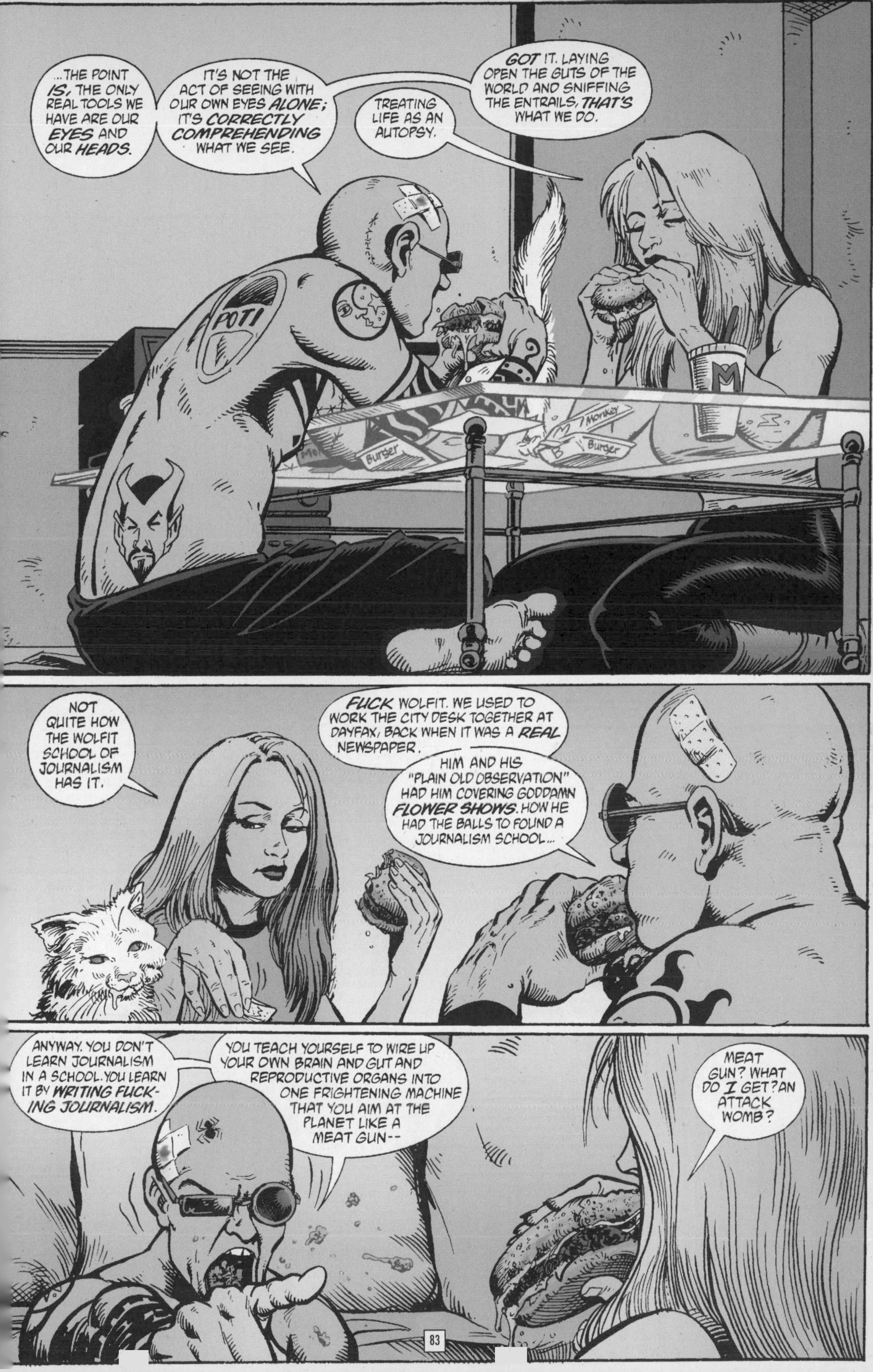
...THE POINT IS, THE ONLY REAL TOOLS WE HAVE ARE OUR EYES AND OUR HEADS.
IT'S NOT THE ACT OF SEEING WITH OUR OWN EYES ALONE; IT'S CORRECTLY COMPREHENDING WHAT WE SEE.
TREATING LIFE AS AN AUTOPSY.
GOT IT. LAYING OPEN THE GUTS OF THE WORLD AND SNIFFING THE ENTRAILS, THAT'S WHAT WE DO.
POTI
Monkey
Burger
Burger
NOT QUITE HOW THE WOLFIT SCHOOL OF JOURNALISM HAS IT.
FUCK WOLFIT. WE USED TO WORK THE CITY DESK TOGETHER AT DAYFAX, BACK WHEN IT WAS A REAL NEWSPAPER.
HIM AND HIS "PLAIN OLD OBSERVATION" HAD HIM COVERING GODDAMN FLOWER SHOWS. HOW HE HAD THE BALLS TO FOUND A JOURNALISM SCHOOL...
ANYWAY. YOU DON'T LEARN JOURNALISM IN A SCHOOL. YOU LEARN IT BY WRITING FUCKING JOURNALISM.
YOU TEACH YOURSELF TO WIRE UP YOUR OWN BRAIN AND GUT AND REPRODUCTIVE ORGANS INTO ONE FRIGHTENING MACHINE THAT YOU AIM AT THE PLANET LIKE A MEAT GUN--
MEAT GUN? WHAT DO I GET? AN ATTACK WOMB?

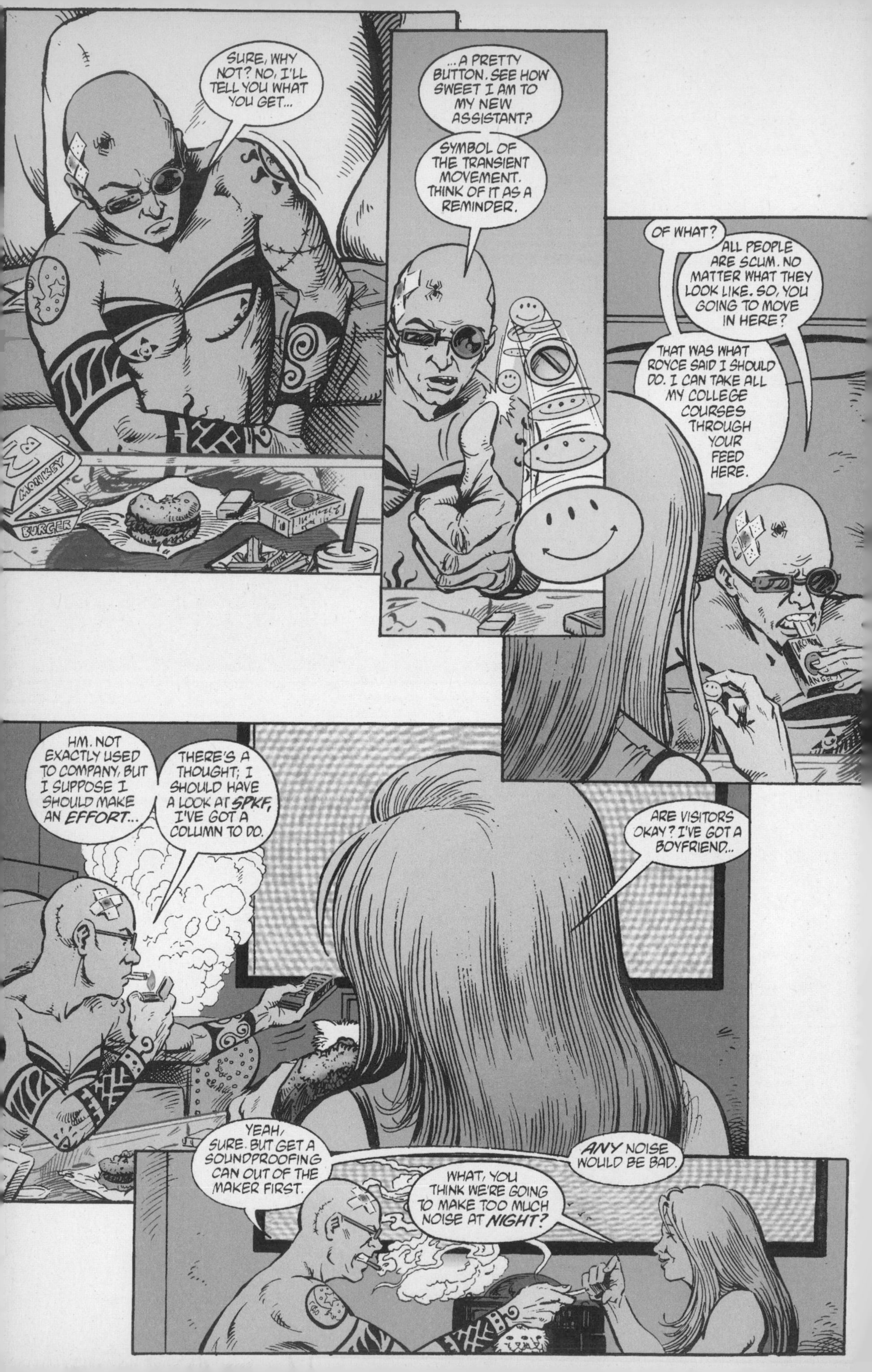
SURE, WHY NOT? NO, I'LL TELL YOU WHAT YOU GET...
...A PRETTY BUTTON. SEE HOW SWEET I AM TO MY NEW ASSISTANT?
SYMBOL OF THE TRANSIENT MOVEMENT. THINK OF IT AS A REMINDER.
OF WHAT?
ALL PEOPLE ARE SCUM. NO MATTER WHAT THEY LOOK LIKE. SO, YOU GOING TO MOVE IN HERE?
THAT WAS WHAT ROYCE SAID I SHOULD DO. I CAN TAKE ALL MY COLLEGE COURSES THROUGH YOUR FEED HERE.
MONKEY
BURGER
HM. NOT EXACTLY USED TO COMPANY, BUT I SUPPOSE I SHOULD MAKE AN *EFFORT*...
THERE'S A THOUGHT; I SHOULD HAVE A LOOK AT *SPKF*, I'VE GOT A COLUMN TO DO.
ARE VISITORS OKAY? I'VE GOT A BOYFRIEND...
YEAH, SURE. BUT GET A SOUNDPROOFING CAN OUT OF THE MAKER FIRST.
ANY NOISE WOULD BE BAD.
WHAT, YOU THINK WE'RE GOING TO MAKE TOO MUCH NOISE AT *NIGHT*?

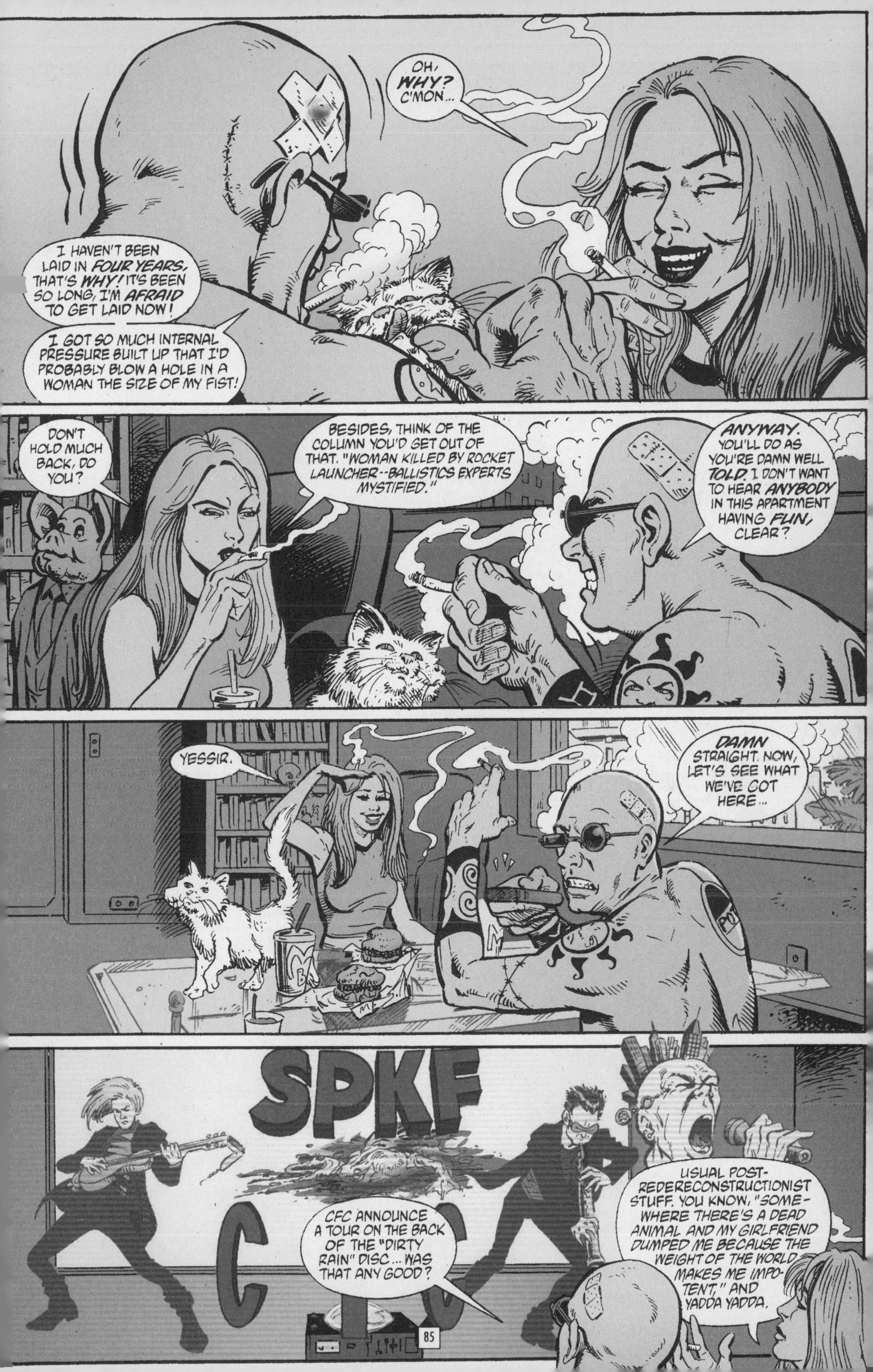
OH, WHY? C'MON...
I HAVEN'T BEEN LAID IN FOUR YEARS, THAT'S WHY! IT'S BEEN SO LONG, I'M AFRAID TO GET LAID NOW!
I GOT SO MUCH INTERNAL PRESSURE BUILT UP THAT I'D PROBABLY BLOW A HOLE IN A WOMAN THE SIZE OF MY FIST!
DON'T HOLD MUCH BACK, DO YOU?
BESIDES, THINK OF THE COLUMN YOU'D GET OUT OF THAT. "WOMAN KILLED BY ROCKET LAUNCHER--BALLISTICS EXPERTS MYSTIFIED."
ANYWAY. YOU'LL DO AS YOU'RE DAMN WELL TOLD. I DON'T WANT TO HEAR ANYBODY IN THIS APARTMENT HAVING FUN, CLEAR?
YESSIR.
DAMN STRAIGHT. NOW, LET'S SEE WHAT WE'VE GOT HERE...
SPKF
CFC ANNOUNCE A TOUR ON THE BACK OF THE "DIRTY RAIN" DISC... WAS THAT ANY GOOD?
USUAL POST-REDERECONSTRUCTIONIST STUFF. YOU KNOW, "SOMEWHERE THERE'S A DEAD ANIMAL AND MY GIRLFRIEND DUMPED ME BECAUSE THE WEIGHT OF THE WORLD MAKES ME IMPOTENT," AND YADDA YADDA.

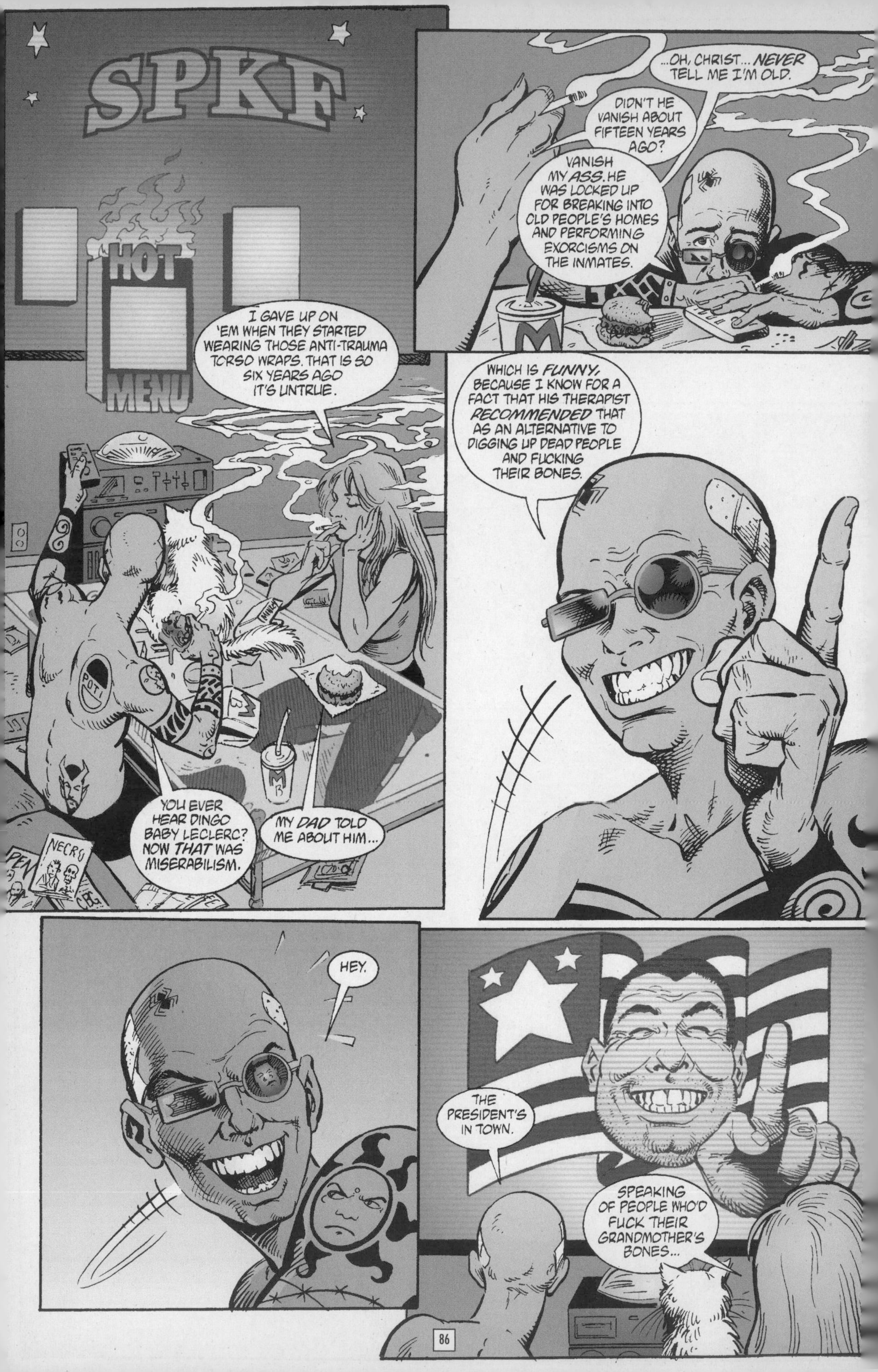
SPKF
HOT
MENU
...OH, CHRIST... NEVER TELL ME I'M OLD.
DIDN'T HE VANISH ABOUT FIFTEEN YEARS AGO?
VANISH MY ASS. HE WAS LOCKED UP FOR BREAKING INTO OLD PEOPLE'S HOMES AND PERFORMING EXORCISMS ON THE INMATES.
I GAVE UP ON 'EM WHEN THEY STARTED WEARING THOSE ANTI-TRAUMA TORSO WRAPS. THAT IS SO SIX YEARS AGO IT'S UNTRUE.
YOU EVER HEAR DINGO BABY LECLERC? NOW THAT WAS MISERABILISM.
MY DAD TOLD ME ABOUT HIM...
NECRO
WHICH IS FUNNY, BECAUSE I KNOW FOR A FACT THAT HIS THERAPIST RECOMMENDED THAT AS AN ALTERNATIVE TO DIGGING UP DEAD PEOPLE AND FUCKING THEIR BONES.
HEY.
THE PRESIDENT'S IN TOWN.
SPEAKING OF PEOPLE WHO'D FUCK THEIR GRANDMOTHER'S BONES...

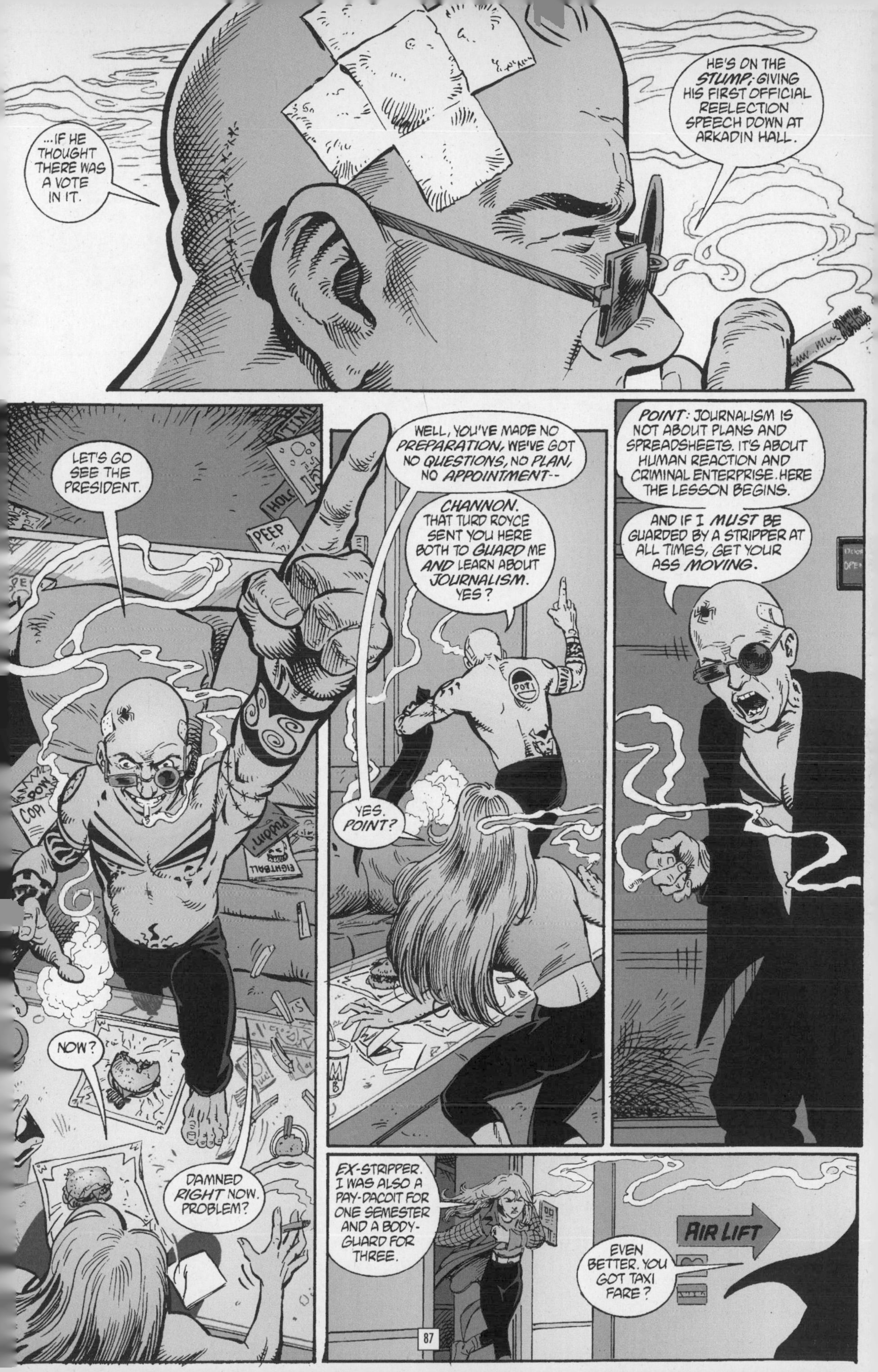
...IF HE THOUGHT THERE WAS A VOTE IN IT.
HE'S ON THE STUMP; GIVING HIS FIRST OFFICIAL REELECTION SPEECH DOWN AT ARKADIN HALL.
LET'S GO SEE THE PRESIDENT.
NOW?
DAMNED RIGHT NOW. PROBLEM?
WELL, YOU'VE MADE NO PREPARATION, WE'VE GOT NO QUESTIONS, NO PLAN, NO APPOINTMENT--
CHANNON. THAT TURD ROYCE SENT YOU HERE BOTH TO GUARD ME AND LEARN ABOUT JOURNALISM. YES?
YES. POINT?
POINT: JOURNALISM IS NOT ABOUT PLANS AND SPREADSHEETS. IT'S ABOUT HUMAN REACTION AND CRIMINAL ENTERPRISE. HERE THE LESSON BEGINS.
AND IF I MUST BE GUARDED BY A STRIPPER AT ALL TIMES, GET YOUR ASS MOVING.
EX-STRIPPER. I WAS ALSO A PAY-DACOIT FOR ONE SEMESTER AND A BODY-GUARD FOR THREE.
AIR LIFT
EVEN BETTER. YOU GOT TAXI FARE?

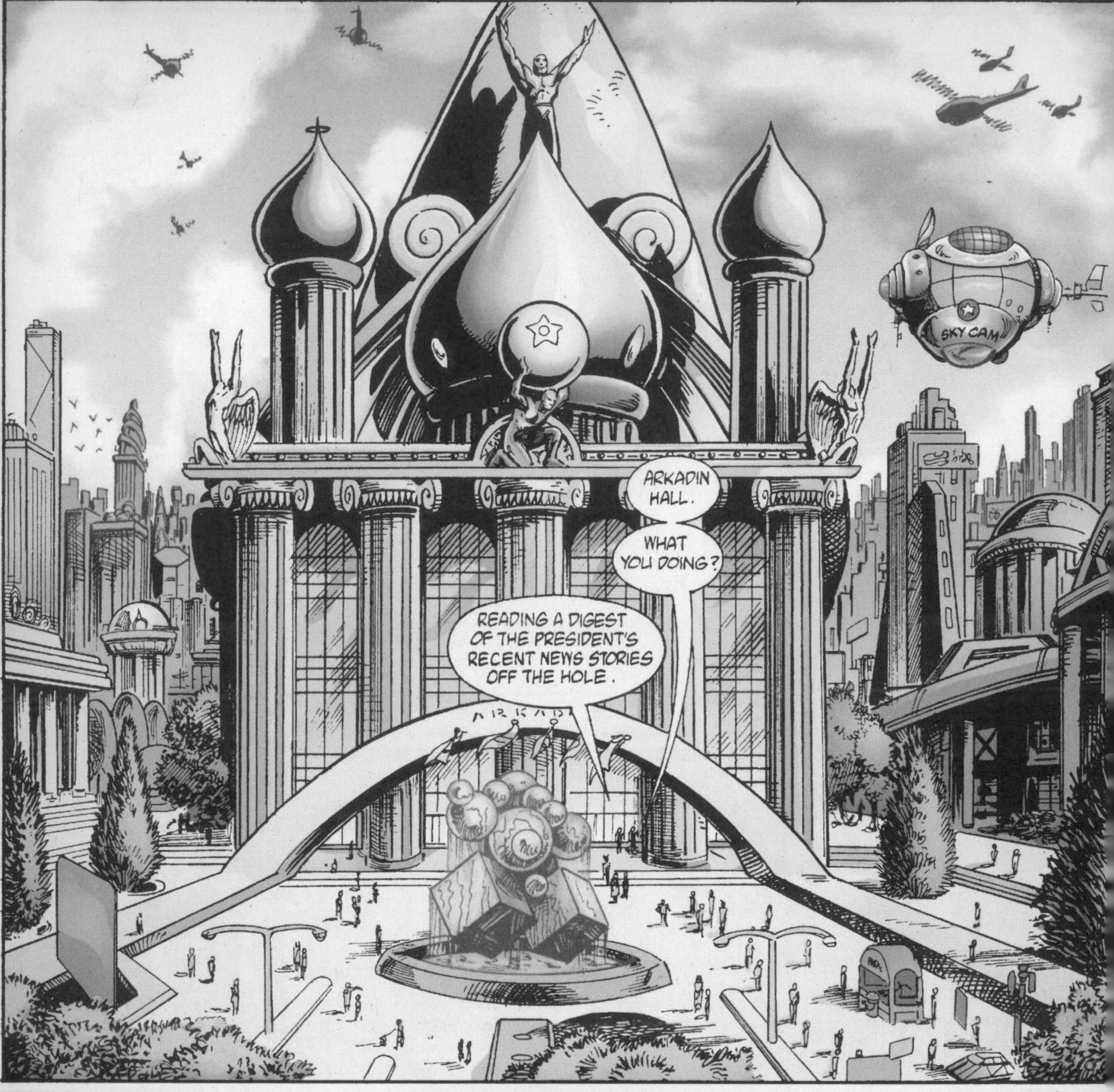
SKY CAM
ARKADIN HALL.
WHAT YOU DOING?
READING A DIGEST OF THE PRESIDENT'S RECENT NEWS STORIES OFF THE HOLE.

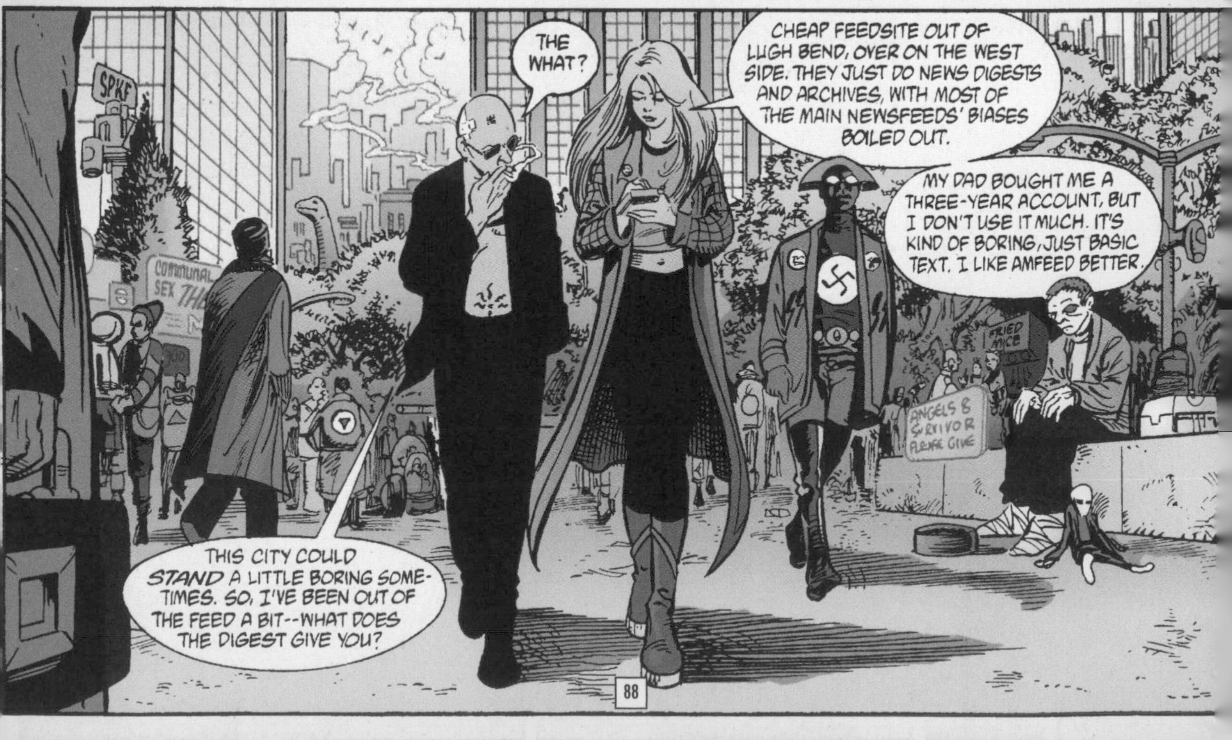
THE WHAT?
CHEAP FEEDSITE OUT OF LUGH BEND, OVER ON THE WEST SIDE. THEY JUST DO NEWS DIGESTS AND ARCHIVES, WITH MOST OF THE MAIN NEWSFEEDS' BIASES BOILED OUT.
MY DAD BOUGHT ME A THREE-YEAR ACCOUNT, BUT I DON'T USE IT MUCH. IT'S KIND OF BORING, JUST BASIC TEXT. I LIKE AMFEED BETTER.
THIS CITY COULD *STAND* A LITTLE BORING SOMETIMES. SO, I'VE BEEN OUT OF THE FEED A BIT--WHAT DOES THE DIGEST GIVE YOU?
SPKF
COMMUNAL SEX
FRIED MICE
ANGELS 8 SURVIVOR PLEASE GIVE

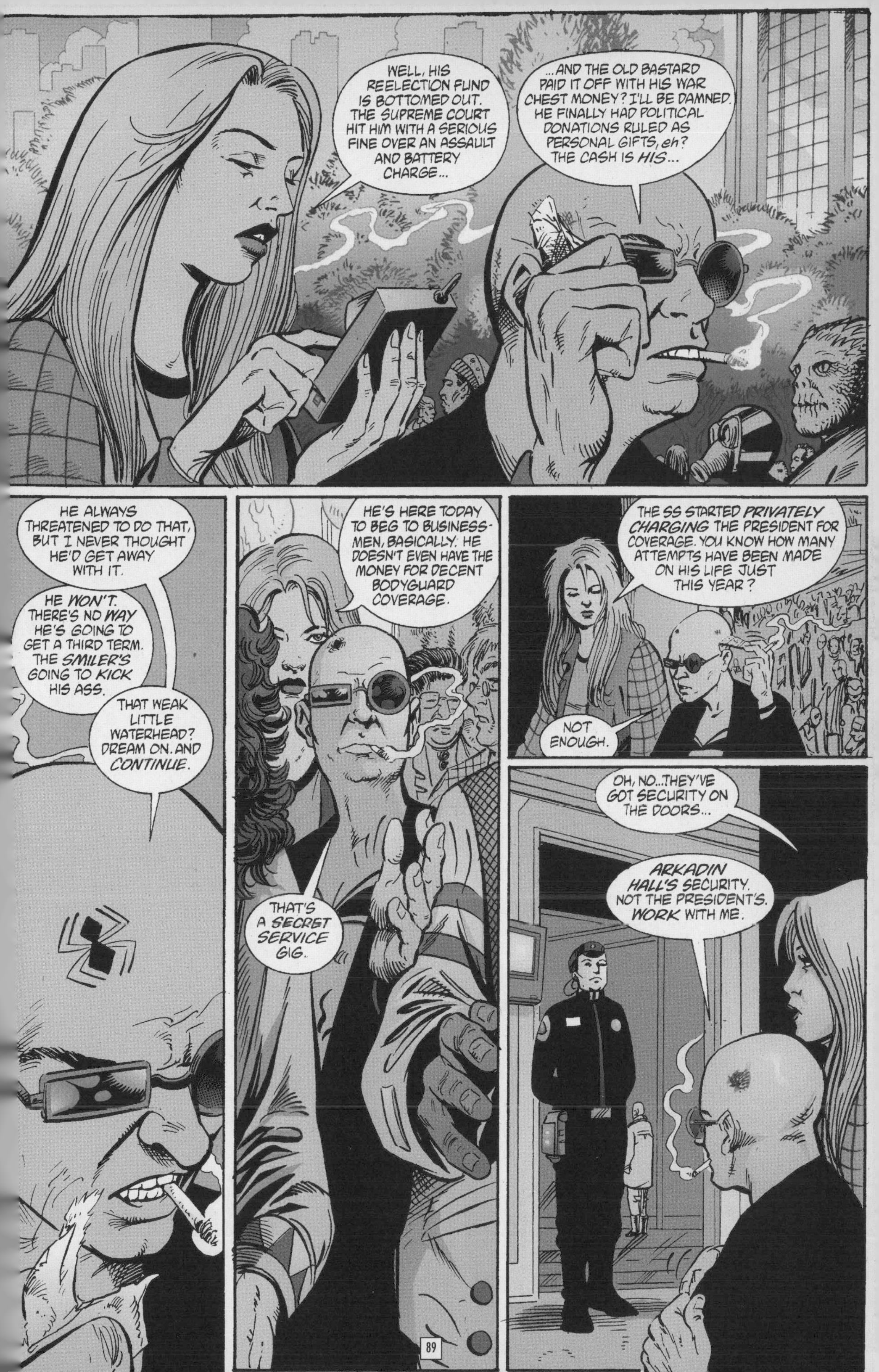
WELL, HIS REELECTION FUND IS BOTTOMED OUT. THE SUPREME COURT HIT HIM WITH A SERIOUS FINE OVER AN ASSAULT AND BATTERY CHARGE...
...AND THE OLD BASTARD PAID IT OFF WITH HIS WAR CHEST MONEY? I'LL BE DAMNED. HE FINALLY HAD POLITICAL DONATIONS RULED AS PERSONAL GIFTS, *eh*? THE CASH IS *HIS*...
HE ALWAYS THREATENED TO DO THAT, BUT I NEVER THOUGHT HE'D GET AWAY WITH IT.
HE *WON'T*. THERE'S NO *WAY* HE'S GOING TO GET A THIRD TERM. THE *SMILER'S* GOING TO *KICK* HIS ASS.
THAT WEAK LITTLE WATERHEAD? DREAM ON. AND *CONTINUE*.
HE'S HERE TODAY TO BEG TO BUSINESSMEN, BASICALLY. HE DOESN'T EVEN HAVE THE MONEY FOR DECENT BODYGUARD COVERAGE.
THAT'S A *SECRET SERVICE* GIG.
THE SS STARTED *PRIVATELY CHARGING* THE PRESIDENT FOR COVERAGE. YOU KNOW HOW MANY ATTEMPTS HAVE BEEN MADE ON HIS LIFE JUST THIS YEAR?
NOT ENOUGH.
OH, NO...THEY'VE GOT SECURITY ON THE DOORS...
ARKADIN HALL'S SECURITY. NOT THE PRESIDENT'S. *WORK* WITH ME.

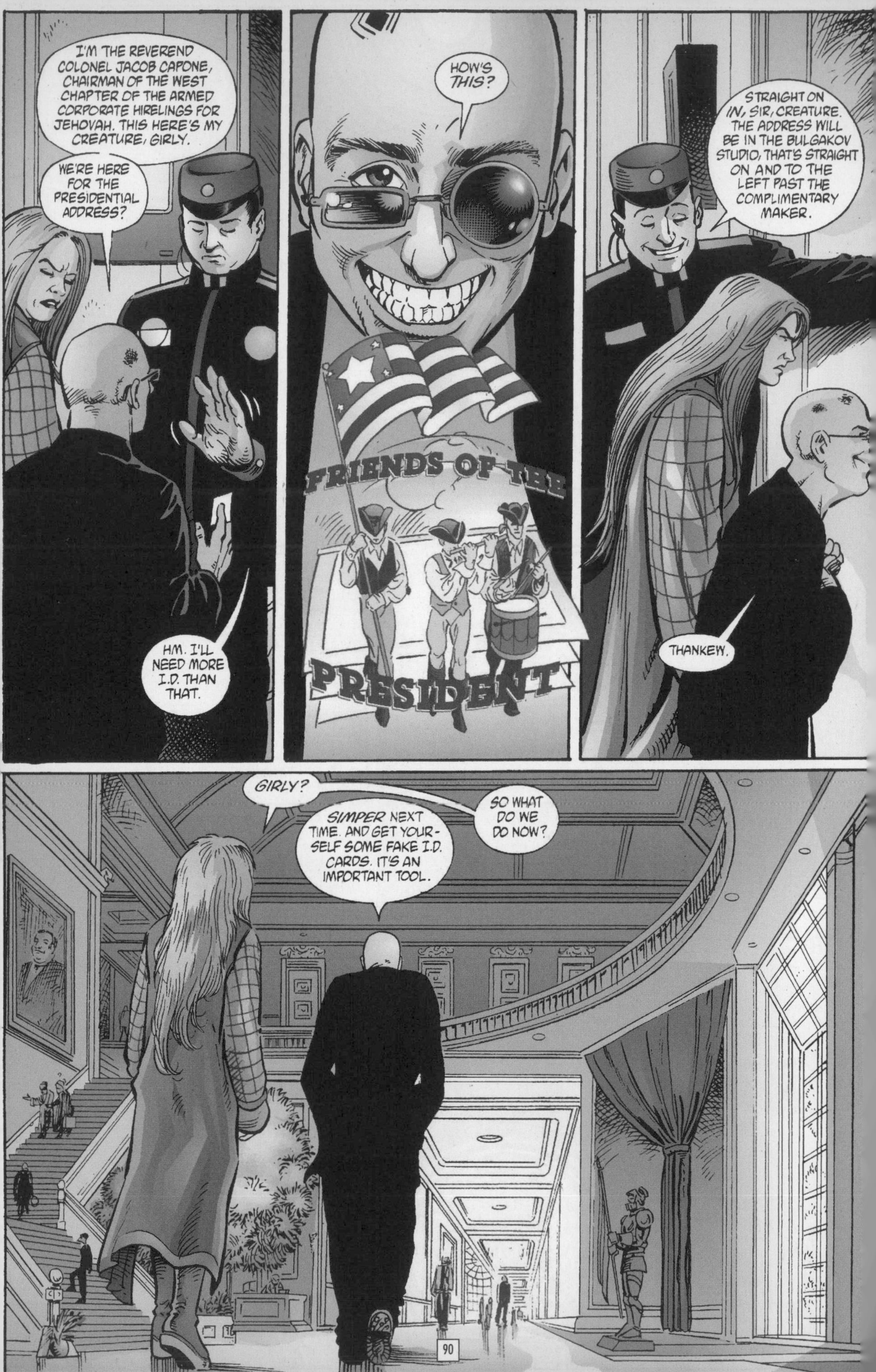

I'M THE REVEREND COLONEL JACOB CAPONE, CHAIRMAN OF THE WEST CHAPTER OF THE ARMED CORPORATE HIRELINGS FOR JEHOVAH. THIS HERE'S MY CREATURE, GIRLY.
WE'RE HERE FOR THE PRESIDENTIAL ADDRESS?
HM. I'LL NEED MORE I.D. THAN THAT.
HOW'S THIS?
FRIENDS OF THE PRESIDENT
STRAIGHT ON IN, SIR, CREATURE. THE ADDRESS WILL BE IN THE BULGAKOV STUDIO, THAT'S STRAIGHT ON AND TO THE LEFT PAST THE COMPLIMENTARY MAKER.
THANKEW.
GIRLY?
SO WHAT DO WE DO NOW?
SIMPER NEXT TIME. AND GET YOURSELF SOME FAKE I.D. CARDS. IT'S AN IMPORTANT TOOL.

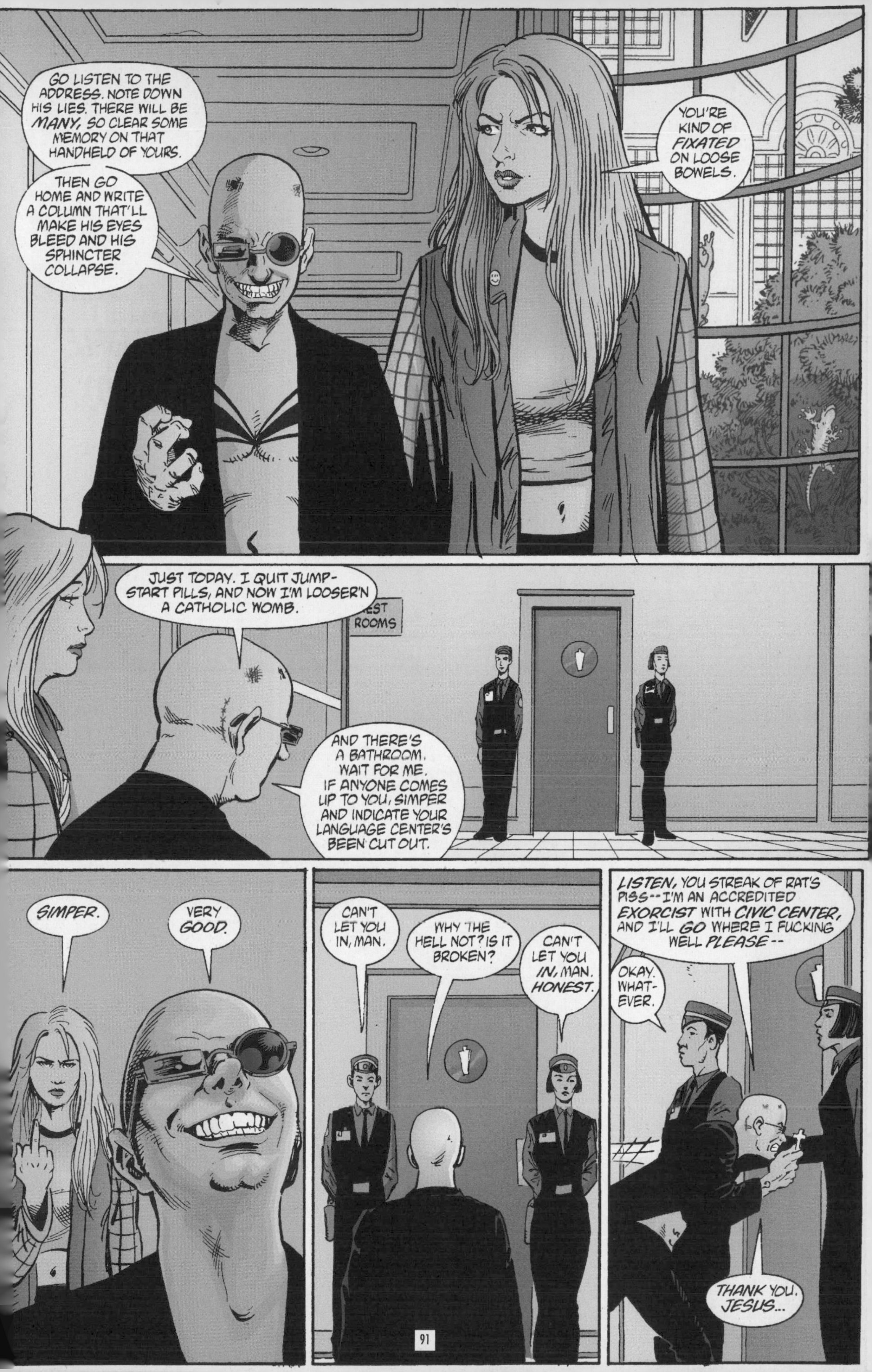

GO LISTEN TO THE ADDRESS. NOTE DOWN HIS LIES. THERE WILL BE MANY, SO CLEAR SOME MEMORY ON THAT HANDHELD OF YOURS.
THEN GO HOME AND WRITE A COLUMN THAT'LL MAKE HIS EYES BLEED AND HIS SPHINCTER COLLAPSE.
YOU'RE KIND OF FIXATED ON LOOSE BOWELS.
JUST TODAY. I QUIT JUMP-START PILLS, AND NOW I'M LOOSER'N A CATHOLIC WOMB.
REST ROOMS
AND THERE'S A BATHROOM. WAIT FOR ME. IF ANYONE COMES UP TO YOU, SIMPER AND INDICATE YOUR LANGUAGE CENTER'S BEEN CUT OUT.
SIMPER.
VERY GOOD.
CAN'T LET YOU IN, MAN.
WHY THE HELL NOT? IS IT BROKEN?
CAN'T LET YOU IN, MAN. HONEST.
LISTEN, YOU STREAK OF RAT'S PISS--I'M AN ACCREDITED EXORCIST WITH CIVIC CENTER, AND I'LL GO WHERE I FUCKING WELL PLEASE--
OKAY. WHAT-EVER.
THANK YOU, JESUS...

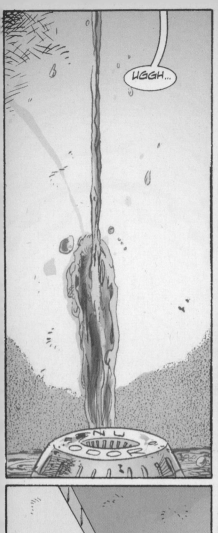

UGGH...

AAHHRR...
GODDAMN CHEAP AUSTRALIAN WHORES...

OTTO FLUSH

JERUSALEM.

MR. PRESIDENT.

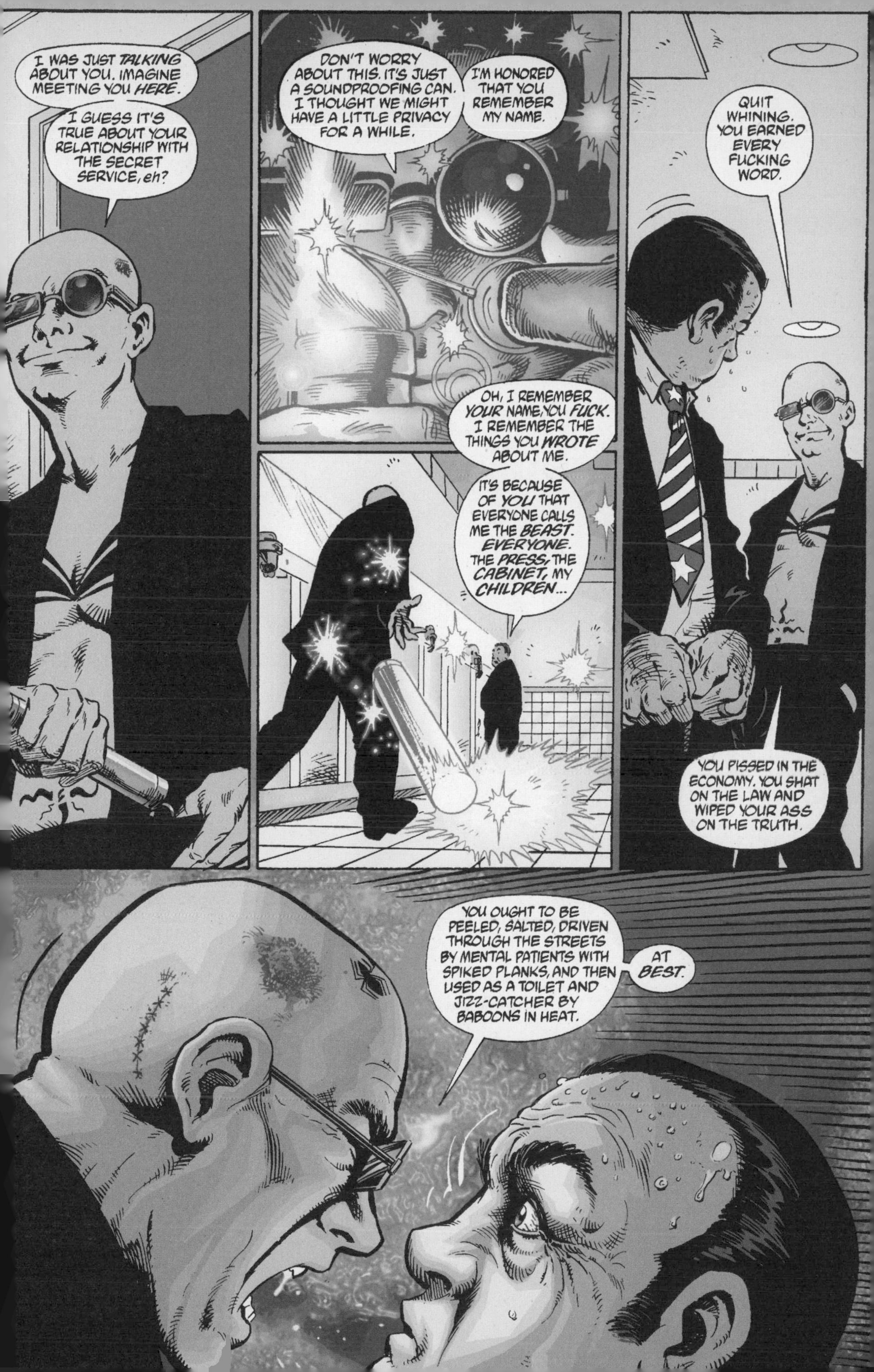

I WAS JUST TALKING ABOUT YOU. IMAGINE MEETING YOU HERE.
I GUESS IT'S TRUE ABOUT YOUR RELATIONSHIP WITH THE SECRET SERVICE, eh?
DON'T WORRY ABOUT THIS. IT'S JUST A SOUNDPROOFING CAN. I THOUGHT WE MIGHT HAVE A LITTLE PRIVACY FOR A WHILE.
I'M HONORED THAT YOU REMEMBER MY NAME.
OH, I REMEMBER YOUR NAME, YOU FUCK. I REMEMBER THE THINGS YOU WROTE ABOUT ME.
IT'S BECAUSE OF YOU THAT EVERYONE CALLS ME THE BEAST. EVERYONE. THE PRESS, THE CABINET, MY CHILDREN...
QUIT WHINING. YOU EARNED EVERY FUCKING WORD.
YOU PISSED IN THE ECONOMY. YOU SHAT ON THE LAW AND WIPED YOUR ASS ON THE TRUTH.
YOU OUGHT TO BE PEELED, SALTED, DRIVEN THROUGH THE STREETS BY MENTAL PATIENTS WITH SPIKED PLANKS, AND THEN USED AS A TOILET AND JIZZ-CATCHER BY BABOONS IN HEAT.
AT BEST.

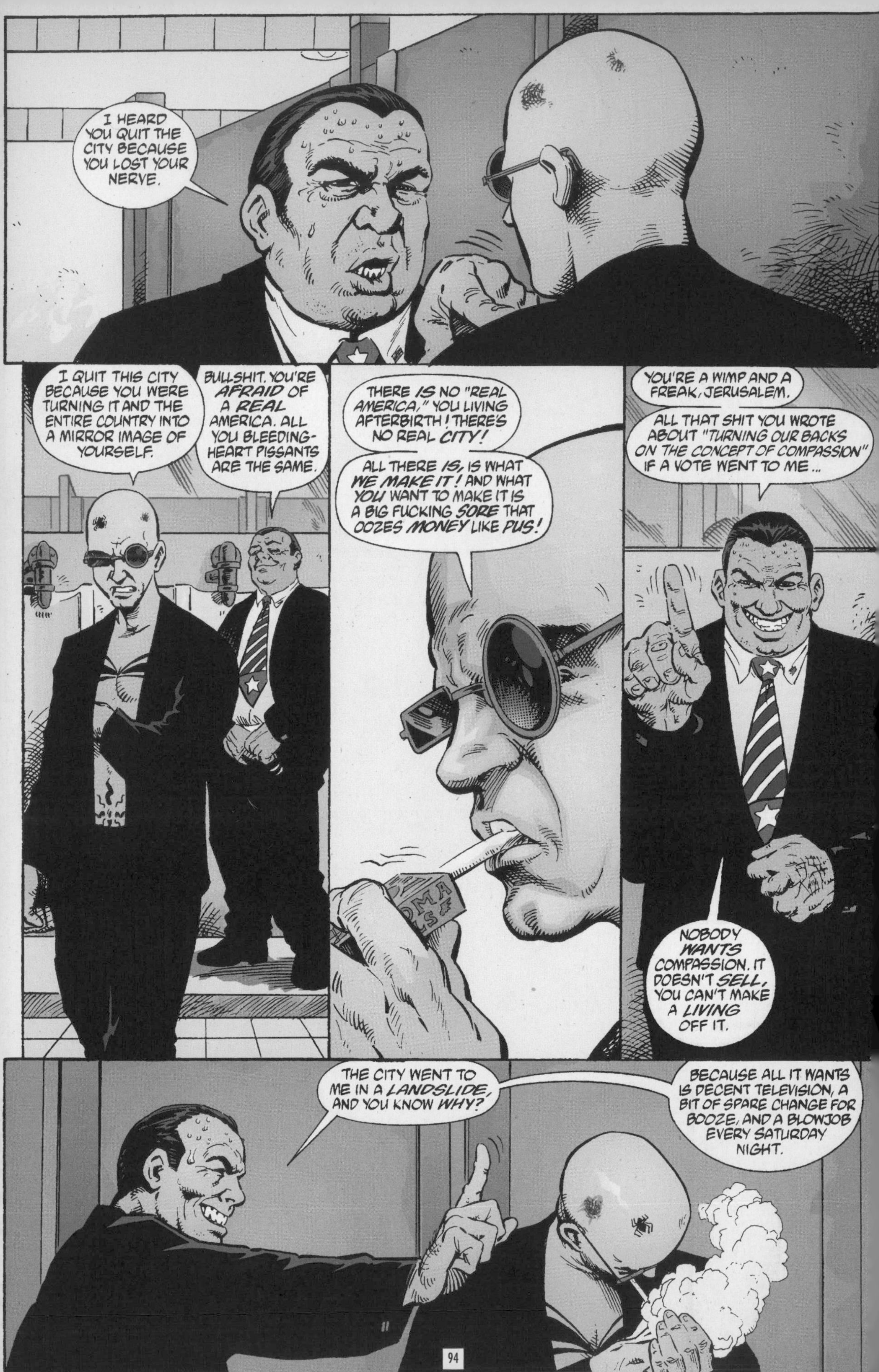
I HEARD YOU QUIT THE CITY BECAUSE YOU LOST YOUR NERVE.
I QUIT THIS CITY BECAUSE YOU WERE TURNING IT AND THE ENTIRE COUNTRY INTO A MIRROR IMAGE OF YOURSELF.
BULLSHIT. YOU'RE *AFRAID* OF A *REAL* AMERICA. ALL YOU BLEEDING-HEART PISSANTS ARE THE SAME.
THERE *IS* NO "REAL *AMERICA*," YOU LIVING AFTERBIRTH! THERE'S NO REAL *CITY*!
ALL THERE *IS*, IS WHAT *WE MAKE IT*! AND WHAT *YOU* WANT TO MAKE IT IS A BIG FUCKING *SORE* THAT OOZES *MONEY* LIKE *PUS*!
YOU'RE A WIMP AND A FREAK, JERUSALEM.
ALL THAT SHIT YOU WROTE ABOUT "*TURNING OUR BACKS ON THE CONCEPT OF COMPASSION*" IF A VOTE WENT TO ME...
NOBODY *WANTS* COMPASSION. IT DOESN'T *SELL*, YOU CAN'T MAKE A *LIVING* OFF IT.
THE CITY WENT TO ME IN A *LANDSLIDE*, AND YOU KNOW *WHY*?
BECAUSE ALL IT WANTS IS DECENT TELEVISION, A BIT OF SPARE CHANGE FOR BOOZE, AND A BLOWJOB EVERY SATURDAY NIGHT.

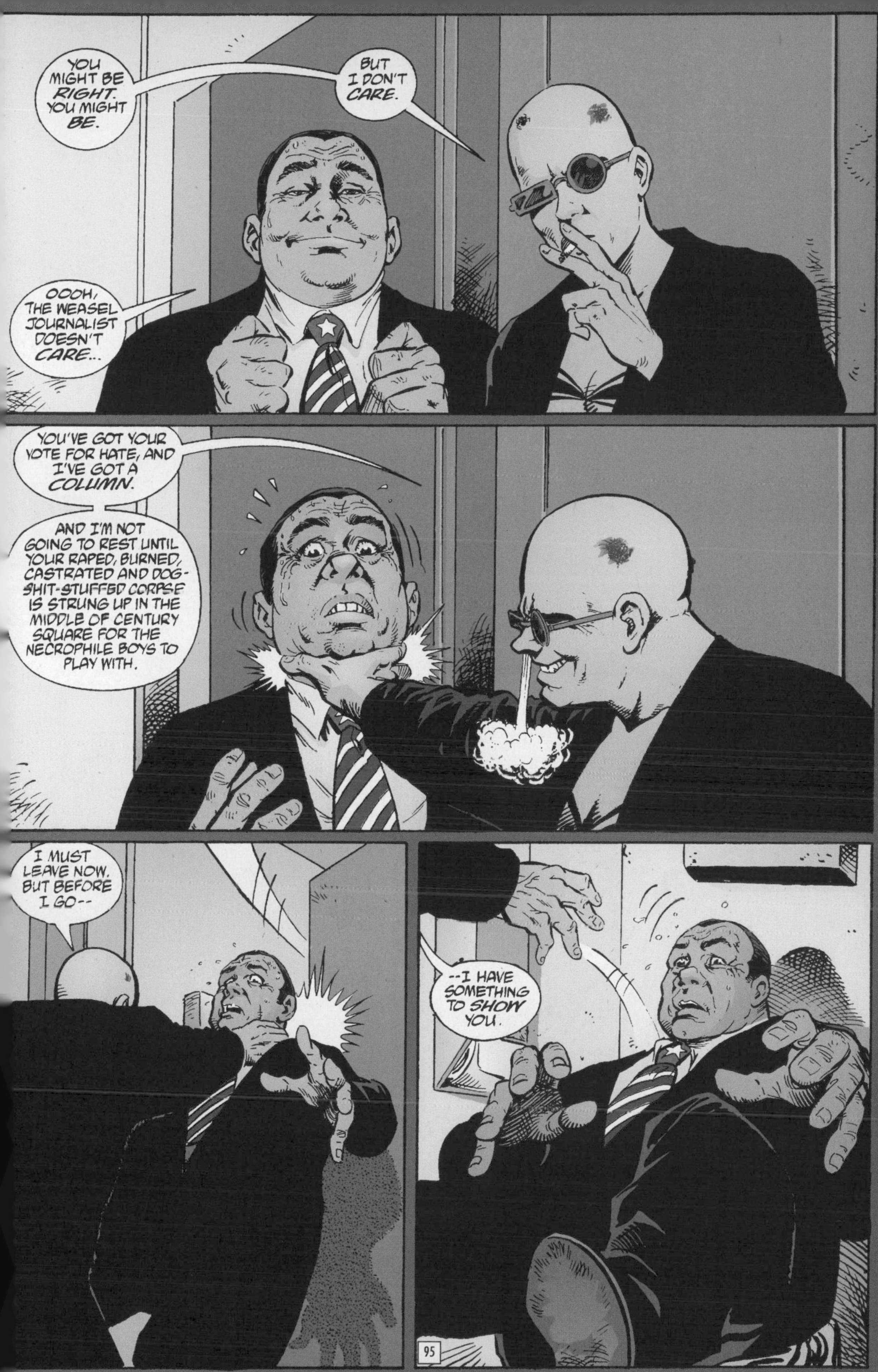

YOU MIGHT BE RIGHT. YOU MIGHT BE.
BUT I DON'T CARE.
OOOH, THE WEASEL JOURNALIST DOESN'T CARE...
YOU'VE GOT YOUR VOTE FOR HATE, AND I'VE GOT A COLUMN.
AND I'M NOT GOING TO REST UNTIL YOUR RAPED, BURNED, CASTRATED AND DOG-SHIT-STUFFED CORPSE IS STRUNG UP IN THE MIDDLE OF CENTURY SQUARE FOR THE NECROPHILE BOYS TO PLAY WITH.
I MUST LEAVE NOW. BUT BEFORE I GO--
--I HAVE SOMETHING TO SHOW YOU.

THIS IS A **BOWEL DISRUPTOR**. IT HAS NO SIGNATURE --YOU CAN'T DETECT ITS USAGE ON A BODY.

IT HAS SEVERAL SETTINGS. SEE THIS DIAL?

LOOSE...

WATERY...

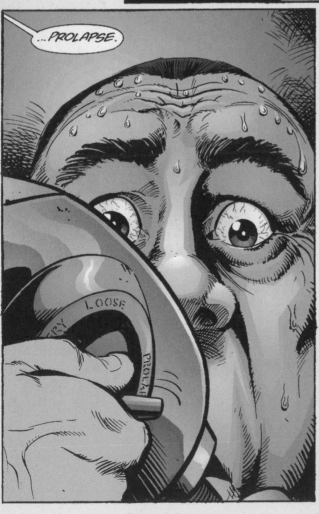

...PROLAPSE.

THERE'S A MAN IN THERE WHO'S HAVING SOME TROUBLE, I THINK. I KNOW YOU'RE NOT ARKADIN HALL SECURITY, BUT...

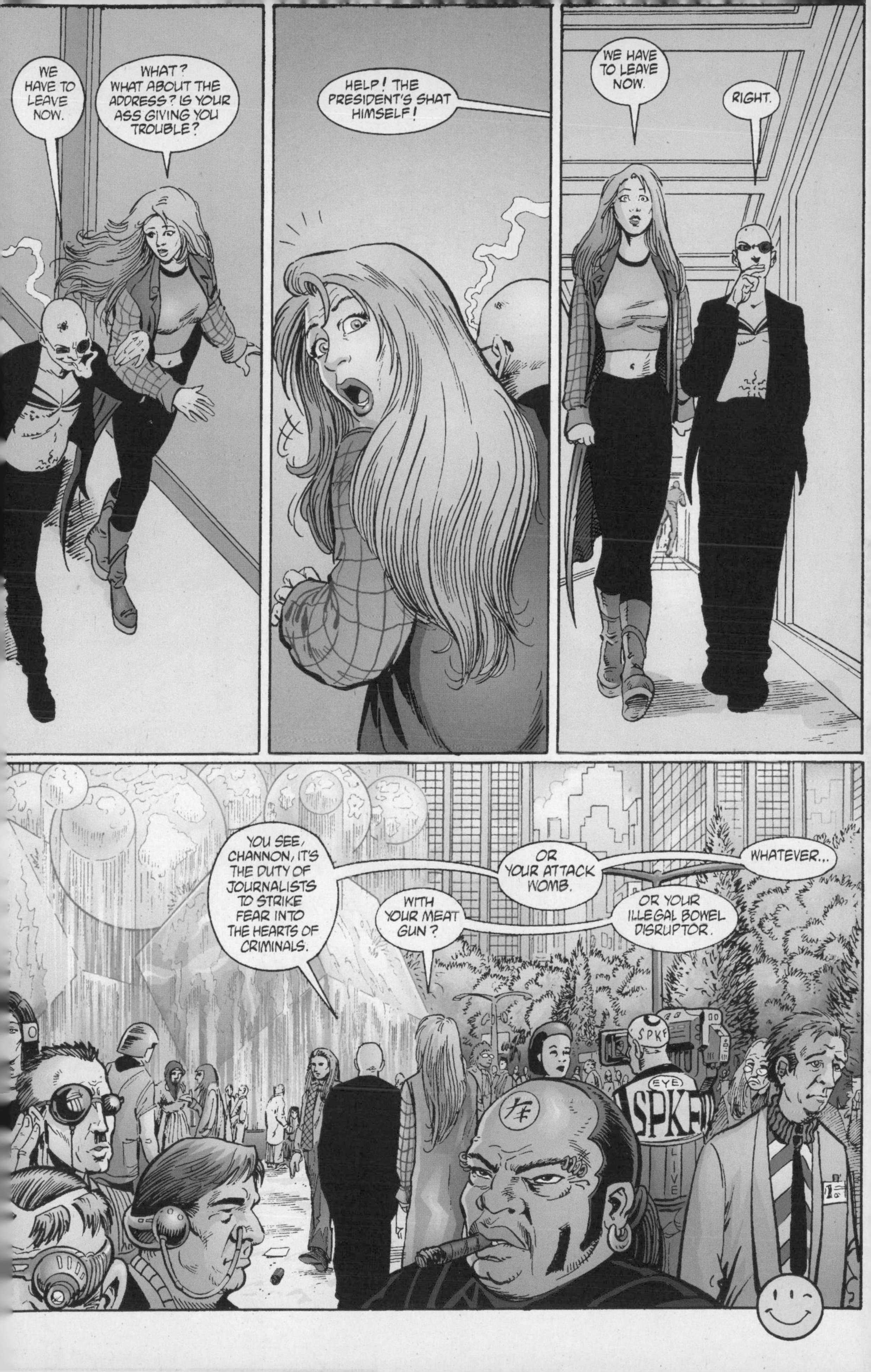
WE HAVE TO LEAVE NOW.
WHAT? WHAT ABOUT THE ADDRESS? IS YOUR ASS GIVING YOU TROUBLE?
HELP! THE PRESIDENT'S SHAT HIMSELF!
WE HAVE TO LEAVE NOW.
RIGHT.
YOU SEE, CHANNON, IT'S THE DUTY OF JOURNALISTS TO STRIKE FEAR INTO THE HEARTS OF CRIMINALS.
WITH YOUR MEAT GUN?
OR YOUR ATTACK WOMB.
OR YOUR ILLEGAL BOWEL DISRUPTOR.
WHATEVER...
SPKF
EYE
SPKF
LIVE

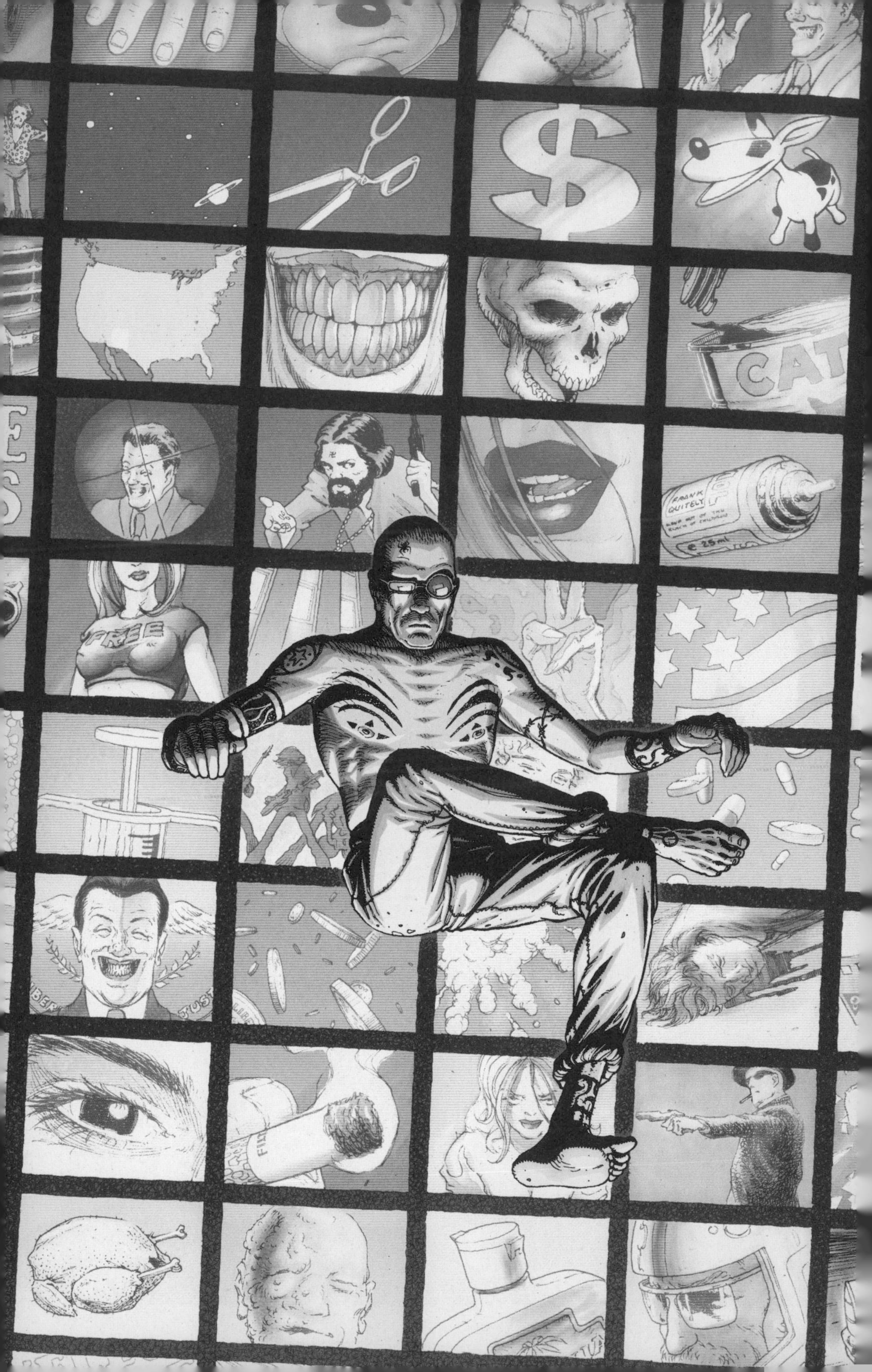
FREE
CAT
FRANK QUITELY

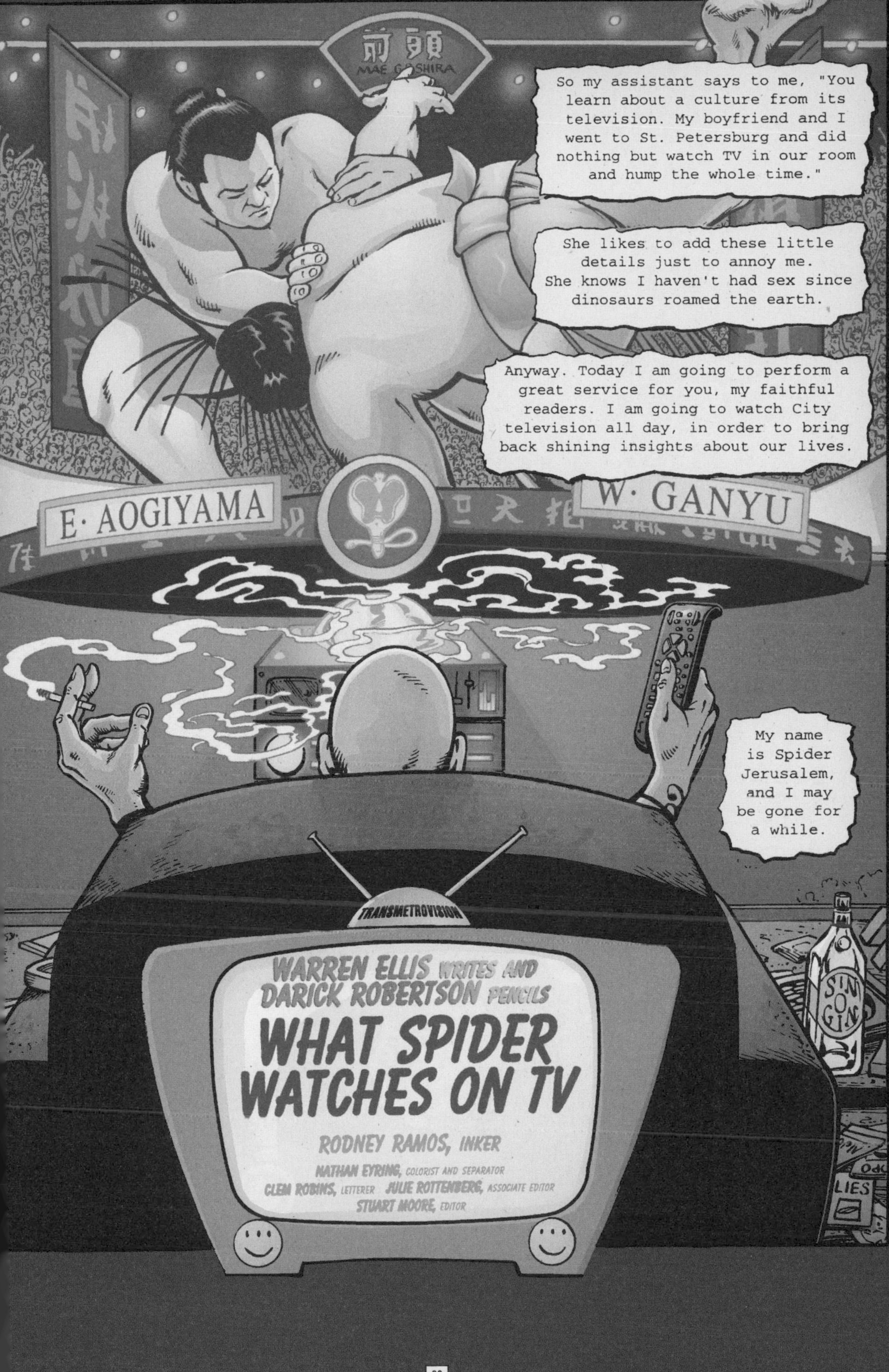

前頭
MAE GASHIRA
So my assistant says to me, "You learn about a culture from its television. My boyfriend and I went to St. Petersburg and did nothing but watch TV in our room and hump the whole time."
She likes to add these little details just to annoy me. She knows I haven't had sex since dinosaurs roamed the earth.
Anyway. Today I am going to perform a great service for you, my faithful readers. I am going to watch City television all day, in order to bring back shining insights about our lives.
E· AOGIYAMA
W· GANYU
My name is Spider Jerusalem, and I may be gone for a while.
TRANSMETROVISION
WARREN ELLIS WRITES AND
DARICK ROBERTSON PENCILS
WHAT SPIDER WATCHES ON TV
RODNEY RAMOS, INKER
NATHAN EYRING, COLORIST AND SEPARATOR
CLEM ROBINS, LETTERER JULIE ROTTENBERG, ASSOCIATE EDITOR
STUART MOORE, EDITOR
SIN O GIN
LIES

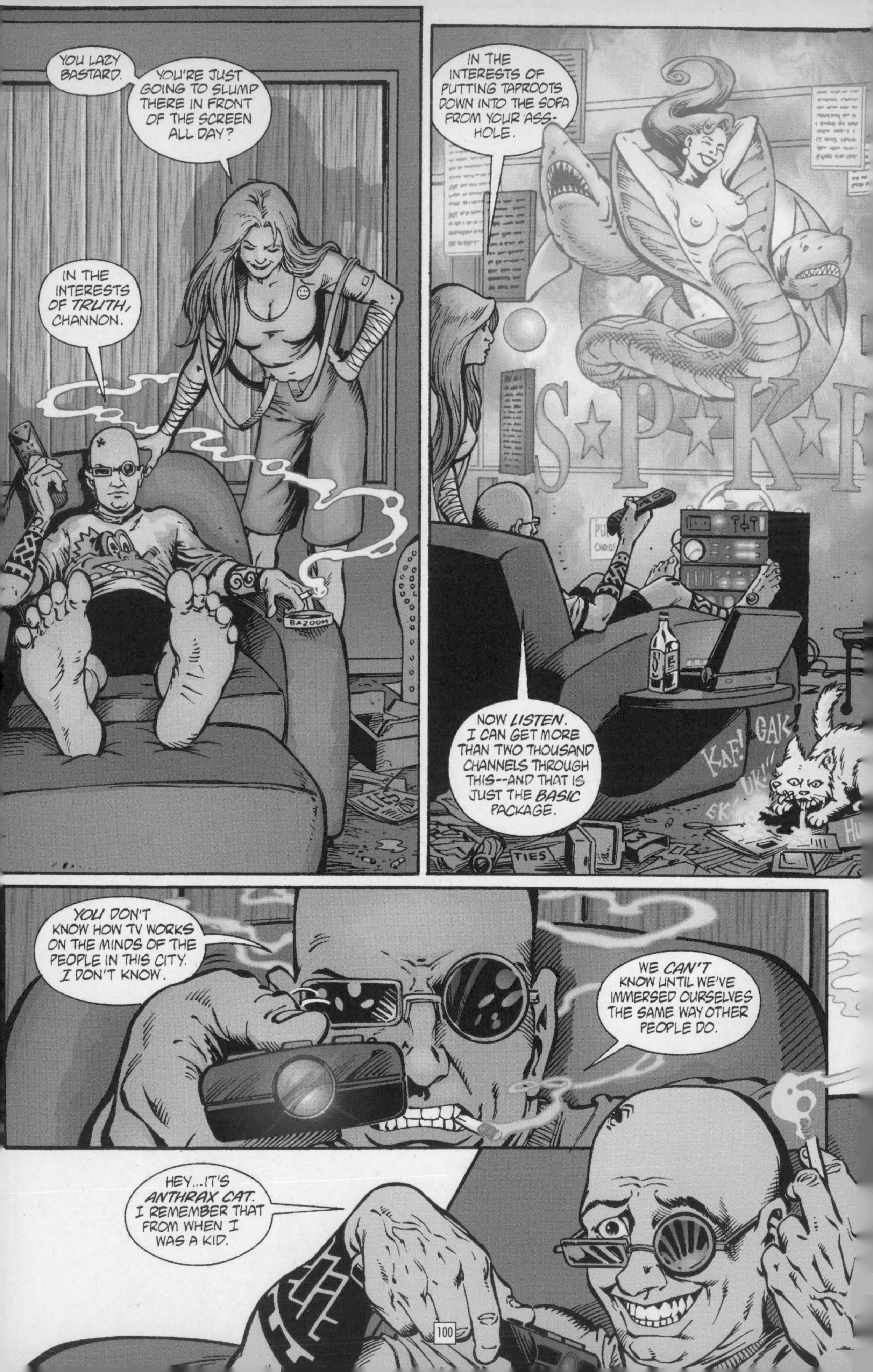
YOU LAZY BASTARD.
YOU'RE JUST GOING TO SLUMP THERE IN FRONT OF THE SCREEN ALL DAY?
IN THE INTERESTS OF *TRUTH*, CHANNON.
BAZOUM
IN THE INTERESTS OF PUTTING TAPROOTS DOWN INTO THE SOFA FROM YOUR ASS-HOLE.
S★P★K★
NOW *LISTEN*. I CAN GET MORE THAN TWO THOUSAND CHANNELS THROUGH THIS--AND THAT IS JUST THE *BASIC* PACKAGE.
KAF! GAK!
EK-UK!!
TIES
YOU DON'T KNOW HOW TV WORKS ON THE MINDS OF THE PEOPLE IN THIS CITY. I DON'T KNOW.
WE *CAN'T* KNOW UNTIL WE'VE IMMERSED OURSELVES THE SAME WAY OTHER PEOPLE DO.
HEY...IT'S *ANTHRAX CAT*. I REMEMBER THAT FROM WHEN I WAS A KID.

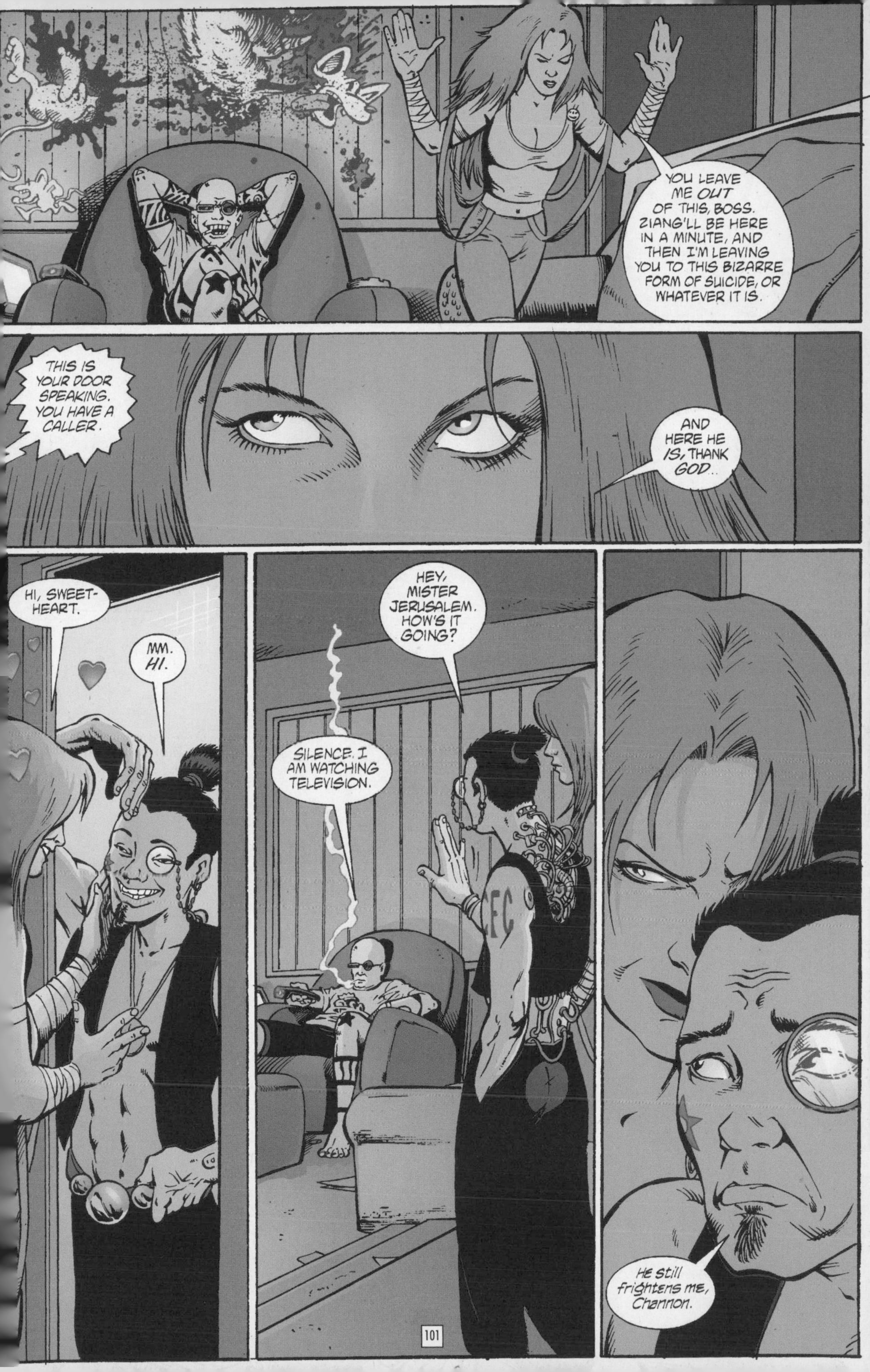
YOU LEAVE ME OUT OF THIS, BOSS. ZIANG'LL BE HERE IN A MINUTE, AND THEN I'M LEAVING YOU TO THIS BIZARRE FORM OF SUICIDE, OR WHATEVER IT IS.
THIS IS YOUR DOOR SPEAKING. YOU HAVE A CALLER.
AND HERE HE IS, THANK GOD...
HI, SWEET-HEART.
MM. HI.
HEY, MISTER JERUSALEM. HOW'S IT GOING?
SILENCE. I AM WATCHING TELEVISION.
He still frightens me, Channon.

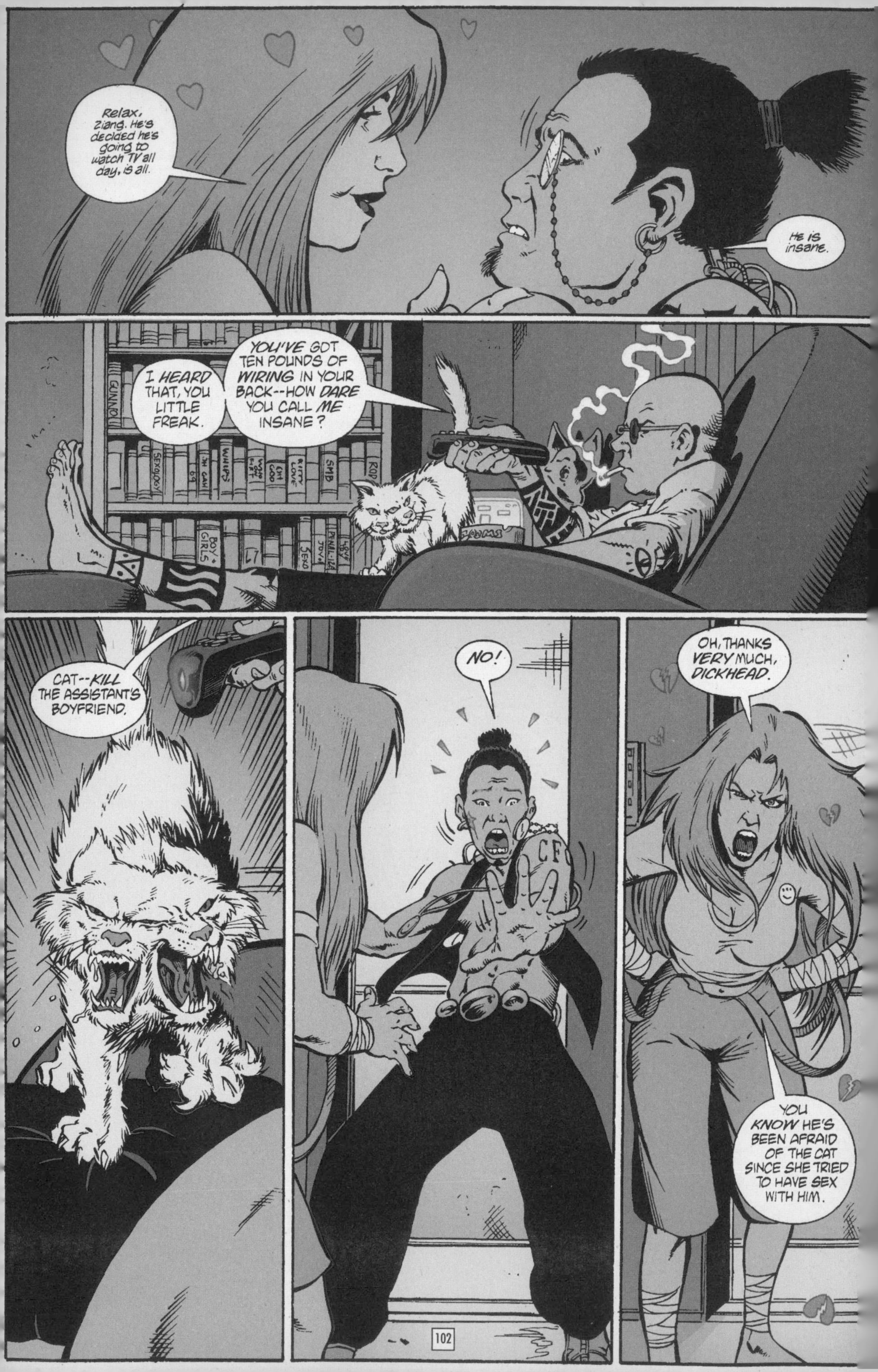

Relax, Ziang. He's decided he's going to watch TV all day, is all.
He is insane.
I HEARD THAT, YOU LITTLE FREAK.
YOU'VE GOT TEN POUNDS OF WIRING IN YOUR BACK--HOW DARE YOU CALL ME INSANE?
CAT--KILL THE ASSISTANT'S BOYFRIEND.
NO!
OH, THANKS VERY MUCH, DICKHEAD.
YOU KNOW HE'S BEEN AFRAID OF THE CAT SINCE SHE TRIED TO HAVE SEX WITH HIM.

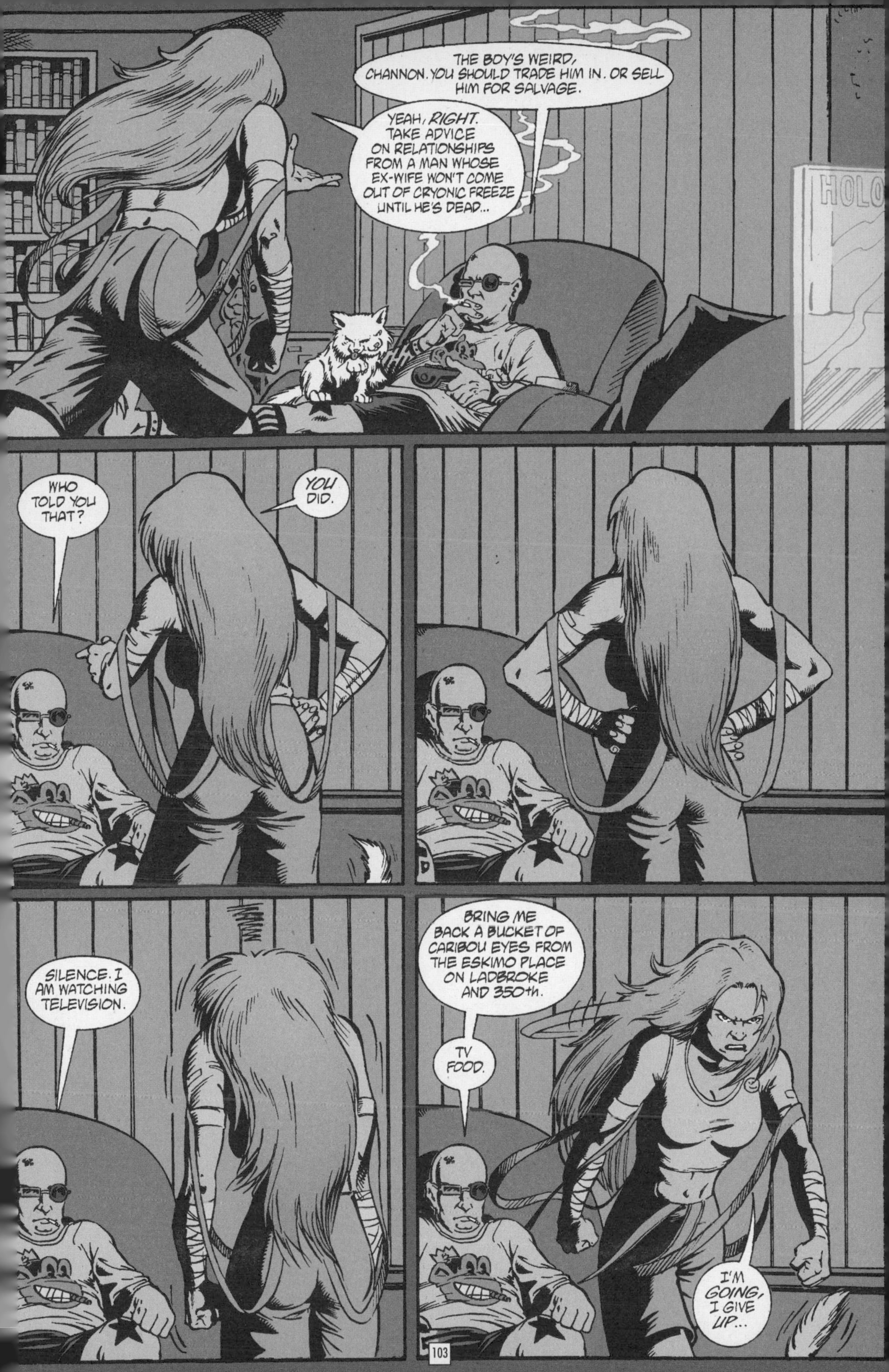
THE BOY'S WEIRD, CHANNON. YOU SHOULD TRADE HIM IN. OR SELL HIM FOR SALVAGE.
YEAH, RIGHT. TAKE ADVICE ON RELATIONSHIPS FROM A MAN WHOSE EX-WIFE WON'T COME OUT OF CRYONIC FREEZE UNTIL HE'S DEAD...
HOLO
WHO TOLD YOU THAT?
YOU DID.
SILENCE. I AM WATCHING TELEVISION.
BRING ME BACK A BUCKET OF CARIBOU EYES FROM THE ESKIMO PLACE ON LADBROKE AND 350th.
TV FOOD.
I'M GOING, I GIVE UP...

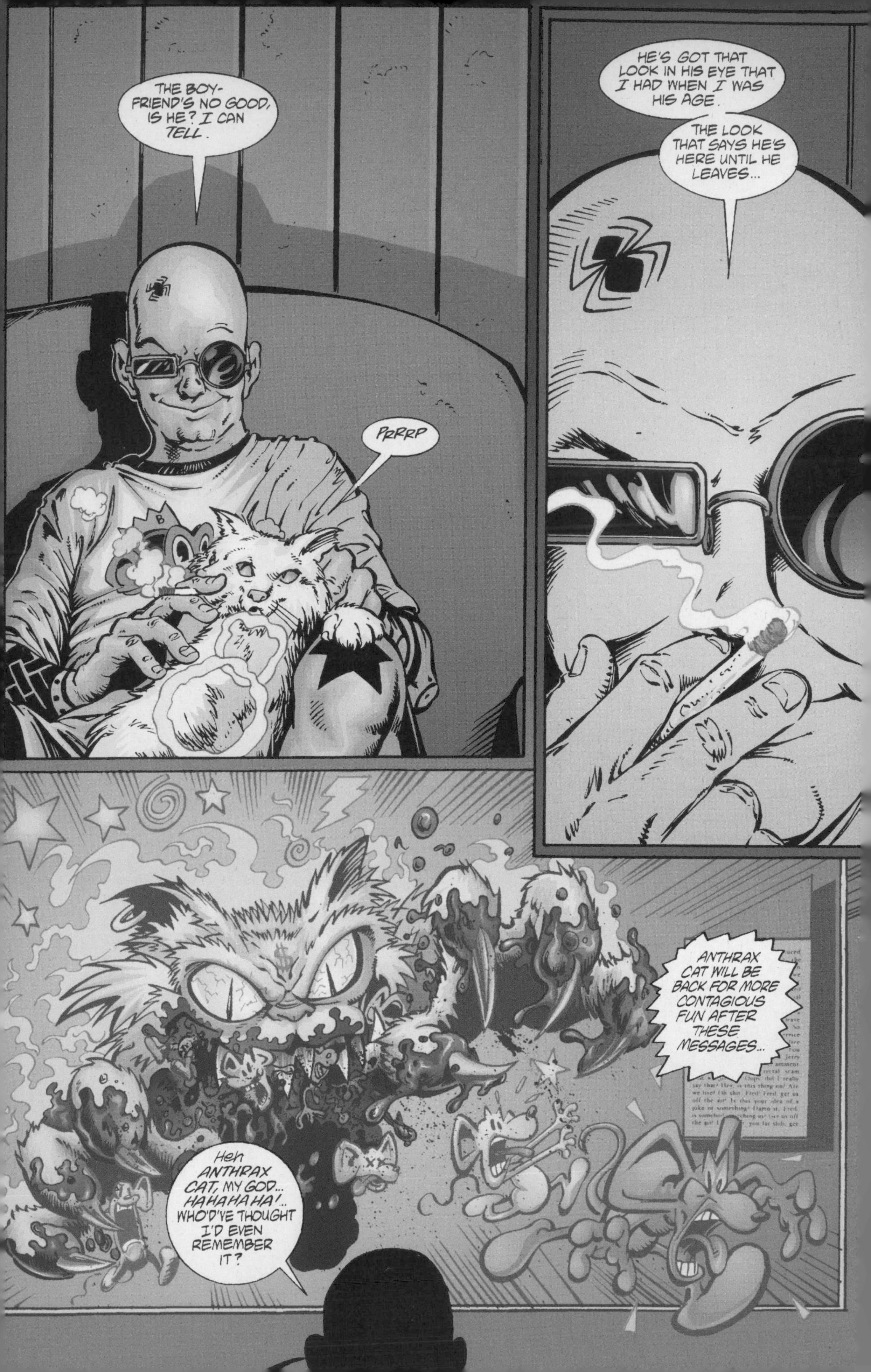
THE BOY-FRIEND'S NO GOOD, IS HE? I CAN TELL.
PRRRP
HE'S GOT THAT LOOK IN HIS EYE THAT I HAD WHEN I WAS HIS AGE.
THE LOOK THAT SAYS HE'S HERE UNTIL HE LEAVES...
ANTHRAX CAT WILL BE BACK FOR MORE CONTAGIOUS FUN AFTER THESE MESSAGES...
Heh ANTHRAX CAT, MY GOD... HAHAHAHA!.. WHO'D'VE THOUGHT I'D EVEN REMEMBER IT?

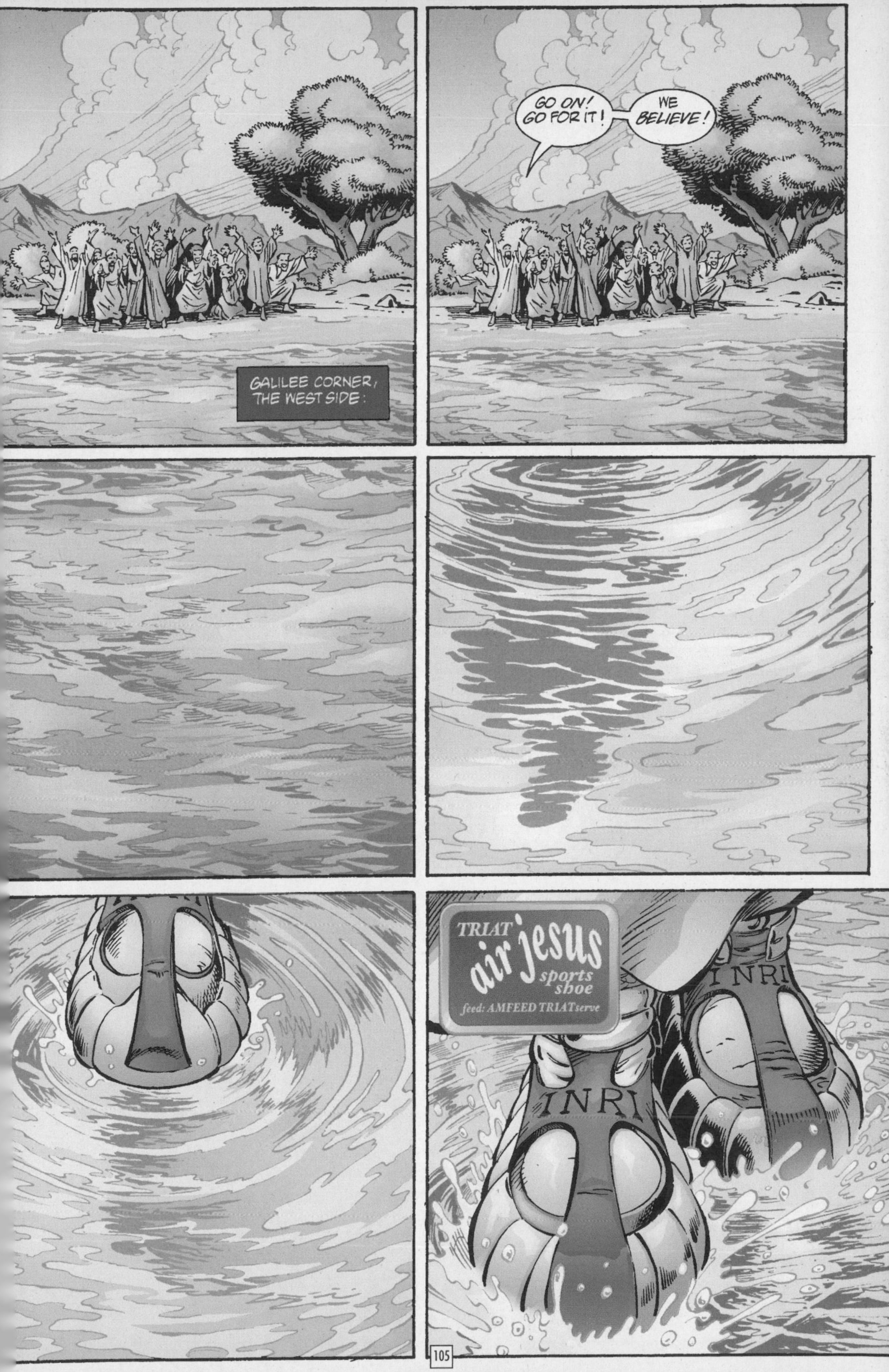
GALILEE CORNER, THE WEST SIDE:
GO ON! GO FOR IT!
WE BELIEVE!
TRIAT air jesus sports shoe
feed: AMFEED TRIATserve
INRI
INRI

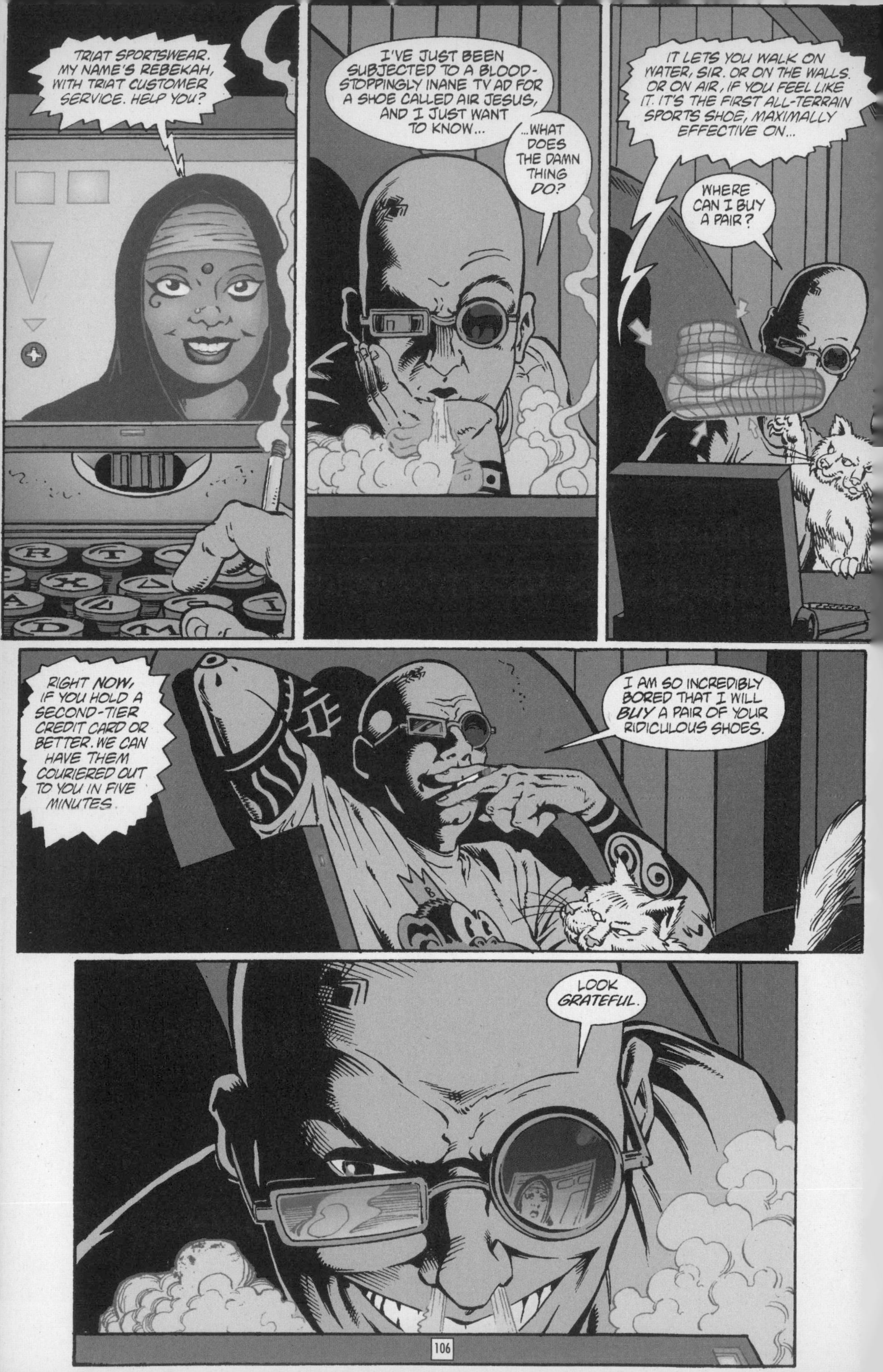
TRIAT SPORTSWEAR. MY NAME'S REBEKAH, WITH TRIAT CUSTOMER SERVICE. HELP YOU?
I'VE JUST BEEN SUBJECTED TO A BLOOD-STOPPINGLY INANE TV AD FOR A SHOE CALLED AIR JESUS, AND I JUST WANT TO KNOW...
...WHAT DOES THE DAMN THING DO?
IT LETS YOU WALK ON WATER, SIR. OR ON THE WALLS. OR ON AIR, IF YOU FEEL LIKE IT. IT'S THE FIRST ALL-TERRAIN SPORTS SHOE, MAXIMALLY EFFECTIVE ON...
WHERE CAN I BUY A PAIR?
RIGHT NOW, IF YOU HOLD A SECOND-TIER CREDIT CARD OR BETTER. WE CAN HAVE THEM COURIERED OUT TO YOU IN FIVE MINUTES.
I AM SO INCREDIBLY BORED THAT I WILL BUY A PAIR OF YOUR RIDICULOUS SHOES.
LOOK GRATEFUL.

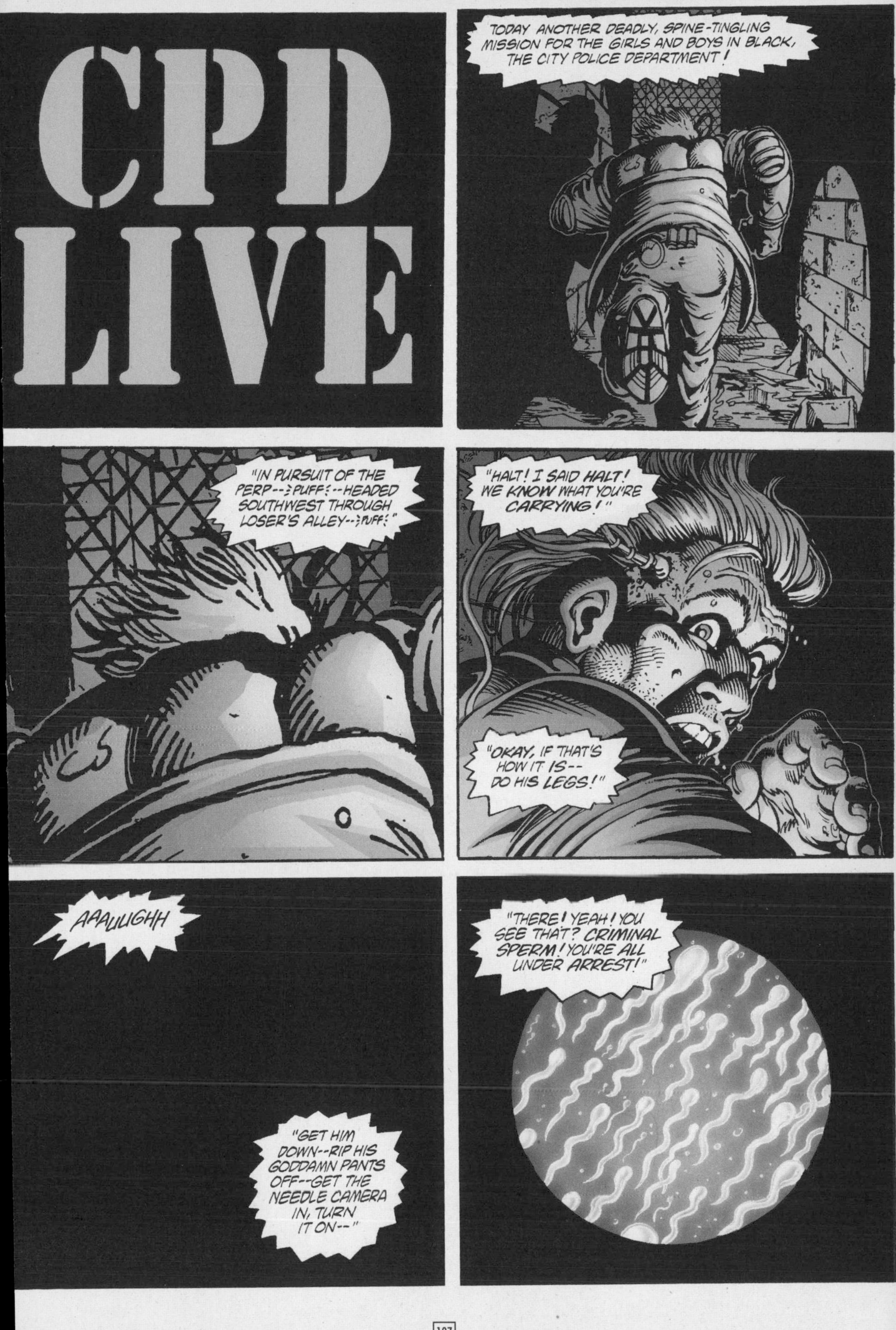
CPD LIVE
TODAY ANOTHER DEADLY, SPINE-TINGLING MISSION FOR THE GIRLS AND BOYS IN BLACK, THE CITY POLICE DEPARTMENT!
"IN PURSUIT OF THE PERP--;PUFF;--HEADED SOUTHWEST THROUGH LOSER'S ALLEY--;PUFF;"
"HALT! I SAID HALT! WE KNOW WHAT YOU'RE CARRYING!"
"OKAY, IF THAT'S HOW IT IS--DO HIS LEGS!"
AAAUUGHH
"GET HIM DOWN--RIP HIS GODDAMN PANTS OFF--GET THE NEEDLE CAMERA IN, TURN IT ON--"
"THERE! YEAH! YOU SEE THAT? CRIMINAL SPERM! YOU'RE ALL UNDER ARREST!"

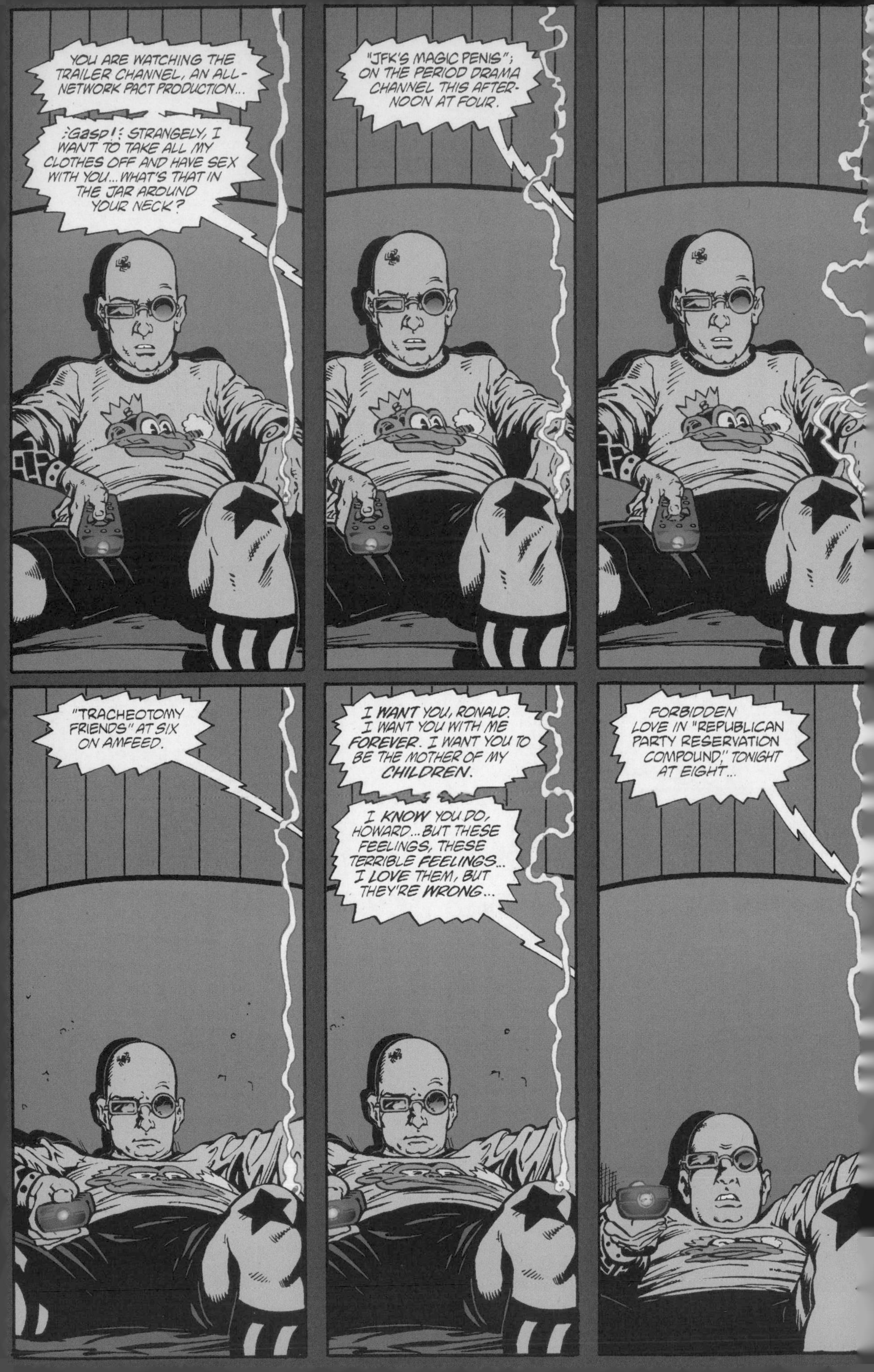
YOU ARE WATCHING THE TRAILER CHANNEL, AN ALL-NETWORK PACT PRODUCTION...
¡Gasp!¡ STRANGELY, I WANT TO TAKE ALL MY CLOTHES OFF AND HAVE SEX WITH YOU... WHAT'S THAT IN THE JAR AROUND YOUR NECK?
"JFK'S MAGIC PENIS"; ON THE PERIOD DRAMA CHANNEL THIS AFTERNOON AT FOUR.
"TRACHEOTOMY FRIENDS" AT SIX ON AMFEED.
I WANT YOU, RONALD. I WANT YOU WITH ME FOREVER. I WANT YOU TO BE THE MOTHER OF MY CHILDREN.
I KNOW YOU DO, HOWARD... BUT THESE FEELINGS, THESE TERRIBLE FEELINGS... I LOVE THEM, BUT THEY'RE WRONG...
FORBIDDEN LOVE IN "REPUBLICAN PARTY RESERVATION COMPOUND," TONIGHT AT EIGHT...

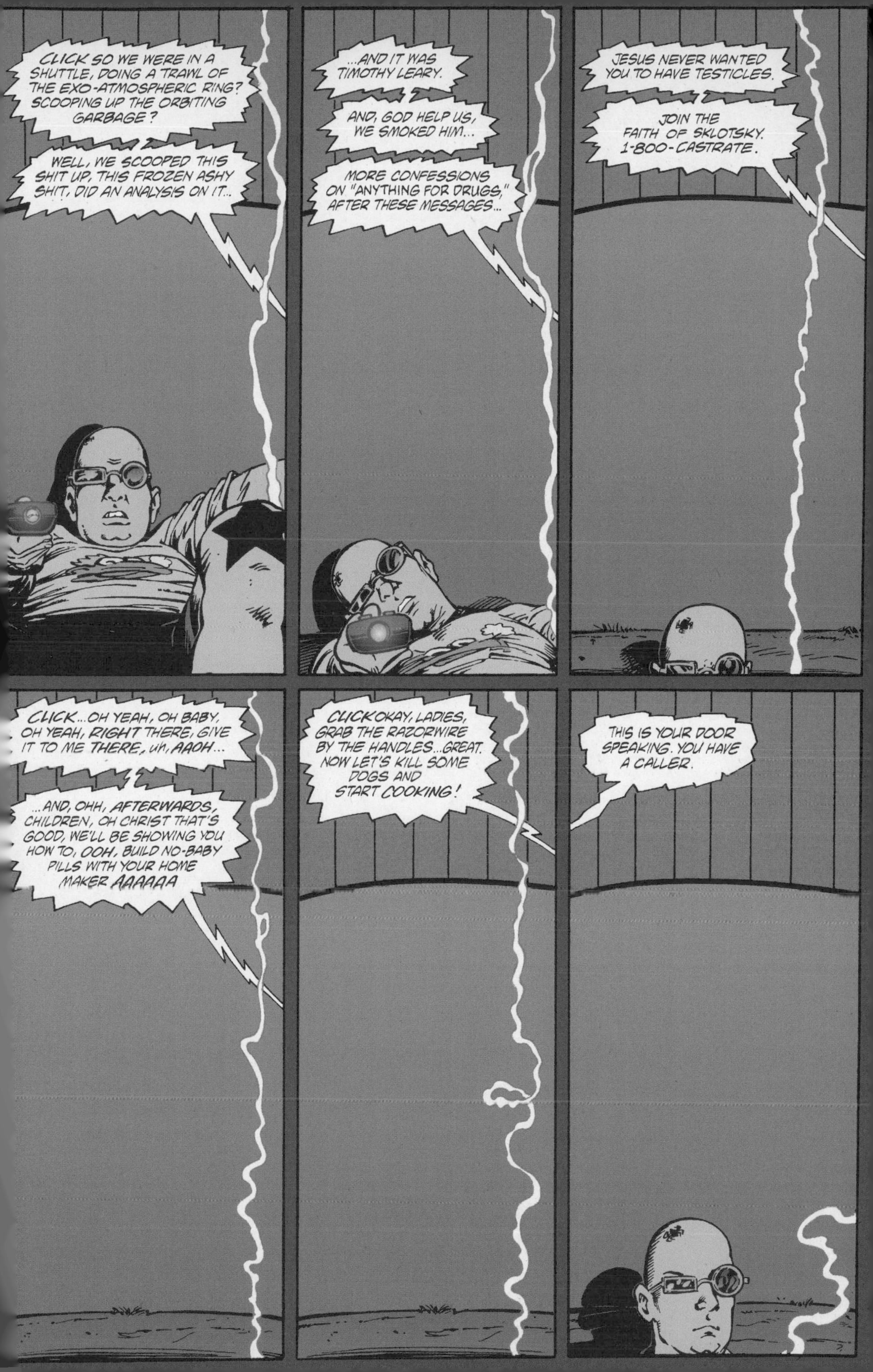
CLICK SO WE WERE IN A SHUTTLE, DOING A TRAWL OF THE EXO-ATMOSPHERIC RING? SCOOPING UP THE ORBITING GARBAGE?
WELL, WE SCOOPED THIS SHIT UP, THIS FROZEN ASHY SHIT, DID AN ANALYSIS ON IT...
...AND IT WAS TIMOTHY LEARY.
AND, GOD HELP US, WE SMOKED HIM...
MORE CONFESSIONS ON "ANYTHING FOR DRUGS," AFTER THESE MESSAGES...
JESUS NEVER WANTED YOU TO HAVE TESTICLES.
JOIN THE FAITH OF SKLOTSKY. 1-800-CASTRATE.
CLICK...OH YEAH, OH BABY, OH YEAH, RIGHT THERE, GIVE IT TO ME THERE, uh, AAOH...
...AND, OHH, AFTERWARDS, CHILDREN, OH CHRIST THAT'S GOOD, WE'LL BE SHOWING YOU HOW TO, OOH, BUILD NO-BABY PILLS WITH YOUR HOME MAKER AAAAAA
CLICK OKAY, LADIES, GRAB THE RAZORWIRE BY THE HANDLES...GREAT. NOW LET'S KILL SOME DOGS AND START COOKING!
THIS IS YOUR DOOR SPEAKING. YOU HAVE A CALLER.

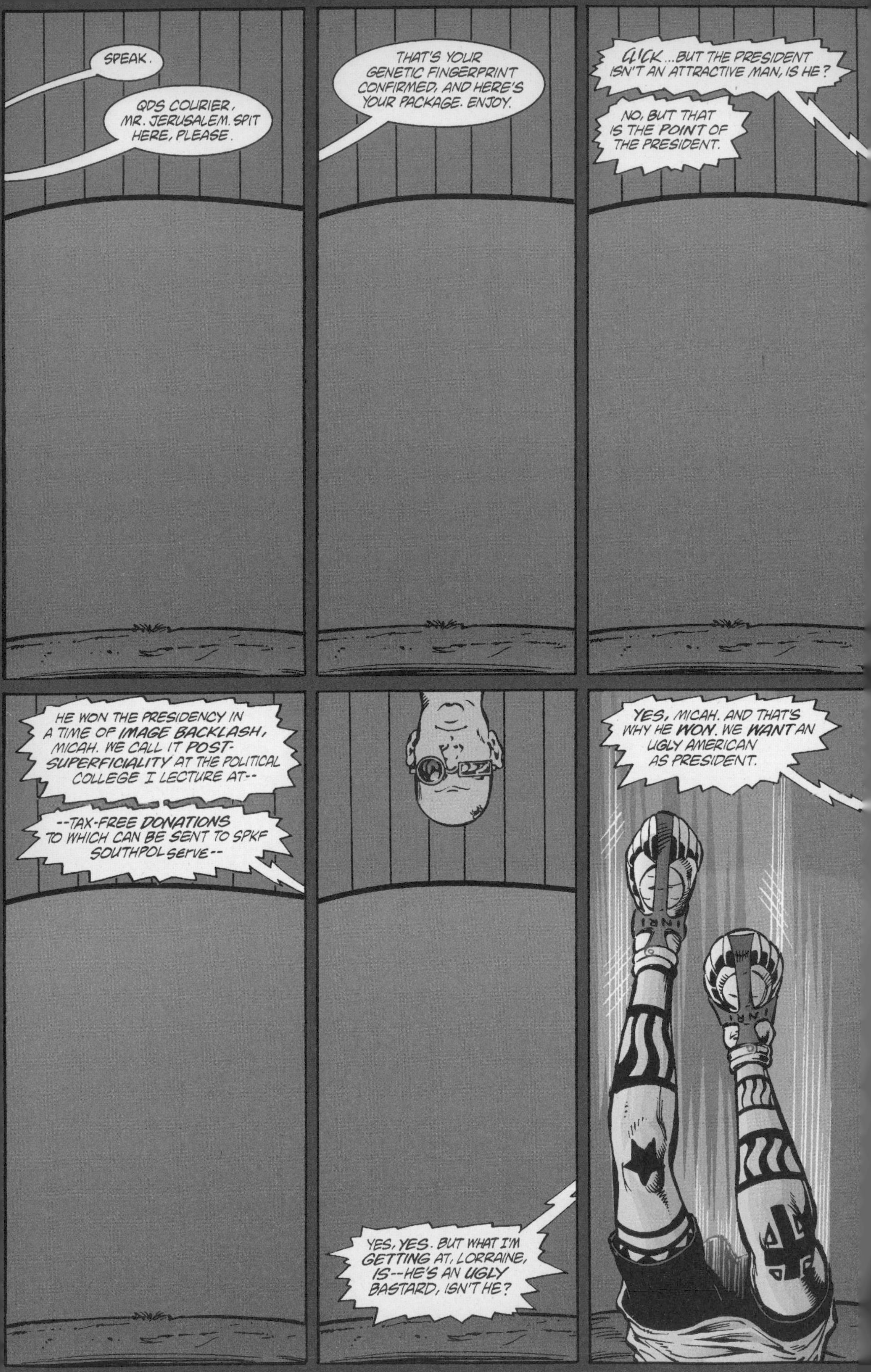
SPEAK.
QDS COURIER, MR. JERUSALEM. SPIT HERE, PLEASE.
THAT'S YOUR GENETIC FINGERPRINT CONFIRMED, AND HERE'S YOUR PACKAGE. ENJOY.
GLICK...BUT THE PRESIDENT ISN'T AN ATTRACTIVE MAN, IS HE?
NO, BUT THAT IS THE POINT OF THE PRESIDENT.
HE WON THE PRESIDENCY IN A TIME OF IMAGE BACKLASH, MICAH. WE CALL IT POST-SUPERFICIALITY AT THE POLITICAL COLLEGE I LECTURE AT--
--TAX-FREE DONATIONS TO WHICH CAN BE SENT TO SPKF SOUTHPOL serve--
YES, YES. BUT WHAT I'M GETTING AT, LORRAINE, IS--HE'S AN UGLY BASTARD, ISN'T HE?
YES, MICAH. AND THAT'S WHY HE WON. WE WANT AN UGLY AMERICAN AS PRESIDENT.

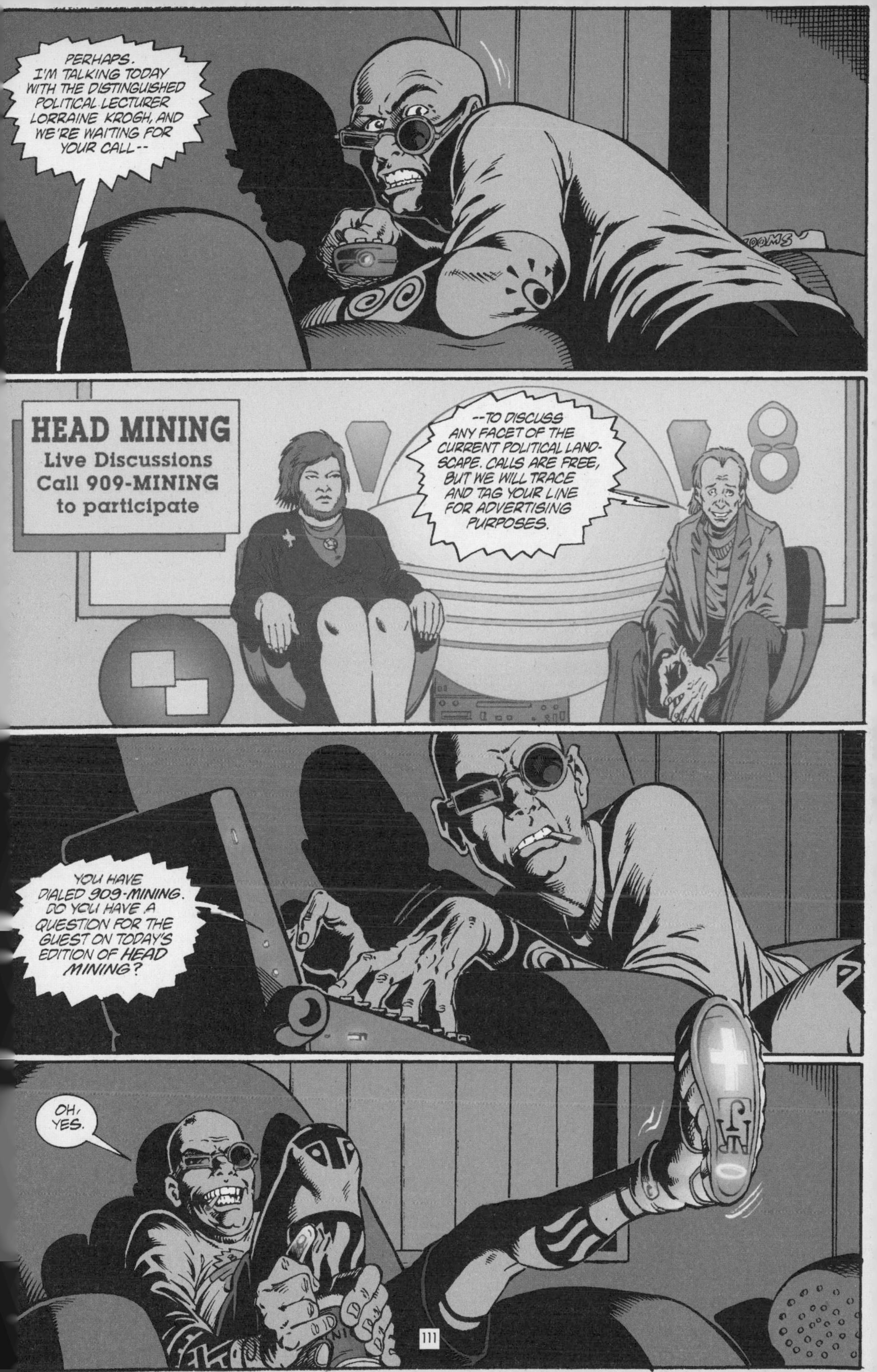
PERHAPS. I'M TALKING TODAY WITH THE DISTINGUISHED POLITICAL LECTURER LORRAINE KROGH, AND WE'RE WAITING FOR YOUR CALL--
HEAD MINING
Live Discussions
Call 909-MINING
to participate
--TO DISCUSS ANY FACET OF THE CURRENT POLITICAL LAND-SCAPE. CALLS ARE FREE, BUT WE WILL TRACE AND TAG YOUR LINE FOR ADVERTISING PURPOSES.
YOU HAVE DIALED 909-MINING. DO YOU HAVE A QUESTION FOR THE GUEST ON TODAY'S EDITION OF HEAD MINING?
OH, YES.

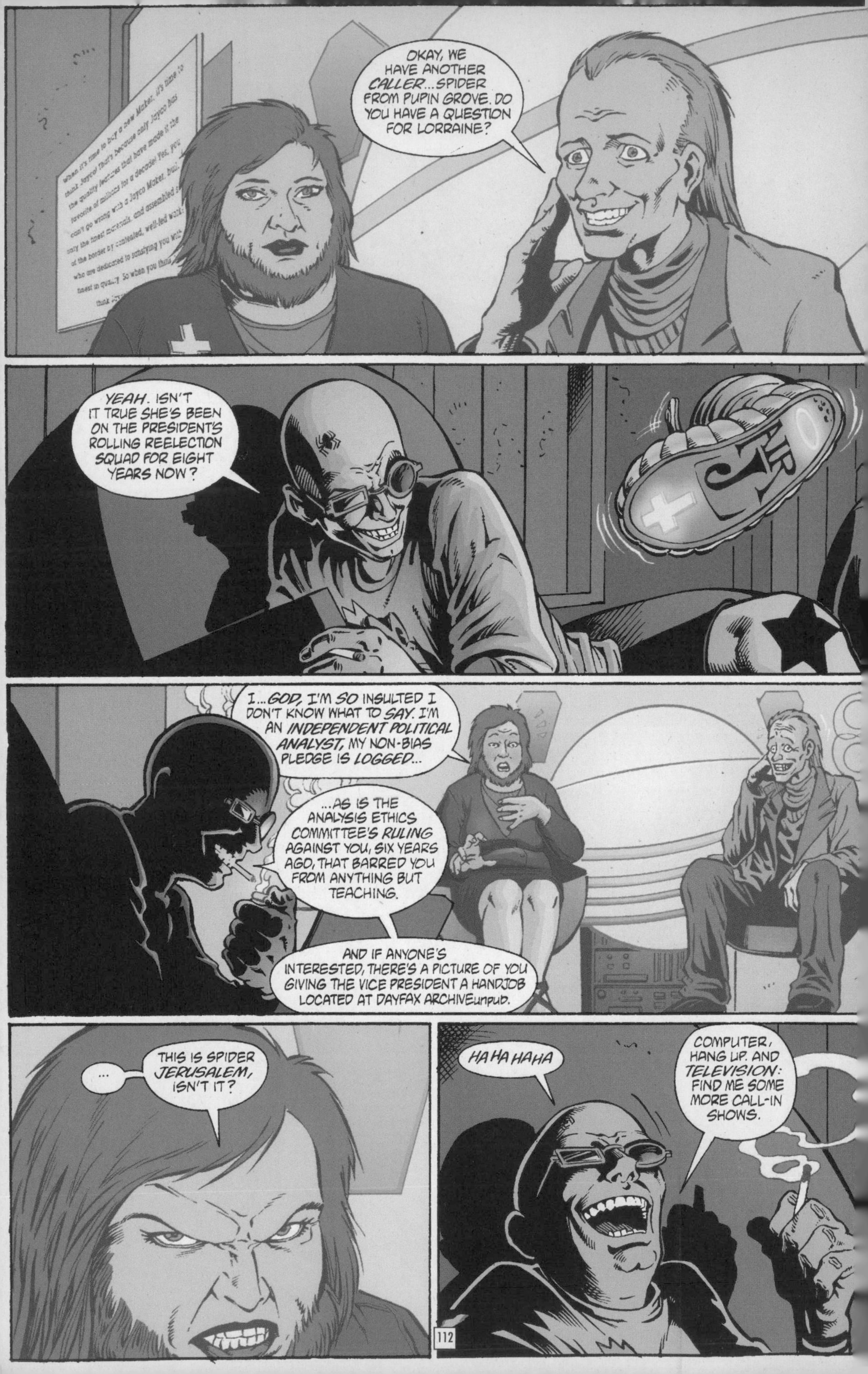

When it's time to buy a new Maker, it's time to
think Jayco! That's because only Jayco has
the quality features that have made it the
favorite of millions for a decade! Yes, you
can't go wrong with a Jayco Maker, buil
only the finest materials, and assembled
of the border by contented, well-fed work
who are dedicated to satisfying you with
finest in quality. So when you think
OKAY, WE HAVE ANOTHER CALLER...SPIDER FROM PUPIN GROVE. DO YOU HAVE A QUESTION FOR LORRAINE?
YEAH. ISN'T IT TRUE SHE'S BEEN ON THE PRESIDENT'S ROLLING REELECTION SQUAD FOR EIGHT YEARS NOW?
AIR J
I...GOD, I'M SO INSULTED I DON'T KNOW WHAT TO SAY. I'M AN INDEPENDENT POLITICAL ANALYST, MY NON-BIAS PLEDGE IS LOGGED...
...AS IS THE ANALYSIS ETHICS COMMITTEE'S RULING AGAINST YOU, SIX YEARS AGO, THAT BARRED YOU FROM ANYTHING BUT TEACHING.
AND IF ANYONE'S INTERESTED, THERE'S A PICTURE OF YOU GIVING THE VICE PRESIDENT A HANDJOB LOCATED AT DAYFAX ARCHIVEunpub.
...
THIS IS SPIDER JERUSALEM, ISN'T IT?
HA HA HA HA
COMPUTER, HANG UP. AND TELEVISION: FIND ME SOME MORE CALL-IN SHOWS.

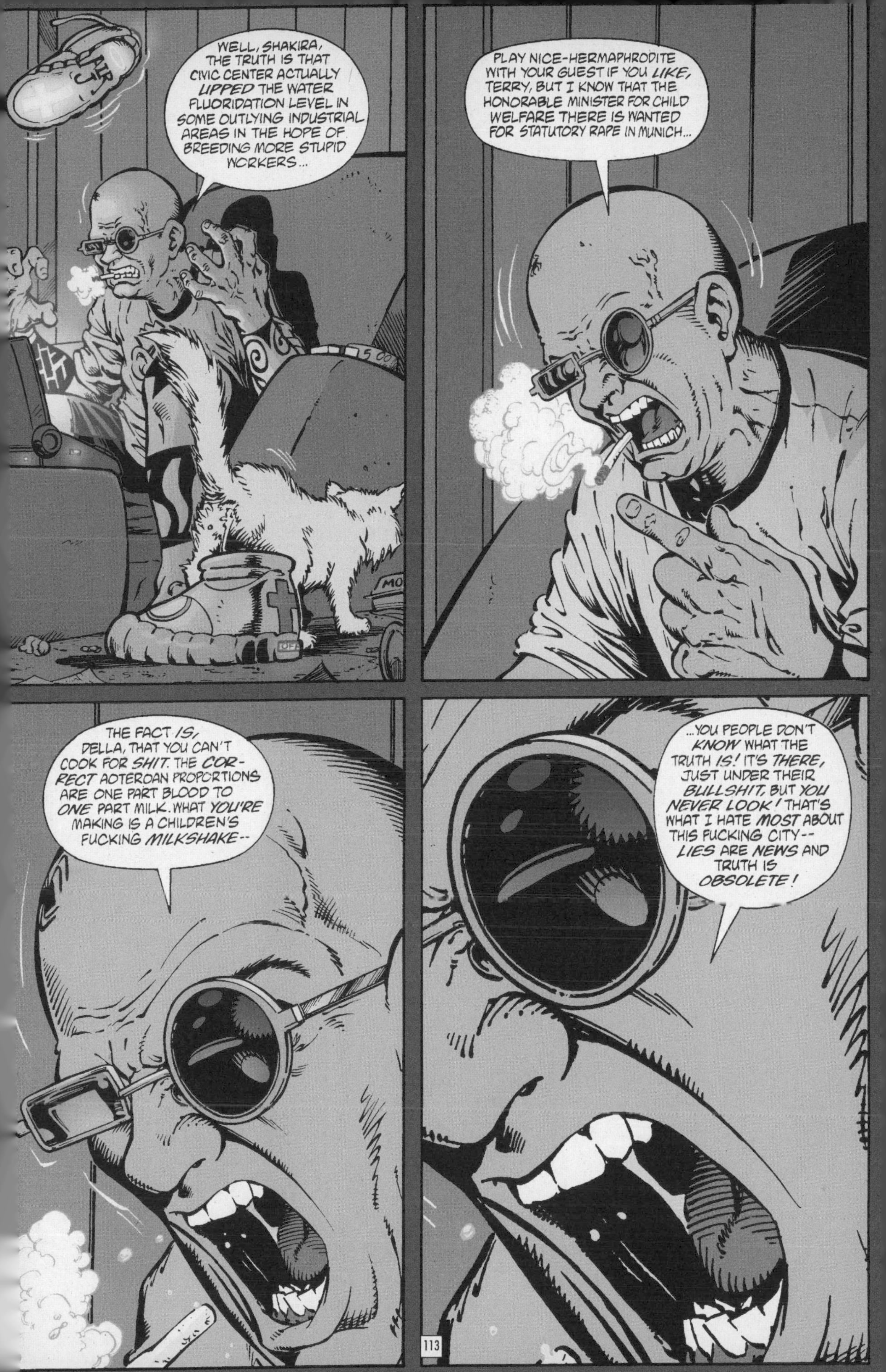
WELL, SHAKIRA, THE TRUTH IS THAT CIVIC CENTER ACTUALLY UPPED THE WATER FLUORIDATION LEVEL IN SOME OUTLYING INDUSTRIAL AREAS IN THE HOPE OF BREEDING MORE STUPID WORKERS...
PLAY NICE-HERMAPHRODITE WITH YOUR GUEST IF YOU LIKE, TERRY, BUT I KNOW THAT THE HONORABLE MINISTER FOR CHILD WELFARE THERE IS WANTED FOR STATUTORY RAPE IN MUNICH...
THE FACT IS, DELLA, THAT YOU CAN'T COOK FOR SHIT. THE CORRECT AOTEROAN PROPORTIONS ARE ONE PART BLOOD TO ONE PART MILK. WHAT YOU'RE MAKING IS A CHILDREN'S FUCKING MILKSHAKE--
...YOU PEOPLE DON'T KNOW WHAT THE TRUTH IS! IT'S THERE, JUST UNDER THEIR BULLSHIT, BUT YOU NEVER LOOK! THAT'S WHAT I HATE MOST ABOUT THIS FUCKING CITY-- LIES ARE NEWS AND TRUTH IS OBSOLETE!

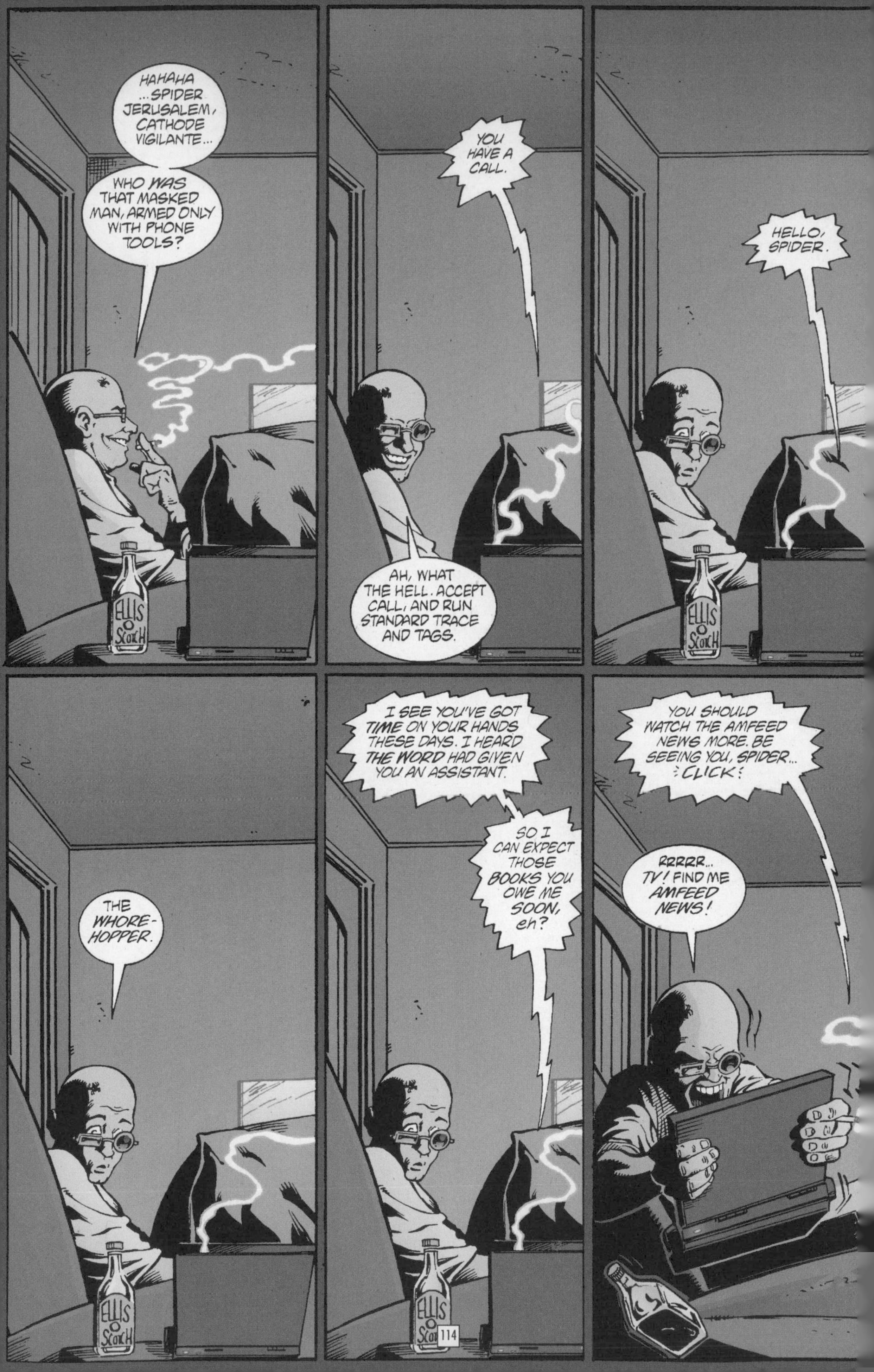
HAHAHA ...SPIDER JERUSALEM, CATHODE VIGILANTE...
WHO WAS THAT MASKED MAN, ARMED ONLY WITH PHONE TOOLS?
ELLIS SCOTCH
YOU HAVE A CALL.
AH, WHAT THE HELL. ACCEPT CALL, AND RUN STANDARD TRACE AND TAGS.
HELLO, SPIDER.
THE WHORE-HOPPER.
I SEE YOU'VE GOT TIME ON YOUR HANDS THESE DAYS. I HEARD THE WORD HAD GIVEN YOU AN ASSISTANT.
SO I CAN EXPECT THOSE BOOKS YOU OWE ME SOON, eh?
YOU SHOULD WATCH THE AMFEED NEWS MORE. BE SEEING YOU, SPIDER... :CLICK:
RRRRR... TV! FIND ME AMFEED NEWS!

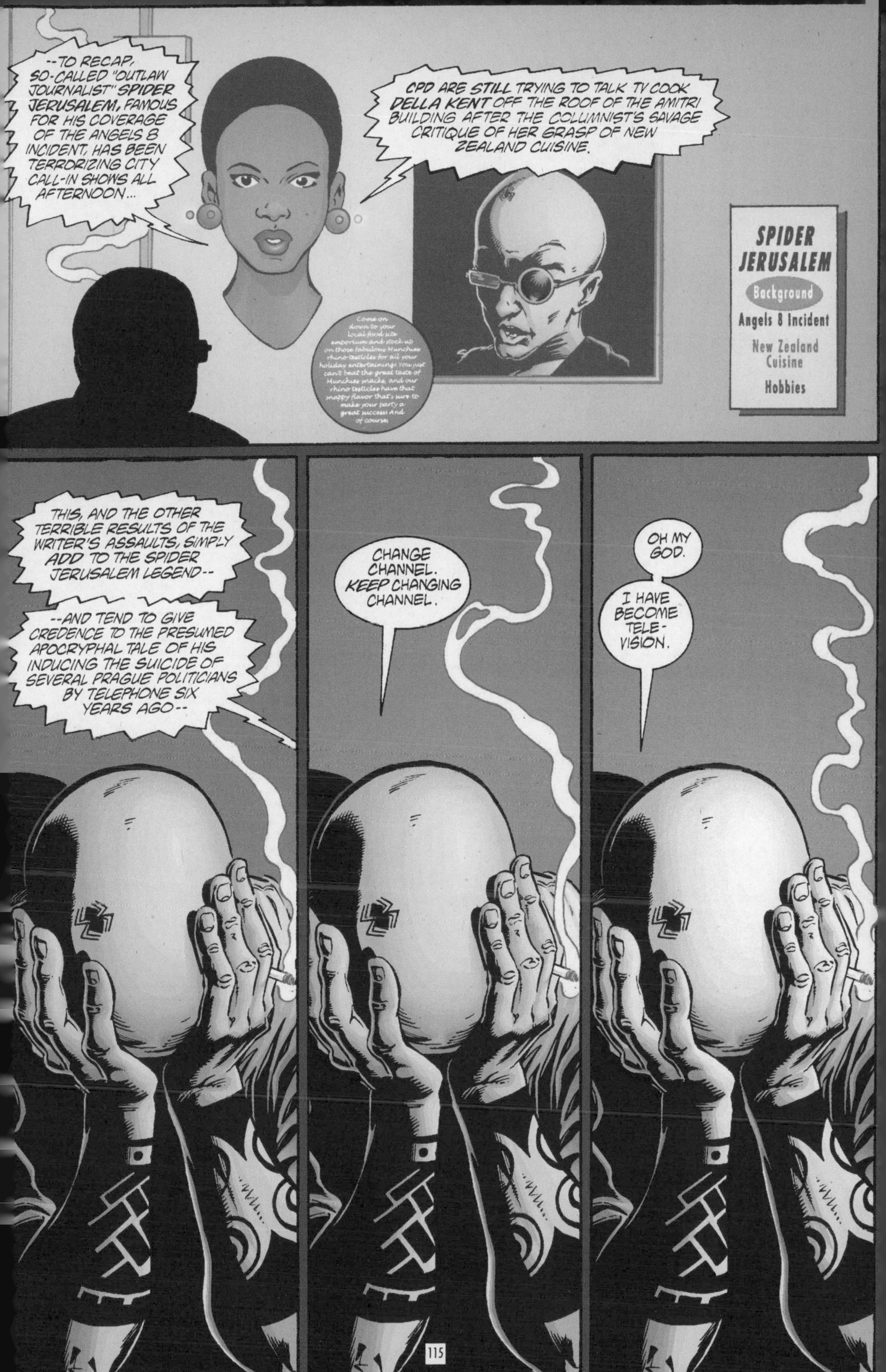
--TO RECAP, SO-CALLED "OUTLAW JOURNALIST" SPIDER JERUSALEM, FAMOUS FOR HIS COVERAGE OF THE ANGELS 8 INCIDENT, HAS BEEN TERRORIZING CITY CALL-IN SHOWS ALL AFTERNOON...
CPD ARE STILL TRYING TO TALK TV COOK DELLA KENT OFF THE ROOF OF THE AMITRI BUILDING AFTER THE COLUMNIST'S SAVAGE CRITIQUE OF HER GRASP OF NEW ZEALAND CUISINE.
Come on
down to your
local food
emporium and stock up
on those fabulous Munchies
rhino testicles for all your
holiday entertaining! You just
can't beat the great taste of
Munchies
rhino testicles have that
flavor that's sure to
make your party a
great success! And
of course,
SPIDER JERUSALEM
Background
Angels 8 Incident
New Zealand Cuisine
Hobbies
THIS, AND THE OTHER TERRIBLE RESULTS OF THE WRITER'S ASSAULTS, SIMPLY ADD TO THE SPIDER JERUSALEM LEGEND--
--AND TEND TO GIVE CREDENCE TO THE PRESUMED APOCRYPHAL TALE OF HIS INDUCING THE SUICIDE OF SEVERAL PRAGUE POLITICIANS BY TELEPHONE SIX YEARS AGO--
CHANGE CHANNEL. KEEP CHANGING CHANNEL.
OH MY GOD.
I HAVE BECOME TELE-VISION.

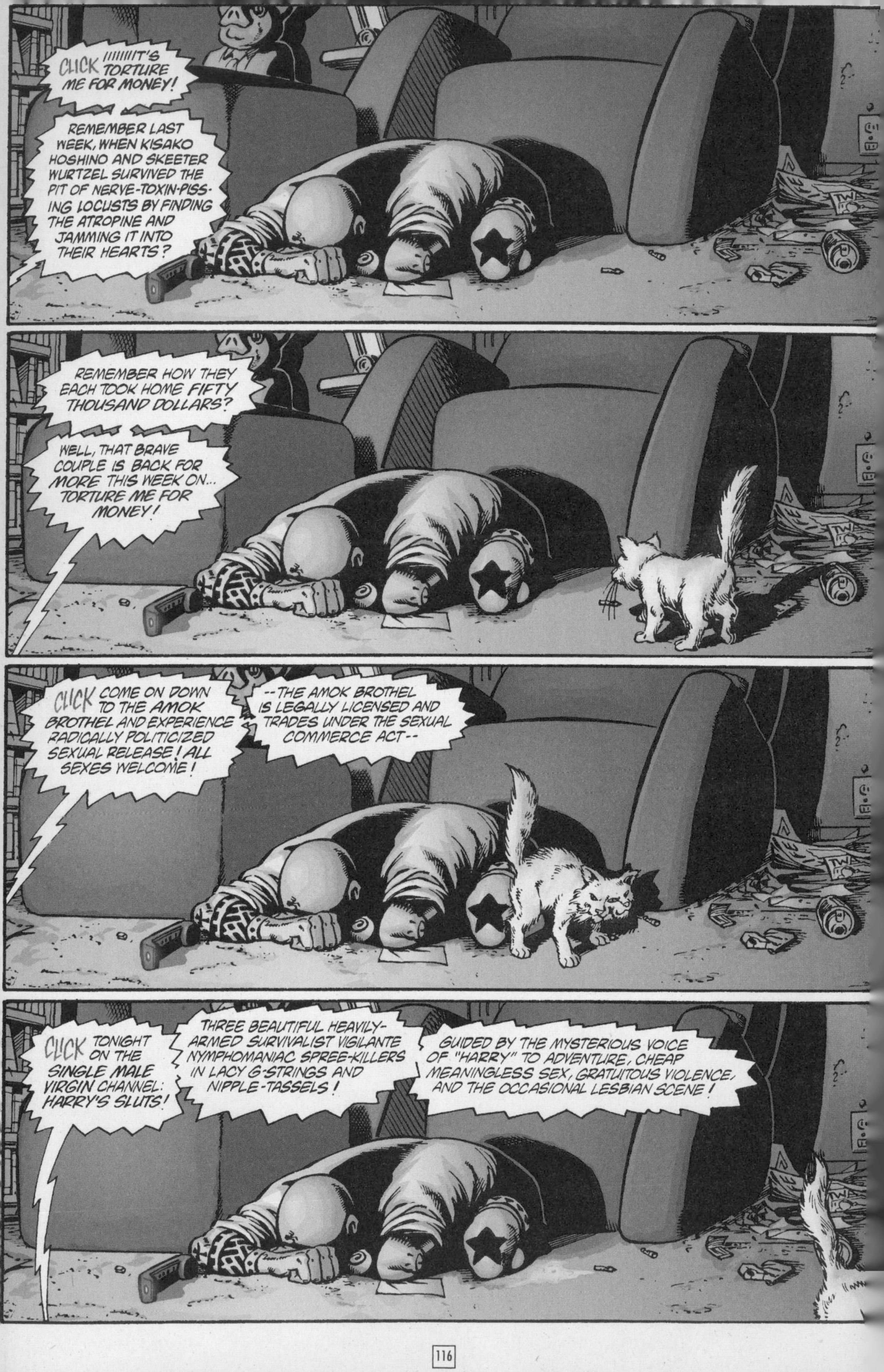
CLICK !!!!!!!!IT'S TORTURE ME FOR MONEY!
REMEMBER LAST WEEK, WHEN KISAKO HOSHINO AND SKEETER WURTZEL SURVIVED THE PIT OF NERVE-TOXIN-PISSING LOCUSTS BY FINDING THE ATROPINE AND JAMMING IT INTO THEIR HEARTS?
REMEMBER HOW THEY EACH TOOK HOME FIFTY THOUSAND DOLLARS?
WELL, THAT BRAVE COUPLE IS BACK FOR MORE THIS WEEK ON... TORTURE ME FOR MONEY!
CLICK COME ON DOWN TO THE AMOK BROTHEL AND EXPERIENCE RADICALLY POLITICIZED SEXUAL RELEASE! ALL SEXES WELCOME!
--THE AMOK BROTHEL IS LEGALLY LICENSED AND TRADES UNDER THE SEXUAL COMMERCE ACT--
CLICK TONIGHT ON THE SINGLE MALE VIRGIN CHANNEL: HARRY'S SLUTS!
THREE BEAUTIFUL HEAVILY-ARMED SURVIVALIST VIGILANTE NYMPHOMANIAC SPREE-KILLERS IN LACY G-STRINGS AND NIPPLE-TASSELS!
GUIDED BY THE MYSTERIOUS VOICE OF "HARRY" TO ADVENTURE, CHEAP MEANINGLESS SEX, GRATUITOUS VIOLENCE, AND THE OCCASIONAL LESBIAN SCENE!

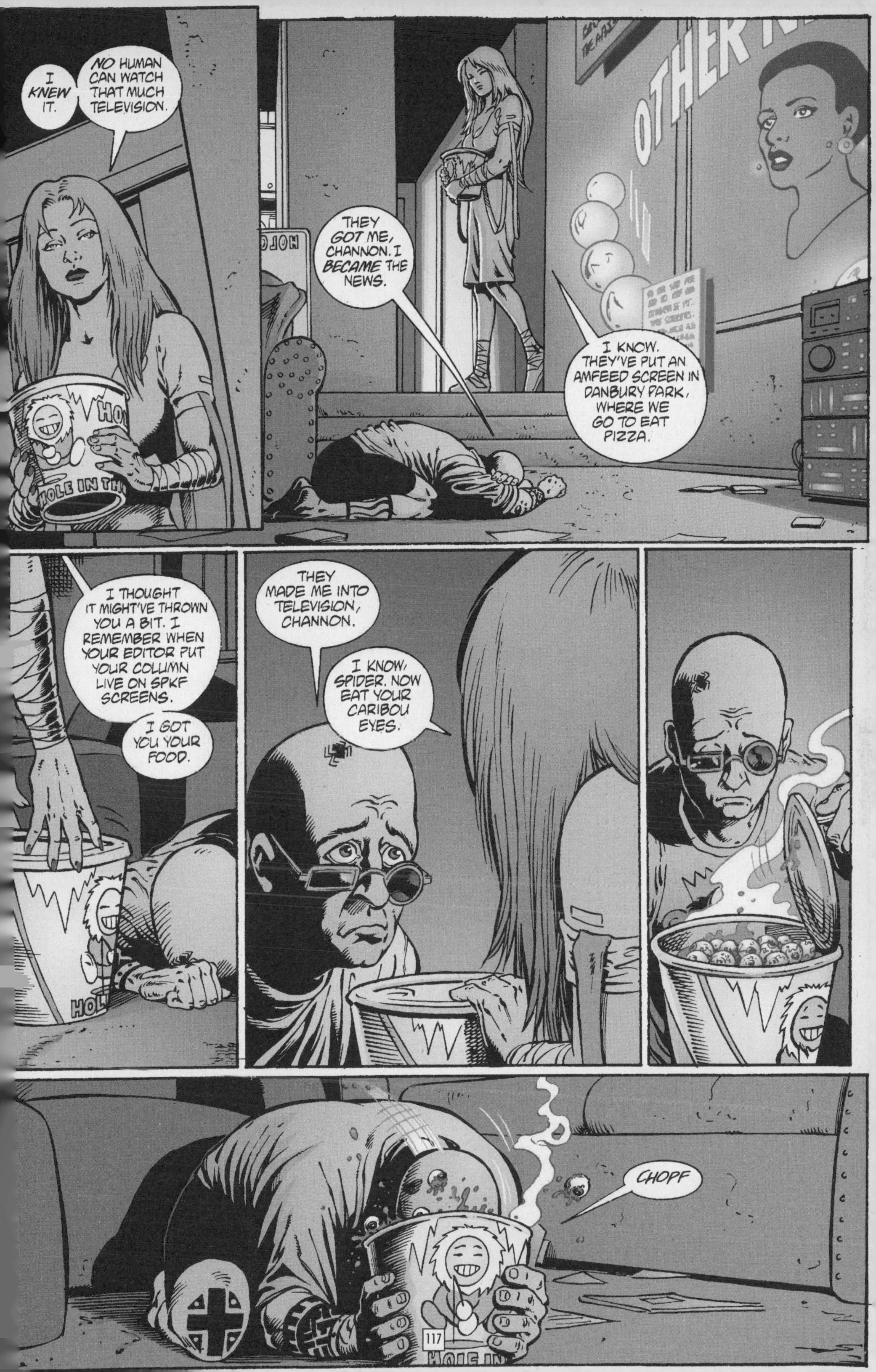
I KNEW IT.
NO HUMAN CAN WATCH THAT MUCH TELEVISION.
THEY GOT ME, CHANNON. I BECAME THE NEWS.
I KNOW. THEY'VE PUT AN AMFEED SCREEN IN DANBURY PARK, WHERE WE GO TO EAT PIZZA.
OTHER N
HOLE IN TH
I THOUGHT IT MIGHT'VE THROWN YOU A BIT. I REMEMBER WHEN YOUR EDITOR PUT YOUR COLUMN LIVE ON SPKF SCREENS.
I GOT YOU YOUR FOOD.
THEY MADE ME INTO TELEVISION, CHANNON.
I KNOW, SPIDER. NOW EAT YOUR CARIBOU EYES.
CHOPF
HOLE IN

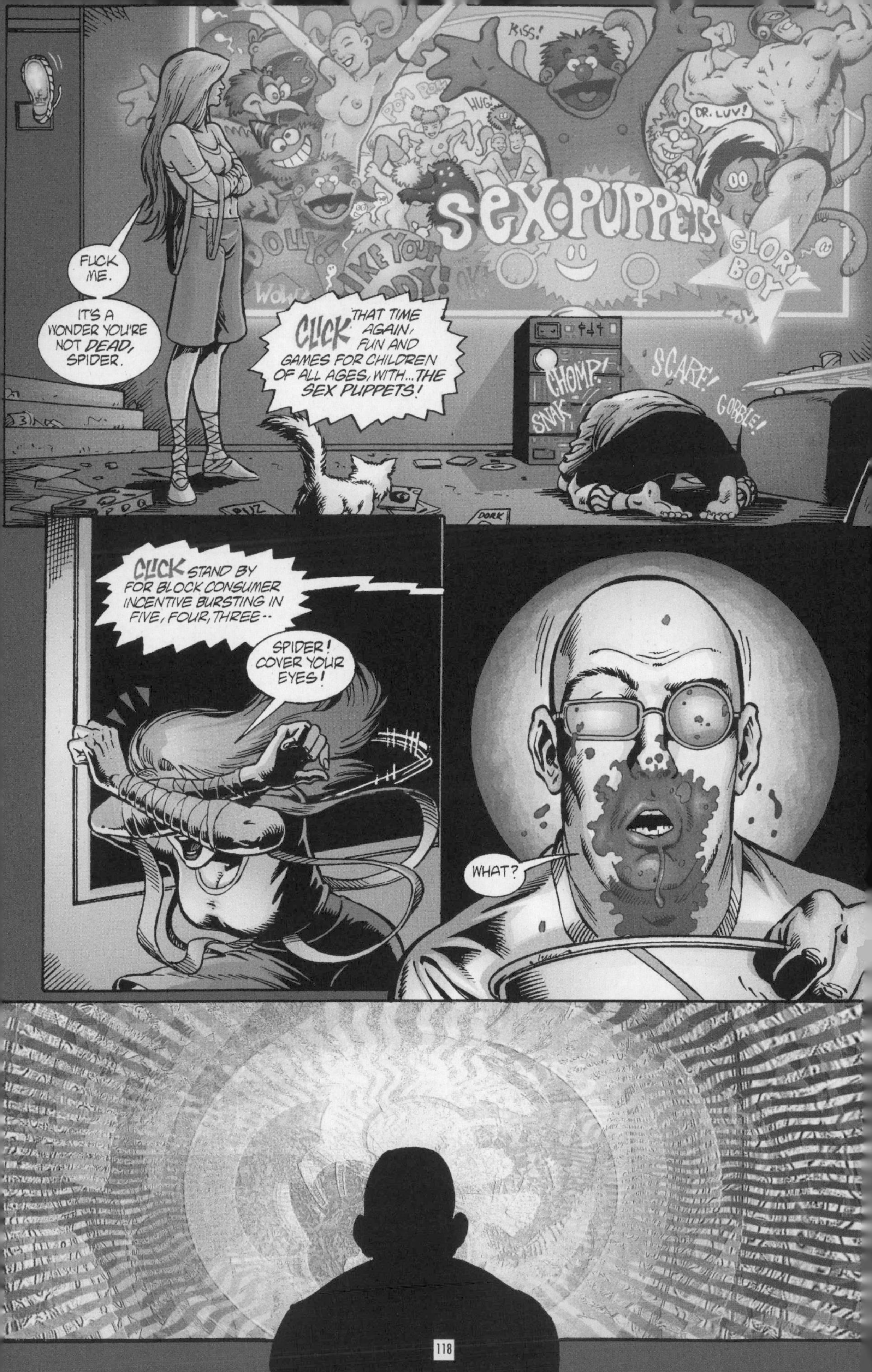
KISS!
POM POM
HUG!
DR. LUV!
SEX-PUPPETS
DOLLY!
GLORY BOY
FUCK ME.
IT'S A WONDER YOU'RE NOT DEAD, SPIDER.
CLICK THAT TIME AGAIN, FUN AND GAMES FOR CHILDREN OF ALL AGES, WITH... THE SEX PUPPETS!
CHOMP!
SNAK
SCARF!
GOBBLE!
PDQ
PUZ
DORK
CLICK STAND BY FOR BLOCK CONSUMER INCENTIVE BURSTING IN FIVE, FOUR, THREE--
SPIDER! COVER YOUR EYES!
WHAT?

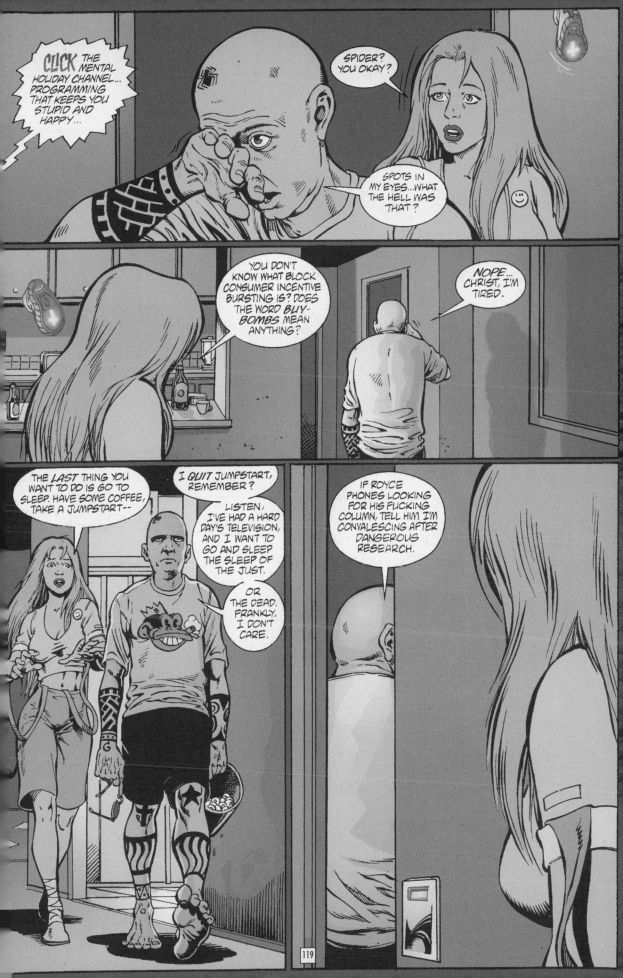

CLICK THE MENTAL HOLIDAY CHANNEL... PROGRAMMING THAT KEEPS YOU STUPID AND HAPPY...

SPIDER? YOU OKAY?

SPOTS IN MY EYES...WHAT THE HELL WAS THAT?

YOU DON'T KNOW WHAT BLOCK CONSUMER INCENTIVE BURSTING IS? DOES THE WORD BUY-BOMBS MEAN ANYTHING?

NOPE... CHRIST, I'M TIRED.

THE LAST THING YOU WANT TO DO IS GO TO SLEEP. HAVE SOME COFFEE, TAKE A JUMPSTART--

I QUIT JUMPSTART, REMEMBER?

LISTEN, I'VE HAD A HARD DAY'S TELEVISION, AND I WANT TO GO AND SLEEP THE SLEEP OF THE JUST.

OR THE DEAD. FRANKLY, I DON'T CARE.

IF ROYCE PHONES LOOKING FOR HIS FUCKING COLUMN, TELL HIM I'M CONVALESCING AFTER DANGEROUS RESEARCH.

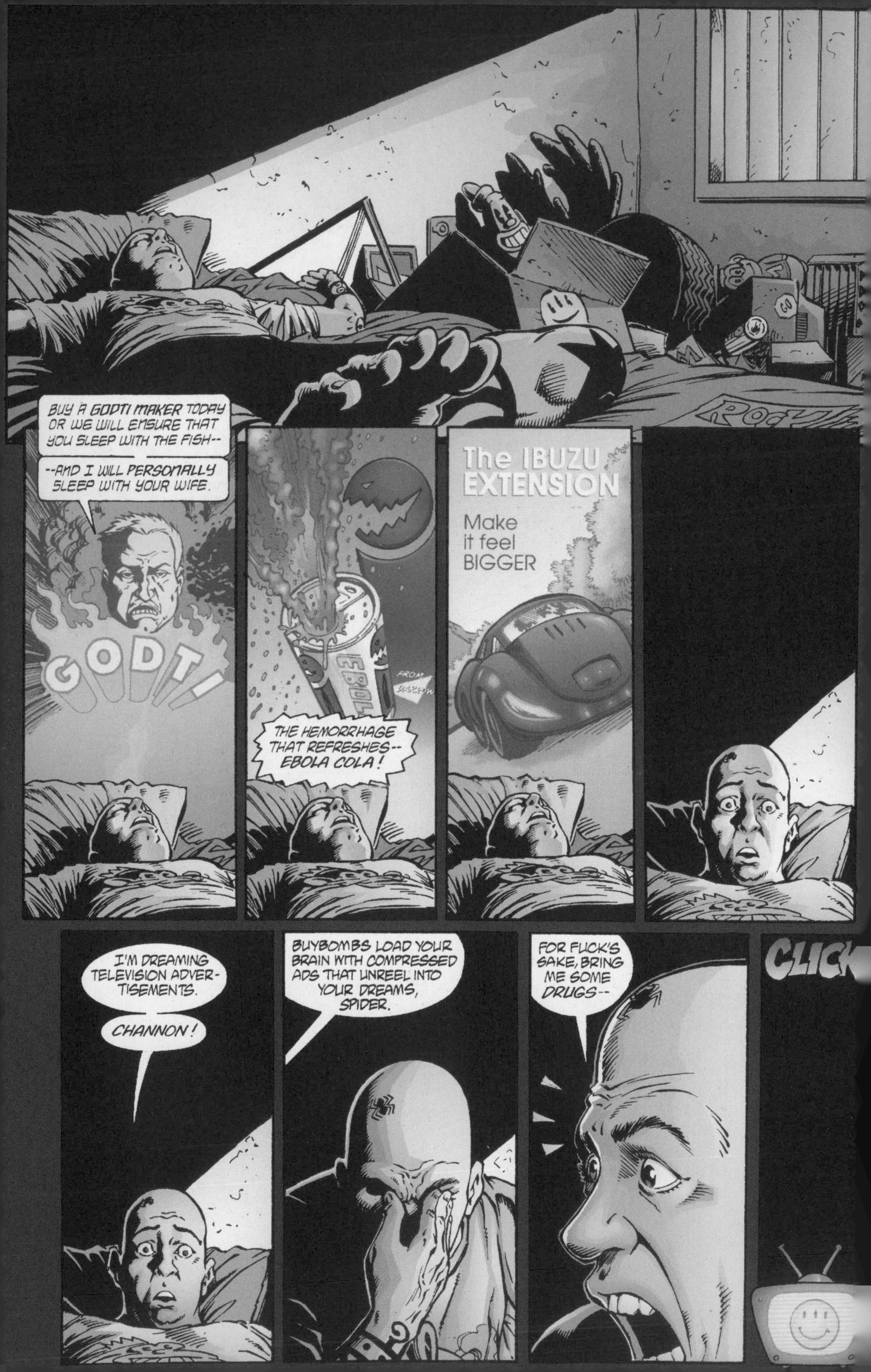

BUY A GODTI MAKER TODAY OR WE WILL ENSURE THAT YOU SLEEP WITH THE FISH--
--AND I WILL PERSONALLY SLEEP WITH YOUR WIFE.
GODTI
EBOLA
THE HEMORRHAGE THAT REFRESHES-- EBOLA COLA!
The IBUZU EXTENSION
Make it feel BIGGER
I'M DREAMING TELEVISION ADVERTISEMENTS.
CHANNON!
BUYBOMBS LOAD YOUR BRAIN WITH COMPRESSED ADS THAT UNREEL INTO YOUR DREAMS, SPIDER.
FOR FUCK'S SAKE, BRING ME SOME DRUGS--
CLICK

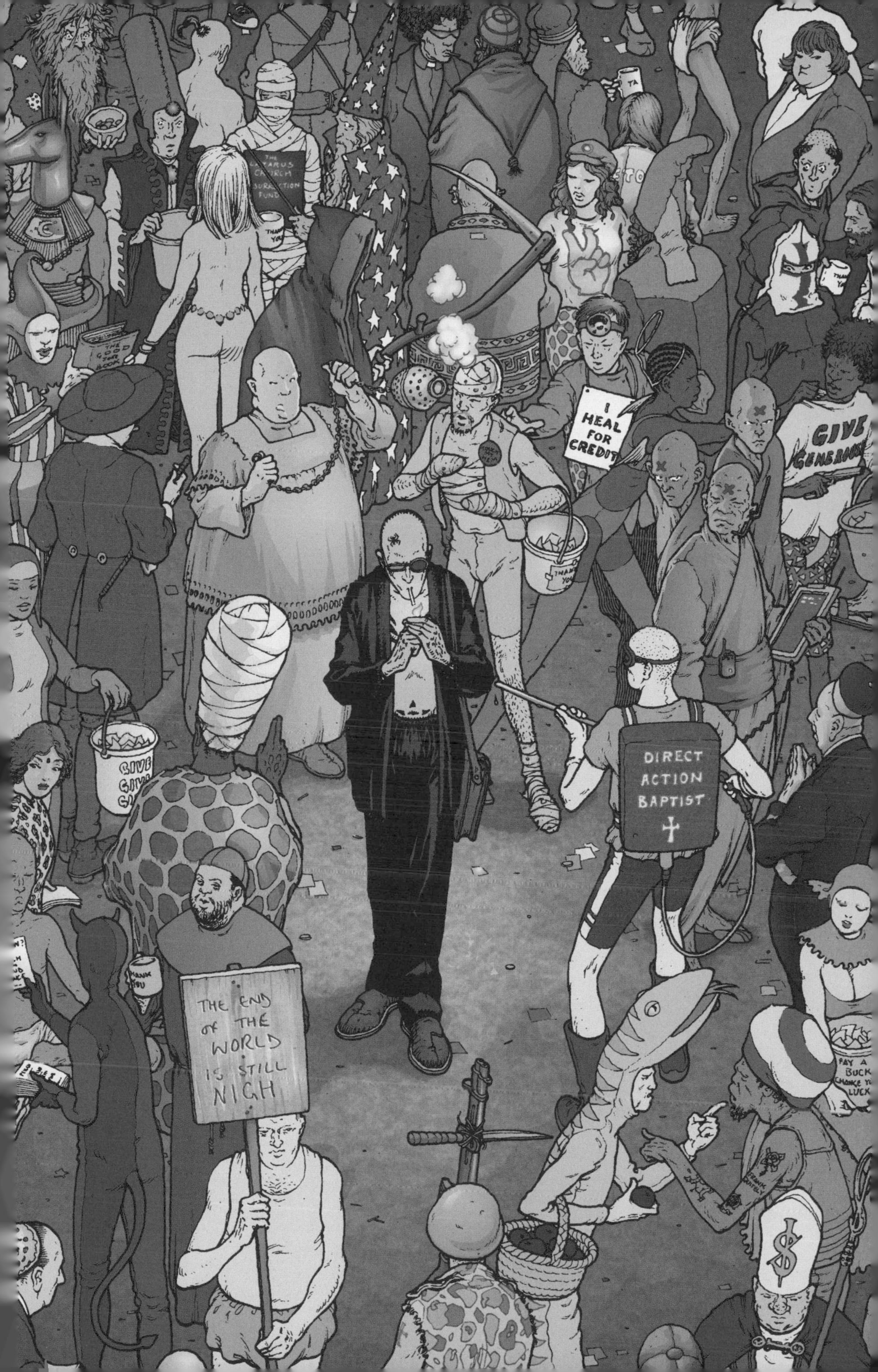
THE GOOD BOOK
I HEAL FOR CREDIT
GIVE
THANK YOU
DIRECT ACTION BAPTIST
THE END OF THE WORLD IS STILL NIGH
PAY A BUCK

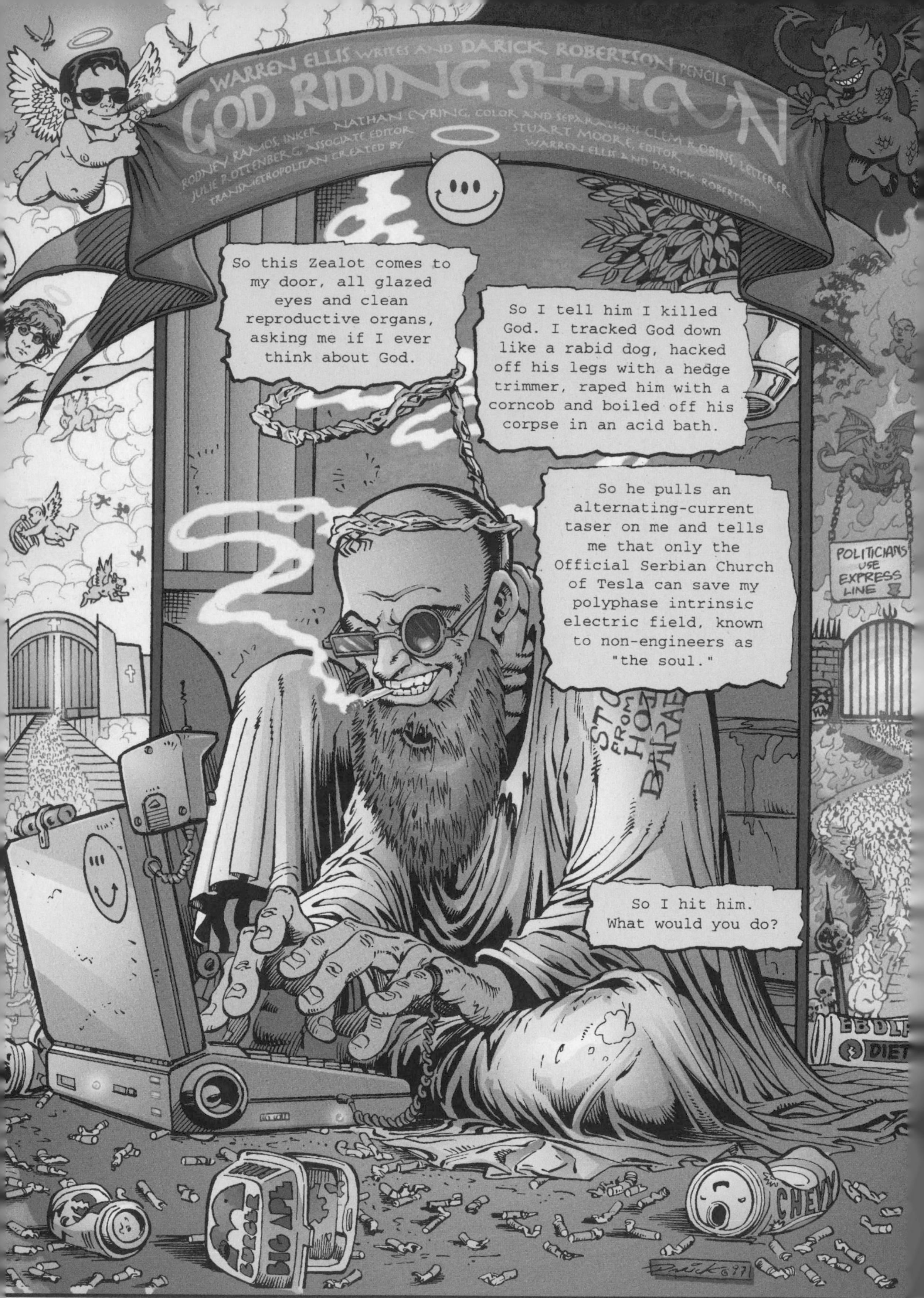

WARREN ELLIS WRITES AND DARICK ROBERTSON PENCILS
GOD RIDING SHOTGUN
RODNEY RAMOS, INKER NATHAN EYRING, COLOR AND SEPARATIONS CLEM ROBINS, LETTERER
JULIE ROTTENBERG, ASSOCIATE EDITOR STUART MOORE, EDITOR
TRANSMETROPOLITAN CREATED BY WARREN ELLIS AND DARICK ROBERTSON
So this Zealot comes to my door, all glazed eyes and clean reproductive organs, asking me if I ever think about God.
So I tell him I killed God. I tracked God down like a rabid dog, hacked off his legs with a hedge trimmer, raped him with a corncob and boiled off his corpse in an acid bath.
So he pulls an alternating-current taser on me and tells me that only the Official Serbian Church of Tesla can save my polyphase intrinsic electric field, known to non-engineers as "the soul."
POLITICIANS USE EXPRESS LINE
So I hit him. What would you do?
CHEVY

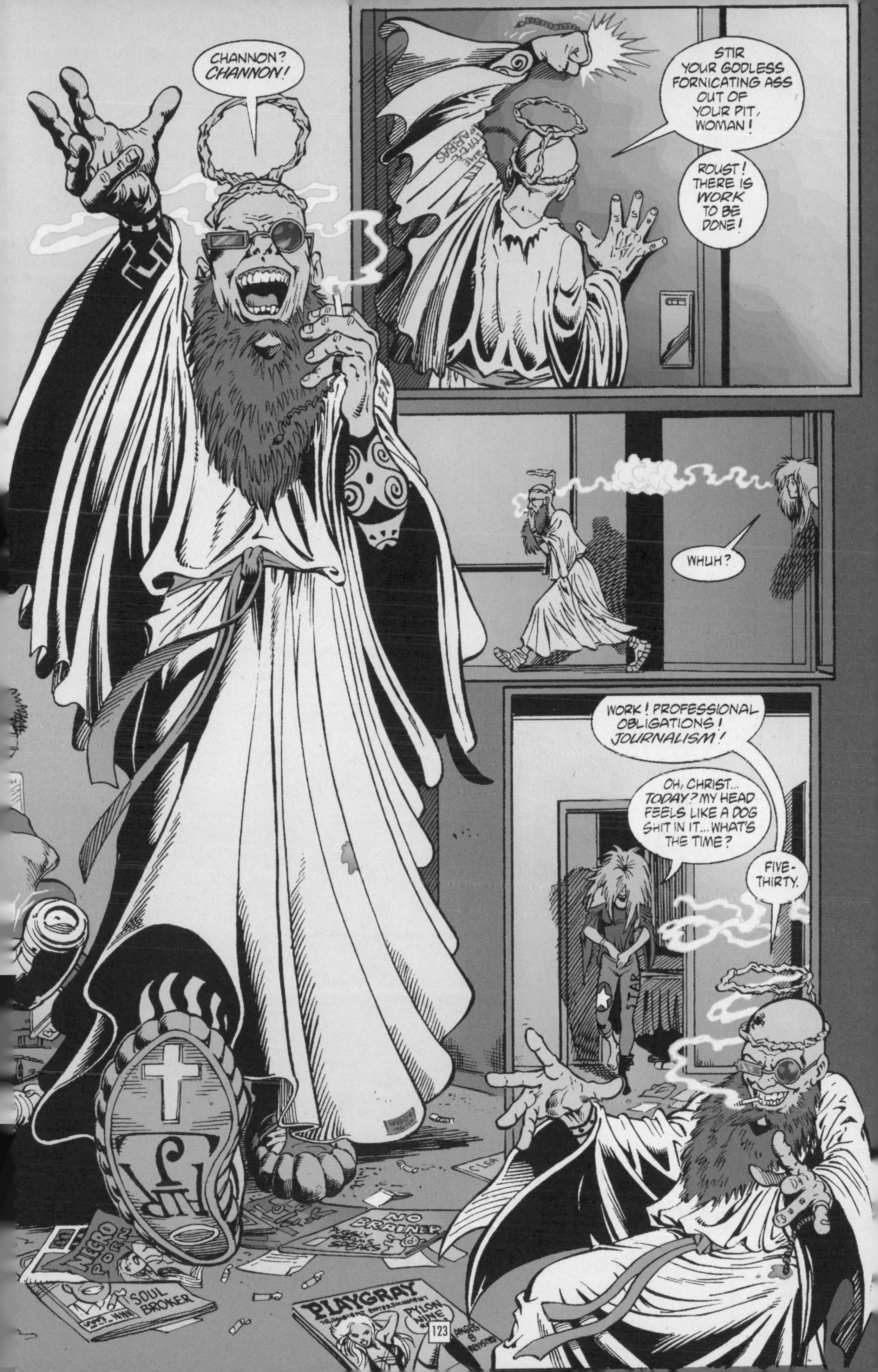
CHANNON? CHANNON!
STIR YOUR GODLESS FORNICATING ASS OUT OF YOUR PIT, WOMAN!
ROUST! THERE IS WORK TO BE DONE!
WHUH?
WORK! PROFESSIONAL OBLIGATIONS! JOURNALISM!
OH, CHRIST... TODAY? MY HEAD FEELS LIKE A DOG SHIT IN IT... WHAT'S THE TIME?
FIVE-THIRTY.
NO BRAINER
NECRO PORN
SOUL BROKER
PLAYGRAY
PYLON NINE
STAR

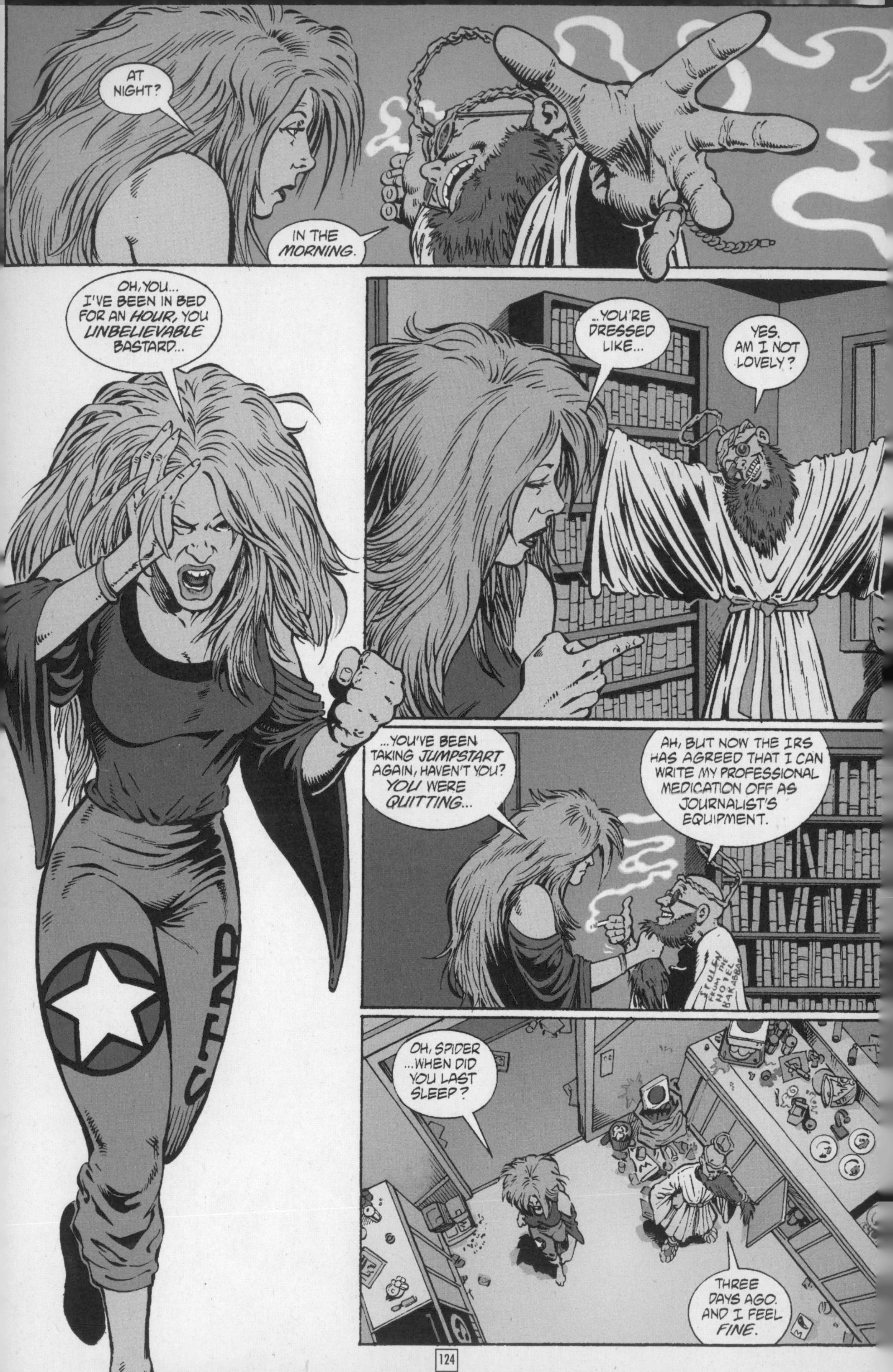
AT NIGHT?
IN THE MORNING.
OH, YOU... I'VE BEEN IN BED FOR AN HOUR, YOU UNBELIEVABLE BASTARD...
...YOU'RE DRESSED LIKE...
YES. AM I NOT LOVELY?
...YOU'VE BEEN TAKING JUMPSTART AGAIN, HAVEN'T YOU? YOU WERE QUITTING...
AH, BUT NOW THE IRS HAS AGREED THAT I CAN WRITE MY PROFESSIONAL MEDICATION OFF AS JOURNALIST'S EQUIPMENT.
STOLEN FROM THE HOTEL BAKABAKA
STAR
OH, SPIDER ...WHEN DID YOU LAST SLEEP?
THREE DAYS AGO. AND I FEEL FINE.

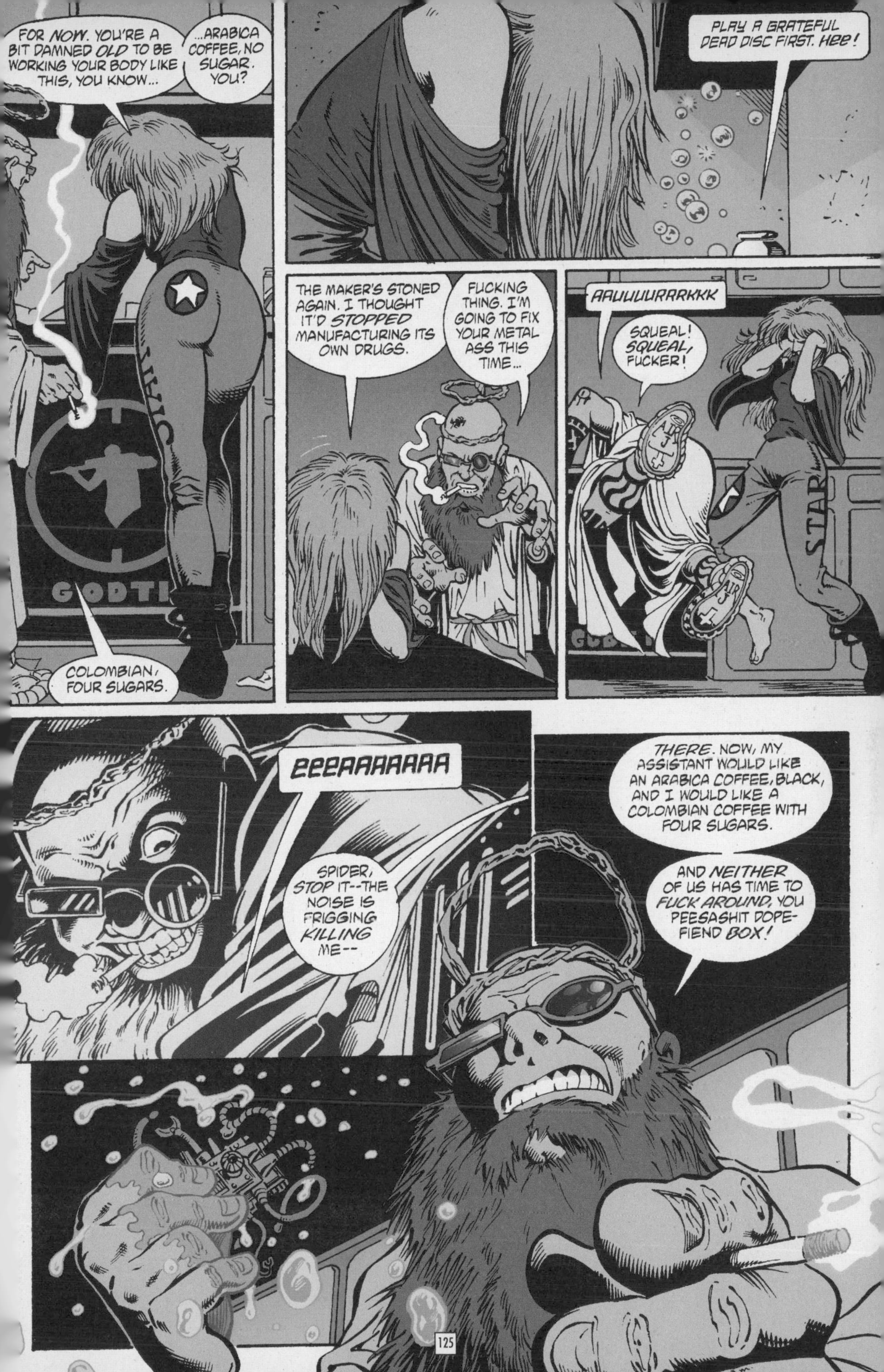
FOR NOW. YOU'RE A BIT DAMNED OLD TO BE WORKING YOUR BODY LIKE THIS, YOU KNOW...
...ARABICA COFFEE, NO SUGAR. YOU?
COLOMBIAN, FOUR SUGARS.
PLAY A GRATEFUL DEAD DISC FIRST. HEE!
THE MAKER'S STONED AGAIN. I THOUGHT IT'D STOPPED MANUFACTURING ITS OWN DRUGS.
FUCKING THING. I'M GOING TO FIX YOUR METAL ASS THIS TIME...
AAUUUURRRKKK
SQUEAL! SQUEAL, FUCKER!
EEEAAAAAAAA
SPIDER, STOP IT--THE NOISE IS FRIGGING KILLING ME--
THERE. NOW, MY ASSISTANT WOULD LIKE AN ARABICA COFFEE, BLACK, AND I WOULD LIKE A COLOMBIAN COFFEE WITH FOUR SUGARS.
AND NEITHER OF US HAS TIME TO FUCK AROUND, YOU PEESASHIT DOPE-FIEND BOX!

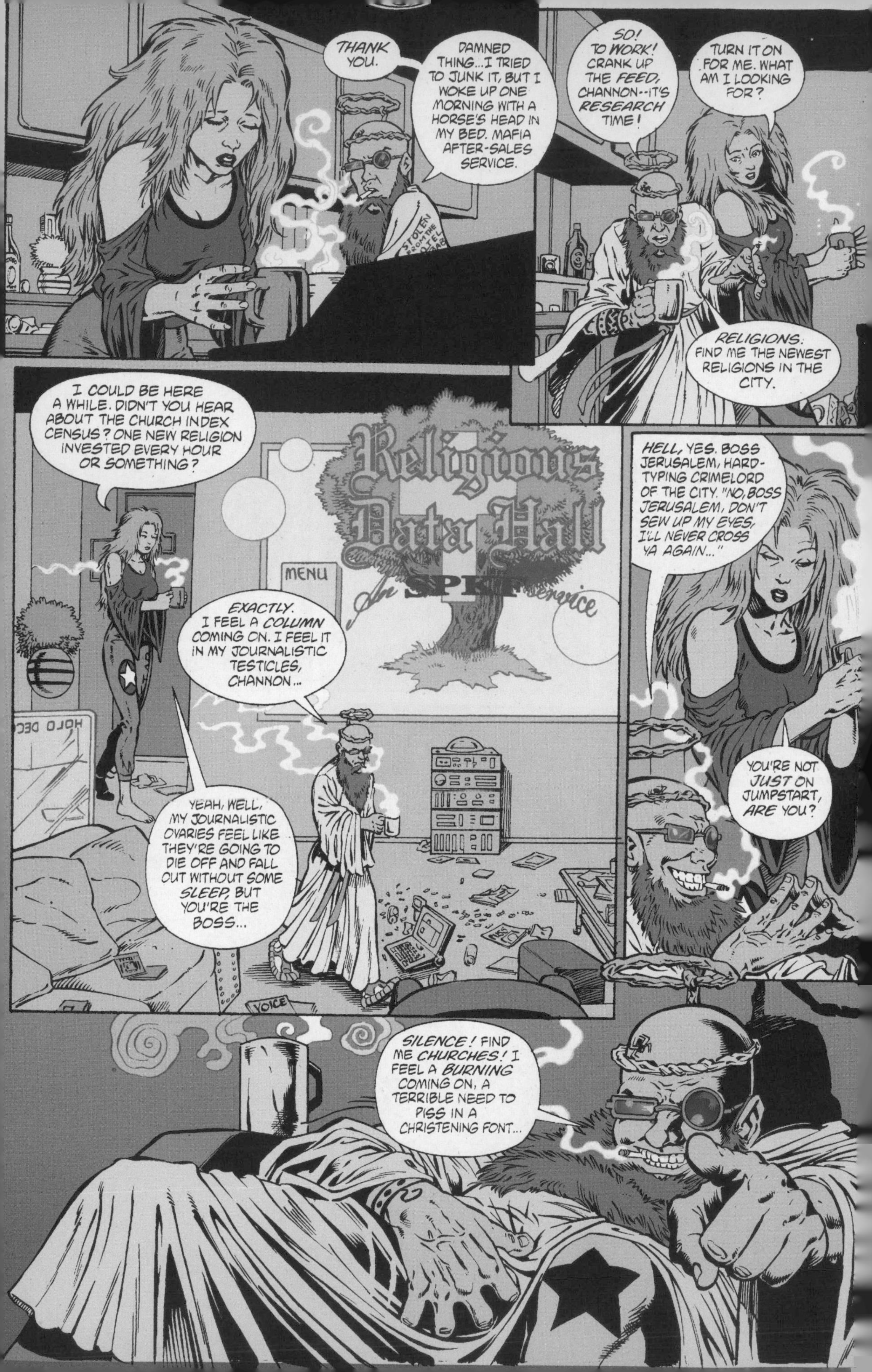
THANK YOU.
DAMNED THING...I TRIED TO JUNK IT, BUT I WOKE UP ONE MORNING WITH A HORSE'S HEAD IN MY BED. MAFIA AFTER-SALES SERVICE.
SO! TO WORK! CRANK UP THE FEED, CHANNON--IT'S RESEARCH TIME!
TURN IT ON FOR ME. WHAT AM I LOOKING FOR?
RELIGIONS: FIND ME THE NEWEST RELIGIONS IN THE CITY.
I COULD BE HERE A WHILE. DIDN'T YOU HEAR ABOUT THE CHURCH INDEX CENSUS? ONE NEW RELIGION INVESTED EVERY HOUR OR SOMETHING?
Religious Data Hall
An SPKF service
MENU
EXACTLY. I FEEL A COLUMN COMING ON. I FEEL IT IN MY JOURNALISTIC TESTICLES, CHANNON...
YEAH, WELL, MY JOURNALISTIC OVARIES FEEL LIKE THEY'RE GOING TO DIE OFF AND FALL OUT WITHOUT SOME SLEEP, BUT YOU'RE THE BOSS...
HELL, YES. BOSS JERUSALEM, HARD-TYPING CRIMELORD OF THE CITY. "NO, BOSS JERUSALEM, DON'T SEW UP MY EYES, I'LL NEVER CROSS YA AGAIN..."
YOU'RE NOT JUST ON JUMPSTART, ARE YOU?
VOICE
SILENCE! FIND ME CHURCHES! I FEEL A BURNING COMING ON, A TERRIBLE NEED TO PISS IN A CHRISTENING FONT...

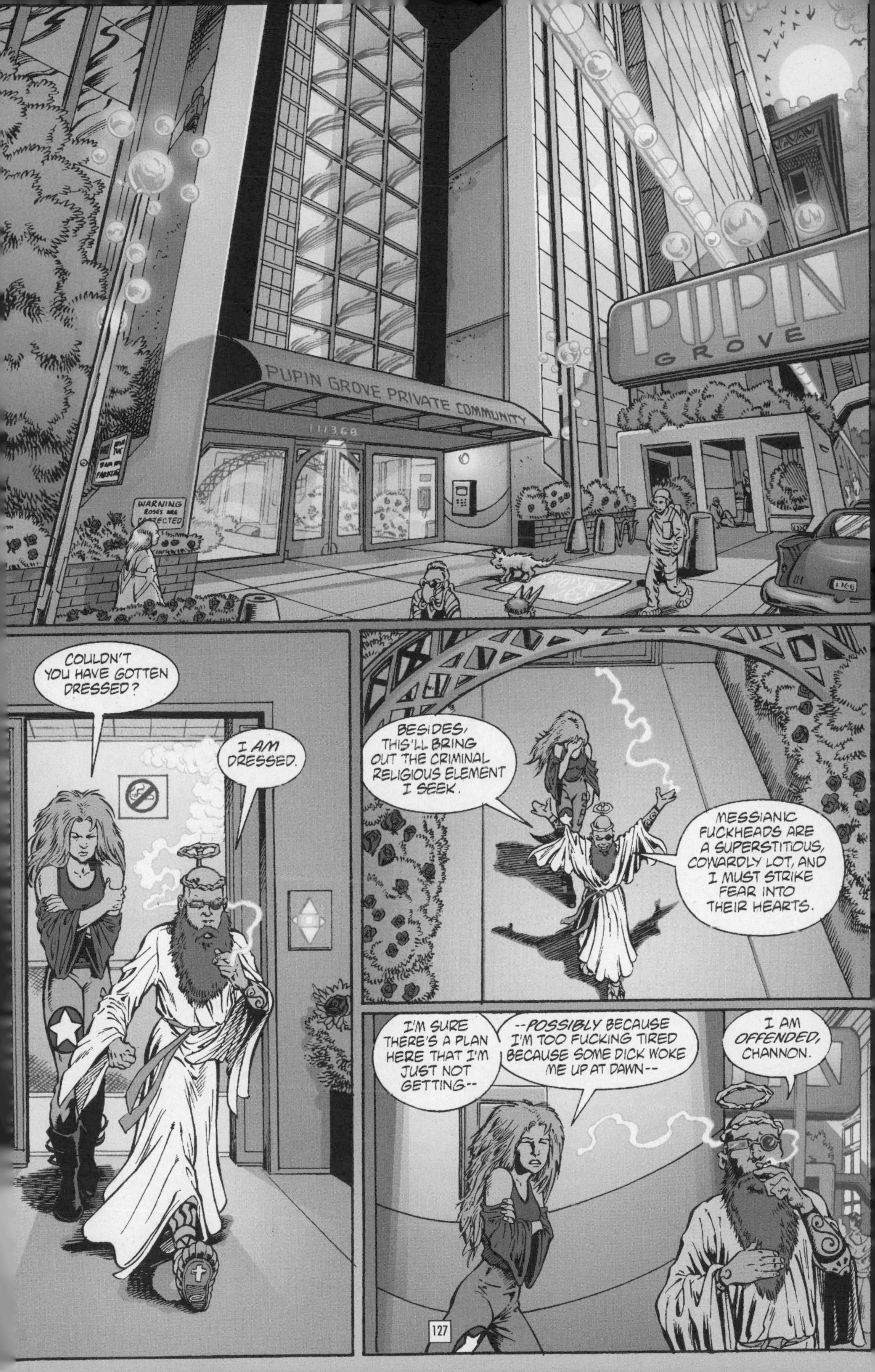
PUPIN GROVE PRIVATE COMMUNITY
111368
PUPIN
GROVE
WARNING
COULDN'T YOU HAVE GOTTEN DRESSED?
I AM DRESSED.
BESIDES, THIS'LL BRING OUT THE CRIMINAL RELIGIOUS ELEMENT I SEEK.
MESSIANIC FUCKHEADS ARE A SUPERSTITIOUS, COWARDLY LOT, AND I MUST STRIKE FEAR INTO THEIR HEARTS.
I'M SURE THERE'S A PLAN HERE THAT I'M JUST NOT GETTING--
--POSSIBLY BECAUSE I'M TOO FUCKING TIRED BECAUSE SOME DICK WOKE ME UP AT DAWN--
I AM OFFENDED, CHANNON.

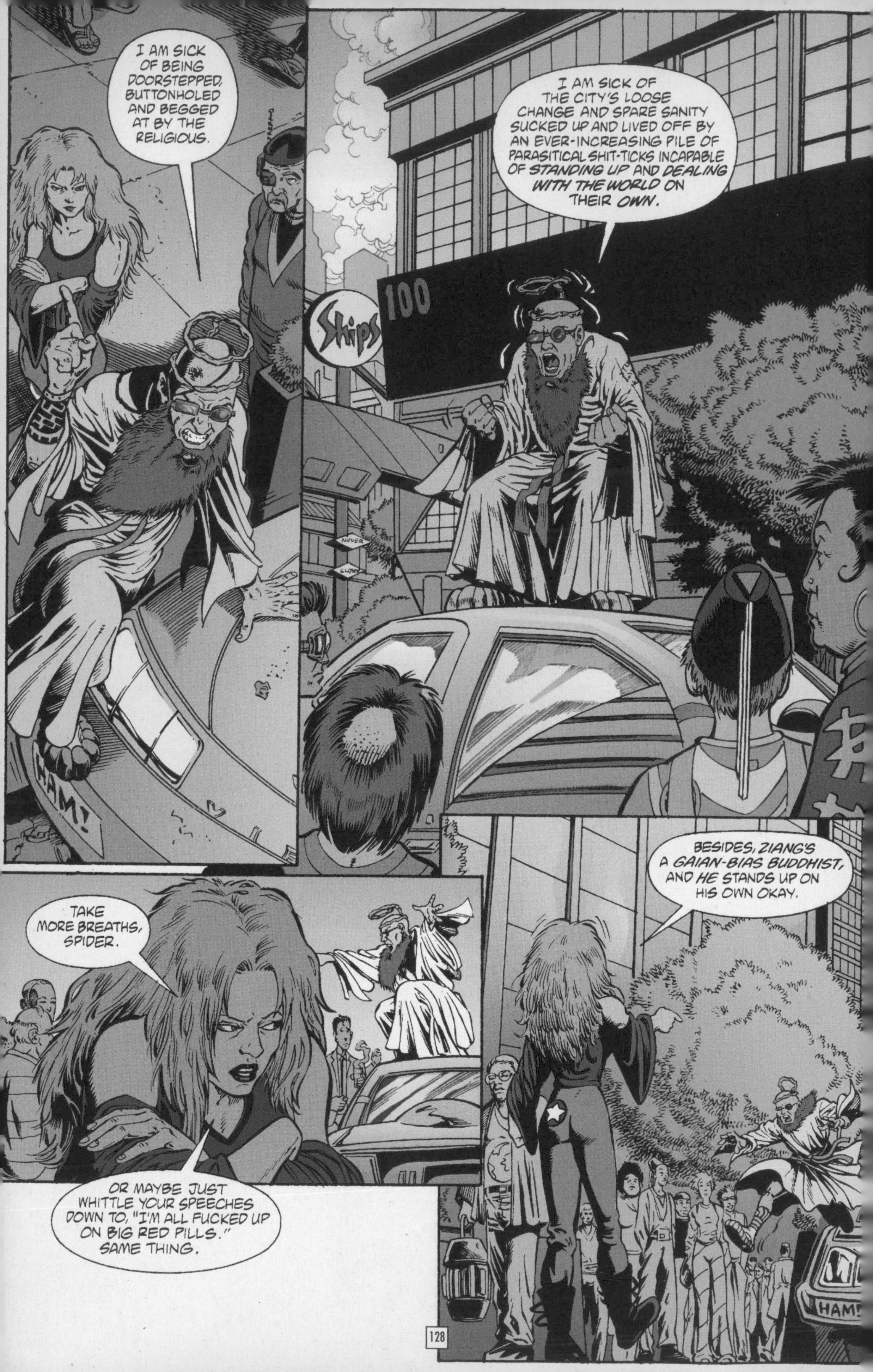
I AM SICK OF BEING DOORSTEPPED, BUTTONHOLED AND BEGGED AT BY THE RELIGIOUS.
I AM SICK OF THE CITY'S LOOSE CHANGE AND SPARE SANITY SUCKED UP AND LIVED OFF BY AN EVER-INCREASING PILE OF PARASITICAL SHIT-TICKS INCAPABLE OF STANDING UP AND DEALING WITH THE WORLD ON THEIR OWN.
100
Ships
HAM!
TAKE MORE BREATHS, SPIDER.
OR MAYBE JUST WHITTLE YOUR SPEECHES DOWN TO, "I'M ALL FUCKED UP ON BIG RED PILLS." SAME THING.
BESIDES, ZIANG'S A GAIAN-BIAS BUDDHIST, AND HE STANDS UP ON HIS OWN OKAY.
HAM!

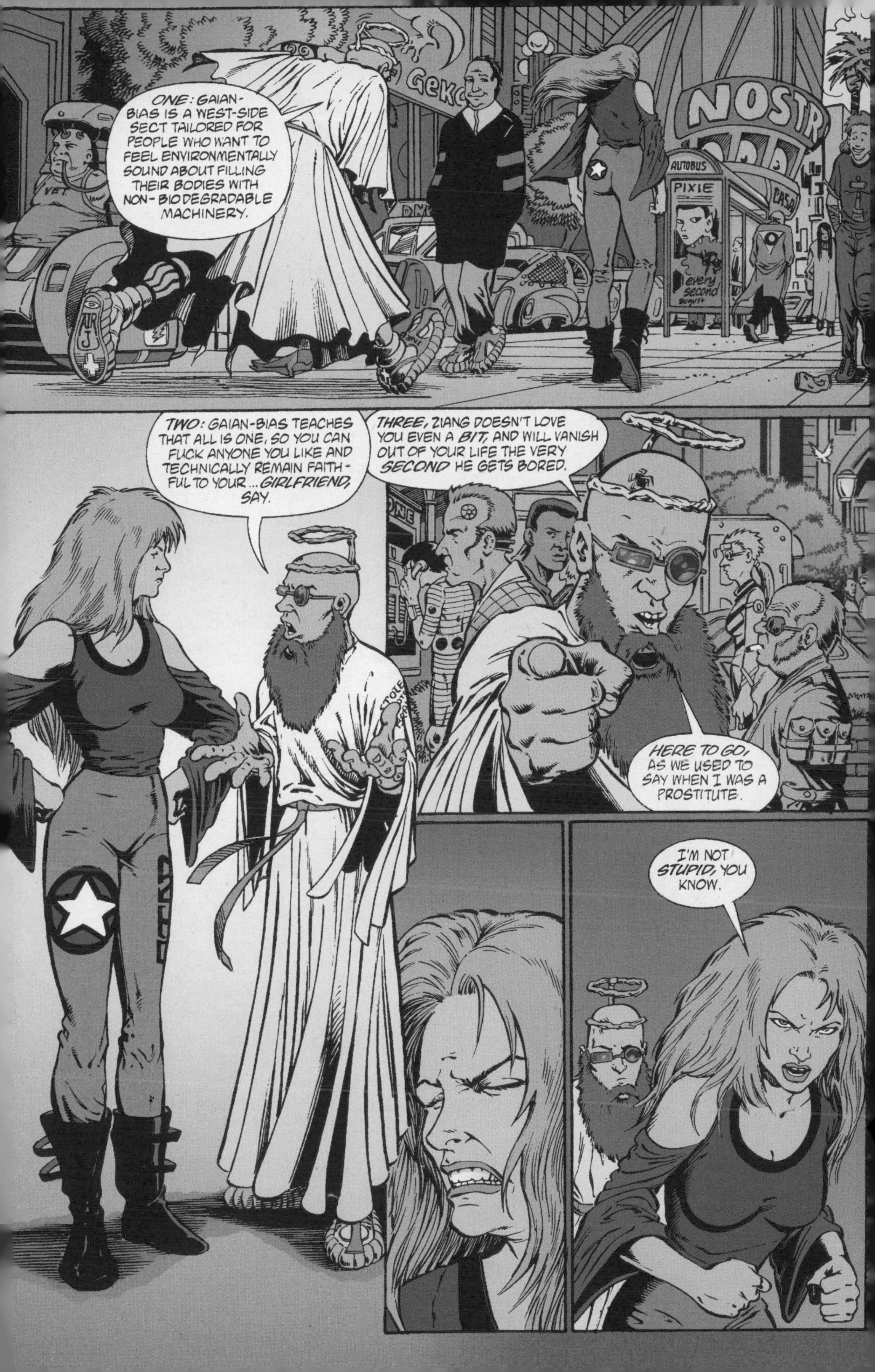
ONE: GAIAN-BIAS IS A WEST-SIDE SECT TAILORED FOR PEOPLE WHO WANT TO FEEL ENVIRONMENTALLY SOUND ABOUT FILLING THEIR BODIES WITH NON-BIODEGRADABLE MACHINERY.
NOSTR
AUTOBUS
PIXIE
every second
TWO: GAIAN-BIAS TEACHES THAT ALL IS ONE, SO YOU CAN FUCK ANYONE YOU LIKE AND TECHNICALLY REMAIN FAITH-FUL TO YOUR ...GIRLFRIEND, SAY.
THREE, ZIANG DOESN'T LOVE YOU EVEN A BIT, AND WILL VANISH OUT OF YOUR LIFE THE VERY SECOND HE GETS BORED.
HERE TO GO, AS WE USED TO SAY WHEN I WAS A PROSTITUTE.
I'M NOT STUPID, YOU KNOW.

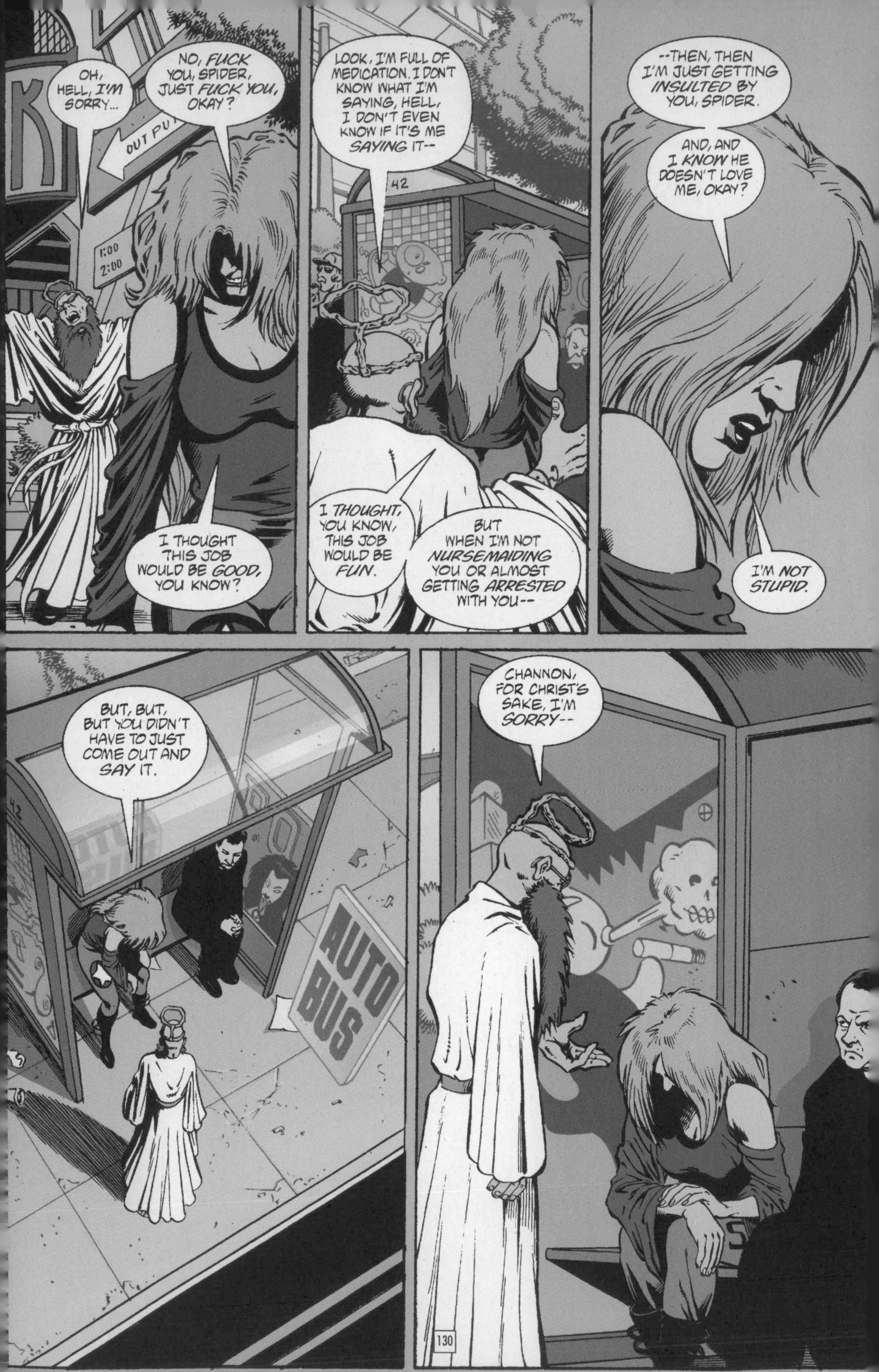
OH, HELL, I'M SORRY...
NO, FUCK YOU, SPIDER, JUST FUCK YOU, OKAY?
OUT PUT
1:00
2:00
I THOUGHT THIS JOB WOULD BE GOOD, YOU KNOW?
LOOK, I'M FULL OF MEDICATION. I DON'T KNOW WHAT I'M SAYING, HELL, I DON'T EVEN KNOW IF IT'S ME SAYING IT--
42
I THOUGHT, YOU KNOW, THIS JOB WOULD BE FUN.
BUT WHEN I'M NOT NURSEMAIDING YOU OR ALMOST GETTING ARRESTED WITH YOU--
--THEN, THEN I'M JUST GETTING INSULTED BY YOU, SPIDER.
AND, AND I KNOW HE DOESN'T LOVE ME, OKAY?
I'M NOT STUPID.
BUT, BUT, BUT YOU DIDN'T HAVE TO JUST COME OUT AND SAY IT.
42
AUTO BUS
CHANNON, FOR CHRIST'S SAKE, I'M SORRY--

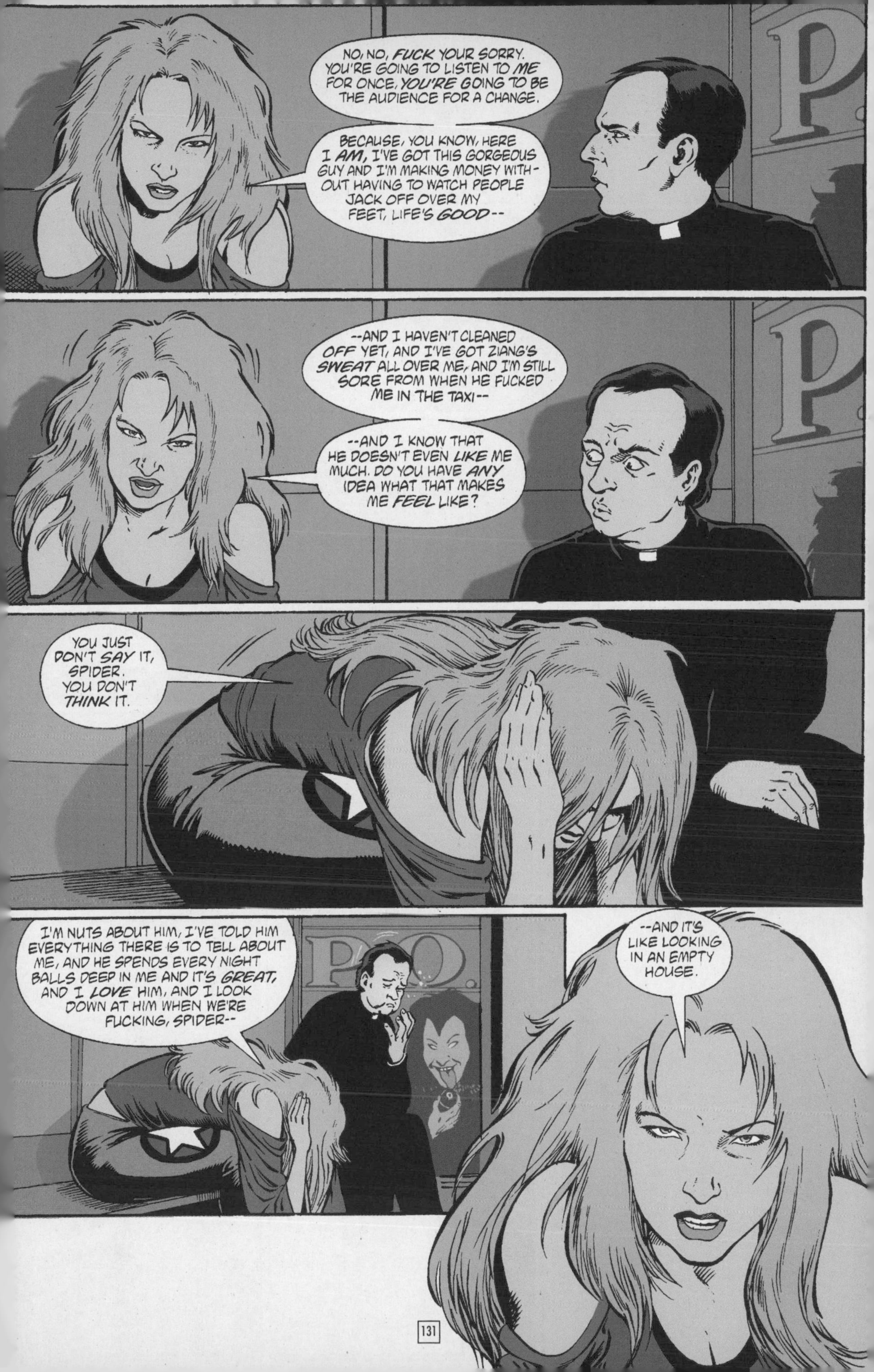
NO, NO, *FUCK* YOUR SORRY. YOU'RE GOING TO LISTEN TO *ME* FOR ONCE. *YOU'RE* GOING TO BE THE AUDIENCE FOR A CHANGE.
BECAUSE, YOU KNOW, HERE I *AM*, I'VE GOT THIS GORGEOUS GUY AND I'M MAKING MONEY WITH-OUT HAVING TO WATCH PEOPLE JACK OFF OVER MY FEET, LIFE'S *GOOD*--
--AND I HAVEN'T CLEANED *OFF* YET, AND I'VE GOT ZIANG'S *SWEAT* ALL OVER ME, AND I'M STILL SORE FROM WHEN HE FUCKED ME IN THE TAXI--
--AND I KNOW THAT HE DOESN'T EVEN *LIKE* ME MUCH. DO YOU HAVE *ANY* IDEA WHAT THAT MAKES ME *FEEL* LIKE?
YOU JUST DON'T *SAY* IT, SPIDER. YOU DON'T *THINK* IT.
I'M NUTS ABOUT HIM, I'VE TOLD HIM EVERYTHING THERE IS TO TELL ABOUT ME, AND HE SPENDS EVERY NIGHT BALLS DEEP IN ME AND IT'S *GREAT*, AND I *LOVE* HIM, AND I LOOK DOWN AT HIM WHEN WE'RE FUCKING, SPIDER--
--AND IT'S LIKE LOOKING IN AN EMPTY HOUSE.

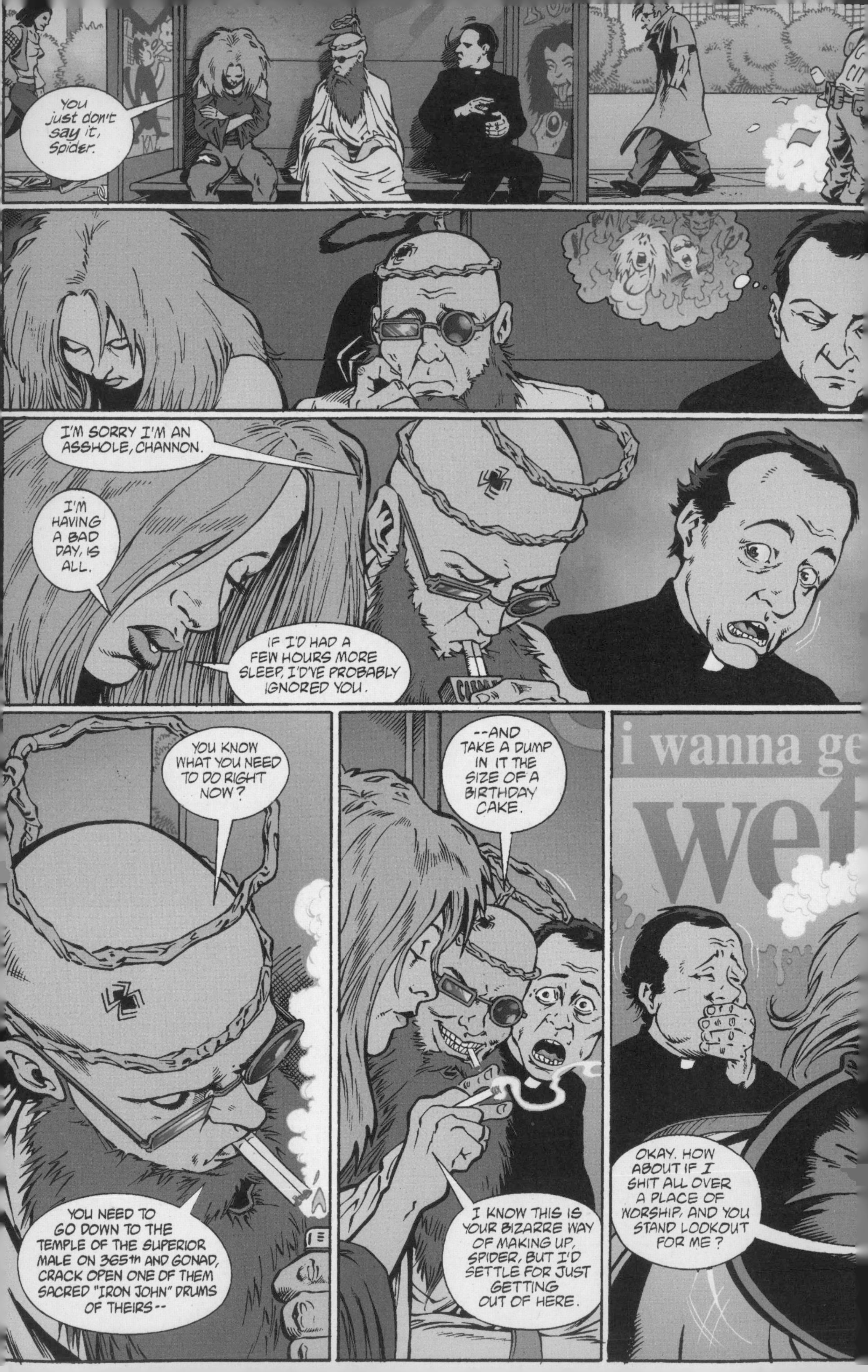
You just don't say it, Spider.
I'M SORRY I'M AN ASSHOLE, CHANNON.
I'M HAVING A BAD DAY, IS ALL.
IF I'D HAD A FEW HOURS MORE SLEEP, I'D'VE PROBABLY IGNORED YOU.
YOU KNOW WHAT YOU NEED TO DO RIGHT NOW?
YOU NEED TO GO DOWN TO THE TEMPLE OF THE SUPERIOR MALE ON 365th AND GONAD, CRACK OPEN ONE OF THEM SACRED "IRON JOHN" DRUMS OF THEIRS--
--AND TAKE A DUMP IN IT THE SIZE OF A BIRTHDAY CAKE.
I KNOW THIS IS YOUR BIZARRE WAY OF MAKING UP, SPIDER, BUT I'D SETTLE FOR JUST GETTING OUT OF HERE.
i wanna ge
wet
OKAY. HOW ABOUT IF I SHIT ALL OVER A PLACE OF WORSHIP, AND YOU STAND LOOKOUT FOR ME?

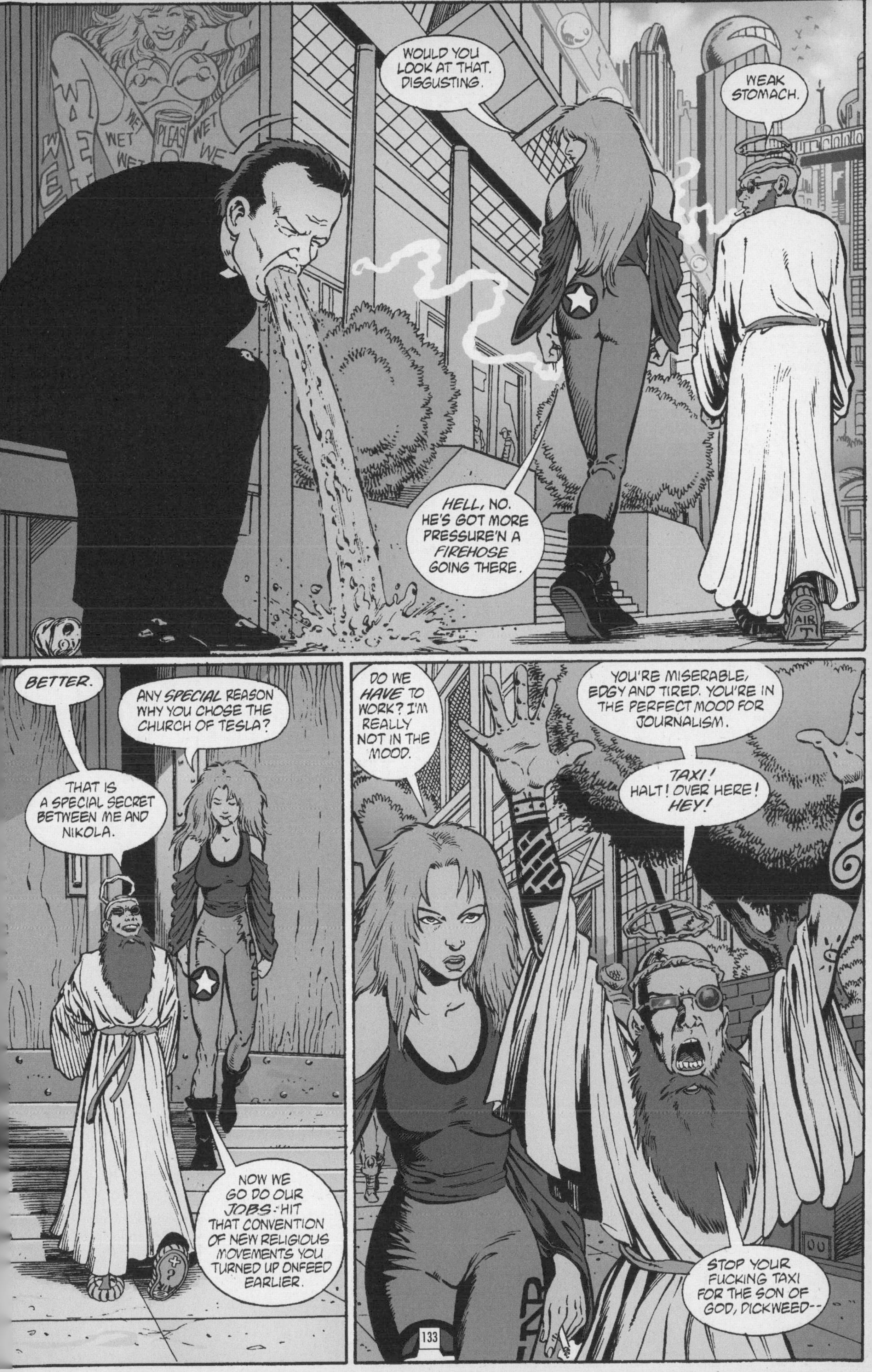
WOULD YOU LOOK AT THAT. DISGUSTING.
WEAK STOMACH.
HELL, NO. HE'S GOT MORE PRESSURE'N A FIREHOSE GOING THERE.
BETTER.
ANY SPECIAL REASON WHY YOU CHOSE THE CHURCH OF TESLA?
THAT IS A SPECIAL SECRET BETWEEN ME AND NIKOLA.
NOW WE GO DO OUR JOBS: HIT THAT CONVENTION OF NEW RELIGIOUS MOVEMENTS YOU TURNED UP ONFEED EARLIER.
DO WE HAVE TO WORK? I'M REALLY NOT IN THE MOOD.
YOU'RE MISERABLE, EDGY AND TIRED. YOU'RE IN THE PERFECT MOOD FOR JOURNALISM.
TAXI! HALT! OVER HERE! HEY!
STOP YOUR FUCKING TAXI FOR THE SON OF GOD, DICKWEED--

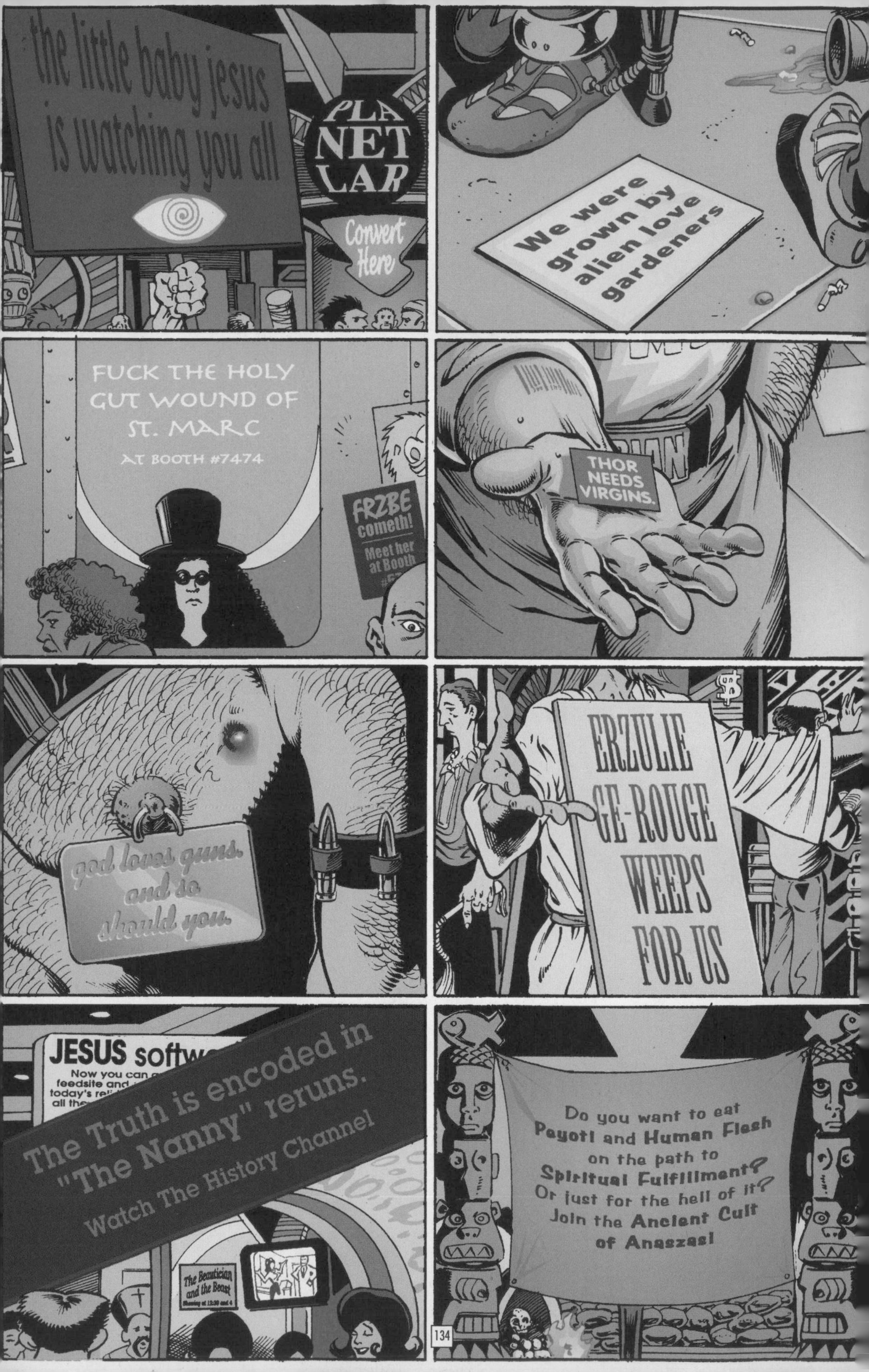

the little baby jesus is watching you all
PLA NET LAR
Convert Here
We were grown by alien love gardeners
FUCK THE HOLY GUT WOUND OF ST. MARC
AT BOOTH #7474
FRZBE cometh!
Meet her at Booth
THOR NEEDS VIRGINS.
god loves guns. and so should you.
ERZULIE GE-ROUGE WEEPS FOR US
JESUS softw
Now you can
feedsite and
today's reli
all the
The Truth is encoded in "The Nanny" reruns.
Watch The History Channel
The Beautician and the Beast
Do you want to eat Peyotl and Human Flesh on the path to Spiritual Fulfillment? Or just for the hell of it? Join the Ancient Cult of Anaszasi

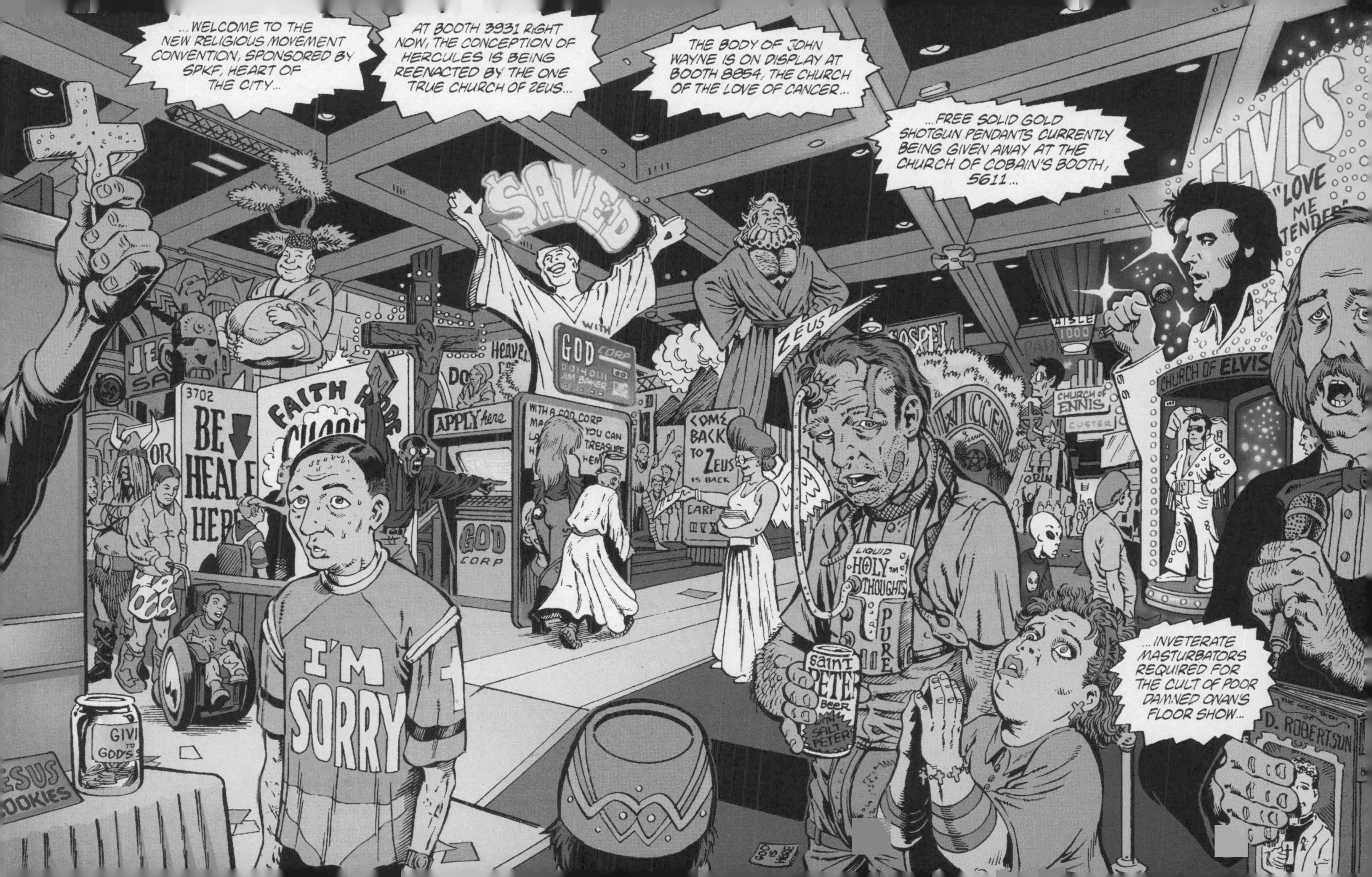
...WELCOME TO THE NEW RELIGIOUS MOVEMENT CONVENTION, SPONSORED BY SPKF, HEART OF THE CITY...
AT BOOTH 3931 RIGHT NOW, THE CONCEPTION OF HERCULES IS BEING REENACTED BY THE ONE TRUE CHURCH OF ZEUS...
THE BODY OF JOHN WAYNE IS ON DISPLAY AT BOOTH 8854, THE CHURCH OF THE LOVE OF CANCER...
...FREE SOLID GOLD SHOTGUN PENDANTS CURRENTLY BEING GIVEN AWAY AT THE CHURCH OF COBAIN'S BOOTH, 5611...
...INVETERATE MASTURBATORS REQUIRED FOR THE CULT OF POOR DAMNED ONAN'S FLOOR SHOW...
SAVED
ELVIS
"LOVE ME TENDER"
GOD CORP
JIM BAKER
3702
BE HEALED HERE
FAITH
APPLY here
WITH A GOD CORP
YOU CAN TREASURE
GOD CORP
COME BACK TO ZEUS
ZEUS IS BACK
ZEUS
AISLE 1000
CHURCH OF ENNIS
CUSTER
CHURCH OF ELVIS
LIQUID HOLY THOUGHTS
PURE
SAINT PETER BEER
SALT PETER
I'M SORRY
GIVE TO GOD'S
JESUS COOKIES
D. ROBERTSON
GOD IS HERE

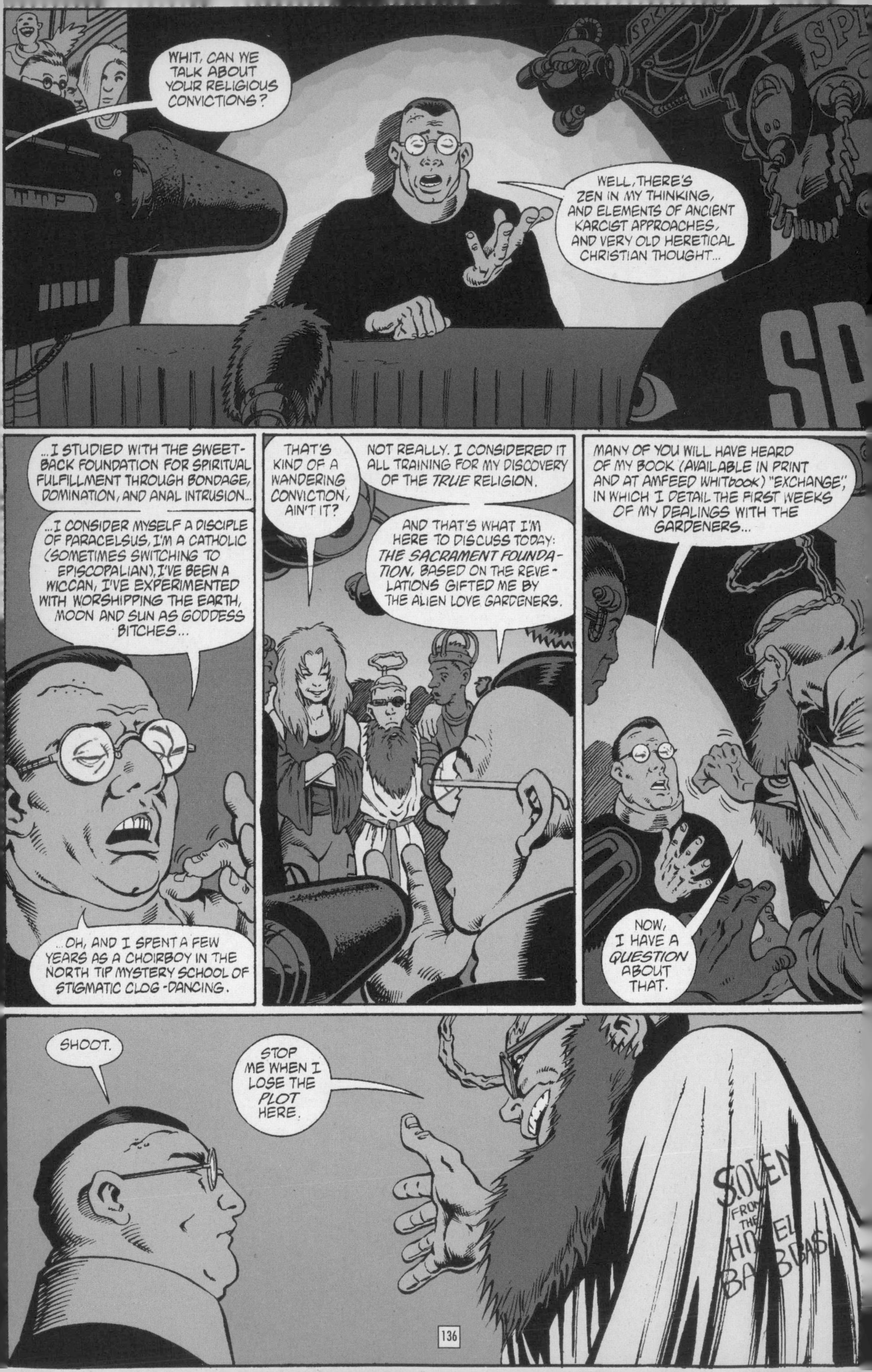
WHIT, CAN WE TALK ABOUT YOUR RELIGIOUS CONVICTIONS?
WELL, THERE'S ZEN IN MY THINKING, AND ELEMENTS OF ANCIENT KARCIST APPROACHES, AND VERY OLD HERETICAL CHRISTIAN THOUGHT...
SPK
...I STUDIED WITH THE SWEET-BACK FOUNDATION FOR SPIRITUAL FULFILLMENT THROUGH BONDAGE, DOMINATION, AND ANAL INTRUSION...
...I CONSIDER MYSELF A DISCIPLE OF PARACELSUS, I'M A CATHOLIC (SOMETIMES SWITCHING TO EPISCOPALIAN), I'VE BEEN A WICCAN, I'VE EXPERIMENTED WITH WORSHIPPING THE EARTH, MOON AND SUN AS GODDESS BITCHES...
...OH, AND I SPENT A FEW YEARS AS A CHOIRBOY IN THE NORTH TIP MYSTERY SCHOOL OF STIGMATIC CLOG-DANCING.
THAT'S KIND OF A WANDERING CONVICTION, AIN'T IT?
NOT REALLY. I CONSIDERED IT ALL TRAINING FOR MY DISCOVERY OF THE *TRUE* RELIGION.
AND THAT'S WHAT I'M HERE TO DISCUSS TODAY: *THE SACRAMENT FOUNDATION*, BASED ON THE REVELATIONS GIFTED ME BY THE ALIEN LOVE GARDENERS.
MANY OF YOU WILL HAVE HEARD OF MY BOOK (AVAILABLE IN PRINT AND AT AMFEED WHIT*book*) "EXCHANGE", IN WHICH I DETAIL THE FIRST WEEKS OF MY DEALINGS WITH THE GARDENERS...
NOW, I HAVE A *QUESTION* ABOUT THAT.
SHOOT.
STOP ME WHEN I LOSE THE *PLOT* HERE.
S.OLEN FROM THE HOTEL BABBAS

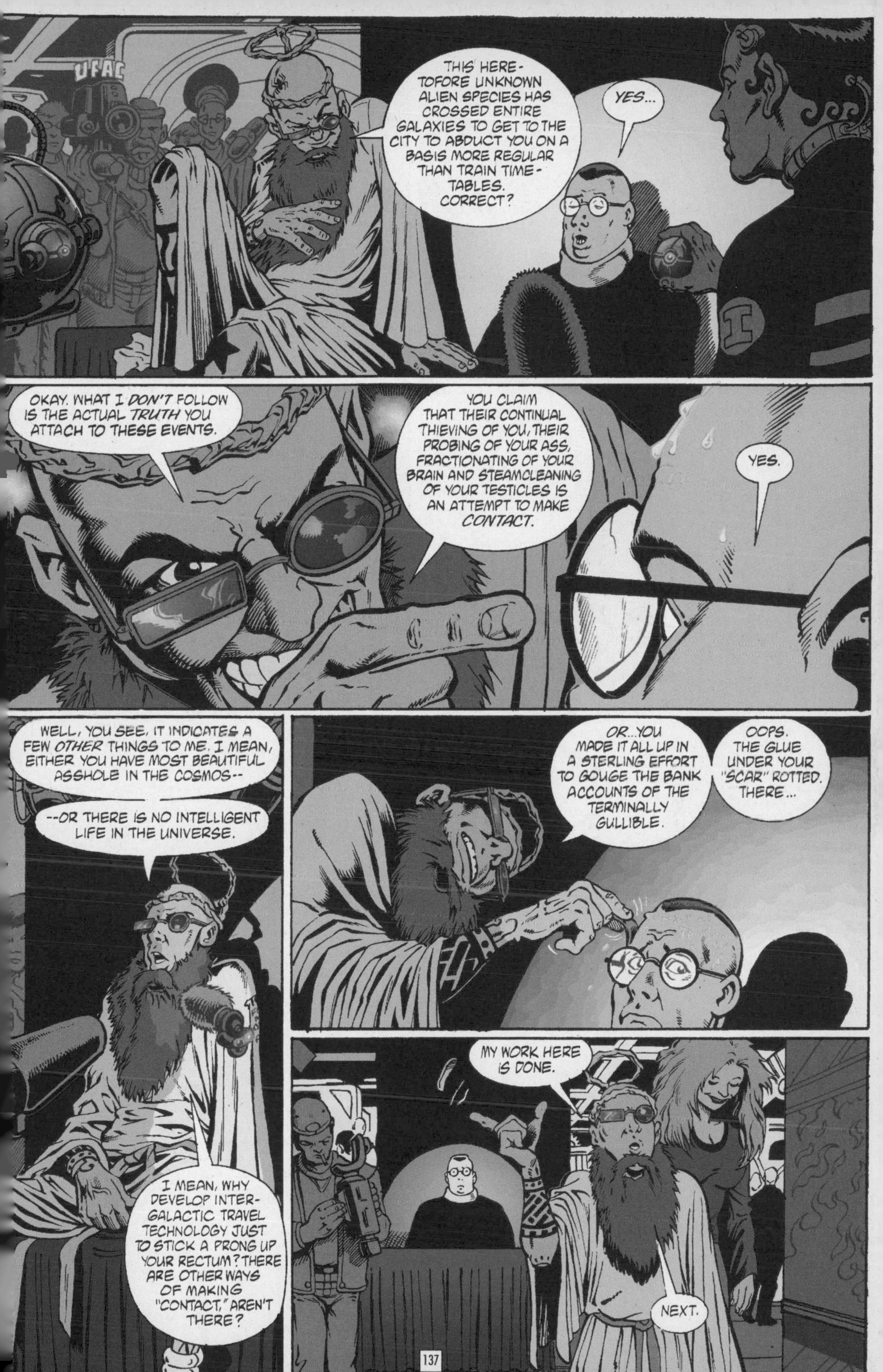
UFAC
THIS HERE-TOFORE UNKNOWN ALIEN SPECIES HAS CROSSED ENTIRE GALAXIES TO GET TO THE CITY TO ABDUCT YOU ON A BASIS MORE REGULAR THAN TRAIN TIME-TABLES. CORRECT?
YES...
OKAY. WHAT I DON'T FOLLOW IS THE ACTUAL TRUTH YOU ATTACH TO THESE EVENTS.
YOU CLAIM THAT THEIR CONTINUAL THIEVING OF YOU, THEIR PROBING OF YOUR ASS, FRACTIONATING OF YOUR BRAIN AND STEAMCLEANING OF YOUR TESTICLES IS AN ATTEMPT TO MAKE CONTACT.
YES.
WELL, YOU SEE, IT INDICATES A FEW OTHER THINGS TO ME. I MEAN, EITHER YOU HAVE MOST BEAUTIFUL ASSHOLE IN THE COSMOS--
--OR THERE IS NO INTELLIGENT LIFE IN THE UNIVERSE.
I MEAN, WHY DEVELOP INTER-GALACTIC TRAVEL TECHNOLOGY JUST TO STICK A PRONG UP YOUR RECTUM? THERE ARE OTHER WAYS OF MAKING "CONTACT," AREN'T THERE?
OR...YOU MADE IT ALL UP IN A STERLING EFFORT TO GOUGE THE BANK ACCOUNTS OF THE TERMINALLY GULLIBLE.
OOPS. THE GLUE UNDER YOUR "SCAR" ROTTED. THERE...
MY WORK HERE IS DONE.
NEXT.

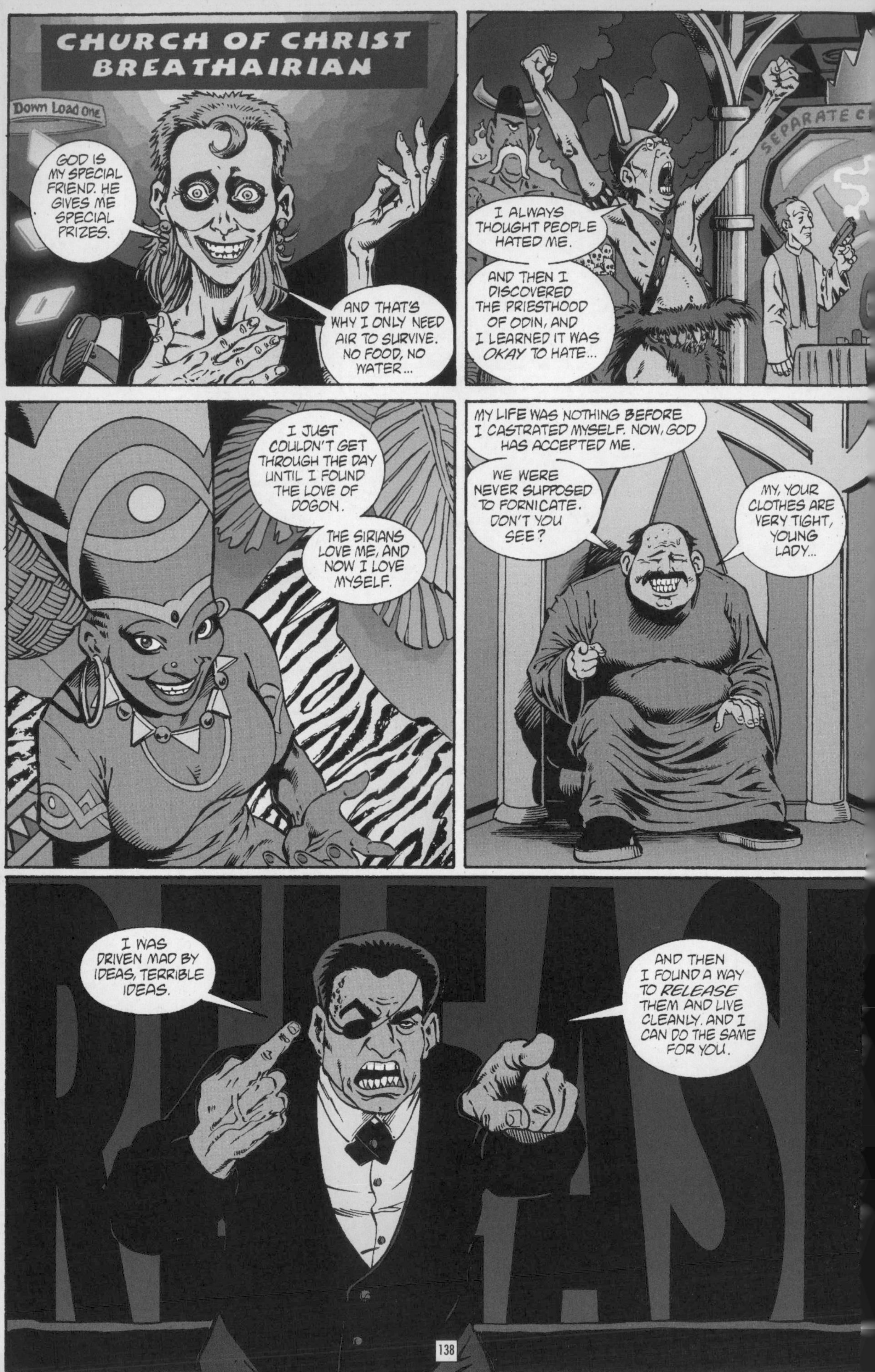
CHURCH OF CHRIST BREATHAIRIAN
Down Load One
GOD IS MY SPECIAL FRIEND. HE GIVES ME SPECIAL PRIZES.
AND THAT'S WHY I ONLY NEED AIR TO SURVIVE. NO FOOD, NO WATER...
I ALWAYS THOUGHT PEOPLE HATED ME.
AND THEN I DISCOVERED THE PRIESTHOOD OF ODIN, AND I LEARNED IT WAS OKAY TO HATE...
SEPARATE C
I JUST COULDN'T GET THROUGH THE DAY UNTIL I FOUND THE LOVE OF DOGON.
THE SIRIANS LOVE ME, AND NOW I LOVE MYSELF.
MY LIFE WAS NOTHING BEFORE I CASTRATED MYSELF. NOW, GOD HAS ACCEPTED ME.
WE WERE NEVER SUPPOSED TO FORNICATE. DON'T YOU SEE?
MY, YOUR CLOTHES ARE VERY TIGHT, YOUNG LADY...
I WAS DRIVEN MAD BY IDEAS, TERRIBLE IDEAS.
AND THEN I FOUND A WAY TO RELEASE THEM AND LIVE CLEANLY. AND I CAN DO THE SAME FOR YOU.

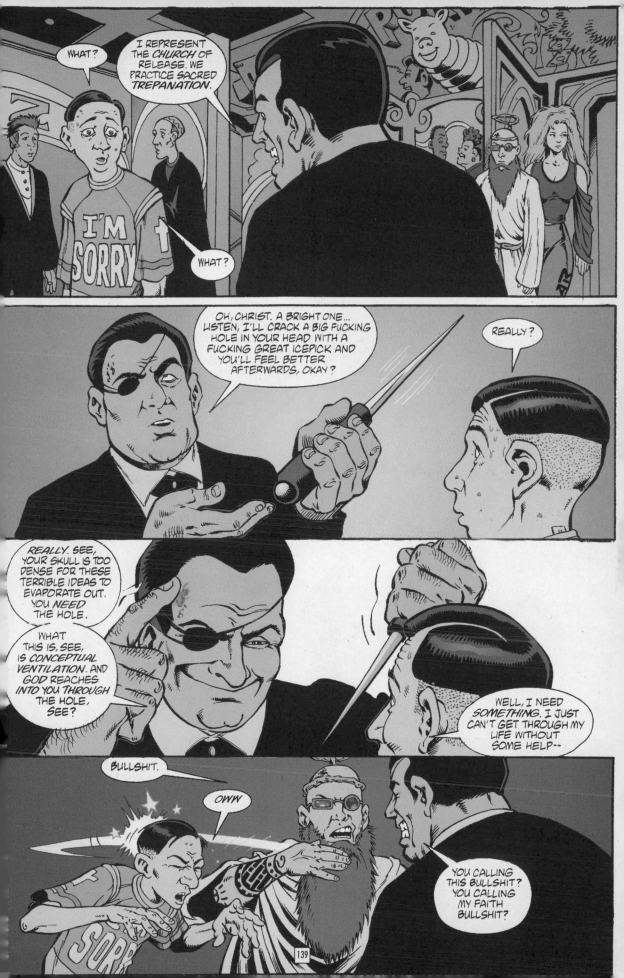

WHAT?

I REPRESENT THE *CHURCH OF RELEASE*. WE PRACTICE SACRED *TREPANATION*.

WHAT?

OH, CHRIST. A BRIGHT ONE... LISTEN, I'LL CRACK A BIG FUCKING HOLE IN YOUR HEAD WITH A FUCKING GREAT ICEPICK AND YOU'LL FEEL BETTER AFTERWARDS, OKAY?

REALLY?

REALLY. SEE, YOUR SKULL IS TOO DENSE FOR THESE TERRIBLE IDEAS TO EVAPORATE OUT. YOU *NEED* THE HOLE.

WHAT THIS IS, SEE, IS *CONCEPTUAL VENTILATION.* AND GOD REACHES INTO YOU *THROUGH* THE HOLE, SEE?

WELL, I NEED *SOMETHING.* I JUST CAN'T GET THROUGH MY LIFE WITHOUT SOME HELP--

BULLSHIT.

OWW

YOU CALLING THIS BULLSHIT? YOU CALLING MY FAITH BULLSHIT?

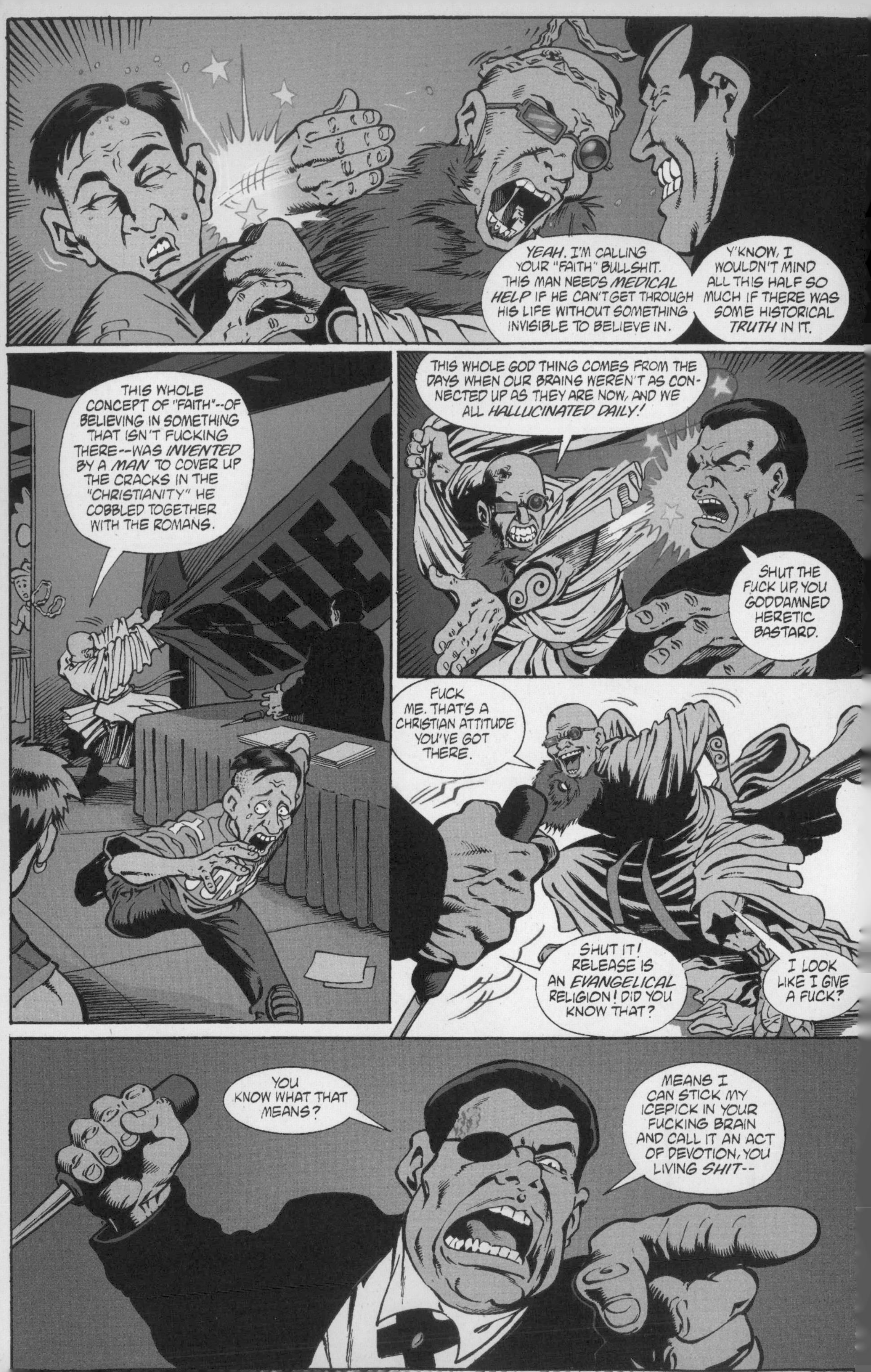
YEAH. I'M CALLING YOUR "FAITH" BULLSHIT. THIS MAN NEEDS MEDICAL HELP IF HE CAN'T GET THROUGH HIS LIFE WITHOUT SOMETHING INVISIBLE TO BELIEVE IN.
Y'KNOW, I WOULDN'T MIND ALL THIS HALF SO MUCH IF THERE WAS SOME HISTORICAL TRUTH IN IT.
THIS WHOLE CONCEPT OF "FAITH"--OF BELIEVING IN SOMETHING THAT ISN'T FUCKING THERE--WAS INVENTED BY A MAN TO COVER UP THE CRACKS IN THE "CHRISTIANITY" HE COBBLED TOGETHER WITH THE ROMANS.
THIS WHOLE GOD THING COMES FROM THE DAYS WHEN OUR BRAINS WEREN'T AS CONNECTED UP AS THEY ARE NOW, AND WE ALL HALLUCINATED DAILY!
SHUT THE FUCK UP, YOU GODDAMNED HERETIC BASTARD.
FUCK ME. THAT'S A CHRISTIAN ATTITUDE YOU'VE GOT THERE.
SHUT IT! RELEASE IS AN EVANGELICAL RELIGION! DID YOU KNOW THAT?
I LOOK LIKE I GIVE A FUCK?
YOU KNOW WHAT THAT MEANS?
MEANS I CAN STICK MY ICEPICK IN YOUR FUCKING BRAIN AND CALL IT AN ACT OF DEVOTION, YOU LIVING SHIT--

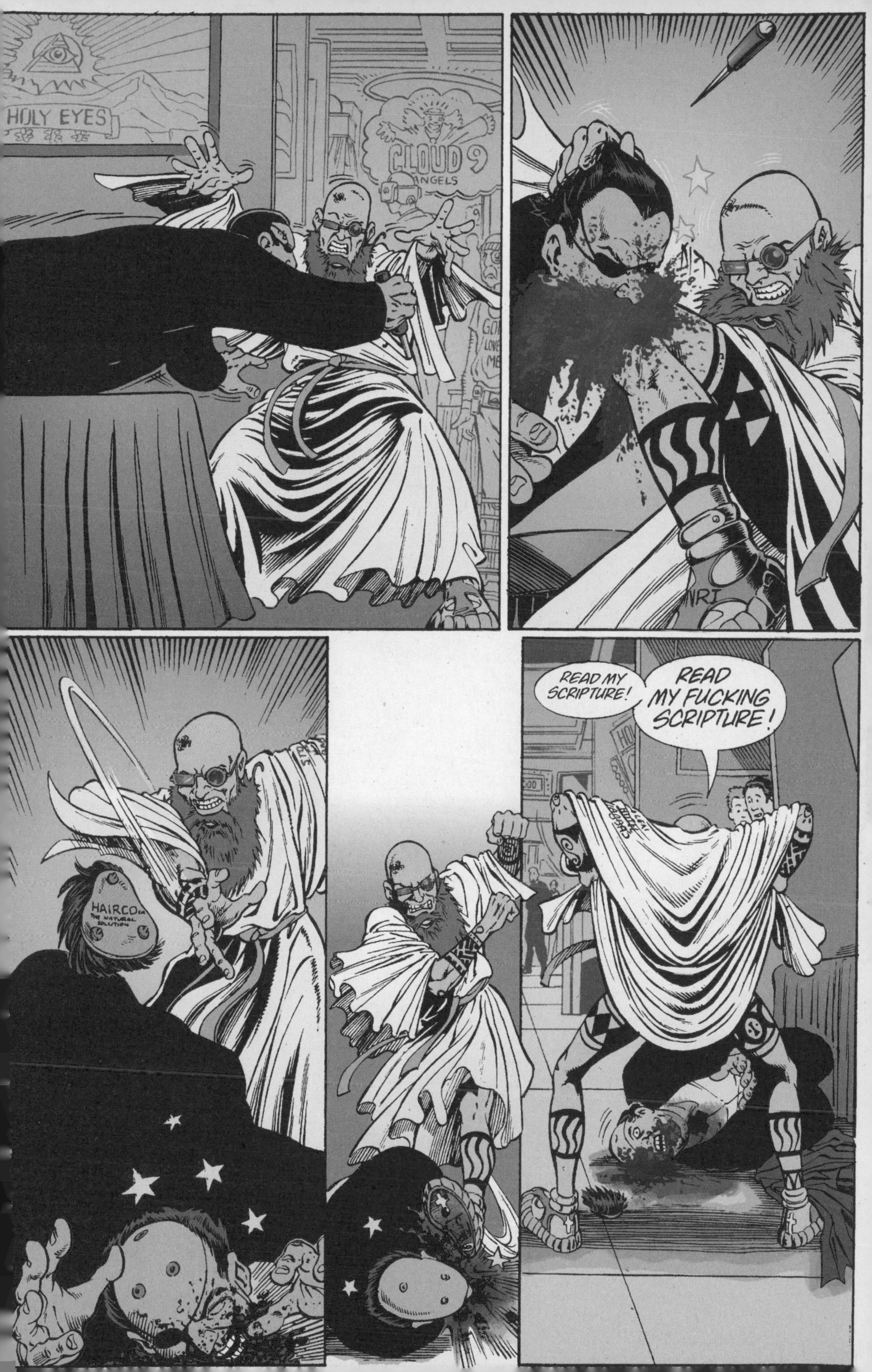
HOLY EYES
CLOUD 9
ANGELS
GOD LOVES ME
INRI
HAIRCO
THE NATURAL SOLUTION
READ MY SCRIPTURE!
READ MY FUCKING SCRIPTURE!

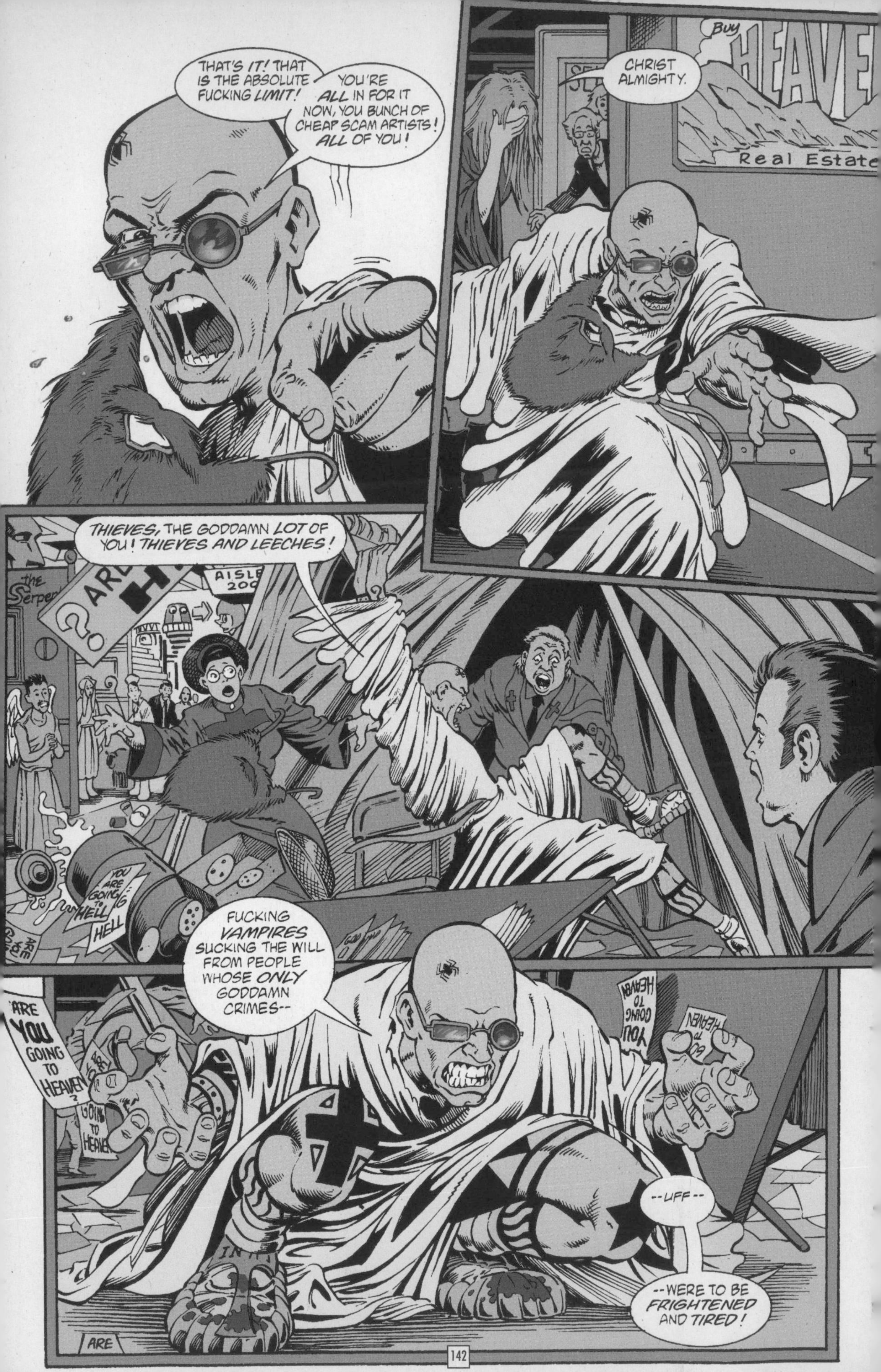
THAT'S IT! THAT IS THE ABSOLUTE FUCKING LIMIT!
YOU'RE ALL IN FOR IT NOW, YOU BUNCH OF CHEAP SCAM ARTISTS! ALL OF YOU!
Buy HEAVEN
Real Estate
CHRIST ALMIGHTY.
THIEVES, THE GODDAMN LOT OF YOU! THIEVES AND LEECHES!
AISLE 200
the Serpent
YOU ARE GOING TO HELL
FUCKING VAMPIRES SUCKING THE WILL FROM PEOPLE WHOSE ONLY GODDAMN CRIMES--
ARE YOU GOING TO HEAVEN?
GOING TO HEAVEN
YOU GOING TO HEAVEN
GO TO HEAVEN
--UFF--
--WERE TO BE FRIGHTENED AND TIRED!
ARE

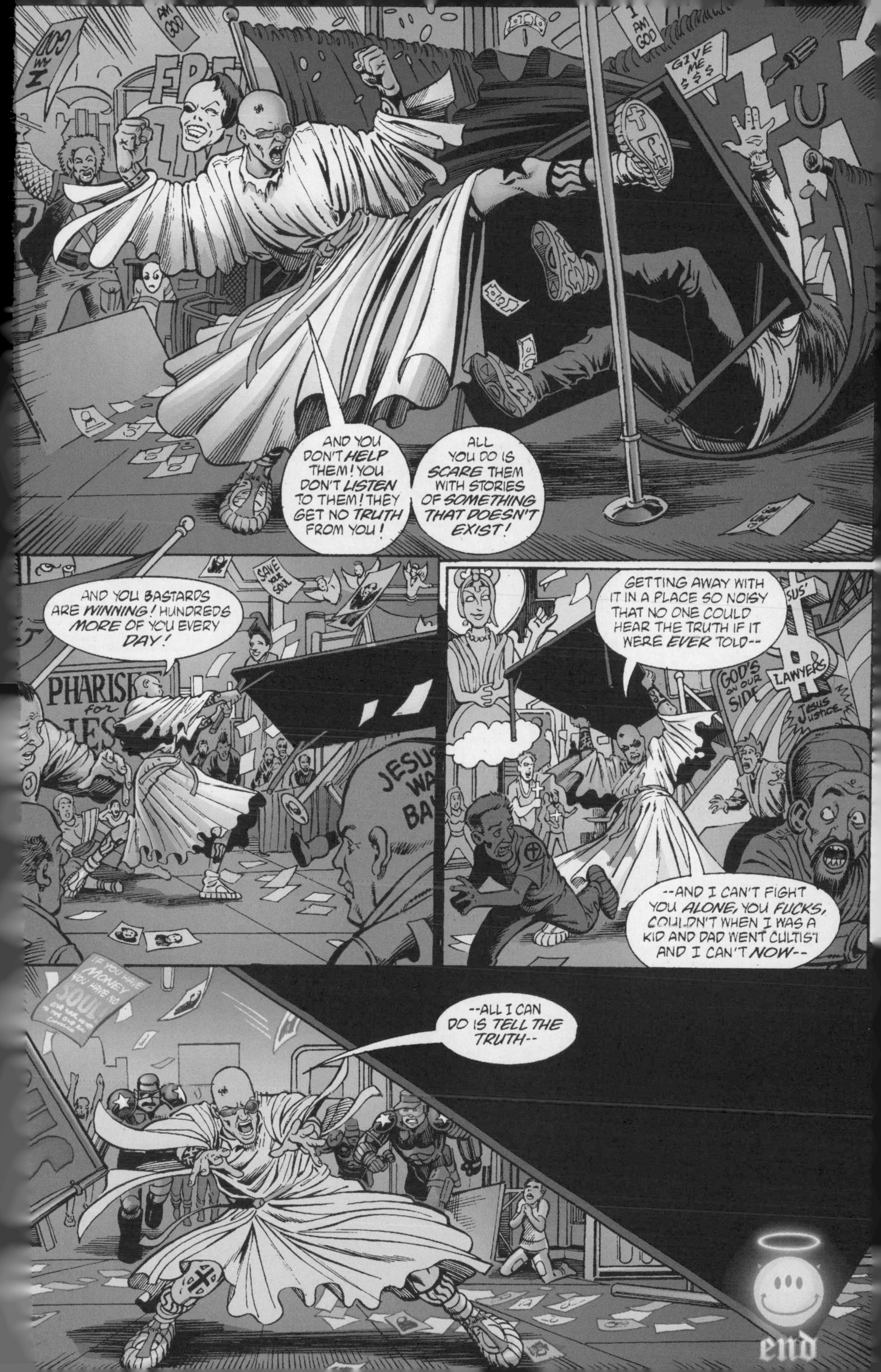
I AM GOD
GIVE ME $$$
AND YOU DON'T HELP THEM! YOU DON'T LISTEN TO THEM! THEY GET NO TRUTH FROM YOU!
ALL YOU DO IS SCARE THEM WITH STORIES OF SOMETHING THAT DOESN'T EXIST!
SAVE YOUR SOUL
AND YOU BASTARDS ARE WINNING! HUNDREDS MORE OF YOU EVERY DAY!
GETTING AWAY WITH IT IN A PLACE SO NOISY THAT NO ONE COULD HEAR THE TRUTH IF IT WERE EVER TOLD--
GOD'S on our SIDE
LAWYERS
Jesus Justice
--AND I CAN'T FIGHT YOU ALONE, YOU FUCKS, COULDN'T WHEN I WAS A KID AND DAD WENT CULTIST AND I CAN'T NOW--
IF YOU HAVE MONEY YOU HAVE NO SOUL
--ALL I CAN DO IS TELL THE TRUTH--
end

VERTIGO

"Transmet is brilliant future-shock commentary."
—SPIN MAGAZINE

"It's angry political sci-fi and it's funny as hell."
—PLAYBOY

TRANSMETROPOLITAN VOL. 2: LUST FOR LIFE

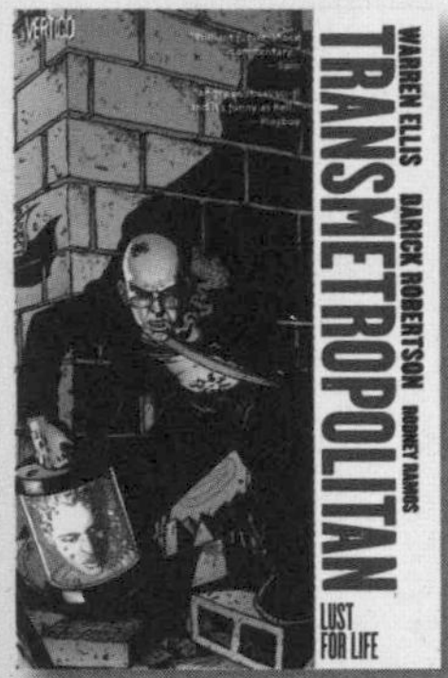
VERTIGO
WARREN ELLIS
DARICK ROBERTSON
RODNEY RAMOS
TRANSMETROPOLITAN
LUST FOR LIFE

TRANSMETROPOLITAN VOL. 3: YEAR OF THE BASTARD

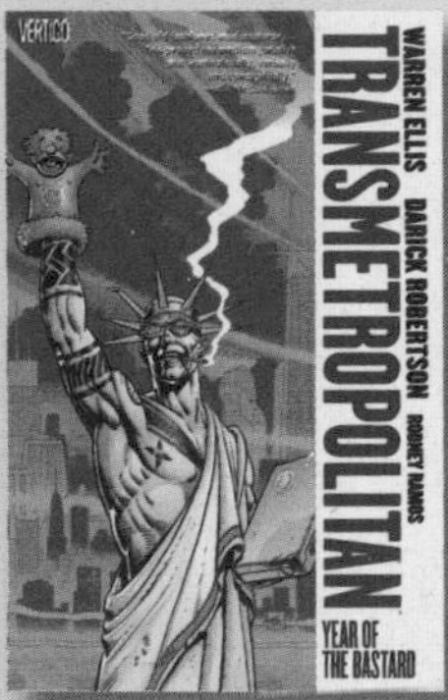
VERTIGO
WARREN ELLIS
DARICK ROBERTSON
RODNEY RAMOS
TRANSMETROPOLITAN
YEAR OF THE BASTARD

Read the Entire Series!

TRANSMETROPOLITAN VOL. 1: BACK ON THE STREET

TRANSMETROPOLITAN VOL. 2: LUST FOR LIFE

TRANSMETROPOLITAN VOL. 3: YEAR OF THE BASTARD

TRANSMETROPOLITAN VOL. 4: THE NEW SCUM

TRANSMETROPOLITAN VOL. 5: LONELY CITY

TRANSMETROPOLITAN VOL. 6: BACK ON THE STREET

TRANSMETROPOLITAN VOL. 7: SPIDER'S THRASH

TRANSMETROPOLITAN VOL. 8: DIRGE

TRANSMETROPOLITAN VOL. 9: THE CURE

TRANSMETROPOLITAN VOL. 10: ONE MORE TIME

FROM THE WRITER OF *PLANETARY*

WARREN ELLIS
TRANSMETROPOLITAN
with DARICK ROBERTSON

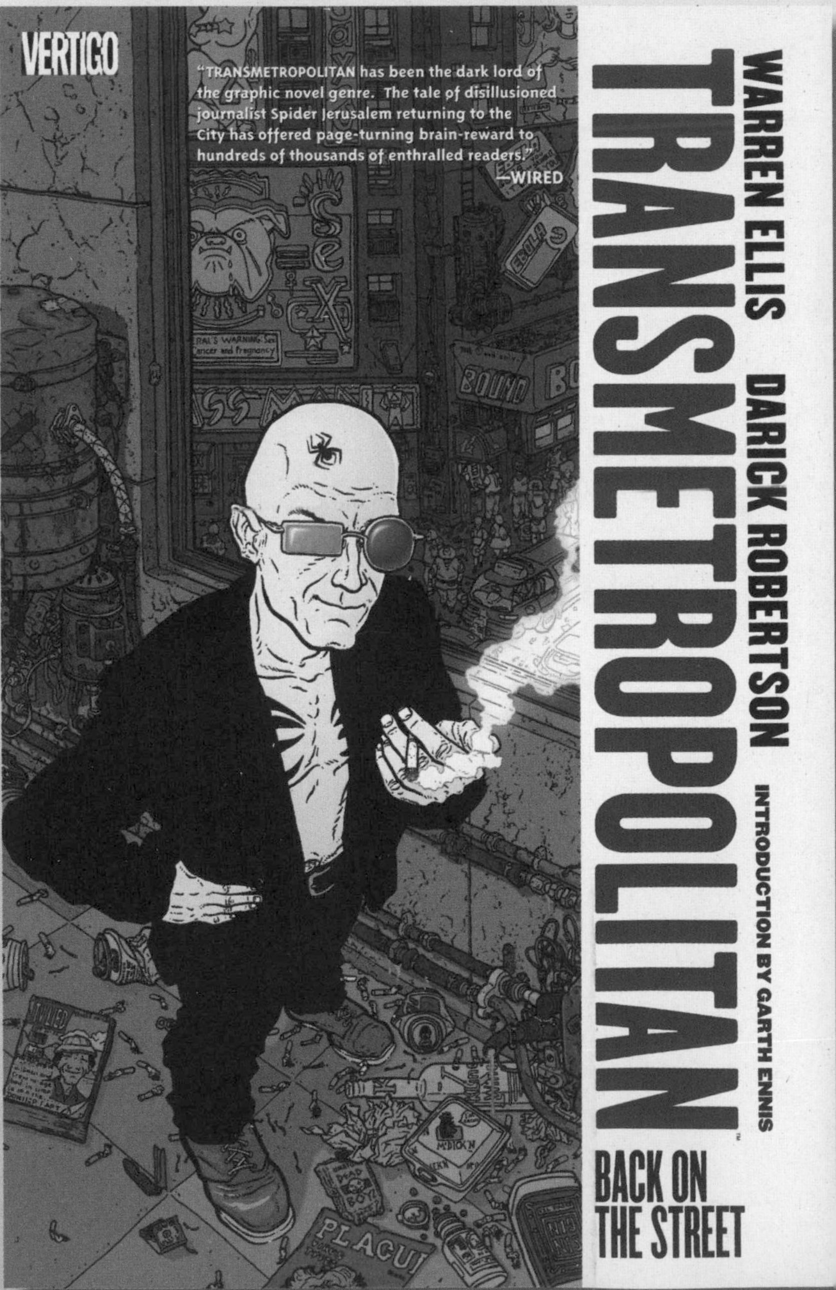
VERTIGO
"TRANSMETROPOLITAN has been the dark lord of the graphic novel genre. The tale of disillusioned journalist Spider Jerusalem returning to the City has offered page-turning brain-reward to hundreds of thousands of enthralled readers."
—WIRED
WARREN ELLIS
DARICK ROBERTSON
TRANSMETROPOLITAN
INTRODUCTION BY GARTH ENNIS
BACK ON THE STREET